CONCEPTS OF COMMUNICATION

UNIVERSITY OF CALIFORNIA
ENGINEERING AND PHYSICAL
SCIENCES EXTENSION SERIES

CONCEPTS OF COMMUNICATION:
INTERPERSONAL, INTRAPERSONAL,
AND MATHEMATICAL

The Authors

CHARLES B. TOMPKINS
RAY L. BIRDWHISTELL
DAVID G. HAYS
H. P. EDMUNDSON
THEODORE H. BULLOCK
W. ROSS ADEY
E. ROY JOHN
RICHARD L. MASLAND
WILLIAM J. McGILL
WILLIAM K. ESTES
JOHN L. BARNES
LEO BREIMAN
EDWARD C. CARTERETTE
DONALD A. NORMAN

The Editors

EDWIN F. BECKENBACH
Professor of Mathematics
University of California
Los Angeles

CHARLES B. TOMPKINS
Professor of Mathematics
University of California
Los Angeles

JOHN WILEY AND SONS, INC., NEW YORK•LONDON•SYDNEY•TORONTO

Library of Congress Catalog Card Number: 70-161492

ISBN 0-471-06120-4

Printed in the United States of America.

10 9 8 7 6 5 4 3 2 1

THE AUTHORS _____

W. ROSS ADEY, M.D., Professor of Anatomy and Professor of Physiology, Space Biology Laboratory, Brain Research Institute, University of California, Los Angeles, California

JOHN L. BARNES, Ph.D., Professor of Engineering and Applied Science, University of California, Los Angeles, California

RAY L. BIRDWHISTELL, Ph.D., Professor of Communications, Anneberg School of Communications, University of Pennsylvania; Senior Research Scientist, East Pennsylvania Psychiatric Institute, Philadelphia, Pennsylvania

LEO BREIMAN, Ph.D., Consultant, Topanga, California

THEODORE H. BULLOCK, Ph.D., Professor of Neurosciences, University of California, San Diego, California

EDWARD C. CARTERETTE, Ph.D., Professor of Psychology, University of California, Los Angeles, California

H. P. EDMUNDSON, Ph.D., Professor of Computer Science and Mathematics, University of Maryland, College Park, Maryland

WILLIAM K. ESTES, Ph.D., Professor of Psychology, Rockefeller University, New York, New York

DAVID G. HAYS, Ph.D., Professor of Linguistics, State University of New York, Buffalo, New York

E. ROY JOHN, Ph.D., Professor of Psychiatry, Brain Research Laboratories, New York Medical College, New York, New York

RICHARD L. MASLAND, M.D., Chairman, Department of Neurology, Columbia University Neurological Institute, New York, New York

v

WILLIAM J. McGILL, Ph.D., President, Columbia University, New York, New York

DONALD A. NORMAN, Ph.D., Associate Professor of Psychology, University of California, La Jolla, California

CHARLES B. TOMPKINS, Ph.D., Professor of Mathematics, University of California, Los Angeles, California

FOREWORD ────────────────────────

A most exciting, promising, and already significantly productive branch of scientific inquiry is the relatively new but burgeoning field of socio-biomathematics. Possibilities of biological analysis vastly greater than ever before have emerged with the advent of the computer age, and the medical and communicative aspects of space travel have made new demands and opened new vistas. These and other current developments are increasingly forcing social and life scientists into mathematics classrooms and enticing mathematicians into scientific laboratories, thus engendering a new breed of scientists—the socio-biomathematicians.

Since the various communication sciences are central to much of this ferment, Physical Sciences Extension, Engineering Extension, and Continuing Education in Medicine and Health Sciences, University of California Extension, Los Angeles, and Engineering Extension, Berkeley organized and, in the spring of 1965, presented a statewide lecture series entitled *Conceptual Bases and Applications of the Communications Sciences*. The objective of the series was to present an integrated and balanced view of the many fields that comprise the communication sciences, bound together through mathematical models and analyses. This book is an outgrowth of that series.

RALPH W. GERARD
Dean of Graduate Division,
University of California
Irvine

FREDERICK T. WALL
Vice Chancellor Graduate Studies and Research
University of California
San Diego

HORACE W. MAGOUN
Dean of Graduate Division
University of California
Los Angeles

EDWARD B. ROESSLER
Dean of University Extension
University of California
Berkeley

PREFACE

... Heine's music can be heard only in the original German. This is true of any translation: for the combination of music and meaning which is poetry—the metamorphosis into a new thing complete in itself, final and self-defining—cannot be paraphrased. The translator can only hope to render the meaning of the poem at a sacrifice of its music, or attempt, by writing an entirely new poem, to suggest the music at the expense of meaning. . . .

Apart from the verbal melodies, which cannot be expressed in any but their own terms, the words themselves present sufficient problems. It is a curious linguistic phenomenon that most of the abstractions, e.g., Love, Faith, Truth, Joy, Grief, Life—those so-convenient English monosyllables—become "*Liebe*," "*Glaube*," "*Wahrheit*," "*Freude*," "*Kummer*," "*Leben*" in the dissyllabic German.

From *Heinrich Heine, Paradox and Poet, The Poems*, translated by Louis Untermeyer, copyright, 1937, by Harcourt, Brace & World, Inc.; renewed 1965 by Louis Untermeyer. Reprinted by permission of the publishers.

One objective of this book is to give, in as quantitative a manner as is feasible, a description of both extent and content of communication sciences.

Communications may be simple or complex in nature. The behavior of the neuron is elementary, but difficulties of measurement and the enormous numbers of cooperating cells render its study difficult and introduce a requirement for ingenuity and subtlety. Communication by means of written language presents obvious complexities.

Communication may be explicit and deterministic, as in a paper concerning mathematics, or it may be implicit, as in the use of gestures and facial expressions as adjuncts to communication or even as total communication facilities. Communications may also be probabilistic, as in the communication of subtle symptoms from the body to the diagnostician involved in diagnosing disease.

Communication may be addressed to the reason or to the emotions—a mathematical paper versus a poem by Heine.

The objective as stated above is incomplete; there should be a statement concerning the value of the accomplishment attempted. The general understanding of natural processes has always been considered to be a valuable goal of scientists. So it is that the papers in the section of this book devoted to Intrapersonal Communication Systems contribute valuably to our objective by describing much that is known concerning the structure and behavior of biological apparatus from the neuron through the central nervous system.

The improvement of communications concerning the field quantified is classically accorded value. Thus we hope in this book to improve communication about communication. The beginning may be to obtain methods of recording aspects of communication which resist deterministic and precise numerical or other quantitative description. This beginning, comparable with the construction of an alphabet in connection with natural languages, is found in Dr. Birdwhistell's paper in the section concerning Interpersonal Communication Systems.

The elementary syllable counting process reported by Louis Untermeyer at the beginning of this Preface contributes to the identification of some communication difficulties, but it would be foolish to suggest that the full meaning of the quotation could be clarified by complete quantification. Similarly, it may be a long time before anything but advances in recording techniques contribute to a quantitative understanding of the generation, use, and interpretation of gestures, intonations, stresses, and other implicit communication devices. In the case of Heine's poems, it is important to recognize that they are at least a combination of meaning and metrical form. More than that, they were intended for impact on a set of readers with whose emotional and living background Heine had a great sympathy. It may be true that we reverse this impact today so that at least the meaning of the poems is interpreted (far from quantitatively) to give some picture of this background in life. It is clearly out of the question to translate this art and music and feeling to precise quantitative figures. So it is and so it will be for a considerable time with much of communication. However, this is no reason for not pursuing the precise, albeit probabilistic, quantification of those aspects of communication sciences that are amenable to such description.

In some cases this has been done, and a part of this book is devoted to Mathematical Aspects of Communication Sciences. Here diverse topics, ranging from Counting Processes in Psychophysics to Discrete Signaling and Coding Systems, are discussed. The degree of precision which has been introduced with value in the study of Learning and Memory is remarkable; this precision led us to classify Dr. Estes' paper as mathematical rather than biological; this (from a couple of mathematicians) was intended as a compliment to the workers in this field for having attained so precise an expression of their ideas, and by no means is it an implication of departure from reality or practicality.

The ultimate objective in the study of communications lies in an understanding of the Uses of Sensory Information by Animals and Men, and a paper devoted to this concludes the book.

The arrangement of this book more or less reflects the degree of quantitative abstraction reported in the papers. Part 1, Interpersonal Communication Systems, reports on communication (mainly) among humans. The concepts are complicated, and generally the substantial knowledge of these concepts reported in the papers of this part is less quantified than is the case in later parts. Part 2, Intrapersonal Communication Systems, generally speaking, is more quantitative than the preceding part, and Part 3, Mathematical Aspects of Communication Sciences, is highly abstract. Within the individual parts the more abstract papers are placed later than the less abstract. It should be noted that the degree of abstraction attained in any study is by no means a measure of the depth of the study; some matters are more nearly abstract in original concept than others. We feel that our colleagues on the advisory committee did a remarkable job of finding subjects which have been developed in the interesting ways described so lucidly by the authors of this volume.

Two papers stand alone; they are not included in any of the three parts comprising the main material in the volume.

The first of these, Chapter 1, is devoted to a quantitative probabilistic description of communication processes. This chapter is abstract to an extent which, with the present state of knowledge and computing power, borders on the unrealistic. Nevertheless, it was included because we feel that it has value in the total abstraction process, which in turn has value mentioned earlier.

The other chapter that stands alone is the last chapter, which presents a means of appraising the value of communications. Here the emphasis is on the decision process which the communication system supports.

In some sense the first chapter of this book presents a model into which the material of the chapters comprising the major parts of the book may be fitted, frequently with intolerable strain or with little gain. The last chapter can be read as justifying the exposition undertaken in the volume in terms of the contributions made by communication to the decision process.

This book is a direct outgrowth of activities by Dean Horace W. Magoun and his colleagues in focusing attention on Conceptual Bases and Applications of the Communications Sciences, the title of a Statewide Lecture Series sponsored by University of California Extension during the spring of 1965. This Statewise Lecture Series was preceded in October 1962 by a Conference on Conceptual Aspects of Communications Theory, suggested originally by Dean Magoun, organized by its Chairman, Dr. Mary A. B. Brazier, and held at UCLA. An attempt was made to document this conference, but the material was so diverse that it was decided to sponsor the ensuing lecture series instead.

Statewide Lecture Series as a tool for exposition on timely topics of interest to Engineering and Physical Sciences Extension of the University of California were developed under the leadership of John C. Dillon and the late Clifford Bell. Planning for such a series is carried out by an advisory committee, and we are grateful to the Advisory Committee of the 1965 Series for bringing to this volume the distinguished authors who have contributed papers. The Advisory Committee consisted of John L. Barnes, Helen Barry, Edwin F. Beckenbach, the late Clifford Bell, Graeme S. Bond, Mary A. B. Brazier, Jack W. Carlyle, Edward C. Carterette, John C. Dillon, H. P. Edmundson, Leonard Farber, Ralph W. Gerard, Horace W. Magoun, the late Clay L. Perry, Thomas H. Sternberg, Charles B. Tompkins, Frederick T. Wall, and Roger H. L. Wilson. All the papers of this book with the exception of the paper by Dr. Adey grew out of this lecture series.

EDWIN F. BECKENBACH
CHARLES B. TOMPKINS

University of California
Los Angeles
March, 1971

CONTENTS ————————————————————————

CONCEPTS OF COMMUNICATION

INTRODUCTION

*A mathematician who is not also
something of a poet will never be
a complete mathematician.*

KARL WILHELM THEODOR WEIERSTRASS

CHAPTER 1

Probabilistic Models of Communications

CHARLES B. TOMPKINS

Professor of Mathematics, University of California, Los Angeles

Contents

1.1 GENERALITIES

Communications is a subject almost unrivaled in breadth, subtlety, and elusiveness. In studying communications, we encounter interplays between more or less implicit natural reactions and explicit actions designed purposely and carefully to transmit information about these reactions. One source of difficulty is that the natural reactions that are likely to furnish the motivation for the communications are not carefully formed in the light of precisely stated postulates chosen to provide easy translation to the medium used in the transmission. Figure 1.1 shows seven components of communications. We shall examine these factors, attempting to provide constructive and productive quantitative descriptions of parts of the communications process.

The message originates in order to describe some status, or it is created by the existence of some status in the originating organism. Not all messages are purposely originated, nor are they necessarily of positive utility. Muscular activity of the heart creates a status which generates an electrical description. This description may be detected as a quasi-periodic potential difference between two areas on the surface of the body; the description is

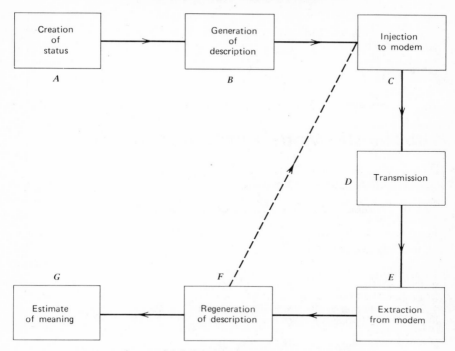

Fig. 1.1 A superficial sketch of components of communication.

partially regenerated, and it is studied by a cardiologist to estimate the meaning of the status signal in terms of muscular and valve action.

The generation of the description may be implicit or explicit; the description itself may identify the status completely if it can be regenerated accurately, or it may furnish only an incomplete classification. The parameters whose values are reported (numerically or otherwise) may be arbitrarily chosen, or they may be carefully assigned to facilitate the communications process; they may originate naturally (as is the case with the electrocardiogram) so that the final estimate of meaning must be made in a way to exploit the information offered in its naturally occurring form, or they may be deliberately chosen with some effective operation in the mind of the person responsible for the communications (as should be the case with the assignment of a call number to a book in a library).

If the parameters result from a scientific or technical choice, the chosen data may be reduced before introduction to the transmitting modem[1] as

---

[1] The word "modem" is one used by communicators to denote the terminal equipment of automatic communications systems; it is a contraction of "modulate-demodulate."

part of the description process. The block labeled C in Figure 1.1 signifies the equipment used and the operations involved in injecting the signal to be transmitted into the transmission system. The modem is a transducer, frequently with fairly complicated programs to carry out in order to assure reliable, convenient, and economical communication.

The transmission channel itself may be almost anything. It is true, however, that many channels may be treated by widely applicable studies involving bandwidth, the Shannon notion of channel capacity, and other developments of modern information theory.

The signal-extraction modem and its immediately neighboring devices are intended to receive the transmitted signal and to present it for regeneration in a suitable form. The purpose here is described as regeneration, at least for general discussion; indeed, I. J. Good [4] makes the plausible point that the major effort in communications is always regeneration. Without laboring this, we can accept for the time being that the receiver of the transmitted data usually will endeavor to regenerate the description originally injected to the transmission system, or at least some transform of this description.

If the transmission system involves repeaters or relay stations, the dotted line from F to C in Figure 1.1 may be followed one or more times; in this case, regeneration of the original description may be incomplete at a repeater station.

Finally comes the step of estimating the meaning of the message received. Frequently this estimate leaves some uncertainty about the status described by the message. In this case, the estimate may involve an explicit or an implicit a posteriori assignment of probabilities to the various statuses which might plausibly have initiated the message.

The estimate may require use of esoteric information. Messages may be encoded for purposes of economy or efficiency in transmission, they may be enciphered for purposes of privacy, or they may require special knowledge, intuition, education, or experience for best interpretation. Moreover, in at least some cases, information may be accumulated from several messages to provide a store of esoteric knowledge in a facility formerly lacking it. This is one description of the learning process; it could also apply to cryptanalysis. A somewhat simpler example is the use of a call number as a stereotyped encoding of the identity of a book in a library. In the Library of Congress system, the assignment of the prefix QA to mathematics books is made arbitrarily. If, however, a user could postulate a systematic assignment of call numbers to classical disciplines, then a few samples would convince him that QA is assigned to mathematics, that QA611 is assigned to books which the classifier felt pertained principally to topology, etc. The self-taught learner could confirm his hypothesis by sampling, and he might even develop enough confidence to reject outliers detected among the classifications assigned by librarians who had exceeded their technical capacity or who had otherwise erred in assigning call numbers. Furthermore, the learner could estimate with some confidence that books with neighboring call letters are likely to be on related subjects; without recovery of fairly explicit information about the meaning of call numbers, however, he would not be inclined to risk too much on this judgment, for he would realize that the assignment of call numbers is in essence a one-dimensional description of a many-dimensional population; that is, he would realize that there are many subjects that might be considered to lie close to topology in one way or another, and that some arbitrary choice of relative significance of properties must have been made in the assignment of single call numbers to each book.

This observation brings another principle of information retrieval to mind. Classification of any document or other information container is a process intended to facilitate recovery of the information contained in the item. The classification scheme, to be useful, must represent the information contained in the source; and since the shortening in abstraction is expected to exceed the redundancy of the original document, the document must be expected to contain information not directly available from the classification. In an informal way, we could regard the classifications of all available documents as information concerning the contents of the documents, but this information is incomplete. Thus we might be able to estimate some probability or some number to be used like a probability that the information sought is in a particular document. It is not inconceivable that the classification of a document will guarantee the presence of the sought information in the document, but since we assume that some information is lost in the classification process, cases must arise in which there is no more than a high probability (not certainty) that the desired information is in a document if no more than the classification of the document is known.

This may become clearer with a class of examples. Suppose a set of records is classified according to several different characteristics. To put the file in serial order requires assignment of relative significance to the various characteristics. Now suppose that we are somehow furnished partial information about a document in the file. To make matters more concrete, suppose that the file contains fingerprints of a large number of people, made under ideal conditions and filed according to measurements of outstanding characteristics. Thus, it might be almost trivial to draw from the file on the basis of the classification a single set of fingerprints matching a newly discovered fingerprint if the outstanding characteristics were certain to be left in the new fingerprint. On the other hand, if partial prints are recovered, the matching process becomes more difficult. There still may be characteristics that rule out many possibilities, but the amount of measurable information may be considerably less than is required for automatic matching on the basis of classification alone. Yet, since the classification scheme is not perfect, there is a chance that the partial print can be matched by full comparison with prints from the file. What is required to assure arriving at any possible match is that all prints whose characteristics are measurably different from those of the partial print in hand be excluded as not possibly interesting. The remaining records are of interest, and they are to be examined thoroughly.

It is clearly not necessary always to require complete assurance that the record sought will not be missed; in many cases, economic arguments make it desirable to accept some risk of failure and to examine fewer than all the records that cannot be surely rejected. If there is a reasonable estimate of the probability that any file record is the one desired, the high-probability candidates can be examined first, and the search can be abandoned when the expected gain from continued search is less than the cost of continuation.

Before turning to more quantitative descriptions of communications and to an examination of some of the tools available for analyzing communications processes, we should note the extent to which probability infuses the whole structure of communication sciences. Because of this infusion, we shall develop our exposition in terms of probabilities, and the analysis to be presented will be mainly probabilistic in nature.

1.2 COMMUNICATIONS—A PROBABILISTIC MODEL

The model discussed here has been used elsewhere [10] to describe communication processes. Later we describe some of the formulas and procedures that might be considered in treating a communications system based on this model.

We assume that the communications are between two organisms, one an *originator* and the other an *addressee*. We assume further that the originator and the addressee have agreed about the elementary factors of the system.

We examine first the activities at the originating end of the communications system. We describe these activities in terms of three sets:

1. *S* is a *set of statuses* which can be observed by the originator and which may stimulate transmission of messages.

2. *A* is a *set of nonredundant descriptors* of the elements of *S*.

3. *B* is a *set of redundant descriptors* to accompany the nonredundant descriptors in describing elements of *S*.

A message is initiated when the originator observes an element s of S. The mechanism of description is assumed to be a choice by the originator of some element a of A; this element is chosen to describe s, and the choice depends on the element s of S which stimulated the message, but it is assumed that any one of several elements a of A might be chosen to describe a single element s of S.

Now, with s and a determined, the rules of the communication system itself dictate a choice of an element b of B. This element is assumed to be uniquely determined by the pair (s,a). The pair (a,b) are the *originator's description of the status s*. It is not necessarily true that this description is unambiguous; in other words, it may be true that the same pair (a,b) can be used to describe any one of several different elements of S.

The final step by the originator is that of injecting the description (a,b) into the transmitting modem (C in Figure 1.1) for transmission to the addressee.

We now examine the activities of the addressee. For purposes of convenient identification, we assign Greek letters to denote his elements. We assume that the transmission channel leading from input to modem C through output from modem E to the description regenerator F is imperfect. The addressee receives from his description regenerator, F, a description (α,β), where α or β or both may differ (by more than a purposely introduced transformation which we allowed in discussing Figure 1.1) from the corresponding element a or b. We assume, however, that α is an element of A (or of the transform of A in the more general case) and that β is an element of B or its transform.

The estimation step now occurs. The addressee must at least choose some element σ of S as the most probable status to have stimulated the message. In many cases, more will be required. This might involve the selection of a subset of S made up of elements which are likely to have stimulated the message; then relative probabilities might be assigned to elements of this set to give an a posteriori estimate, based on the regenerated description (α,β) of the probability that any one of the elements of the chosen subset stimulated the message. In some cases, the estimate should be made explicitly for the whole set S rather than some subset chosen on plausibility arguments. In infinite cases, the probabilities may have to be assigned to measurable subsets of S, or a probability density function assigned over S.

The varying demands outlined in the preceding paragraph indicate the nature of risk the addressee must agree to accept. In the simplest case, he somehow estimates the most probable stimulus and arbitrarily assigns (so far as his later actions are concerned) a zero probability to any other potential stimulus. In the medium case, he determines a set of probable candidates, evaluates relative probabilities among the elements of this set, and in effect assigns zero probability to the complement of this set. In the exhaustive case, he extracts all the information available to him from the message.

We shall see shortly that this communications system leads to practically insurmountable computational difficulties in many cases, even though it is naively simple.

Part of this "naive simplicity" stems from the fact that this communications model ignores the role of service messages—messages that request repetition of part of a transmission or seek other clarification when the addressee has reason to believe that his information is more degraded than is necessary. Consideration of details of this type would complicate this descriptive model and the resulting calculations; for example, what rule should the addressee follow in requesting clarification?

We still need some rules for occurrence of statuses, choice of element a, determination of element b, and garbling of description (a,b) into description (α,β). We take these rules to be mainly probabilistic in nature. The terms used to describe them are explained in more detail in later sections; a few examples will be given before leaving this description.

If S is finite (that is, if the number of elements of S is finite), we assume that a probability function is defined over S (One in which the addressee has faith!) so that for each element s of S the probability that the next stimulating status will be s is well defined; we denote this probability by $\Pr[s]$. For countably infinite sets S (that is, for sets with an infinitude of elements that can be numbered completely by the positive integers) this same type of probability function is applicable. For larger sets S, comparable in size to the set of real numbers, a somewhat more complicated approach is necessary, as noted earlier. In any event, we assume that an appropriate probability function is accepted by the addressee as governing the appearance of the statuses, always in the sense that the particular stimulating status appears as a random choice made under this probability function.

Similarly, if A is finite, we assume a family of probability functions with values denoted by $\Pr[a \mid s]$ (to be read "the probability of a, given s"). Specifically, in mathematical language, such a function is a function whose domain is the Cartesian product of A and S and whose range is the set of nonnegative real numbers; it is further required that for every fixed s the sum of the values taken over A is 1. The interpretation is that for every value $s \in S$ (s an element of S) the addressee is confident that if the originator observes the status s, the value $\Pr[a \mid s]$ is the probability that the originator will choose the descriptor a.

The next step is the determination of b. This is the first deterministic element of the model. The element b is determined by the randomly selected elements s and a for any particular message. Thus we can stipulate the existence of a function (again confidently accepted by the addressee) from the Cartesian product of S and A to B governing the choice of b in a deterministic manner. (By a *function* from a Cartesian product of two sets to a third set, we mean a rule that is given for selecting an element of the third—or *range*—set as the image of any ordered pair of elements, the first from the first factor of the Cartesian product and the second from the second factor; the set of ordered pairs makes up the Cartesian product of the two sets, and this compound set is called the *domain* of the function.)

We now have completed the description of the activities of the originator. The description (a,b) has been prepared, and all that remains for the originator of this description is to introduce it to the transmitting modem. The action of the transmission system is again assumed to be random. The description (a,b) may be imperfectly transmitted and received as a description (α,β). Again the rules for this possible garbling are stated through use of a probability function. If the set $A \times B$ (the Cartesian product of A and B) is finite, then we need a probability function with value $\Pr[\alpha,\beta \mid a,b]$ [the probability of (α,β), given injection of (a,b)] accepted by the addressee.

With all these functions described, the task of the addressee is to estimate the probabilities of the occurrence of the various possible stimuli to initiate the communication.

We now turn to some examples. Unprecisely, we may take S to be a set of ideas from which the originator is to choose one for transmission. Once an idea has been chosen, the frame of a descriptive sequence of words is chosen; the nature of this choice may be governed by the nature of the originator—a poet is likely to choose an outline form different from that chosen by a nonpoetical mathematician. Once this frame (an element of A) is chosen, various redundant words come along by rule. The transmission channel may be a printed page, a telephone wire, or any other device for communicating words. The words, of course, may be misunderstood, and an incorrect description may be regenerated.

Again, consider a program for a computer. Suppose that the set S contains arithmetic or logical operations of considerable sophistication which a computer may be able to carry out when they are properly described in machine language. Let A be a set of PL/I (a programming language different from machine language) programs, and let b be a compiled machine language program corresponding to any $a \in A$. Here there is some degeneracy, for b depends only on a and not on s. We now discard the PL/I program a and retain only the machine-language program b. The model described above is broad enough to accept this as a communications system in which the object is to pick up the machine-language program and to learn what the original assignment (from S) to the machine was. In this, it is clear that the compiled program depends deterministically on s and a, and indeed the dependence on s is only formal. The choice of a (the PL/I program) is not completely predictable, and the programmer may choose between several alternatives. The lost PL/I program is depicted in the model by stipulating that the transmission of a is so garbled that no information is transferred, and the availability of the completely correct machine program is depicted by stipulating that b is transmitted completely without error. The assignment to the addressee is the usual one of estimating the status stimulating the message; in this case, the requirement is that the mathematical purpose of the program be deduced. The answer, except for unessential equivalent choices of labels for variables and equivalent overlapping compound steps, is unique; but the decipherment of the machine-language program into the much stronger language of mathematics may not be immediately obvious.

A reason for this lack of clarity is the absence of context in most machine language. Context may be defined in either of two ways. The easiest definition, which has been accorded some preferential position in the use of indexes of "key words in context," is that the context of a chosen word is the word itself and a connected set of neighboring words. This definition has merit in that it is easy to present a word in context; it is somewhat unsatisfactory in that it presents no specific instrument for deciding how to use context or even how big a neighborhood of the word being taken in context is required. A second definition is more attractive from the point of view of this chapter. This definition conceives of a description of *strength of a language.* This concept is a little too demanding for presentation here, but, roughly speaking, one language is stronger than another if the first language never requires a greater number of simple statements and sometimes requires fewer simple statements than the second language to express a thought. Then, if both languages express a thought so that there is a mapping from sets of statements in the weaker language to statements in the stronger, *the context of any given statement in the weaker language is the statement in the stronger language which includes the meaning of the given statement in the weaker language.*

Now it is not true that machine language (as described above) is weaker than PL/I, for there are single machine-language statements that require several statements for expression in PL/I. However, the part of machine language that can be obtained by compilation of PL/I is weaker than PL/I under our description. Thus, what happened in our lost PL/I example above was *the destruction of context of the statements in the comparatively weak machine language.* It is clear that this context, if it can be recovered at all, can be recovered by examining a set of neighborhoods of the statement whose context is to be determined and by extracting from this set of neighborhoods a maximal one which can be represented by a single *PL/I* statement. This observation bridges the gap between the two descriptions of context above.

All this may be important in connection with natural languages as well as with machine languages. We describe a *compiler* as a translator from a stronger language to a weaker. Compilation is fairly easy to accomplish, now that its nature is understood. The reverse process, however, is not at all easy, since, as noted previously, retention of the statements only in a weaker language destroys context. One might conjecture that the translation of natural languages follows the course implied earlier. For the validity of this conjecture, it is necessary to assume that the two natural languages involved are weak languages in the system. We assume further that a language stronger than either exists, perhaps implicitly in the mind of the translator. Then *the translator's assignment is first to decompile from one of the weak natural languages to the strong implicit language and then to compile from the strong implicit language to the other weak natural language.* The first step is relatively difficult, for it seems to involve the process of regenerating the general intention from a specific machine-language code. This process, however, is the basic process of communications as we have presented it here, and it is possible to the extent that communications themselves are possible in the weak natural language. After this step, the compilation into the second weak natural language is easy; it is the natural process of description in words—a process many people overdo, so that practice is usually well advanced even though success may be elusive.

We regret that a fuller discussion of this model and its implications is not presently available, and the author hopes to provide this discussion elsewhere. Meanwhile, fairness dictates that we note that many successful and experienced translators are convinced that this is not a model of the process they use; others agree that this is a correct model, and we believe that the tortuous search for a "soft spot" in a sentence to be attacked in machine translation is a search for context in very much the way it has been described here. Thus we present the model hopefully as a model for at least some translation of natural languages into other natural languages.

1.3 PROBABILITY CALCULATIONS

Our purpose in this section is to develop, without detail, methods available for studying the calculation of a posteriori probabilities. By omitting details, we are able to offer a discussion of reasonable length rather than a complete book. The omitted details are well documented, and they constitute one of the most notable developments of mathematics in the first half of the twentieth century. We suggest that the reader who is well versed in mathematics consult at least the prefaces to [5] and [7], and perhaps that he browse through [3] for an elementary exposition and consult [1], [2], and [11] for detailed development of various concepts needed to complete this exposition. To the reader who feels that he already has been subjected to enough of the details of the mathematical approach, we suggest that he accept as axiomatic the statements made here which are fundamental to the development of our theme (they are not hard to understand and to accept, with the possible exception of statements concerning nonmeasurable sets).

We start with a finite set S; it is representative, among other things, of the set S which appeared as the set of statuses at the beginning of Section 1.2. For finite sets, probability calculations offer no conceptual difficulties, although they may be too extensive for realistic execution. A *probability function over S* is a function which assigns a nonnegative number to each element of S, with the further restriction that the sum of all the real numbers assigned is 1. The idea of probability abstracts the idea of frequency (without requiring an infinitude of repetitions). In what is probably the oldest sense with which the word "probability" is used, an experiment is visualized in which a single element is selected from S. The elements are not identical, and it is assumed that some attribute of the element affects the chances of its being selected. After the element is selected, it is returned to the population, and the experiment is repeated, without having bias introduced because of the outcome of the first experiment. The probability assigned to each element s of S is the limit of the fractional frequency with which it is selected:

$$(1.1) \qquad \Pr[s] = \lim_{n \to \infty} \frac{n_s}{n},$$

where n is the number of performances of the experiment and n_s is the number of times s is selected.

In the spirit of mathematics, this description of the intended meaning of probability functions can be presented through the use of axioms that describe the arithmetic calculations required for what we regard as rigorous reasoning for intelligent behavior under probabilistic conditions. Under these axioms, the limit in (1.1) can be proved to exist in a satisfactory sense. This sense is no more definitive in its application than the following example will lead one to believe.

Let the set S consist of two elements, a and b. Assume that each of these elements is equally likely to be selected, so that $\Pr[a] = \Pr[b] = \frac{1}{2}$. Now consider the repeated selection experiment above, and extend the idea of "equally likely" to finite sequences (s_k), where k takes values $1, 2, \ldots, n$, and, for each value of k, s_k is either a or b. There are 2^n possible sequences of length n, and we assume that each of these sequences is equally probable among all sequences of length n; that is, the probability of selecting any particular sequence named in advance is 2^{-n}. This assumption is completely different from the so-called law of averages, quoted by many sports writers, under which "law" a long series of as would more probably be followed by a b than by an a.

Now, to return to our argument, denote by S_n the set of all sequences of length n whose elements have identity a or b. There are 2^n sequences in S_n. For example, if $n = 4$, eight of the sequences are $aaaa$, $aaab$, $aaba$, $aabb$, $abaa$, $abab$, $abba$, and $abbb$; the other eight are obtainable by replacing a by b and b by a in each of the eight sequences already written.

We continue with the example of S_4. For each nonnegative integer k not exceeding 4, we write $\sigma_{4,k}(a)$ equal to the number of sequences in S_4 in which there are exactly k elements with identity a. We tabulate these as follows:

$$\sigma_{4,0}(a) = 1,$$

$$\sigma_{4,1}(a) = 4,$$

$$\sigma_{4,2}(a) = 6,$$

$$\sigma_{4,3}(a) = 4,$$

$$\sigma_{4,4}(a) = 1.$$

Then, under our assumption of equal probability of each element of S_4, each number constituting the right-hand member of an equation above is 16 times the probability of selecting a sequence of 4 elements with the number of elements of identity a indicated by the second index of the left-hand member.

We now turn our attention back to equation (1.1) and its meaning. In the preceding example, the ratio of the number of elements with identity a in a sequence of length 4 to the total number of elements may take values 0, $\frac{1}{4}$, $\frac{1}{2}$, $\frac{3}{4}$, and 1. Of the 16 possible sequences, only 2 yield a ratio which differs from $\frac{1}{2}$ by a quantity whose absolute value exceeds $\frac{1}{4}$.

This counting argument may be extended. Again, let S_n be a set of sequences of length n, and let $\sigma_{n,k}(a)$ be the number of sequences in S_n in which element a occurs exactly k times. Compute the value $k/2^n$; this is the fraction whose limit is asserted to exist in the discussion of equation (1.1). Actually, of course, the value $k/2^n$ may take any of $(n + 1)$ values, for k may take any integer value between 0 and n, inclusive. We look, however, at the probability of selecting any particular value of k. More directly to our purpose, we may choose a positive number h (as close to zero as we like), we can choose all values of k such that

(1.2)
$$\left| \frac{k}{2^n} - \frac{1}{2} \right| > h,$$

and we can compute the probability of selecting a sequence with k having one of these values. This probability is just the sum of $\sigma_{n,k}(a)$ over all values of k satisfying (1.2). We denote this probability as

(1.3)
$$\Pr\left[\left| \frac{k}{2^n} - \frac{1}{2} \right| > h \right] = \sum_{k < \frac{1}{2} - h} \frac{\sigma_{n,k}(a)}{2^n} + \sum_{k > \frac{1}{2} + h} \frac{\sigma_{n,k}(a)}{2^n}.$$

The sense in which (1.1) is valid is that *for any positive numbers h_1 and h_2, however small, there exists an integer N such that if $n > N$, then*

(1.4)
$$\Pr\left[\left| \frac{k}{2^n} - \frac{1}{2} \right| > h_1 \right] < h_2.$$

In (1.2) to (1.4), the symbol $|k/2^n - \frac{1}{2}|$ denotes the absolute value of the quantity inside the vertical bars.

In (1.4), the quantity h_1 is a tolerance, and h_2 is the fraction of selections for which the difference between the attained value of $k/2^n$ is allowed to differ from its expected value by more than this tolerance. *If a large enough value of n (the value depending on h_1 and h_2) guarantees that the probability of exceeding the stated tolerance h_1 is less than h_2, the process is said to converge in probability.* This is the sense of equation (1.1). There can be no more than one limit in probability to any process.

Before continuing, we should note that the abstract theory of probability is completely consistent in itself, but applications to reality are not part of this consistent theory. The theory, applied over a finite set S, permits arbitrary assignments of nonnegative probabilities to each element s of S, with the only restriction being that the assigned probabilities sum to 1. For example, there is no abstract inconsistency in assigning the probability 1/21 that the face of a cubical die with a single dot will be the top face after a random roll, the probability 2/21 that the face with two dots will be on top, and generally $i/21$ that the face with i dots will be on top. This assumption, however, seems to be unrealistic when applied in a game of craps. The theory is broad enough to accept any realistic set of probabilities, and it is easy to conceive of a population with an attribute which takes six values distributed in ratios $1:2:3:4:5:6$; this would lead to the probability assignments suggested above as being inappropriate to dice.

Sets of probability axioms have been stated in many works, including [5] and [7]. We are less formal in summarizing the procedures illustrated here.

First, consider a finite set S with a probability function. Let a and b be two different elements of S and consider the probability of selecting either a or b in one selection. We take this probability to be

$$(1.5) \qquad \Pr[a \lor b] = \Pr[a] + \Pr[b].$$

The symbol $\lor$ is to be read "or." If we consider a sequence of two selections (either from the same population or from different populations) and describe the probability of selecting first a and then b, we take

$$(1.6) \qquad \Pr[a \land b] = \Pr[a] \cdot \Pr[b],$$

where the symbol $\land$ is to be read "and," and where the probabilities are chosen from the appropriate populations.

Each of the formulas (1.5) and (1.6) can be extended to any finite number of selections.

We now turn to a formula attributed to Bayes. Let P be a finite set whose elements are finite populations, and let a probability function be taken over P; that is, let a probability be assigned to each element of P. We assume also that a probability function is defined over each population which is an element of P. We do not insist that the elements of two different populations of P be different; and if the same element occurs in different populations, it may have different probabilities under the probability functions assigned to these populations.

As an example, consider two cubical dice, one with faces numbered 1 through 6 and the other with faces numbered 1 through 3, with each label used twice. These may be considered to be two elements which make up P; and to be specific, we denote the first die by p_1 and the second by p_2. The probability function over P can be any pair of nonnegative numbers summing to 1; for example, let us arbitrarily assign $\Pr[p_1] = 19/20$ and $\Pr[p_2] = 1/20$.

We assume that either element p_1 or p_2 is itself a population, in the sense that either die can be selected and rolled any number of times to furnish selections from the total set of elements (1,2,3,4,5,6). We assume that the faces are all equally probable to be selected (as the top face after the random roll), so we have probability functions which we can write as follows:

$$\Pr[1 \,|\, p_1] = \frac{1}{6}, \qquad \Pr[4 \,|\, p_1] = \frac{1}{6}, \qquad \Pr[1 \,|\, p_2] = \frac{1}{3},$$

$$\Pr[2 \,|\, p_1] = \frac{1}{6}, \qquad \Pr[5 \,|\, p_1] = \frac{1}{6}, \qquad \Pr[2 \,|\, p_2] = \frac{1}{3},$$

$$\Pr[3 \,|\, p_1] = \frac{1}{6}, \qquad \Pr[6 \,|\, p_1] = \frac{1}{6}, \qquad \Pr[3 \,|\, p_2] = \frac{1}{3}.$$

These are called *conditional probabilities*, and the symbol $\Pr[n\,|\,p_k]$ is to be read "the probability of n, given p_k."

Now visualize a two-step process in which first a population is selected and then an element of this population is selected, each selection being random under the probability distributions given. We seek a new probability function over the set of numbers assigned to the faces $(1,2,3,4,5,6)$. From formula (1.6), we can write 12 probabilities:

$$\Pr[p_1 \wedge 1] = \frac{19}{20} \cdot \frac{1}{6} = \frac{19}{120}, \qquad \Pr[p_2 \wedge 1] = \frac{1}{20} \cdot \frac{1}{3} = \frac{1}{60},$$

$$\Pr[p_1 \wedge 2] = \frac{19}{120}, \qquad \Pr[p_2 \wedge 2] = \frac{1}{60},$$

$$\Pr[p_1 \wedge 3] = \frac{19}{120}, \qquad \Pr[p_2 \wedge 3] = \frac{1}{60},$$

$$\Pr[p_1 \wedge 4] = \frac{19}{120}, \qquad \Pr[p_2 \wedge 4] = \frac{1}{20} \cdot 0 = 0,$$

$$\Pr[p_1 \wedge 5] = \frac{19}{120}, \qquad \Pr[p_2 \wedge 5] = 0,$$

$$\Pr[p_1 \wedge 6] = \frac{19}{120}, \qquad \Pr[p_2 \wedge 6] = 0.$$

It should be noted that the sum of the probabilities over the complete set of 12 compound probabilities is 1. We now apply formula (1.5) to compute 6 new probabilities:

$$\Pr[(p_1 \wedge 1) \vee (p_2 \wedge 1)] = \frac{19}{120} + \frac{1}{60} = \frac{7}{40},$$

$$\Pr[(p_1 \wedge 2) \vee (p_2 \wedge 2)] = \frac{7}{40},$$

$$\Pr[(p_1 \wedge 3) \vee (p_2 \wedge 3)] = \frac{7}{40},$$

$$\Pr[(p_1 \wedge 4) \vee (p_2 \wedge 4)] = \frac{19}{120} + 0 = \frac{19}{120},$$

$$\Pr[(p_1 \wedge 5) \vee (p_2 \wedge 5)] = \frac{19}{120},$$

$$\Pr[(p_1 \wedge 6) \vee (p_2 \wedge 6)] = \frac{19}{120}.$$

Again it should be noted that the sum of these six probabilities is 1, the summation being over all the marks which can be selected by the compound action of randomly selecting a die and then randomly selecting a face of the die, under the probability functions applying to each of the elementary actions. These six probabilities might appropriately be denoted Pr[1], Pr[2], Pr[3], Pr[4], Pr[5], and Pr[6].

We now state the general rule for generating a table of probabilities from a compound action.

Rule for Compound Probabilities. *Let P be a finite population of populations p_k over a finite set S with a probability function given over P, and for each k let there be given a probability function over S (with $\Pr[s_i|p_k] = 0$ if the element s_i does not occur in the population p_k). Then the probability of selecting any element s_i of S by selecting a population randomly and then selecting an element from this population randomly is*

$$(1.7) \qquad \Pr[s_i] = \sum_k \Pr[p_k] \cdot \Pr[s_i | p_k].$$

The proof is straightforward, in the manner of the example just given. The terms in the sum are the probabilities of selecting the element s_i from a particular population p_k, complying with formula (1.6), and the sum over k conforms with formula (1.5) (extended to any finite case) for the probability of selecting s_i by any compound selection of population and element of the population.

If we now return to our example with the two dice, we may carry out a compound selection of a die and a mark on the face of this die, and from the result of this experiment we can deduce information about which die was actually selected. For example, if the mark is 4, 5, or 6, then the die p_1 was certainly selected, for the die p_2 does not have these marks. On the other hand, if the mark is 1, 2, or 3, then the probability of p_2 may be greater than the a priori assigned probability of $1/20$, for p_2, if selected, has a greater probability of furnishing any of these marks than does p_1 if it is selected.

The general question here is whether the roles of P and S above can be reversed. If an element s_i of S is selected, this element was certainly selected from one of the original populations of P. Thus it is appropriate to seek a probability function over P which depends on the element s_i selected. This is entirely analogous and dual to the original idea that a selection from P led to a probability function over S. If this dual point of view is acceptable, then we should be able to assign probability functions $\Pr[p_k|s_i]$ to satisfy the relation dual to (1.7),

$$(1.8) \qquad \Pr[p_k] = \sum_i \Pr[s_i] \cdot \Pr[p_k | s_i].$$

It is obvious that (1.8) is satisfied if we write

$$(1.9) \qquad \Pr[p_k | s_i] = \frac{\Pr[p_k] \cdot \Pr[s_i | p_k]}{\Pr[s_i]},$$

where $\Pr[s_i]$ is to be computed according to (1.7), and where $\Pr[s_i] > 0$. In connection with this computation, it should be noted that the summation index written k in (1.7) is a "dummy index," and that the final result of the summation does not depend on k. Indeed, the summation formula (1.7) is to be read "the probability of any selection s_i is the sum over all elements of P of the probability of selection of an element of P multiplied by the probability of selection of s_i if that element of P is chosen." This omits all reference to the index shown as k in the formula, thus permitting the index to be denoted by any other symbol, say j; this change might be made in order to avoid confusion with the meaningful symbol k in (1.9).

Formula (1.9) is the only general formula which will establish the duality sought. This may be shown by taking special cases with only one conditional probability positive. *This is the formula of Bayes. The quantity* $\Pr[p_k | s_i]$ *is the a posteriori probability of* p_k, *given* s_i.

The formula of Bayes is consistent with all the requirements we have placed on the abstract structure of probability, and we accept it. The formula is reasonable in application also, for if we think in terms of frequencies, discussed in connection with (1.1), then the numerator of (1.9) is the frequency with which the combination $p_k \wedge s_i$ occurs, and the denominator is the frequency with which s_i itself occurs. Thus the right-hand member of (1.9) is analogous to the fraction of all the selections of s_i arrived at by a selection of p_k.

For most applications which arise in this book, attention can be restricted to finite sets P and S. We might note in passing, however, that the ideas of Lebesgue integration permit a probability theory in which infinite sets are admissible. If the infinite set is countable (that is, if the elements of the set can be exhaustively numbered using the set of positive integers for the numbering), then the only requirement is that convergent infinite sums be used in place of the finite sums used here. Although any function defined over a finite set has a finite mean, this may not be true for infinite sets. In particular, let f be a real-valued function defined over a finite population S with a probability function. This means that some number $f(s)$ is attached to each element s of S. Then the mean value of f (weighted in accordance with the probability function over S) is

$$(1.10) \qquad \bar{f} = \sum_{s} f(s) \cdot \Pr[s],$$

the summation being over all elements of S. If S is a countable set whose kth element is s_k, and if $\Pr[s_k] = 2^{-k}$, then S with its probability function is admissible to the theory developed above and expanded to countable sets. If the function f is taken to have values $f(s_k) = 2^k$, then the mean value of f is infinite. This fact may be accepted without detracting from the utility of the theory. If the function f is taken to have value 2^k for k odd and -2^k for k even, no mean value $\bar{f}$, finite or infinite, exists.

If the set S is a continuum—a line segment, a ray, a whole line, or a plane, for example—then a more general summation operation must be used. Notice, first, that not more than a countable set of elements can have positive probabilities. If a probability theory is to be established over S, it is convenient to think in terms of a probability density function. This is a function with nonnegative values on S, with the further restriction that some generalized sum over S has value 1. This generalized sum may be a Lebesgue integral with respect to some measure function over S, with the measure function of the whole of S having value 1. In this case, the measure of any set of S is the probability of selecting an element of that set. Some sets are not measurable; for examples, see [11, Chapter VII]. Nonmeasurable sets are excluded from probability calculations. This exclusion, which may seem unattractive at first glance, is unavoidable.

Another description of probability over continuous spaces may be made in terms of cumulative distribution functions. In this, there need be no density function; but for a domain of subsets of the space studied, probabilities of selecting from the subsets of the domain are assigned. We shall not go into the axiomatics of such assignment here, but we suggest that an appropriate tool to consider is the Lebesgue-Stieltjes integral.

A probability theory for infinite sets is developed by Kolmogorov [7]. In particular, he establishes a Bayes formula for probability density functions. A detailed discussion of Lebesgue and other related measures is given by von Neumann [11]. An exposition of Lebesgue-Stieltjes integrals is presented by Bochner [1]. Many excellent expositions of probability theory have appeared; an elementary one is by Gnedenko and Khinchin [3].

We shall not try to treat continuous domains fully, but rather shall restrict our attention to introducing a few fairly formal descriptions of a continuous case, with probability density functions treated by standard methods of analysis. These functions are measurable functions over some space with a measure. We might postulate a measure space P of populations with a probability density function $p: P \to \{\text{nonnegative reals}\}$, with

$$(1.11) \qquad \int_P p(k)\ dk = 1.$$

The interpretation of the density function is that for every set $K \subset P$ for which the integral $\int_k p(k) \, dk$ is meaningful,

$$(1.12) \qquad \Pr[k \in K] = \int_K p(k) \, dk.$$

This integral is a clear extension of the function $\Pr[p_k]$ over the finite k domain used heretofore. The rest of this formal development is analogous to other parts of the development for the finite case.

Similarly, for almost every $k \in P$ we are given a density function $s: S \rightarrow \{\text{nonnegative reals}\}$, where S is the union of elements belonging to at least one population (that is, element) of P. For fixed k and for $i \in S$, denote the value of s by $s(i|k)$. When $s(i|k)$ is defined, require

$$(1.13) \qquad \int_S s(i|k) \, di = 1.$$

Now extend formulas (1.5) and (1.6) to give

$$(1.14) \qquad \Pr[(k \in K) \wedge (i \in I)] = \int_K \int_I p(k)s(i|k) \, di \, dk,$$

whenever the integral is meaningful.

Now expand K to fill P, and write

$$(1.15) \qquad \Pr[i \in I] = \int_P \int_I p(k)s(i|k) \, di \, dk.$$

If we write formally

$$(1.16) \qquad \Pr[k \in K] = \int_S \int_K s(i)p(k|i) \, dk \, di,$$

with, from differentiation of (1.15),

$$(1.17) \qquad s(i) = \int_P p(i)s(i|k) \, dk,$$

we may try to define $p(k|i)$ to be consistent with (1.16) and (1.17); that is, we want

$$(1.18) \qquad \Pr[k \in K] = \int_S \left[\int_K \left(\int_P p(k)s(i|k) \, dk \, p(k'|i) \right) dk' \right] di.$$

Finally, analogously to the Bayes formula, we write formally, from (1.9),

$$(1.19) \qquad p(k'|i) = \frac{p(k')s(i|k')}{\displaystyle\int_P p(k)s(i|k) \, dk}$$

and

$$(1.20) \qquad \Pr[k' \in K \,|\, i] = \int_K p(k' \,|\, i) \, dk'.$$

The extension of the Bayes formula to (1.19), to be interpreted through (1.20), requires a system in which the validity of the limiting processes implied in the preceding formalities can be established. This can be accomplished for a comfortably wide class of operations.

For the most part, however, we can restrict our attention to the finite case; in fact, if such restriction does not give a good approximation to the correct computational results, the validity of the continuous case cannot be established.

1.4 RE-EXAMINATION OF THE PROBABILISTIC MODEL

Our first objective here is to re-examine the probabilistic model of communications offered in Section 1.2 in the light of the development in Section 1.3—and in particular in the light of the formula of Bayes, equation (1.9) or equation (1.19). In doing this, we manage to muddy the water just a bit by noting that there are several factors, each more or less independent of the others, in our model of communications, and that because of this independence these factors can be attacked separately.

In Section 1.2, we were concerned with a set S of statuses, a set A of nonredundant descriptors, and a set B of redundant descriptors. Furthermore, we had several probability functions for study. In this section, we assume that all sets are finite; in view of the closing sentence of Section 1.3, this admits a good approximation to the results we should get for the infinite case, and it permits specialization to equation (1.9). In fact, this assumption of finiteness removes all convergence questions with their requirement of meticulous detail, and it gives a model which seems likely to describe communications adequately to fit our knowledge of communications for some time to come.

One of the probability functions we considered was over the set S of statuses. We stipulated that the addressee had this probability function as an a priori guide to the nature of the report of the originator. In the light of the Bayes formula, this probability function may, at least conceptually, be modified to give an a posteriori probability function over S, since the mechanism of ascribing a population with distribution function to each element s of S is similar to the mechanism used in connection with the dice of Section 1.3. In the case of dice, the rule of procedure was to select a die and by rolling it to select an element of the population it depicted. In the present case, once a status s is established, it leads to the selection of an element a of A randomly, subject to the probability function over A associated with s.

For the time being, omniscience is handy, and we assume explicitly that the originator has randomly selected a status from S and that we know exactly the descriptor he has selected from A. With this knowledge and the knowledge (which we have assumed to be available with or without omniscience) of the deterministic selection from B (when the selections from S and A are known), we can re-estimate a posteriori the probability function over S. It is reasonable, and it should be subject to proof, that our assumption of perfect knowledge of the elements selected from A and B, because it matches or exceeds the knowledge available to the addressee, gives us a means for determining an a posteriori distribution over S with at least the confidence of the addressee. This observation is basic in information theory.

The a posteriori probability function which gives the probability that an element s of S was chosen, given that a choice a was made from the set A to describe the choice, is

(1.21)
$$\Pr[s\,|\,a] \;=\; \Pr[s] \cdot \frac{\Pr[a\,|\,s]}{\Pr[a]}.$$

This is a direct application of the Bayes formula (1.9).

The quality of a good expositor or a good journalist is that he is able to select a in such a way as to favor heavily the correct element s in this *a posteriori probability* function. This favoring of the correct status s in the Bayes calculation can be brought about only by an effective choice of the conditional probability functions $\Pr[a\,|\,s]$. This choice in practical cases depends both on the originator's ability at expression, and on the ability of the originator to identify the status which is presented to him.

This point of view seems to the author to be essential in describing the process of communications. Even if there are no available data to fit the formulas, it seems to be important to recognize the formulas, at least implicitly, as providing a description of the vehicles available for communications.

In short, an ambitious journalist or expositor seeks to improve the rules by means of which he describes an element s of S by choosing an element a of A. It was explicitly noted in Section 1.2 that the a priori probability functions are those of the addressee and not necessarily those of the originator, and one of the subtleties of originating a single communication is to estimate well the probability functions which will be used by the addressee and to exploit this estimate.

As a particular example of this estimation procedure, let us consider the word "eventually." To an audience of citizens of the United States unsullied by contact with other languages, the statement "eventually x," where x is a predictive clause such as "it will snow," means that if we observe through a sufficiently long period, the event x will happen with probability 1 or probability very close to 1. In any of several other languages, however, the word which is the clear image of "eventually" carries nowhere near the implication of high probability which is accepted in the purely American language. Thus, for example, in French the word "*éventuellement*" is to be translated "possibly, contingently; should the occasion arise; on occasion" [6].

The good expositor judges the audience he is trying to address. In particular, for example, if he is a quantitative expositor who knows the variation of degree of near certainty assigned by various languages to the "eventually"-stem, and if he is addressing an international audience, then he will avoid use of this word because of its ambiguity and because of the fairly convenient replacements available.

We turn now to the possibility of garbles in the transmission of the pair (a,b) from the originator to the addressee. This study immediately factors into two parts. The first factor is concerned with the behavior of a transmission channel which has already been established and with a particular established rule for determining the element b once the elements s and a have been selected. This study will here be called *descriptive transmission theory*. The second factor is directed toward the improvement of the transmission channel and improvement of the rule for determining b. This factor clearly depends on descriptive transmission theory, for without that theory there would be no way to compare results from two different systems; but this second factor, which will be called *transmission mechanics*, explicitly admits a purposeful change of the communication techniques in order to improve quality of transmission. Thus the descriptive theory is concerned with what is in being, and transmission mechanics is concerned with methods of improvement of the transmission channel, including methods of description of the status observed. In particular, transmission mechanics includes concern with error-recognizing and error-correcting codes to be inserted as part of the redundant descriptor, b. The descriptive transmission theory is more subtle than one would realize from this seemingly innocent description, and it contains much of the recently developed information theory. One output of the descriptive theory is a set of implications or even outright suggestions as to how the transmission mechanics can be improved.

Turning first to the descriptive theory, we again consult the formula of Bayes. The first consideration will be one of the means available to the addressee to estimate the a posteriori probability that the originator despatched the communication (a,b). This estimate will be based on the observation of the pair (α,β) by the addressee, the a priori probability of a pair (a,b) having been introduced to the modem, and application of the formula of Bayes. In connection with the formula of Bayes, it is true that many statisticians prefer to use it sparingly or not at all, and that this group contains many of the world's most distinguished statisticians; use of the Bayes approach is not absolutely required, and indeed it may be replaced by axioms providing another perfectly adequate foundation, but we find the formula convenient in furnishing a central foundation on which to base our abstract structure, and we shall use it in this development.

We should first attempt to find an a priori probability function for the pair (a,b). This is closely related to the probability value Pr[a] appearing in the denominator of equation (1.21). The quantity Pr[a] was to be computed by application of formula (1.7). In the present case, it is necessary that the process of generation of the component b of the message be taken into account; specifically, it was assumed that b might depend on both a and s. If the dependence has been on a alone, we should have Pr[a], as calculated for equation (1.21), as the a priori probability of an (a,b) pair. Because of the admissibility of dependence on both a and s, however, we must use a different calculation for the a priori probability function. In our general discussion here, the precise values of this function are not important or computable. All that is necessary is that we assume that the population of (a,b) pairs is finite, that we can compute a probability function to be accepted as the probability of any particular pair, given any status s, and that an a priori probability function over the finite set S of states is available. With this information, we are able to write the a priori probability of occurrence of a pair (a,b):

$$(1.22) \qquad \Pr[(a,b)] \;=\; \sum_{s} \Pr[s]\cdot\Pr[(a,b)\,|\,s].$$

So far as the addressee is concerned, this is the only information about (a,b) available a priori. Thus he is forced to use this probability as his a priori probability with regard to input messages. The estimate is to be modified into an a posteriori probability function through use of the extracted pair (α,β) and assumptions about the transmission channel. In order to avoid unrevealing complications, we assume for this discussion that the extracted pair is intended to match the injected pair rather than some convenient transform of the injected pair.

The characteristics of the transmission which are immediately applicable under the formulation we have presented are the entries in a table of conditional probabilities. Again, it is not necessary to know what the mechanism of possible garbling is, or whether the components of the pair are garbled independently (as was the case with the PL/I example mentioned earlier, in which the component *a* was completely garbled and the component *b* completely ungarbled).

Thus we require the probability functions $\Pr[(\alpha,\beta)\,|\,(a,b)]$, the probability of extraction of (α,β), given injection of (a,b). With this, an observation of (α,β), and the usual understanding about why selection of any (a,b) for injection is responsible for a probability function over the set of pairs (α,β), we can write the a posteriori probability function over the set of pairs (α,β):

$$(1.23) \qquad \Pr[(a,b)\,|\,(\alpha,\beta)] = \frac{\Pr[a,b]\cdot\Pr[(\alpha,\beta)\,|\,(a,b)]}{\Pr[\alpha,\beta]},$$

where $\Pr[a,b]$ is computed according to (1.22), $\Pr[(\alpha,\beta)\,|\,(a,b)]$ is a description of characteristics of the transmission channel, and the denominator $\Pr[\alpha,\beta]$ is given by

$$(1.24) \qquad \Pr[\alpha,\beta] = \sum_{(a,b)} \Pr[a,b]\cdot\Pr[(\alpha,\beta)\,|\,(a,b)].$$

The material down through equation (1.24), but in particular equation (1.23), furnishes the best description of the transmission channel available from the material attainable under the assumptions of this section. With this information and information about the speed of transmission, the information theorist can define channel capacity and formulate approaches to optimal use of the channel. If the channel capacity seems inadequate, then classical (frequently Fourier-transform) analysis of bandwidth, power, noise, and similar concepts may serve to suggest a remedy.

It is clear also that selection of a status *s* starts a process which is transitive, in the sense that selection of *s* dictates a probability distribution over pairs (a,b), and this in turn yields a selection which dictates a probability distribution over pairs (α,β). If we are not interested in determining the characteristics of the isolated transmission channel, we can study the probability function over S, under which *s* is selected, in terms of conditional probabilities over extracted pairs (α,β); from this we can indicate a direct calculation of the a posteriori probability imposed on S by extraction of a pair (α,β).

We choose an element *s* of S, a pair (α,β), and a pair (a,b). Since we know $\Pr[(a,b)\,|\,s]$ and $\Pr[(\alpha,\beta)\,|\,(a,b)]$, we may use formula (1.6) to compute the probability of a transit from *s* to (α,β) by way of the pair (a,b):

$$(1.25) \quad \Pr[\{(a,b)\,|\,s)\,\wedge\,[(\alpha,\beta)\,|\,(a,b)\}] = \Pr[(a,b)\,|\,s]\cdot\Pr[(\alpha,\beta)\,|\,(a,b)].$$

Now we can apply formula (1.5) to compute the probability $\Pr[(\alpha,\beta)\,|\,s]$ for every possible route from *s* to (α,β). The possible routes are via the various admissible pairs (a,b), so we write

$$(1.26) \qquad \Pr[(\alpha,\beta)\,|\,s] = \Pr[\bigvee_{(a,b)}\{[(a,b)\,|\,s]\,\wedge\,[(\alpha,\beta)\,|\,(a,b)]\}],$$

where the symbol $\bigvee_{(a,b)}$, is intended to be a large "or" symbol with index (a,b), to be used analogously to a summation symbol, and the right-hand member of the equation denotes the probability that there is some pair (a,b) through which the transit from s to (α,β) is made, given s. By (1.5) and (1.25), this probability is

$$(1.27) \qquad \Pr[(\alpha,\beta)\,|\,s] \;=\; \sum_{(a,b)} \Pr[(a,b)\,|\,s]\cdot\Pr[(\alpha,\beta)\,|\,(a,b)].$$

This last equation (1.27) establishes S as a set of populations with elements which are pairs (α,β). Since we start with a probability distribution over S, and since we have the probability distribution imposed on the set of pairs (α,β), given selection of any element of S, we are in a position to apply the Bayes formula again and to present a formula for the a posteriori probability function over S, given an observation (α,β):

$$(1.28) \qquad \Pr[s\,|\,(\alpha,\beta)] \;=\; \Pr[s] \;\cdot\; \frac{\Pr[(\alpha,\beta)\,|\,s]}{\Pr[(\alpha,\beta)]}.$$

This is the formula of Bayes (1.9) applied to the data available here. On the right, the factor $\Pr[s]$ is the original assigned probability, the factor $\Pr[(\alpha,\beta)\,|\,s]$ is to be computed using (1.27), and $\Pr[(\alpha,\beta)]$ is to be computed through equations (1.24) and (1.22).

This formally solves the problem faced by the addressee. Realistically, however, in any sizable communications system, the evaluations are far too extensive for economical execution, and we look for fractions of the total problem which can be attacked reasonably. Some of the more interesting of these fractions will be treated in later chapters of this book.

1.5 STOCHASTIC POPULATION PROCESSES

The only communications model which has been treated thus far in this chapter assumed orderly progression through a small number of elements from an originator to an addressee who is supposed to exercise intelligence to estimate the status stimulating the message. In this model, the originator need exercise no intelligence; the message may be a by-product of some other activity. The electrical potential differences produced on the skin by muscles of the heart is an example of valuable communications accidentally generated.

We shall now turn our attention to a different aspect of communications. Here it might be well to think of large numbers of active participants. The model to be produced is vague, but in some sense it should apply to the central nervous system of the human, with a large number of neurons. Our purpose in noting this model is not so much to treat any particular problem, but rather to present another probabilistic description that may be handled in some useful cases.

We again consider a set S of statuses. Further, we restrict our attention to a finite set S, although the argument may be modified in some cases, as was indicated in connection with the formula of Bayes. We assume that each status has a set of neighbors. We consider transitions from one status to another. We need sufficient stability to assure that a time period can be found which is so short that the probability of a transition to a non-neighbor during that period is uniformly dominated by a constant times the square of the time duration.

Specifically, we seek the probability that the status $s_i \in S$ is attained at some time $(t + h)$, where t and h are to be fixed for the moment. We denote this probability by $y_i(t + h)$. We refer this probability back to the status existing at time t. We now demand that h be close to 0, so that h^2 is dominated to any desired degree by h. Now let $N(i)$ be the set of values which index the neighbors of s_i; that is, $N(i) = \{j \,|\, s_j \text{ neighbors } s_i\}$. (This last is set notation, and it should be read "$N(i)$ is the set of values j such that s_j neighbors s_i.")

We now return to the usual product and sum rules. We write $y_j(t)$ as the probability that the jth status exists at time t; and we assume that we know functions $c_{j,i}$, depending on time, which estimate the probability of transition from the status s_j to s_i during the time period of duration h starting at time t, given that the status s_j occurs at time t:

(1.29) $\Pr[s_i \text{ at time } (t + h) \,|\, s_j \text{ at time } t] = c_{j,i} h + O(h^2)$.

Here $O(h^2)$ denotes some quantity which is uniformly bounded by some constant times h^2 as h tends to zero. By straightforward application of the rules already stated for compound probabilities, we immediately get

(1.30) $y_i(t + h) = \sum_i c_{j,i}(t) \cdot y_j(t) \cdot h$

$$+ \left[1 - \sum_i c_{i,j}(t) \cdot h\right] y_i(t) + O(h^2).$$

Here the first term on the right-hand side is the probability of occurrence of a status neighboring s_i at time t times the probability of transition from that status to s_i, estimated to within $O(h^2)$; the second term is the probability that the status s_i occurs at time t and that no transition to a neighboring status occurs during the period from t to $t + h$, also estimated to within $O(h^2)$; and the final term is the error from using the linear estimates.

By rearranging (1.30) and dividing by h, we easily get

(1.31) $\dfrac{y_i(t + h) - y_i(t)}{h} = \sum_i [c_{j,i}(t) \cdot y_j(t) - c_{i,j}(t) \cdot y_i(t)] + O(h),$

and by permitting h to vary and by taking limits as h tends to zero, we obtain

$$(1.32) \qquad \frac{dy_i}{dt} = \sum_i (c_{j,i}y_j - c_{i,j}y_i).$$

Equation (1.32) is typical of stochastic processes of the general nature described here. If the set S is continuous rather than finite, and if it is endowed with suitable structure of transition probabilities, then the right-hand member of (1.32) may be replaced by space derivatives so that the stochastic behavior of the continuous model may be depicted by a partial-differential-equation model, generally parabolic in nature. If the size of S is great, a partial-differential-equation model may give a good approximation to the stochastic model developed into equations (1.32), for solutions of these equations may present a finite-grid approximation to the solution of an analogous partial differential equation.

Finally, before noting the nature of applications of techniques of this general type, we should consider the nature of transition probabilities. It is true that we may consider transitions to be fundamentally probabilistic in nature, so that we may believe that the model actually is consistent with reality. Views including probabilistic transitions are generally held to be valid in quantum mechanics, for example. On the other hand, we may be forced to accept a model involving probabilistic transitions because of ignorance or because of the cost in time, effort, or deleterious effects which would be involved in distinguishing between several different statuses.

More fully (and symbolically), suppose that the set S is naturally indexed over two sets, so that its elements would be denoted naturally by marks such as s_{ik}. Suppose further that the transitions from each status s_{ij} of S to the next status to occur is completely deterministic, so that (for example) status $s_{i_1k_1}$ is invariably followed at a determined age of $s_{i_1k_1}$ by status $s_{i_2k_2}$, at least when the system is not subjected to unnatural outside influence. Suppose, however, that sets of statuses are aggregated in the model, so that all statuses with the same value of the first index i are treated as identical. The reasons stated above for this type of identification include ignorance of the second index or its nature, laziness, or, perhaps most important, inability to carry out the measurements required to observe the value of the second index without subjecting the system to unnatural outside influences which would unacceptably affect its behavior. Under any of these conditions, if there is reasonably stationary distribution of values of the second index among elements with equal first-index values, then the false but practicable stochastic model may be introduced and used.

Models of this type may be applied in studies of large nervous systems for some time to come, whether the elementary statuses are actually probabilistic or not. Deep brain surgery to determine whether or not a patient with a serious brain injury will later be subject to epileptic seizures may be a bit heroic and dangerous.

Our applications of stochastic processes are likely to resemble life-and-death processes. Thus signals or parts of signals may be created or lost stochastically during transmission, and the state of transmission may be described conveniently in terms of population of quanta of signal energy, the quanta being either the natural indivisible physical quanta or quanta of convenience introduced to facilitate computational study of a system. If the model used permits births without restraint or without serious effect on the death rate (perhaps through starvation or its analog), then the possibility of infinitely many statuses must be contemplated.

It should also be noted that transient solutions of problems involving differential equations of the type of (1.32) are frequently required. (The most elementary analyses in queuing theory generally seek equilibrium solutions.) An amusing model involving beetles was presented by Neyman, Park, and Scott [9]. Here the model must lead to extinction with probability 1, and the only nontransient solution would be one where the size of each of the two populations considered in the paper is zero; however, approximate methods were used to determine a transient but remarkably persistent quasi-stability, in which one population becomes extinct and the other seemingly stabilizes for an expected period which I. J. Good and the present author have estimated roughly to exceed the assumed evolutionary period of the animals involved.

Those who are interested in the mathematics of stochastic population processes may consult a mathematically demanding expository paper by Moyal [8].

REFERENCES

1. Bochner, Salomon, *Lectures on Fourier Integrals*, Annals of Mathematics Studies, No. 42, Princeton, 1950.
2. Feller, William, *An Introduction to Probability Theory and Its Applications*, Vol. I, 3rd ed., Wiley, New York, 1968.
3. Gnedenko, B. V., and A. Ia. Khinchin, *An Elementary Introduction to the Theory of Probability*, Dover, New York, 1962.
4. Good, I. J., A paper presented at a Conference on Conceptual Aspects of Communications Theory, University of California, Los Angeles, October, 1962.
5. Good, I. J., *Probability and the Weighing of Evidence*, Hafner, New York, 1950.
6. *Heath's Standard French and English Dictionary*, J. E. Mansion (editor), 2nd ed., D. C. Heath and Company, Boston, 1939.
7. Kolmogorov, A. N., *Foundations of the Theory of Probability*, Chelsea, New York, 1956.
8. Moyal, J. E., "The General Theory of Stochastic Population Processes," *Acta Math.*, **108**, (1962), 1–31.

9. Neyman, Jerzy, Thomas Park, and Elizabeth L. Scott, "Struggle for Existence: The Tribolium. Model: Biological and Statistical Aspects," *Proceedings of the Third Berkeley Symposium on Mathematical Statistics and Probability*, **4**, (1959), 4–79.

10. Tompkins, C. B., "Methods of Successive Restrictions in Computational Problems Involving Discrete Variables," in *Experimental Arithmetic, High Speed Computing and Mathematics, Proceedings of Symposia in Applied Mathematics*, Vol. **15**, American Mathematical Society, Providence, 1963, pp. 95–106.

11. von Neumann, John, *Functional Operators*, Vol. I, Annals of Mathematics Studies, No. 21, Princeton, 1959.

FURTHER READINGS

1. Bartlett, M. S., *An Introduction to Stochastic Processes, with Special Reference to Methods and Applications*, Cambridge University Press, New York, 1966.

2. Beckenbach, Edwin F., "Combinatorics for School Mathematics Curricula," in Lennart Råde (editor), *The Teaching of Probability and Statistics*, Almquist and Wiksell, Uppsala; Wiley, New York, 1970, pp. 17–51.

3. Breiman, Leo, *Probability*, Addison-Wessley, Reading, Mass., 1968.

4. Feller, William, *An Introduction to Probability Theory and Its Applications*, Vol. II, Wiley, New York, 1966.

5. Grenander, Ulf, "Toward a Theory of Patterns," in *Symposium on Probability Methods in Analysis*, Springer Verlag, Berlin, 1967, pp. 79–111.

6. Kolmogorov, Andrei N., "Logical Basis for Information Theory and Probability Theory," *IEEE Trans. Inform. Theory*, **IT-14** (1968), 662–664.

7. Moran, P. A. P., *An Introduction to Probability Theory*, Clarendon, Oxford, 1968.

PART 1

INTERPERSONAL COMMUNICATION SYSTEMS

Veracity does not cocsist in saying, but in the intention of communicating truth.

SAMUEL TAYLOR COLERIDGE
Bibliographia Literaria
CHAPTER 9
FENNER, LONDON, 1817

CHAPTER 2

Communication:
A Continuous Multichannel Process

RAY L. BIRDWHISTELL

Professor of Communications, Annenberg School of Communications, University of Pennsylvania; Senior Research Scientist, East Pennsylvania Psychiatric Institute, Philadelphia

Contents

2.1   INTRODUCTION

As a new area of knowledge emerges or as old knowledge is re-examined from new perspectives, sections of the formalized intellectual world stir restlessly in absorbtive and divisory activity. Established disciplines disown or lay competitive claim to the new ideas as trivial to or as extensions of their special interests. Since novel approaches to a major area of phenomena are seldom the results of the efforts of a single discipline, at times historical accident seems to determine the initial placement in a particular field of interest. Such placement may not preclude multidisciplinary concern with the new area, but it does inevitably shape the early course of its theory and its investigatory procedures. New developments may be sufficiently novel or incomprehensible, however, that they resist disciplinary capture; the early history is one of crescive activity in the interstices between disciplines.

As an approach gains acceptance, it may bloom into a discipline with its own identity, if its concepts are not defined in the jargon and restrained by the logic of particular disciplines. It is not unique in the history of science for such a new discipline to bifurcate even in the process of formation: it reproduces at a very early stage of growth. This may very well be the phenomenon observable today in that every-man's land which stretches from revised stimulus-response (S-R) theory through cybernetics, information theory, sign theory, systems theory, and mathematical communication theory into social interactional, semantic, psycholinguistic, and human communicational theory.

To be conversant with the literature of information transmission and of human communication is to be impressed with the fact that no matter how divergent may be the approaches there represented, the literature is characterized by fresh, pioneering, and productive thought and investigation. Premature unification or integration of these ideas would certainly abort or cripple them. To make explicit the approach used in this chapter, certain guidelines may be useful in appraising this diverse body of theory, data, and investigatory procedures. An overview of the total area indicates that two general foci or theoretical emphases have been evolving.

2.2 DIVERGENT APPROACHES

The first of these foci is concerned with the investigation and development of general theory about the nature of and the conditions for the transmission of intermittent signals along a particular channel within a limited field. The investigatory procedures here range from the logical-speculative to the classically experimental. The language tends toward the mathematical; the premises, stochastic; the ideal, quantification. The subject matter of this focus is largely in terms of models. The interpart behavior of machines, of neural arcs, and of experimental animals, including human beings, provides the data for examination, abstraction, and generalization. Human or animal social behavior is seldom examined except in as-if models, say, of "dominance structures," "games," "war," or "economic rings" and mock-ups of an administrative structure. In general, telecommunication is of greater concern than face-to-face interaction.

As always, it is difficult to generalize along disciplinary lines about those who have pioneered in or been attracted to this focus of interest. Review of the literature, however, indicates that mathematicians, engineers, some philosophers, many experimental psychologists, and a number of linguists with a particular emphasis on the formal properties of linguistic systems feel particularly comfortable with this approach. The majority, regardless of primary disciplinary loyalty, are explicit in their description of their premises and methodology and leave no doubt that they regard their cogitations and investigations as tool-making. As trained and disciplined scholars, they make it clear that, as tools, the emergent concepts cannot transcend the quality of the data to which the instruments are applied.

There is a second major focus of interest, which is, in part, descendent from, related to, and, hopefully, contributory to the logico-experimental emphasis indicated above. The second concern is with the *structure* of the learned and patterned behavior operating in the interconnection of living systems. The space-time field of such interconnectedness is seen as one of the object-matters for research, a function of the structure of the system itself, and only with caution ever delimited for experimentation. The heuristic field of the classical experiment is often regarded with suspicion as destructive of the communicative phenomena it seeks to comprehend. The investigatory procedures tend to be derived from a natural-history approach. Tentatively isolated units are subjected to contrast analysis and tested by explicit procedures, *in situ*, for structural identity. Quantification tends to be utilized as a method for communicating results rather than as a search technique. Beginning with an assumption of derandomized fields of phenomena, workers with this emphasis tend to postpone statistical procedures for the evaluation of particular events as related to the research-derived structure. Proponents of this position place great emphasis on the systematization of observational recording procedures. Although abstractions in the form of models are utilized, by and large the model is seen as emergent from the research procedures rather than as the subject of these procedures.

Again, there is no clear demarcation of the disciplines associated with this approach. Its intensive and specialized training requirements tend to restrict it to sociologists, psychologists, and anthropologists with linguistic and/or kinesic training; to ethologists, social biologists, and comparative psychologists; and to others from a variety of disciplines who are sufficiently conversant with the techniques, conceptuology, and data of linguistics and/or kinesics to use them. The investigators in this field generally are cognizant of the heuristic nature of their conceptual and investigatory tools, are fully aware that their generalizations apply to an abstracted universe, and know that their emergent data reflect the observational and organizing frame which they employ.

2.3 CONTRASTING VIEWS OF THE HUMAN COMMUNICATIVE PROCESS

This chapter is concerned primarily with the second emphasis. It is perhaps overconservative in its insistence that extensive research is needed, both cross-culturally and cross-speciationally, before we can hope for a comprehensive definition of *human* communication. Nor can it be regarded as representative of human communicational studies in its emphasis on communication as multisensorily based. Only recently have the data from a variety of fields forced us from a monochannel theory of communication. Traditionally, as shaped by culturally induced out-of-awareness preconceptions about infrahuman and human nature, theory about human communication has been phrased as though communicational processes were largely a matter of the transmission of lexical, meaning-carrying forms which are organized into larger shapes by grammatical convention. Whether these forms are ablated from the interpersonal behavioral stream as words or sentences, or examined only in their various derivative telecommunicative abstractions, the abstraction process is justified on the premise that the *significant* aspect of communication is contained within these data. Since these verbal or syntactic forms are carried along the audio-aural channel, that channel is examined as *the* communicative channel, and the speech and the auditory apparatuses, by logical extension, *the* organs of communication. Other sensorily based channels of interpersonal connection are either held constant as environmental variables of speech-centered communication, set aside as expressors of individual feeling states, or dismissed as primitive or atavistic contributors of interference. Silence, except in special cases, is defined as noncommunication. Consistent with these premises and according to this logic, communication is defined as a discontinuous, single-channel process, fully comprehensible by experiments which test the efficiency of the passage of new information from transmitter to reactive receiver.

However, a contrasting position is taken here. Communication is seen as a complex system made up of interdependent codes that can be transmitted along all sensorily based channels that can be influenced. It is seen as a continuous process made up of overlapping discontinuous segments which, in multisensory arrangement, maintain the interactive process. Spoken language is regarded as essential to human society as we know it, but is not, in a priori fashion, assigned priority of function in any particular interactive situation. The communicative situation is seen as one in which there is not *a* message in transmission but *several* messages, of different shapes, compositions, and durations. On the basis of data derived from linguistic and kinesic (the study of communicative body motion) analysis, this theory extrapolates to the assumption that not only is *speech* behavior organized and codified, but so also is the information carried over a still indeterminate number of other channels. Furthermore, not only is spoken language *not* treated as *the* communicative system employed by man, but it is regarded as infracommunicational. That is, language does not stand alone but is interdependently meshed with structured infracommunicational behavior from other channels in the communicative stiuation. Finally, the interactive situation in which *new* information is passed between participants of an interaction is seen to be a very specialized case of human communication, interesting and revealing, but a statistical rarity in the continuum of ordered human association.

2.4 THE BEHAVIORAL SCIENCES AND COMMUNICATION THEORY

The theoretical position that stresses the multichannel structure of human communication is of multidisciplinary genesis. It is impossible in this limited space to detail the contributions from the behavioral sciences which led to the demand for such a reappraisal. A few, however, can be outlined. From cultural anthropology and sociology have come various data that demonstrate the innocence of earlier theories which divided human societies into "simple" or "complex" on the basis of myopic appraisals of their technology or the presence or absence of literacy. The complex division of social labor characterizing even the rudest society requires complex communicative activity to socialize the young, to regulate interpersonal activity, and to meet the exigencies of changing and varying environments. *The demands of adaptation require coordinate activity which cannot conceivably be entrusted to a single communicative channel.*

Men must communicate in face-to-face situations and at a distance, in situations of inaudibility as well as those in which there is no interference, in situations in which silence is demanded, and in those in which vocalizations are trivial to the activities being monitored, organized, or developed. Men must exchange information in the dark and under well-lighted conditions, upwind and downwind, in conditions of closed air space and in the open, in situations in which tactile contact is demanded, and in others where it is prohibited. But most importantly, men must receive and contribute information, develop concert activity, and inhibit unwanted processes of action *for which they have neither words nor awareness.* No theory of communication that would leave the division of labor dependent on verbal interchanges can possibly serve to describe the organized, learned, and transmitted behavior observed in even the rudest society.

As previously discussed, archives of data are being collected by the social biologists, the ethologists, and the comparative psychologists which cast doubt upon, if they do not demolish, theories that would reduce animal behavior to preformationistic physiological or genetical diagrams. More importantly, as observational studies have augmented or have been substituted for cage studies, species after species has been demonstrated to have complex group organizations which are clearly dependent on social learning for continuity. Society, from fish to men, is dependent on communicative activity. As a regulator of personal and interpersonal activity, this communicative activity must be ordered. Man may, by his invention of language, be recognized as having made an incalculable contribution to the range of communicative systems, but he can no longer be regarded as *the* communicator.

Psychology and psychiatry have contributed a wealth of empirical, experimental, and observational studies that have opened the way to the comprehension of the mechanisms which underlie man's ability to be influenced and to influence one another. Studies of learning and of perception have proceeded to the point that the patterned and structured nature of man's incorporation of his environment can no longer be relegated to simplistic causal formulas relating to isolated events. The results of thousands of experiments tested against null hypotheses have led us to the point where we recognize the rich lodes in the world once relegated to *ceteris paribus*.

Thus we now have convincing data that men do not act merely in terms of that of which they are aware. Organisms, including man, must learn much of which they are not aware and which cannot be taught. Such matters cannot be taught since none within the surround are aware of it either. More important, an overwhelming proportion of the information necessary to the survival of the individual, the group, and/or the species is transmitted throughout a population or segments of the population without the membership being aware of the transmissional process. One *could* define the subject matter of communicational studies as that behavior which it is possible to transmit on purpose, but to do so would be to omit the data of a half-century of behavioral science.

Since the example presented later (Sections 2.8–2.11) is a linguistic-kinesic one, discussion of certain developments of these fields has been reserved until last. In the prototheory of human communication we have been presenting here, the attempt has been made to restate propositions about communicative processes in a manner more congruent with contemporary knowledge about humans and animals and their social organizations. However, the use of Occam's razor is insufficient. The test of any theory in science must take place in the context of investigation, measurement, and discovery. Not only must a general theory unify old data, but it must lead us toward new. A theory that stresses the examination of behavior is only a piety if it does not lead us to behavior. The theory and research of linguistic anthropology has been exemplary in this regard. From any point of view of communication, the investigations of linguistic scientists are models of rigor and discipline in the investigation of communicative behavior. In fact, if it is possible to speak of a "breakthrough" in the analysis of human communicative *behavior*, the structural and descriptive linguists must be given credit for it.

Even before the turn of this century, students of language who attempted to describe the languages of non-Western peoples were dissatisfied with the universals made about language and communication by scholars preoccupied with the so-called "modern languages." Traditional historistic or intuitionistic approaches proved unsatisfactory when applied to field data. In particular, the linguistic anthropologists found that the oversimplifications of grammarians schooled in Latin or Greek were inappropriate to the task of understanding these new data. Even preliminary analyses were convincing that such languages could not be denigrated as primitive and crude or as atavistic precursors to the modern languages of literate people. The language spoken by "natives" were obviously just as "evolved," just as complex, and just as meaning-transmissional as the languages of the literate. These languages were different in structure, however, and they demanded new investigatory procedures.

From de Saussure on, a number of linguists, including such pioneer American figures as Franz Boas, Edward Sapir, and Leonard Bloomfield, insisted that the speech stream itself must be examined by the linguist. They taught that phonetic, lexicographic, and grammatical abstractions studied in isolation from this stream are misleading if not distortional. These men and their students demonstrated that examinations of the vocalic stream will yield vast stores of data to the descriptive investigator armed with an explicit frame for the segmentation and structuralization of the behavior audible to the skilled researcher. The efficiency, productivity, and explicitness of the descriptive linguistic frame has been demonstrated in the examination of a variety of languages. In the case of English (and the example below, for comprehensibility, is from American English), this method has made it possible to unravel problems which have cursed generations of teachers and learners of the language. If nothing else, the past twenty years of research of the structure of American English makes it clear that we do not yet fully understand it. Further, it makes abundantly evident the fact that experimentation which naively *assumes* a comprehension of American English is at best operational and at worst based on irresponsible ignorance. The insistence of the linguistic anthropologist that the establishment of structural significance at every level of the data takes precedence in research over assignment of social meaning has not always been popular with linguists who would prefer other roads to meaning.

Yet the complexity of the data uncovered by the exhaustive techniques employed by the descriptive linguists gave them confidence that even the most elaborate manipulations of words and sentences were insufficient to describe reliably the meaningful interaction between men. Their research made it clear that a full description of the communicative process was going to have to include data about the other vocalic processes that went on in association with words, in substitution for words, or had other communicative function than words. Since this research is adequately represented in available literature, there is no need for extensive discussion of it here. For the student of communicative behavior to ignore this literature or even to ignore that portion of it which has appeared since World War II is to condemn understanding of language processes to a nineteenth-century model.

The present author, exposed to linguistics as a graduate student, returned to work in close association with linguists as he sought to order the complicated but regular body motion behavior which he observed in interview situations. Field work among the Kutenai Indians of Idaho and British Columbia laid the groundwork for the recognition that human facial expression, body position, and movement were not only orderly, but varied in form and function from society to society. Even the earliest attempt to describe and delineate significant body motion made it clear that such behavior was susceptible to research procedures analogic to, although not identical with, those which were being developed and utilized by the linguistic anthropologists. At first, every attempt was made to study body motion as a system separate and distinct within itself, and to abstract and order segments of behavior without recourse to other signal systems present in the interpersonal field. Only as it became clear that we could speak with confidence of communicative body-motion systems with their own structural rules, and had demonstrated that this system could largely be described without recourse to audible behavior, did we turn to the examination of the relationship between kinesic and linguistic data. Since the data on kinesic research are far less known to students of communication than the linguistic material, there is more need for introduction here. Space limitations permit only the barest outline, however. (The References contain items for the interested student.) The discussion to follow may be too technical for general interest. It is suggested that some readers may want to skip to Section 2.5, "Body Behavior and Speech Behavior."

Kinesic research, like linguistic anthropological research, seeks repetitive elements which seem of consequence in the interactive behavioral stream, tentatively abstracts these, and tests them for structural significance. The research process is essentially one of locating least significant elements of position and movement, of establishing their relevance to larger structural elements by contrast analysis, and then of repeating the process until larger and larger structural segments are analyzed in a hierarchical structure. "Meaning," at each stage of research, is defined as the structural significance of the element in its structural context. Broader definition of "meaning" is postponed by research design until the significant elements are sufficiently analyzed to permit the test of a behavioral complex in the social setting. Thus such problems as those discussed elsewhere regarding the dichotomization of behavior into so-called "emotive" and "cognitive" categories are postponed until the structure of the communicative process is sufficiently known to permit objective test.

The earliest stage of kinesic research was concerned with that behavior commonly called "gesturing." Broad testing revealed that no gesture was universal in its import or meaning. That is, we could find no "natural" or species-wide gestures. In fact, working more specifically with American gestures, it soon became evident that, although informants might agree as to their shapes and "meaning range," such ranges of "meanings" were totally inadequate when examined in the context of an interaction. No lexicography or dictionary is sufficient to define the range of interactional effects of particular words. Comparably, it is impossible from interview or from tests with "judges" to define the range of particular gestures. Further research revealed that "gestures" are not independent forms. That is, they are less like words than they are like stem forms.

Associated with these stem forms are other kinesic forms which function like prefixes, suffixes, infixes, and transfixes. Under investigation, these *kinemorphs* (the affixual forms plus stems) prove to be made up of smaller interchangeable segment classes, the *kinemes*. These abstracted motion packages are directly analogous to the sound-package building blocks for language. Thus the small classes of body motion, the *kinemas*, combine regularly to form *kinemorphs*, which are again analyzable into kinemorphemic classes. (The imposition of these neologisms is regretable but necessary.) We have, in kinesics, forms like the phonemes, the morphemes, and the lexemes which are constituted at various levels of segmentation in the linguistic stream. Finally, research has demonstrated, at least for the American movement system, that these forms combine into variedly complex syntactic structures—again analogic to comparable structures in the vocalic stream.

2.5 BODY BEHAVIOR AND SPEECH BEHAVIOR

In interactive sequences, kinesic forms comparable to words, sentences, and paragraphs have been isolated by direct observation and by the analysis of silenced film. Body behavior continues in systematic fashion, whether or not speech is present in an interaction. Much of kinesic research has been particularly concerned with data gathered without consideration of the presence or absence of linguistically significant sound. Complex kinemorphic constructions occur in association, but not necessarily in concert, with vocalic behavior. That is, a sound camera will record kinemorphic constructions which are coincident with and are bounded in time by the same junctural shape as is the speech stream. Other kinemorphic constructions occur within segments of a given syntactic sentence, while still others may extend well beyond the vocalic shape, beginning before the onset of phonation and extending beyond its termination. In other words, there is no evidence at this point that kinesic behavior is merely duplicative substitute channel behavior for vocalic behavior. Neither does the obverse seem to be substantiated by the data.

Our preliminary investigations of *sound* movie material give us no reason to believe that there is any simple *one-to-one* relationship between linguistic and kinesic data at this level. One channel may "appear" to reenforce the message of the other, it may "seem" to modify an aspect of the other, or it may "seem" to negate the other. We have isolated and analyzed a number of situations in which, *within a limited observational time*, the segments of behavior carried along the two channels have no immediately demonstrable relationship to each other. On the other hand, we have been unable to detect evidence of *channel independence* which held up as we continued the enlargement of the observational present; as might be expected, there was always a cue in the system that somehow integrated the two.

The methodologies employed by both kinesics and linguistics dictate exhaustive investigation of their particular channels before any attempt can be made to correlate the data of the two. There is an expectable tendency on the part of the linguist to be interested in kinesic data which are directly relevant to spoken behavior. The kinesicist, too, as he exhausts the body-motion behavioral stream, is specially interested in vocalic behavior which has a measurable effect on kinesic structure. Joint research has demonstrated that when the interaction rather than the message structure of a particular channel is the focus of research, it is easier to resist the temptation to regard one channel as "central," the other as "modificatory."

In the discussion to follow, we would like to present data which demonstrate an intimate and possibly necessary relationship between certain structured body-motion and spoken-language forms. Although technical, the data should be comprehensible to native or skilled speakers of American English. The example *abstracts* certain behaviors from the spoken and moved stream; the reader is urged to remember that these abstracted pieces of structure do not exhaust the communicative activity in an interaction.

Among the more important linguistic investigations in spoken American English of the past twenty-five years have been those concerned with pitch,[1] stress, and juncture. Contrastive research revealed that structurally significant variations in loudness and intensity are required for the production of meaningful lexemes, clauses, phrases, and syntactic sentences. These discoveries, when combined with new insights into the junctural conventions of American speech, expedited the behavioral examination of the utterance situation. Since stress and juncture are technical phenomena, a brief and very simplified introduction follows (Sections 2.6 and 2.7).

2.6 LINGUISTIC JUNCTURE

A number of linguists now agree that American English can be described as having three *terminal* junctures. These are often relatable to punctuation conventions in writing.

The first, usually at a cessation point in phonation, the $/\#/$, is described as an off-glide in pitch, plus some elongation of terminal phonemes (characteristic of, but not limited to, a standard "declarative" sentence).

The second, usually at a cessation point in phonation, the $/\|/$, is described as a rise in pitch, plus some elongation of terminal phonemes (characteristic of, but not limited to, certain interrogatory sentences).

The third, more difficult to handle, the $/|/$, is described as sustained pitch, with some shift in phoneme length, often, but not always, at a pause point and in anticipation of continuation of phonation.

2.7 LINGUISTIC STRESS

Many linguists agree that the speaker of American English utilizes combinations of four significant degrees of loudness in the production of

---

[1] For clarity and simplicity, little attention is given in this example to intonation patterns. The relationship between kinesic behavior and linguistic intonation behavior is still undergoing analysis. It seems likely from preliminary data that some kind of systematic relationship exists between certain stretches of kinesic behavior and certain aspects of American English intonation behavior. The data are exceedingly elusive, however, and must be investigated further before even tentative generalizations can be made.

various lexemes, phrases, clauses, and syntactic sentences. These, from loudest to most weak, are primary / ´ /, secondary / ^ /, tertiary / ` / and weak / ˇ /. These four degrees of American English stress are relative, not absolute, distinctions. The auditor makes his contrasts within a given utterance on the basis of the points of relative loudness in the particular stream as measured against his internalized code.

In the discussion to follow (Section 2.8), it is hoped that by a series of contrasts of the phrase "forty fives," uttered in a variety of contexts, to sensitize the reader, unacquainted with linguistic and kinesic conventions, to some of the relationships that have been discovered to exist between linguistic and kinesic structure. In each case, "forty fives" is to be tested as a complete sentence, the response to an appropriate question. To orient the reader, the linguistic stresses and junctures are isolated in contrast exercises. Next, the kinesic stresses and junctures are noted (Section 2.9), and an example is given (Section 2.10). After some tentative correlations, the frame is enlarged to demonstrate how utterance strings are tied together, linguistically and kinesically (Section 2.11). Finally, the intimate relationship between body motion and spoken behavior is demonstrated by some contrastive examples from spoken and moved mathematics. For the reader easily (and understandably) wearied by the detail and technicality of this discussion, the following generalization can be made as the point of the exercises to follow. *Since regularities appear in the stream of movement and in the stream of audible behavior around certain syntactic forms, it is possible to state that body motion and spoken "languages" do not constitute independent systems at the level of communication. By a logic not yet known, they are interinfluencing and probably interdependent.*

2.8 AN EXERCISE IN LINGUISTIC-KINESIC ANALYSIS

Consider the following expressions:

a. "Forty fives."   As in a list made up of forty numerals of the shape of five.

b. "*Forty* fives."   As in the case where the speaker is distinguishing between a list made up of forty, not thirty, fives.

c. "Forty *fives*."   As in the case of a list of forty numerals in the shape of fives, not forty numerals in the shape of sixes.

d. "Forty-fives."   As in the case of guns of a particular caliber.

e. "Forty-*fives*."   As in the case where the speaker is distinguishing guns of .45 caliber from guns of a .44 caliber.

The question is: How (in the sense of what code does he possess) does a normal speaker of English (without recourse to larger contexts in which these appear) make these distinctions when he *perceives* them as sentences in response to direct questions? If we attend only to degrees of loudness and annotate them with the linguistic symbol, we get some immediate contrasts:[2] In examples (a), (d), and (e), our informants spoke "fives" louder than "forty." We assign primary stress / ´ / to "fives."

When we then compare the production of the initial lexeme in these three forms, we can perceive that "forty" in (a) is in contrast with (stronger than) "forty" in either (d) or (e). We assign secondary stress / ^ / to the stronger "forty" in (a). Thus (a) is recordable as /fôrty fíves/. The "for-" in "forty" in (d) and (e) is demonstrable not under weak stress and can be recorded as tertiary / ` /. We now have (d) and (e) as /fòrty fíves/:

a. fôrty   fíves#   As in a list of the numeral five.

d. fòrty⁺ fíves#   As in the guns of a given caliber.

e. fòrty⁺ fíves#   As in .45s, not .44s.

Further information is required to distinguish (d) from (e). One solution is to note that some informants hear "fives" in (e) as having a higher pitch than in (d) and to note this by an arbitrary convention (*).[3] Thus (e) is recorded as /fòrty ⁺ *fíves#/. Since, however, a number of informants cannot, when listening to tape, distinguish (d) from (e), we shall pay special attention to this later when we combine the linguistic and kinesic data. Thus: (d) /fòrty ⁺ fíves#/; (e) /fòrty ⁺ *fíves#/.

We find that when stress only is considered, "forty" and "fives" appear equally loud in (b) and (c). Thus: (b) /fórty fíves/ and (c) /fórty fíves/. The single bar juncture, described above, is involved, and we get /fórty| fíves#/ for both (b) and (c). Again, pitch seems to play a special role, and,

---

[2] According to linguists concerned with American English structure, every stretch of phonation bounded by terminal junctures contains a primary stress against which other stress activity can be weighted.

[3] The fact that we do not attend to pitch *patterning* in these examples does not make them artificial but rather leaves them incomplete. For purposes of explication, however, we omit such data. It must be emphasized, though, that no informant did *or could* omit the intonation profiles from his speech. The inclusion of (*) and the linguistic junctures are only part of the significant intonational material necessary to the production of syntactic sentences.

even though a number of our informants cannot hear it, we add our pitch
distinctions as one solution to the problem. Our corpus now reads:

a. /fôrty   fíveš/   d. /fòrty + fíveš/

b. /fŏrty | fíveš/   e. /fòrty + fíveš/

c. /fórty | fíveš/

These represent the most common responses in the informant-test
situation. The informant may vary his responses, however, and some informants seem to prefer alternate contrasts. These are linguistically contrasted below:

a. /fôrty   fíveš/   a'. "fórty | fíveš"

b. /fŏrty | fíveš/   b'. "fórty   fíveš"

c. /fórty | fíveš/   c'. "forty   fíveš"

d. /fòrty + fíveš/   d'. "forty + fíveš"   d''. /fórty   fíveš/ (rare)

e. /fòrty + fíveš/   e'. "forty + fíveš"

It is to be remembered that these are only several of the possible vocalic
variations. If the original questioner gives some signal that he has not
perceived the distinctions between (b) and (c) or between (d) and (e),
the informant may add paralinguistic or parakinesic behavior as he repeats
for clarification. For instance, he may put *drawl, overhigh,* or *overloud* on the
lexeme indicated above by the arbitrary pitch symbol (*); or he may put
oversoft on the weaker stress to emphasize the stronger stress.

2.9   KINESIC STRESS AND JUNCTURE

As stated previously, early work in kinesics concentrated on the isolation
of kinemes, kinemorphemes, and complex kinemorphemic constructions
discovered in silenced interaction. As research proceeded, body-motion
behavior of a different order was detected in association with volcalization.
Embedded in the complex stream, such behavior was noted as part of
the microkinesic record. At first, since the motions seemed inconsequential
to the structure of the kinesic stream, they were dismissed as artifacts of
muscular, skeletal, or skin involvements in speech production. They were
to take on new significance when research energies were turned to the correlation of spoken and moved behavior in sound-filmed sequences of interaction. The regularity and the systematic nature of these eye-blinks, nods,
and hand and foot movements became apparent, and they could be ac-

counted for only by analysis in the larger frame. At first, these segments were called kinesic *markers*. When, however, research revealed that these could be analyzed into classes of movements (in intensity or body position) in free variation, they were elevated to the status of kinemes of stress.

There are four kinesic stress kinemes: *primary* / ˇ /, *secondary* / ˆ /, *tertiary* or *unstressed* / ¯ /, and *destressed* / ° /. Earlier research in *kine-morphology* demonstrated that American kinesics has at least four kinesic terminal junctures. The first, which terminates a complex kinemorphic stream with a lowering, plus a slight lengthening of movement, is termed *kinesic double cross* /k # /. The second, *kinesic double bar*, /k‖/ has a raise and hold of body part. The third, *kinesic single bar* /k|/ involves a hold in position. Finally, the *kinesic triple cross* / # /, which usually but not always occurs coincident with a kinesic double cross, following a series of passages marked by double crosses, involves a major shift in body position.

As we shall see in the examples below, there are one and perhaps two *internal* kinesic junctures. The first, a *kinesic plus juncture*, /+/, occurs to change the positioning of the primary kinesic stress as it binds certain forms. The second, still under analysis, has been termed a *hold juncture*, / ˆ /. The hold juncture, under special conditions, ties together two or more kinesic primary stresses or a primary and a secondary.

As in the case of linguistic phenomena, theoretically, there is only one kinesic primary stress between any two kinesic terminal junctures. The hold junctures / ˆ /, however, may subsume a kinesic single-bar juncture between two primary kinesic stresses. The hold juncture also operates to tie several syntactic sentences together—that is, it can cover several stretches bounded by terminal / # / or /‖/ junctures. The author suspects the hold-juncture category as too inclusive. It may, under further study, in certain situations be an allokine of a single bar; in others, it may be a separate terminal juncture which operates across /|/, /‖/, and / # / within triple-cross junctures.

As this data developed, we were suspicious of the parallel to linguistic phenomena. It seemed quite possible that we were forcing the body-motion data into a pseudolinguistic frame. The more experience we have with the recording and analysis of utterance situations, however, the more confident have we become of the utility if not the final validity of this formulation. There is, after all, no reason why the two systems must, at this level of structure, have two different logics.

The kinesic stress and juncture material customarily concurrent with our five contrast examples is presented in Section 2.10. First stress and juncture kinemes, as derived from the behavior of informants in the question-answer environment, are presented. There is insufficient space here to detail the articulatory variations which are involved in the performance of either the kinesic stress or junctures. The reader who is a native or skilled speaker of American English, interested in perceiving these, can speak the examples *in response to the appropriate questions* and, by restricting his movement to his head, "feel" the body involvement.

2.10   KINESIC STRESS-AND-JUNCTURE RESPONSES

Now consider the following expressions:

a. "fôrty fĭves"   As in a list made up of forty numerals of the shape of five.

b. "fŏrty⌢fîves"   As in a case where the speaker is distinguishing between a list made up of *forty*, not thirty, fives.

c. "fôrty⌢fĭves"   As in a case where the speaker is distinguishing between a list made up of forty *fives*, not sixes.

d. "fôrty⁽⁺⁾fîves"   As in the case of guns of a particular caliber.

e. "fôrty⁽⁺⁾fîves"   As in a case where the speaker is distinguishing between guns of .45 caliber, not .44 caliber.

These represent the most common responses in the informant-test situation. The informant may vary his responses, however, and some informants seemed to prefer alternate responses. These are kinesically contrasted as follows:

a. "fôrty fĭves"   (or)   a'. "fŏrty | fĭves"   (or)   a". "fŏrty⌢fĭves"

b. "fŏrty⌢fîves"   (or)   b'. "fŏrty⚌ fĭves"   (or)   b". "fŏrty | fĭves"

c. "fôrty⌢fĭves"   (or)   c'. "fôrty↑fĭves"

d. "fôrty⁽⁺⁾fîves"

e. "fôrty⁽⁺⁾fîves"

Some informants characteristically utilize parakinesic "overstrong" or "overintense" or parakinesic "drawl" in making distinctions; others appear to turn to parakinesics only when the questioner seems confused. Some informants characteristically use paralinguistic phenomena; others seem to employ parakinesics as a primary tool for contrast distinctions. Still others "pile up" parabehavior from both channels. There is some temptation to regard these variations as items of "style" or personality, as functions of larger interpersonal relationship patterns. Until we know a great deal more about the structure of both parakinesic and paralinguistic behavior, such extrapolations must remain unjustified by our evidence.

2.11 KINESIC-LINGUISTIC CORRELATION

When the data are assembled, we get interesting, if inconclusive, results. Although the general form of the kinesic material is predictable from knowledge about the linguistic, and the general form of the linguistic material is predictable from knowledge of the kinesic, there is some variation in the subshapes. There do not seem to be *absolute* and nonvariable correlations between particular junctures or stresses at the phonemic and kinemic level. Some correlations, however, are possible when regular combinations of stress kinemes are examined. Certain combinations of the stress kinemes form regular structures, which under analysis are revealed to be members of form classes, the *suprasegmental kinemorphemes*.

The allokinemorphs of stress and the kinemorphemes of which they are members are listed below:

Allokinemorphs of Stress	*Kinemorphemes*
/ ˅ /	/ ˅ /
/ ∧˅ / or / − ˅/ or / − ∧/	/ ⌐˅/
/ ˅∧ / or / ˅ −/ or /∧ −/	/ ⌐ /
/− ˅̟ −/ or / ˅̟/ − ˅̟∧	/⌐⌐/
/ ˅	/ or / ˅#˅ / / ˅⌒˅ /	/˅⌐˅/[4]
/ook / or /ook#/ or /ook‖/	/−o−/
/oo˅ /	/ ⌐˅/
/ ˅oo/	/˅⌐/

When we analyze our corpus, noting the suprasegmental kinemorphemes, the interdependent patterning becomes clearer:

A. ⌐˅k#   *A'.*˅⌐˅k#   *A''.*˅⌐˅k#

A. ∧ ˅k#   A'. ˅ | ˅k#   A''. /fŏrty⌒fĭve˅s K# /

a. /fôrty fíve#s/   a'. /fórty fíve#s/

---

[4] /˅⌐˅/ may, as research proceeds, turn out to be a syntacteme or even an "uttereme." Only as we know more about kinesic junctures can we be sure about its form and function.

B.⌣—k #   *B'.*⌵⌢k #   *B''.*⌵⌢k #

B. ∨ ⇡ ∧ k#   B'. ∨ ⌢ ∨ k#   B''. /fŏrty | fĭves/

b. /fŏrty | fíves/   b'. /fórty# fíves/

C. ⌢⌿   *C'.* —⌿k #   *C''.*⌵⌢⌿k #

C. ∧ ⇡ ∨ k#   C'. ∧ ⇡ ∨ k#   C''. /fŏrty⌢fĭves/

c. /fórty | fíves/   c'. /fórty # fíves/

D. ⌶—k #   *D'.*⌵⌢k #

D. — ⌄⁺ — k#   D'. ∨ ⇡ ∨k #

d. /fôrty + fíves/   d'. /fôrty + fíves/

E. ⌶— k #   *E'.*⌣—k #

E. — ⌄ ∧ k#   E'. ∨ ∧ k#

e. /fôrty + fíves/   e.' /fôrty fíves/

Further perspective is provided on (d) /forty fives/ and on (e) /forty fives/ when we put them in contrast with another form. In these, we are dealing with an example in which crescendo stress sequences of tertiary-plus juncture-primary operate. Let us contrast them with a form in which we invert the stresses to the dimuendo sequence of primary-plus-tertiary. This is characteristic over forms like "tenpins," "suitcase," and "baseball." We singularize both forms:

D. ⌶— k#   F. ⌶— k#

D. ∨ k#   F. ⌄ k#

d. /fórty + five/   f. /báse + ball/

In both cases the kinesic / + /juncture pulls the primary stress to tie the two lexical items into a "nominal." Let us extend this example:

G. —————⌿   *G'.* ⌣——⌢——⌿

G. ∧   ∨   k #   G'. ∨ ⇡   ∧   ∨k #

g. /tên + fòrty + fíves/   g'. /tén | fòrty + fivés/

H. ⌒‿ ⟋ k #   *H'.* ⟍‿⌢‿ ⟋ k #

H. ∧   ∨ k #   H'. ∨ ⌢↑   ∨ #

h. tên + bâse + bàlls   h'. tén | báseballs

I. ‿‿‿⟋   *J.* ‿‿‿⟋

I. ∧   ∨   k #   J. ∧   ∨   k #

i. /fòrty fîve cáliber/   j. /báseball + gâmes/

And further:

K. ⟍‿⌢‿⟋   *L.* ⟍‿⌢‿⟋ k #

K. ∨ ⫴ ∧ ∨ k #   L. ∨ ⌢↑ ∧ ∨ k #

k. /tén#fòrty fîve revólvers/   l. /tén#báseball gâmes/

M. ‿‿‿⟋ k #   *N.* ⟍‿⌢‿⟋ k #

M. ∧   ∧ ∨ k #   N. ∧ ∨ ¦ ∨ k #

m. /fòrty fîve câliber revôlvers/   n. /báseball gâme | stréet càr/

    or   or

M'. ‿‿‿∨ k #   *N'.* ‿‿‿∨ k #

M'. o o o k¦∨ k #   N'. o o o ⌢↑ ∨ k #

m'. /fòrty fîve câliber revôlvers/   n'. /báseball gâme stréet càr/

From these examples, it becomes clear that *linear* survey of particular body movements as related to particular degrees of loudness will not yield significant data about phrase, clause, and sentence formation. Examination of the relationship between the *patternment* of the linguistic material and the *patternment* of the kinesic material illustrates, however, how each contributes structure to the comprehensible utterance. In these examples, an exceedingly limited corpus of linguistic material was utilized for purposes of demonstration. Had we been interested in showing the *range of variability* of the production of American English sentences of these shapes, our corpus would have been much larger. Even with variations of pitch and paralanguage, however, the suprasegmental kinemorphemes would remain stable.

That kinesic patterning contributes to the comprehensibility of utterances at the syntactic level seems evident. Whether this contribution is to be assessed as "redundant" will depend largely on the definition of redundancy—and particularly on the definition of the role of redundancy in the social situation. An excellent term and a useful tool in informational theory, "redundancy" remains but little understood in communication theory. It makes a great deal of difference whether we are interested in *a message* sent by *an individual* to *an individual* or in *messages* and *patterns of messages* transmitted between the membership of a human group of whatever shape. Multichannel contributions not only support continuity in order performance by overlapping codes of various sizes and durations, but they increase the likelihood of message reception from variably readied sense perceptors.

2.12 A MATHEMATICAL EXAMPLE

In the preceding examples, the lexemes "forty" and "fives" were selected as relatively colorless, numeral lexemes. The five examples with their varying semological contexts were used to show how simple constructions and clauses are structured morphologically and syntactically. As a final example, a series of contrasts will be drawn from our continuing research on "spoken and moved mathematics." Association with Beberman and Hendrix of the Illinois Mathematics Project studies of the teaching of mathematics, and examination of their very good films on the teaching situation, led to the conviction that there was considerable range of skill (or technique) to be seen in the performance of mathematics teachers. This range, from our point of view, cannot be understood by such subjective and crude or poetic descriptions as "a matter of personality" or in paradigms which define "good" teaching as a matter of "innate" skill or of the even looser concept "experience." Even less rewarding are discussions of degrees of "motivation."

It seems that we need to be able to describe objectively certain differences in the *behavior* of a "successful" teacher as contrasted to that of the less "successful" teacher. ("Success" here is measured either by professional reputation or by the comparative performance of groups of pupils.) Thus far, the present author has been concerned as an investigator with only one very limited aspect of this monumental problem. Preliminary examination of a film made of one person regarded as an excellent teacher led us to observe other teachers (but, unfortunately, without benefit of film) whose teaching performances seemed to leave room for improvement. One of the behavioral differences which we observed between these teachers was that the "better" teacher enunciated his mathematical propositions as though he were speaking standard American English, while the others varied between such enunciation and a peculiarly ambiguous variety of spoken "written" mathematics. It seemed likely that this would occasion some distress in students who perceived mathematical concepts in other than the written frame.

At best, this was an impressionistic conclusion. Since that time, as part of other research into the structure of American movement patterns, the behavior which is characteristic of spoken formulas has been under scrutiny. The research is far from completed, but certain of the findings may be illustrative of the points being made here. The examples below illustrate certain organizational functions of kinesic stress and juncture. The linguistic data are incomplete for these contrasts. Suffice it to say that such data, thus far analyzed, are consistent with those presented in Sections 2.8–2.11.

Common responses given in the context of "answers to particular mathematical problems" appear below:

    ∨k #
    ∨k #
a. "*A*"   as in *A*

    ⌐⌐⌐∨k #   ⌐⌐ k #
  ∧   ∨   or ∨   ∧
b. "*A* squared"   "*A* squared"   as in *A*²

     ⌐⌐∨k #   ⌐⌐∨ k #
  ∧ – ∨   or   ∨ ⁀ ∧ ∨
c. "*A* plus *B*"   "*A* plus *B*"   as in *A* + *B*

   ⌐⌐∨ | ⌐⌐∨ k #
  ∧ ∨ | ∧ ∨ k #
d. "*A* squared plus *B*"   as in *A*² + *B*

 ∨k #   ⌐⌐∨ k #   ∨|k ⌐⌐∨ k #
 ∨k # – ∧   ∨   or ∨| ∧ ∧ ∨
e. "*A* plus *B* squared"   "*A* plus *B* squared"   as in *A* + B²

 -o-| ∨ k #
 o o| ∨ k #
f. "*A* plus *B* squared"   as in (*A* + *B*)²

‾‾‾‾‾‾V | ‾‾‾‾⌵ k #

o   o   ∨ | ∧   ∨ k #

g. "*A* plus *B* squared minus one"   as in $(A + B)^2 - 1$

∨ k # -o- | ‾‾‾‾⌵ k

∨ k # o o o | ∧   ∨

h. "*A* plus *B* squared minus one"   as in $A + B^2 - 1$

∨ k #‾‾‾∨ k #   ⌢⌢‾‾‾⌵ k #

∨ k # o ∨ k # ∧ ∨⌢‒   ∨

i. "*A* plus *B* squared minus one over two"   as in $A + B^2 - \dfrac{1}{2}$

∨ k # -o-   ⌢ ‾‾‾⌵ k #

∨ k # o o o o o ⌢̣ ‒   ∨ $A + \dfrac{B^2 - 1}{2}$

j. "*A* plus *B* squared minus one over two"   as in $A + \dfrac{B^2 - 1}{2}$

∨‾‾‾ k # ⌢⌵ k #

v o o o k # ‒ ∨

k. "*A* plus *B* squared minus one over two"   as in $\dfrac{A + B^2 - 1}{2}$

Some students, when shown these examples, suggest that the body-motion behavior evident in these performances may be an artifact of eye movement or head movement in reading or writing behavior. Although some informants do "move" their reading, they appear to be as rare as those who move their lips while reading silently. Others upon viewing these examples tend to view them as "mathematical behavior." Some evidence that these are special cases of more general principles of organization may be demonstrated by the following paired contrasts. For simplicity, only the suprasegmental kinemorphemes are shown. Punctuational conventions are coded to assist the reader.

∨ k #   ∨ k #

a. "*A*"   = "John"

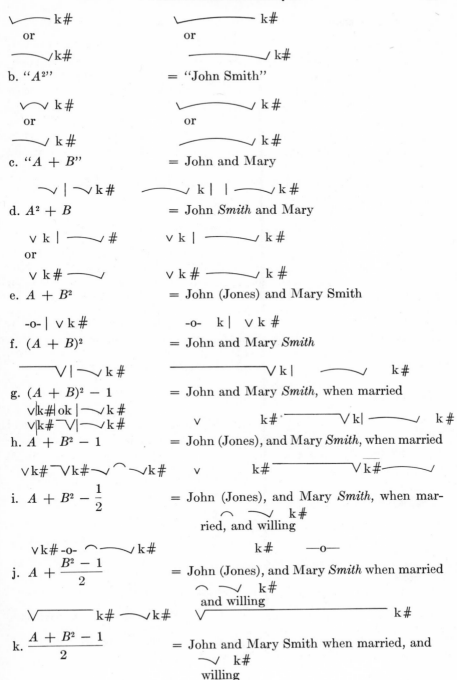

⌣————k#   ⌣————————k#
 or   or
——⌣k#   ————————⌣k#

b. "A^2"   = "John Smith"

⌄⌣ k#   ⌣————⌣ k#
 or   or
——⌣ k#   ————————⌣ k#

c. "$A + B$"   = John and Mary

⌄ | ⌄k#   ——⌣ k | | ——⌣k#

d. $A^2 + B$ = John *Smith* and Mary

∨ k | ——⌣#   ∨ k | ————⌣ k#
 or
∨ k#——⌣   ∨ k#————⌣ k#

e. $A + B^2$ = John (Jones) and Mary Smith

-o- | ∨ k#   -o- k | ∨ k#

f. $(A + B)^2$ = John and Mary *Smith*

————∨ | ⌣k#   ————————∨ k | ——⌣   k#

g. $(A + B)^2 - 1$ = John and Mary *Smith*, when married

∨|k#| ok |⌣k#
∨|k#⌐∨|⌣k#   ∨   k#·————∨ k | ——⌣ k#

h. $A + B^2 - 1$ = John (Jones), and Mary *Smith*, when married

∨k#⌐∨k#⌣ ⌢ ⌣k#   ∨   k#————∨ k#——⌣

i. $A + B^2 - \dfrac{1}{2}$ = John (Jones), and Mary *Smith*, when mar-
⌢ ⌣ k#   ried, and willing

∨k#-o- ⌢——⌣k#   k#   —o—

j. $A + \dfrac{B^2 - 1}{2}$ = John (Jones), and Mary *Smith* when married
⌢ ⌣ k#   and willing

∨———— k# ——⌣k#   ∨————————————k#

k. $\dfrac{A + B^2 - 1}{2}$ = John and Mary Smith when married, and
⌣ k#   willing

2.13   CONCLUSION

These examples have been designed to illustrate certain definable relationships between body-motion behavior, as kinesically analyzed, and
spoken American English. A more complete treatment would have to deal
with the relationships between the body motion during silence as related
to other modalities as well as that which is demanded for the performance of
spoken language. We know far too little about the other communicative
modalities to do more than hypothesize about such relationships. If we
extrapolate from even the limited data presented above, however, it would
seem that we have good reason to be deeply suspicious of any theory of
human communication which accounts only for the behavior carried on
the audio-aural channel.

We can do no better than conclude with the words of Colin Cherry from
his excellent book, *On Human Communication* (p. 127):

> In all experiments carried out upon people, involving their sensations, it is of
> the greatest importance to record all the conditions of the test; only too frequently,
> results are vitiated because an experimenter has failed to record some significant
> attribute of the stimulus or of the environment. The human senses . . . do not
> possess one set of constant parameters, to be measured independently, one at a
> time. It is even questionable whether the various "senses" are to be regarded as
> separate, independent detectors. The human organism is one integrated whole,
> stimulated into response by physical signals; it is not to be thought of as a box,
> carrying independent pairs of terminals labeled "ears," "eyes," "nose," et cetera.

REFERENCES

This is a list of publications designed to acquaint the reader with some of
the background to this chapter. Although it is weighted in support of the
point of view represented here, the listing includes some discussion of
alternative solutions.

General Theory

1. Bateson, G., Ray L. Birdwhistell, Henry Brosin, Frieda Fromm Reichmann, Chas.
   Hockett, and Norman A. McQuown, *The Natural History of an Interview*, U. of
   Chicago Library, 1971.
2. Cherry, Colin, *On Human Communication*, M. I. T. Press and Wiley, New York,
   1957.
3. Carpenter, Edmund, and Marshall McLuhan (editors), *Explorations in Communication: An Anthology*, Beacon Press, Boston, 1960.
4. Goffman, Erving, *Behavior in Public Places; Notes on the Social Organization of
   Gathering*, The Free Press of Glencoe: Collier MacMillan, London, 1963.
5. Goffman, Erving, *Presentation of the Self in Everyday Life*, University of Edinburgh,
   Social Science Research Center, Monograph No. 2, Edinburgh, 1956.

6. LaBarre, Weston, *The Human Animal*, University of Chicago Press, Chicago, 1954.
7. Mead, George, *Mind, Self and Society*, University of Chicago Press, Chicago, 1940.
8. Mead, Margaret, *Continuities in Cultural Evolution*, Yale University Press, New Haven and London, 1964.
9. Miller, George A., Eugene Galanter, and Karl Pribram, *Plans and the Structure of Behavior*, Henry Holt and Co., New York, 1960.
10. Osgood, C. E., and T. A. Sebeok, "Psycholinguistics: a Survey of Theory and Research Problems," *J. Abnorm. Soc. Psychol.*, **49**, No. 4, Part 2, 1954, Morton Prince Memorial Supplement.
11. Ruesch, Jurgen, and Gregory Bateson, *Communication: The Social Matrix of Psychiatry*. Norton, New York, 1951.
12. Sapir, Edward, "The Unconscious Patterning of Behavior in Society" in E. S. Dummer (editor), *The Unconscious, a Symposium*, Knopf, New York, 1927.
13. Scheflen, A. E., "Natural History Method in Psychotherapy: Communicational Research," in Gottschalk, L., and A. H. Auerbach (editors), *Methods of Research in Psychotherapy*, Appleton-Century-Crofts, New York, 1966.
14. Sebeok, Thomas A., Alfred S. Hayes, and Mary C. Bateson, *Approaches to Semiotics*, Mouton and Co., London, The Hague, Paris, 1964.

Linguistics

15. Bloch, Bernard, and George E. Trager, *Outline of Linguistic Structure*, Linguistic Society of America, Waverly Press, Baltimore, 1942.
16. Bloomfield, Leonard, *An Introduction to the Study of Language*, New York, Holt, 1914.
17. Bloomfield, Leonard, *Language*, Henry Holt and Co., New York, 1933.
18. Carroll, John B., and Joseph B. Casagrande, "The Function of Language Classifications in Behavior," in Eleanor Macoby, T. H. Newcomb, and E. L. Hartley (editors), *Readings in Social Psychology*, 3rd ed., Holt, New York, 1958.
19. Chomsky, Naom, *Syntactic Structures*, Mouton and Co., Gravenhage, 1957.
20. de Saussure, F., *Cours de linguisitique generale*, Ballcy and A. Sachehaye (editors), (collaboration of de A. Riedlinger, Payot), Paris, 1949.
21. Fries, Chas. Carpenter, *The Structure of English, An Introduction to the Construction of English Sentences*, Harcourt Brace, New York, 1952.
22. Gleason, Henry A., *An Introduction to Descriptive Linguistics*, rev. ed., Holt, Rinehart and Winston, New York, 1961.
23. Harris, Zelig S., *Structural Linguistics*, University of Chicago Press, Chicago (Phoenix Books), 1961.
24. Hill, Archibald A., *Introduction to Linguistic Structure*, Harcourt Brace, New York, 1958.
25. Hill, Archibald A. (editor), *First-Second-Third Conference on Problems of Linguistic Analysis in English*, The University of Texas, Austin, 1962.
26. Joos, Martin, "Description of Language Design," *J. Acoust. Soc. Amer.*, **22**, No. 6, 1950, 701–709.
27. King, Harold V., "English Internal Juncture and Syllable Divisions," in Marckwardt, Albert H. (editor), *Studies in Language and Linguistics—in Honor of Charles C. Fries*, English Language Institute, University of Michigan, 1964.
28. Sapir, Edward, *Selected Writings of Edward Sapir*, Mandelbaum, David G. (editor), University of California Press, Berkeley and Los Angeles, 1951.

29. Trager, George L., and Henry Lee Smith, Jr., *An Outline of English Structure* (Studies in Linguistics, Occasional Papers, No. 3), Battenburg, Norman, Okla., 1951.
30. Trager, George L., and Henry Lee Smith, Jr., "Paralanguage: A First Approximation," *Studies in Linguistics*, Vol. 13, Nos. 1–2, Spring 1958, 1–13, Department of Anthropology and Linguistics, University of Buffalo.

Body Motion and Gesture

31. Darwin, Charles, *Expression of the Emotions in Man and Animals*, D. Appleton and Company, New York, 1873.
32. Efron, David, *Gesture and Environment, A Tentative Study of Some of the Spatio-Temporal and "Linguistic" Aspects of the Gestural Behavior of Eastern Jews and Southern Italians in New York City, Living under Similar as Well as Different Environmental Conditions*, Kings Crown Press, New York, 1941.
33. Hall, Edward T., *The Silent Language*, Doubleday, New York, 1959.
34. Hall, Edward T., "A System for the Notation of Proxemic Behavior," *American Anthropologist*, **65,** No. 5, 1963.
35. Harrison, Randall, *Pictic Analysis: Toward a Vocabulary and Syntax for the Pictorial Code; with Research on Facial Communication*, a thesis submitted to Michigan State University, Department of Communication, 1964.
36. Hayes, Francis, "Gestures: a Working Bibliography," *Southern Folklore Quarterly*, **21,** 1957, 218–317.
37. Hewes, Gordon, "World Distribution of Certain Postural Habits," *American Anthropologist*, **57,** No. 2, 1955.
38. Nielsen, Gerhard, *Studies in Self Confrontation*, Munksgaard, Copenhagen, 1962.
39. Ruesch, Jurgen, and Weldon Kees, *Nonverbal Communication*, University of California Press, Berkeley and Los Angeles, 1956.
40. Saitz, Robert L., and Edmond Cervenka, "Columbian and North American Gestures, A Contrastive Inventory," *Centro Columbo Americano*, Canero 7, Nos. 23–49, 1962.
41. Scheflen, A. E., W. W. Hampe, and A. Auerbach, in O. Spurgeon English (editor), *Strategy and Structure in Psychotherapy: Three Research Approaches to the Whitaker and Malone Multiple Therapy*, Eastern Pennsylvania Psychiatric Institute Press, Philadelphia, 1965.
42. Scheflen, A. E., *Stream and Structure in Communication: Context Analysis of a Psychotherapy Session*. Eastern Pennsylvania Psychiatric Institute Press, Philadelphia, 1965.

Recordings

43. Same as [1]. Scholars may examine extensive recordings at the University of Chicago, Dept. of Anthropology, by permission of Norman A. McQuown; at Western Psychiatric Institute, by permission of Henry Brosin; or at Eastern Pennsylvania Psychiatric Institute, by permission of Ray L. Birdwhistell.
44. McQuown, Norman A., "Linguistic Transcriptions and Specification of Psychiatric Interview Material," *Psychiatry*, **20,** 1957, 79–86.
45. Pittenger, Robt. E., Charles F. Hockett, and John J. Danehy, *The First Five Minutes, A Sample of Microscopic Interview Analysis*. Paul Martineau, Ithaca, N. Y., 1960.

Kinesics

46. Birdwhistell, R. L., *Introduction to Kinesics*, U. of Louisville Press, 1952. Available in microfilm from University Microfilms Incorporated, 313 North First Street, Ann Arbor, Michigan.
47. Birdwhistell, R. L., "Background to Kinesics," *ETC* (*A Review of General Semantics*), **13**, 1955, 10–18.
48. Birdwhistell, R. L., "Contribution of Linguistic-Kinesic Studies to the Understanding of Schizophrenia," in Auerbach, Alfred (editor), *Schizophrenia*, Ronald Press, New York, 1959, pp. 99–123.
49. Birdwhistell, R. L., "Kinesics and Communication," in Carpenter, Edmund, (editor), *Explorations in Communication*, Beacon Press, Boston, 1960, pp. 54–64.
50. Birdwhistell, R. L., "Paralanguage: 25 Years After Sapir," in Brosin, Henry W. (editor), University of Pittsburgh Press, Pittsburgh, 1961.
51. Birdwhistell, R. L., "A Development in Communication Research and Evolutionary Theory," in Austin, William (editor), *Proceedings of the Georgetown Roundtable in Anthropology and Linguistics*, 1961.
52. Birdwhistell, R. L., "An Approach to Communication," *Family Process*, **1**, No. 2, 1962, 194–201.
53. Birdwhistell, R. L., "Critical Moments in the Psychiatric Interview," in Tourlentes, Thomas T., Seymour L. Pollack, and Harold E. Himwich (editors), *Tenth Annual Symposium on Biological, Psychological, and Sociological Problems, State Research Hospital, Galesbury, Illinois, 1960*, Grune and Stratton, New York, 1962, pp. 179–188.
54. Birdwhistell, R. L., "The Kinesic Level in the Investigation of the Emotions," in Knapp, Peter H. (editor), *Expression of the Emotions in Man*, International Universities Press, New York, 1963, pp. 123–139.
55. Birdwhistell, R. L., "Communication Without Words," in *L'Aventure Humaine*, Encyclopedie des sciences de l'homme, Kister S. A., Geneva; De La Grange Baterliere S. A., Paris, Vol. 5, pp. 157–166, 1968.
56. Birdwhistell, R. L., "Body Behavior and Communication," *International Encyclopedia of the Social Sciences*, New York, 1965.
57. Birdwhistell, R. L., "Communication as a Multi-Channel System," in Sills, David L. (editor), *International Encyclopedia of the Social Sciences*, Macmillan, New York, 1968.

FURTHER READINGS

1. Birdwhistell, R. L., *Kinesics and Context: Essays on Body Motion Communication*, The University of Pennsylvania Press, Philadelphia, 1970.
2. Dance, Frank E. X. (editor), *Human Communication Theory, Original Essays*, Holt, Rinehart and Winston, New York, 1967.
3. Lomax, A., *Folksong Style and Culture*, American Association for the Advancement of Science, Publication No. 88, Washington, D. C., 1968.
4. Meerloo, Joost A. M., *Unobtrusive Communication, Essays in Psycholinguistics*, Royal Van Gorcum, Assen, 1964.
5. Miller, George A., *The Psychology of Communication, Seven Essays*, Basic Books, New York, 1967.
6. Parry, John, *The Psychology of Human Communication*, University of London Press, London, 1967.

CHAPTER 3

Representation of Meaning
in Natural Languages

DAVID G. HAYS

Professor of Linguistics, State University of New York, Buffalo

Contents

3.1 INTRODUCTION

It is surprising that a phenomenon so widespread and so fundamental in human life as the conveyance of meaning by natural language should remain almost wholly outside our understanding in a century that has brought rapid progress in fields that we had considered hopeless. In the 1925 edition of *Compton's Pictured Encyclopedia*, the article on radium is headed "Nature's Mystery." Two years earlier, a book called *The Meaning of Meaning* [13] was published. Radium has been unmasked, but the meaning of "meaning" is still hidden from us.

We can trace our tardiness in this domain to many origins. Few significant practical applications have awaited knowledge of semantics. The conceptual tools, in the form of mathematical theories of language structure, were lacking until recently, and the physical tools—computers—were developed just two decades ago. Those who have looked into semantical problems despite these formidable handicaps have too often been seeking capsule cures for diseases of universal proportions; by setting their goals so much too high, they sometimes prevented themselves from making the short steps forward that would have been possible. Moreover, we have been lazy in the past, not accepting the painful conclusion that if we want more precise specification of the meanings of words than are given in dictionaries, we must do more work than the usual dictionary makers. Instead of massive empirical studies from which generalizations eventually might have come, there have been searches for truths of an order that other sciences have attained, if at all, only after extensive work at the level of natural history.

If the formalizations of linguistics, the use of the computer, and a willingness to pursue knowledge in detail scientifically, rather than in general philosophically, can be brought together, then perhaps rapid progress in semantics will be made at last. If results are obtained, they will be put to work in psychology, sociology, and other fields that study mankind largely by examining the communication that flows unceasingly among men; the results will be used to design more effective messages, for advertising and perhaps other purposes as well; and they will serve the designers of automatic systems for translation, indexing, abstracting, and other parts of the scientific, commercial, and governmental information-processing network.

3.2 LINGUISTIC FORMALISMS

A common feature of several contemporary theories of language is the recognition of multiple levels, or strata. Each stratum has an alphabet and a grammar; in some fashion, varying from one theory to another, the elements of each stratum are mapped onto those of adjacent strata (for example, by transduction). The lowest stratum is that of sounds or written marks; the highest is the stratum where language is most intimately connected with the cognitive and emotional systems of language users. Between lowest and highest are an as yet undetermined number of levels of grammatical and semantical organization.

The elements of the lowest stratum occur in linear order, to a very close approximation. Short sequences of sounds or letters represent words, which are the elements of a new level. A dictionary defines words and gives some of their properties. The defined entities are abstractions; the standard spelling and the common pronunciation of the word are merely two of its properties. Thus the purpose of the dictionary is to tabulate the mapping of one stratum onto another.

A sentence is a string of words, representable by a sequence of sounds or letters. Applied to a given sentence, the grammar of a language identifies syntactic relationships among the words; the result is a structural diagram of the sentence. Some examples are given below.

The grammatical facts of a language are not identical with the semantical facts; another stratum must be recognized, for several reasons. The same meaning can be conveyed by two sentences with different grammatical structures and different parts of speech: "He is happy," "His happiness is obvious." English and other natural languages offer many ways of tailoring the expression of an idea to the grammatical context. Again, the properties of units that are relevant to their syntactic compatibility are not always semantically interpretable. Gender in French or Spanish is more closely associated with the sounds and spellings of words than with their meanings—except, of course, for words that denote living things. Even the units of syntactic and semantical structure are often different. Usually the semantical unit is larger, a compound word or idiom: *snowman* or *look up*.

Thus it seems clear that at least three strata must be recognized in natural languages. Sequences of sounds or letters represent words, which are the units of syntactic structures. Combinations of words represent semantical units, which also occur in structures somewhat different from the grammatical structures of the same language. (For a general discussion, see [11].)

3.3 CONTEXT-FREE PHRASE-STRUCTURE GRAMMAR

Several models of syntactic structure have recently been proposed. According to the model of phrase structure [17], the immediate constituents of a sentence are two or more phrases, for example, the subject and the predicate. Each of these in turn has constituents, and so on, until the ultimate constituents are reached, the smallest units that are syntactically relevant. An immediate-constituent diagram is presented in Figure 3.1. Formally, a phrase-structure grammar characterizes a set of finite strings and assigns structures to them by means of rewrite rules [4].

Consider an alphabet A and the set F of all finite strings f over the alphabet; for example, let $A = \{a,b\}$, and $F = \{a,b,aa,ab,ba,bb,aaa, \ldots\}$. A context-free phrase-structure grammar is a 4-tuple, $G = \langle X,A,S,R \rangle$; here A is an alphabet, X an auxiliary alphabet, S an element of X, and R a set of rewrite rules of the form

$$x \to f$$

with $x \in X$ and f a nonnull string (at least one character) over the joint alphabet $A \cup X$.

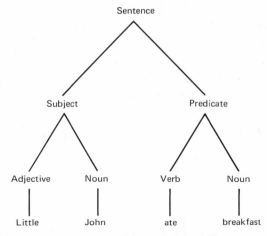

Fig. 3.1 An immediate-constituent diagram.

To generate a string using G, start with the special symbol S (= sentence). Find a rule in R with S on the left, say $S \to f_1$, and rewrite S as the string that appears on the right in that rule: $S \Rightarrow f_1$. Now, recursively, if the string obtained consists entirely of elements of A, the string belongs to the language characterized by G; otherwise, the string has the form $f_{11}x_i f_{12}$, with $x_i \in X$. Find a rule in R with the form $x_i \to f_2$, and rewrite:

$$f_{11}x_i f_{12} \Rightarrow f_{11}f_2 f_{12}.$$

For example, let the grammar be $\langle \{x,y,z,S\}, \{a,b,c\}, S, \{S \to xy, x \to xz, z \to yx, y \to a, x \to bc\} \rangle$. A possible *derivation* is

$$
\begin{aligned}
S &\Rightarrow xy \\
&\Rightarrow xzy \\
&\Rightarrow xyxy \\
&\Rightarrow bcyxy \\
&\Rightarrow bcaxy \\
&\Rightarrow bcabcy \\
&\Rightarrow bcabca.
\end{aligned}
$$

A context-free derivation corresponds to a phrase-structure diagram, as in Figure 3.2. Every substring derived from a single symbol is a phrase; thus in Figure 3.2 the phrases are bc, a, bc, a, abc, $bcabc$, and $bcabca$.

3.4 DEPENDENCY GRAMMAR

According to the model of syntactic dependency [5], one of the smallest units of the sentence plays a central role in its structure—for example, the

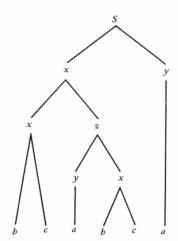

Fig. 3.2 A phrase-structure diagram.

main verb. Some of the other units are directly related to this one, such as the subject, object, and auxiliaries. Each of the smallest units is governed by just one of the other units, with the exception of the one central unit, which has no governor. A dependency diagram is presented in Figure 3.3.

A dependency grammar is a 5-tuple, $\langle A,X,D,X_0,M \rangle$, where A is the terminal alphabet, X is an auxiliary alphabet, D is a set of dependency rules, X_0 is a subset of X, and M is a correspondence of X and A.

To generate a sentence with a dependency grammar, choose any element of X_0, say x_i, and find a rule in D of the form

$$X_i(X_{j_1}, X_{j_2}, \ldots, *, \ldots, X_{j_n}).$$

According to this rule, an occurrence of type X_i can govern simultaneously occurrences of types X_{j_1} up to X_{j_n}, and the occurrences must be in the order given, with X_i in the position of the asterisk. Now choose rules with X_{j_1}, and so on, in the governing position. Whenever a rule is chosen of the form

$$X_i(*),$$

that occurrence governs nothing. Otherwise, the new dependents added at each choice of a rule must be considered as governors. The process stops when every auxiliary symbol introduced has been tested. Then, for every auxiliary, M is used to obtain a corresponding element of A. A dependency diagram, as illustrated in Figure 3.3, is a display of the generation of a sentence.

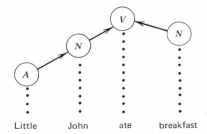

Little   John   ate   breakfast

Fig. 3.3 A dependency diagram.

3.5 TRANSFORMATION RULES

If one level of a language is described with a phrase-structure grammar, an additional level can be treated by the introduction of transformation rules [2, 3]. The first level is called the base; the phrase structures (or *P-markers*) assigned by the base grammar are essential for what follows.

A transformation rule is a rewrite rule of the form $\phi \to \psi$, where ϕ and ψ are structural descriptions. The effect of a transformation is to rewrite one P-marker as another; the left-hand side of the rule determines the class of P-markers to which the rule can be applied, and the right-hand side specifies the shape they take after transformation.

Let f be a string generated in the base with P-marker Q, and let $f = f_1 + f_2 + \ldots + f_n$ be a factorization with each f_i a phrase; then each f_i derives from some auxiliary symbol x_i in Q, and corresponding to the factorization of f there is an *analysis* of Q of the form $x_1 x_2 x_3 \ldots x_n$. For example, in Figure 3.2 the string can be factored in three ways: $bcabc + a$, with structural description xy; $bc + abc + a$, with structural description xzy; and $bc + a + bc + a$, with structural description $xyxy$.

In a transformation rule, the left-hand side can specify a particular structural description, or it can specify a class of them by means of variables or otherwise.

Application of a transformation rule can cause a permutation of factors in the string, deletion of a factor, insertion of a constant factor, and so on. Correspondingly, the P-marker changes, in ways that have not yet been described in full. For example, if a transformation

$$xyxy \to xyyx$$

were applied to the string and P-marker in Figure 3.2, the string would become $bcaabc$, and the P-marker could—perhaps—be converted into either of those shown in Figure 3.4. But in this figure, (II) has the advantage of deriving the final phrase only from symbols that covered it in the

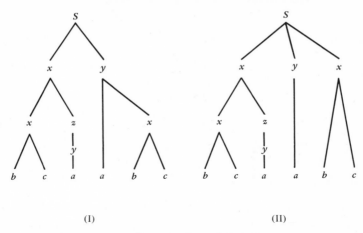

(I)   (II)

Fig. 3.4   Two transformed *P*-markers.

original *P*-marker, whereas (I) makes it derive from a new symbol. Use of such principles may make it possible to avoid stating the full structural effects of transformation rules individually; only their effects on structural descriptions would be given, and the full transformed *P*-marker would be determined in accordance with the general principles.

When a transformational grammar is used to describe the syntax of a natural language, the base is produced with a relatively simple set of phrase-structure rules; the grammatical complexity and diversity of sentences actually used in writing and conversing are the result of transformations. For example, "His happiness is obvious" is obtained by composing two strings from the base: "He is happy" and "[It] is obvious." Applying different transformations to the same pair could yield "His being happy is obvious," "It is obvious that he is happy," and perhaps also "He is obviously happy." Semantical interpretation of the base is therefore less complex than would be the interpretation of the structures attached to real sentences by a phrase-structure grammar.

3.6   SEMEMIC NETWORKS

Two strata can be related through a system of representational rules. Lamb [9, 10] proposes that a sememic stratum be recognized; he uses representational rules to map sememic networks onto dependency trees.

A sememic network consists of nodes and oriented edges. A dependency structure differs from a sememic network only in that it must be a tree; in a dependency diagram, only one edge is directed away from any node and there is always exactly one node from which no edge is directed. (That is to say, every element has just one governor, except for the origin or principal element of the sentence, which has none.) These restrictions do not apply to sememic networks.

The nodes of a sememic network are labeled with elements from a finite set, the sememes of the language. According to Lamb, this alphabet can be established for a language by determining all the semantical distinctions that correlate with differences in expression [9, p. 76]. This task is of course large, but it is incomparably smaller than that of finding all semantical distinctions without regard to language; the second task presumably belongs to science and philosophy.

As an example, Lamb uses the word *big*, which can represent any of four sememes. The first is also represented by *large:* "That's a big boulder," "That's a large boulder." It is also possible to say, without changing the meaning of *big*, "That boulder is big," "This boulder is bigger than that one." But the second sememe represented by *big*, as in "big sister," cannot be used in the other contexts: "I have two big sisters, and Mary is my bigger sister" and "My sister is big" show changes of meaning. The third sememe can occur in comparative contexts: "He's a big fool" and also, without shift of meaning, "He's a bigger fool than I am." But "The fool is big" reverts to the sense of *large*. Finally, "He's a big man around here" represents a network containing the fourth sememe, and "Around here, he's big" and "He's a bigger man on campus than in town" show no change of meaning. Nevertheless, the fourth sememe is distinct from the first: "He's a large man around here" clearly differs in meaning from "He's a big man around here," yet *large* is supposed to represent the first of the four sememes represented by *big*.

The syntax of a language characterizes a set of syntactically well-formed strings, with accompanying phrase-structure or dependency diagrams. It is also necessary to separate the well-formed sememic networks from those disallowed by the language. Lamb has not yet published a formal statement of how this separation is to be made; the following discussion is based partly on conversations with him, but mainly on general considerations of what is necessary and possible. Examples of the kind of network that has to be characterized are presented in Figure 3.5. One is simplified from Lamb [9]; the others illustrate complexities.

The first element of the formalism is, of course, the alphabet of sememes.

A subset of the sememes is distinguished; exactly one element of this subset must appear in each network. A typical element is Lamb's *decl*, identifying its network as representable by a declarative sentence.

Finally, a set Σ of subnetworks is given, and in each a node is distinguished. Every sememe in the alphabet labels the distinguished node in at

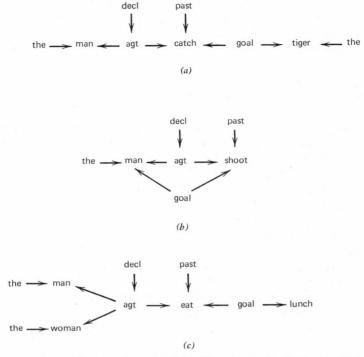

Fig. 3.5 Simplified sememic diagrams. (*a*) "The man caught the tiger." (*b*) "The man shot himself." (*c*) "The man and woman ate lunch."

least one network in Σ, but any sememe can label the distinguished nodes of any number of subnetworks. Each subnetwork defines a legitimate context of occurrence for the sememe labeling its distinguished node. In these subnetworks, edges are labeled with quantifiers: *not, exactly one, at least one*, and perhaps *at most one*. The reasons for using these labels can be shown by examples. A noun that accepts a definite article (*man*, Figure 3.5*a*) accepts exactly one. If a verb is not used reflexively, *agt* and *goal* must not, in its context, point to the same noun (cf. Figure 3.5*b*). Since several entities can be agents of the same action, *agt* points to at least one noun (Figure 3.5*c*).

This formalism characterizes a set of networks if either of two procedures can be given: one for enumerating the set constructively, or one for deciding whether or not an arbitrary given network belongs to the set. A construction procedure is given here; a recognition procedure would be easy to design.

To produce a network, select a sememe belonging to the distinguished subset; such a sememe must label exactly one node in any well-formed network. Now suppose that the label of the first node is s_i; find a subnetwork with s_i as the label of its distinguished node (that is, choose a context for s_i). The subnetwork selected from Σ replaces the single node labeled s_i as the core of a developing network; its distinguished node is now tagged, and this node will not be used again to guide choice of an element of Σ.

Now, recursively, choose any untagged node of the developing network and match its label with the label of the distinguished node of some subnetwork in Σ. The selected network from Σ must be compared, node by node, with the developing network. Let x be the distinguished node, joined to nodes u, v, w in the developing network, and consider x' in the subnetwork of Σ, joined to a, b, and c. If any of a, b, c have labels not identical with labels of u, v, w, edges and nodes with the new labels must be added to the developing network unless the quantifier is *at most one;* then the addition is optional. If the label of, say, a matches that of u, then the quantifiers of edges (x,u) and (x',a) are compared; the outcomes are listed in Table 3.1. If the label of any of a, b, c matches the labels of two or more of u, v, w, the quantifier of (x',a) (or whichever) must be *at least one.* The matching continues until the whole subnetwork chosen from Σ has been examined. If any unacceptable result is obtained, the developing network is rejected (unless another element of Σ, with the same distinguished-node label, can be found). Otherwise, node x is tagged and another node of the developing network is chosen for elaboration.

This formalism is not due to Lamb, and he—or any other student of the question—may well reject it. It has severe shortcomings, some of them

TABLE 3.1

Outcomes when Quantifiers of Edges (x,u) and (x',a) are Compared

(x,u)	(x',a)			
	Not	At Most One	Exactly One	At Least One
Not	A^1	A^1	U	U
At most one	U	A^1	A^1	A^1
Exactly one	U	A^1	A^1	A^1
At least one	U	A^1	A^1	A^2

A = acceptable; U = unacceptable.

[1] Identify node a with node u and apply the more restrictive quantifier.

[2] Either identify node a with node u or add a new node.

remediable. The set of subnetworks Σ clearly is large in any practical application. Every natural language has a large vocabulary, and the number of sememes is bound to be greater than the number of words. In Σ there is at least one subnetwork for every sememe, and it seems plain that there must in fact be a great many. That number can be reduced, however, by modification of the formalism. If each sememe can be replaced with a network of components, and if the alphabet of components is much smaller than the alphabet of sememes, then the number of subnetworks should decrease significantly. The argument relies on two assumptions. First, there would be at least one subnetwork in Σ for each component, rather than for each sememe. Second, the relationships demanded or excluded in natural languages are assumed to be relationships among components. If sememe s_i must be attached to one of sememes $s_{j_1}, \ldots, s_{j_n}$, it is probably because each s_{j_k} contains a certain component; replacing sememes with components reduces n subnetworks of Σ to 1.

There are alternative ways to reduce Σ, but this is not the place to consider them in detail. The object of presenting any formalism is to emphasize the need for one and to suggest, in a very general way, what kind of system might serve.

3.7 LEVELS, STRATA, AND COMPONENTS

Lamb uses the term *strata* for the several parts of a model of language. Each stratum has its own kind of element, assembled in strings, trees, or networks. Each stratum also has its own tactic system, characterizing a set of well-formed assemblies. Connecting the strata are representation rules, which map the elements and connections of one stratum onto those of another. For Lamb, the production of a sentence is to be understood as the production of a network on the highest stratum, followed by a sequence of downward conversions until the lowest stratum is reached. What happens on the highest stratum is intimately connected with the cognitive functioning of the speaker; what happens on the lowest stratum is intimately connected with the neurophysiological mechanisms of articulation.

A multistratal system is potentially more powerful than one with a single level. The strings produced on the lowest stratum must satisfy more than the tactics of that stratum; they must also be representations of assemblies occurring on the next stratum. The same is true, stratum by stratum, all the way to the top. Even if the formalism for the tactics of each stratum is relatively simple, and the formalism for representation rules as simple as possible, the system as a whole ranks with the most powerful.

Chomsky and his collaborators have proposed a system with three components: syntactic, semantic, and phonological [8]. The syntactic component has two parts: phrase structure and transformations. These linguists have been concerned primarily with abstract characterization, not production or recognition. In their formalism, the syntactic component produces strings with two associated structures: one before and one after application of transformations. The pretransformational description is subject to interpretation by the semantic component, and the posttransformational string is converted by the phonological component into something capable of controlling the articulatory mechanism.

Since this model is not supposed to describe the processes of speaking and understanding, but rather to describe what a language user must know in order to perform those processes, it is irrelevant to argue that a speaker does not produce syntactically well-formed strings at random until he arrives at one that can be interpreted as conveying the meaning he intends. This argument is surely true, however, and it must prevent anyone from being tempted to adopt the model of Chomsky and others for the new and unintended purpose of describing the production of speech.

Lamb's model therefore has one potential advantage; it offers an abstract characterization that can be interpreted, without significant modification, as a production mechanism and as a recognition mechanism. This advantage is, of course, conditional on the adequacy of the abstract model and both its interpretations.

The other major difference between Lamb's and Chomsky's models is the difference between rewrite rules and stratal conversions. When a transformation is applied, it replaces one object with another, and the next operation is performed on the new object. What the phrase structure produces is lost as soon as a transformation rewrites it, and likewise for all intermediate steps. On the other hand, conversion from one stratum to another proceeds by repeatedly inspecting some part of an assembly on the first stratum and creating a corresponding part on the second.

When the assemblies on both strata are strings, stratal conversion proceeds by *transduction* [15]. Processes of this kind have been studied, and it seems likely that a *finite-state* machine having strictly limited storage capacity will suffice for descriptions of natural languages. Conversions between trees on one stratum and strings on another can be made, in either direction, by a *pushdown-store* machine having potentially infinite memory but much restricted in other respects, if a context-free phrase-structure (or dependency) grammar would characterize the system [16]. When the assemblies on the two levels are trees, or trees and networks, new problems arise and solutions are not yet available.

3.8 MEANING, TRANSFORMATION, AND PHRASE STRUCTURE

Consider a linguistic system in which a *base* is generated by a phrase-structure grammar and strings of the base (with associated *P*-markers) are converted by transformations into *surface* strings and P-markers. The surface strings are (or can be further converted into) messages. The significance of a message could be attributed to the elements of the alphabet occurring in it, to the phrase-structure rules by which they are interrelated, or to the transformation rules. Current proposals deny any contribution from the transformation rules; the base is so constructed that transformations are predetermined and hence can add nothing to the significance of the base elements to which they apply [8].

Each element of the base alphabet is assumed to have a meaning, that is, to represent or signify some element of another level; ambiguity must be permitted. The meaning of a phrase in a base P-marker is calculated from the meanings of the constituent phrases, but the calculation depends on the rule associated with the phrase.

Specifically, let the rules of the base grammar be of two forms: $x_i \rightarrow a_j$, with $a_j \in A$; or $x_i \rightarrow f$, with f a string on X. For each rule $x_i \rightarrow a_j$ there is given a *dictionary entry* $\langle x_i, a_j, P, R, T \rangle$ [7]. Here P is a string on a finite alphabet of *properties*, R is a *residue*, and T is a Boolean expression composed of strings on the same alphabet of properties (with connectives *and*, *or*, *not*). P describes a_j used grammatically as x_i, insofar as the language systematizes use of a_j; R completes the description of a_j; and T states requirements for agreement.

A *semantic composition rule* (Fodor and Katz say "projection rule") specifies how the meaning of a phrase is to be computed from the meanings of its constituents. One part of each rule is a statement—perhaps a list—of the phrase-structure rewrite rules to which it applies. As an illustration, take the subordination rule used by Fodor and Katz, applicable to rewrite rules such as *Nominal* $\rightarrow$ *Adjective Noun*. The semantic composition rule specifies how to test for agreement and how to amalgamate the descriptions of the constituents of the phrase. With T and P as defined above, let $T(P) = 1$ if P contains all of the properties mentioned (not negated), and none of the properties negated, in at least one of the conjuncts of the disjunct normal form of T. In other words, P satisfies T.

The subordination rule identifies one constituent of any phrase to which it applies as head, the other as subordinate. Its agreement specification is that $T_{\text{sub}}(P_{\text{head}}) = 1$. Other semantic composition rules could differ from this one by specifying, for example, that $T_\alpha(P_\beta) = 1$ and also $T_\beta(P_\alpha) = 1$, where α and β identify the constituents.

The subordination rule also specifies the form of the semantic description of the phrase, namely

$$\langle x_{\text{head}}, \quad a_{\text{sub}}a_{\text{head}}, \quad P_{\text{head}}P_{\text{sub}}, \quad R_{\text{head}}R_{\text{sub}}, \quad T_{\text{head}} \rangle.$$

Obviously, other rules could specify altogether different amalgamations.

The rule suggested by Fodor and Katz for modifier-head phrases is attractive, since the distribution of properties between head and modifier seems arbitrary. In some instances it appears that a single item has the same meaning as a composite of two other items: *vixen* is very like *female fox*. Their amalgamation method is less attractive in other situations; the meaning of a sentence is merely the concatenation of properties originally pertinent to subject, verb, and object. When Katz [6] attempts a definition of *analytic* (true by meaning alone), he is forced to deal with the meanings of parts of strings—with subject and predicate independently, rather than with the meaning of a sentence and parts of the meaning. For some purposes, therefore, it is necessary to have at hand a *P*-marker as a guide to the interpretation of meaning. This situation presumably came about because Fodor and Katz wished to avoid structure within the system of semantic descriptions. There would be structure if, for example, the meaning of a sentence could be segmented, without reference to a *P*-marker, into subject, verb, and object parts.

It is almost self-evident that natural languages do not distribute components of meaning among subject, verbal element, and object in a uniform, systematic fashion—even if the syntactic terms are defined relative to the base. If two sentences can have the same meaning, although one puts a component in the verb and the other puts the same component in the object, clearly readjustments are needed in passing from syntax to semantics. Such questions are begged, not answered, by a formalism that leaves all structure on the syntactic level and puts none into semantic descriptions. Moreover, some components cannot be moved about so freely; if one person strikes another, the meaning of the sentence depends on the properties of the striker and the struck.

Perhaps the difference between the formalism of sememics, in which structure is crucial, and the Fodor-Katz formalism of semantic markers is another difference between stratification and a linguistic description with multiple components. Any single stratum must be complete within itself, whereas a semantic component can furnish markers that cannot be interpreted independently. If such a component is to be adopted, the problem of semantically controlled realignments of syntactic structure must be dealt with.

3.9 TOWARD A THEORY OF MEANINGFUL USE OF LANGUAGE

Preceding sections of this chapter have set forth some of the linguistic apparatus currently being offered for the analysis of how meaning is represented in natural language. Nothing has been said about what meanings are, yet the linguist's approach to that question must be slightly different from the philosopher's (cf. [14]). The linguist is a descriptive scientist; his domain is language as produced and understood by virtually every human being. One task of philosophy is to clarify and justify the methods of science; formal languages, as used in science, bear some relationship to the data of science, and philosophers must examine that relationship, instructing the scientist as far as they can in meaningful use of his formal language. In this philosophical undertaking, concepts of truth, meaning, and reference have been useful; they have also been criticized, and they remain a matter of dispute on a deep technical level. Since the linguist's purpose is different, his theoretical problems may differ from those of the philosopher, as we shall now indicate.

To begin, the linguist requires a semantic theory that can explain certain phenomena. The basic situation is that of the mature monolingual person of normal intelligence. As he moves through relatively familiar surroundings, he is capable of describing the new situations he encounters. Psychologists have noted that each person's background influences his description of an event, but the more fundamental point is the consistency of reports from different observers. A full account of the observer must begin with perceptual processes, go on to cognitive mechanisms, and end with grammatical and phonological systems. Between cognition and grammar, the account must evidently explain how words are chosen, why the reports of a particular event differ slightly in phrasing, and so on; these explanations are evidently within the scope of a semantic theory.

A normal person can report past events, answer questions, and make generalizations. Similarly, he can ask questions and make use of reports; for example, he can draw a scene from a description or follow complicated instructions. In none of these abilities is the normal person perfect. Even the simplest facts can be forgotten, even the most obvious questions can go unanswered, even the most direct generalizations can go unmade. A semantic theory must explain, in part, both the abilities and the inadequacies of human language users.

The knowledge of the normal person changes with time; he knows facts about the world he lives in and also about the use of language, and these facets of his knowledge must be disentangled. For example, a person may very well know that a female of the porcine kind is a sow, and that guinea pigs are divided into male and female, without knowing that the same term, sow, is used for female guinea pigs. However closely interlocked semantic knowledge and other knowledge may be, semantic theory must provide for their essential independence, and for their independent development.

The most dramatic stage of language development is undoubtedly the acquisition of a mother tongue. Once the rudiments are grasped, the language itself becomes a tool for further learning in the first language, and an analogical basis for acquiring new languages. What poses greatest theoretical difficulty is the very beginning, the stage of learning that language has structure and is used for communication. This difficulty is not solved by enunciating innate mechanisms, since the issue is not whether *any* mechanisms are inherent in the species, but rather what precise form they take. Detailed studies of the course of early development are beginning to replace speculation [1, 12] and should eventually impose strong requirements on semantic theory.

Even after the first stage, learning phenomena raise problems for a semantic theory. A person can learn the use of a word or construction gradually, through exposure to its use, or suddenly, by hearing it defined. Semantic theory must explain the recognition of defining contexts, and the alteration of structure that follows.

The linguist's semantic theory is required to explain a very wide range of data; those mentioned here are a scant sampling. In general, these data have to do with the stimuli presented to a person and the responses he makes to them. Hence psychological mechanisms must be postulated to explain the data, and if data of so many kinds are to be accounted for with one homogeneous theoretical construction, it must be one of great complexity. The organization and functioning of the brain are not yet open to direct inspection except in the most limited ways, and they should not be supposed to be more elaborate than necessary to do the work required. Even so, the linguistic theories presented in earlier sections evidently fall short. More, not less, complexity is required.

Theory builders use the conceptual apparatus of their time; they have no other choice. The best analogy available now is the computer, which stores information and carries out algorithms. The meaning of a word (or other unit) is, by this analogy, what the brain stores in order to carry out such algorithms as describing an event, understanding a report, or answering a question. If two words are synonymous, it is because what is stored is the same for both. The meaning of a sentence is what is stored as a result of understanding the sentence; it is approximately what would be stored just before the same sentence was produced as a description or report.

What is stored as the meaning of a word or sentence apparently differs from what is stored as the direct representation of either the sentence itself or the event it describes. Lamb's sememic networks are one suggestion about the abstract form of what is stored, and Katz and Fodor offer another suggestion. To choose between them, or reject both in favor of a present or future competitor, requires collection of data of many different kinds, construction of algorithms for various human processes with language, and analysis of the results: Does the network model facilitate or hinder the design of algorithms? Are experimental data readily explained in terms of presence and absence of semantic markers? And so on.

The representation of meaning in natural languages cannot yet be simulated on a computer, characterized with precision in an abstract model, or placed among the natural phenomena we "understand." But the meaning of meaning is better understood than it was a generation ago, and semantics as a branch of linguistics is gradually falling into place between syntax and the psychology of cognitive processes.

REFERENCES

1. Brown, R., and J. Berko, "Word Association and the Acquisition of Grammar," *Child Development*, **31**, 1960, 1–14.
2. Chomsky, N., *Syntactic Structures*, Mouton and Co., The Hague, 1957, pp. 6–24.
3. Chomsky, N., "On the Notion 'Rule of Grammar,'" in Jakobson, R. (editor), *Structure of Language and Its Mathematical Aspects*, American Mathematical Society, Providence, 1961.
4. Chomsky, N., "Formal Properties of Grammars," in Luce, P., R. Bush, and E. Galanter (editors), *Handbook of Mathematical Psychology*, Vol. II, Wiley, New York, 1963, pp. 323–418.
5. Hays, D. G., "Dependency Theory: A Formalism and Some Observations," *Language*, **40**, 1964, 511–525.
6. Katz, J. J., "Analyticity and Contradiction in Natural Language," Fodor, J. A., and J. J. Katz (editors), *The Structure of Language*, Prentice-Hall, Englewood Cliffs, N. J., 1964, pp. 519–543.
7. Katz, J. J., and J. A. Fodor, "The Structure of a Semantic Theory," *Language* **39**, 1963, 170–210.
8. Katz, J. J., and P. M. Postal, *An Integrated Theory of Linguistic Descriptions*, The M.I.T. Press, Cambridge, 1964.
9. Lamb, S. M., "The Semenic Approach to Structural Semantics," *Amer. Anthropologist*, **66**:3:2, 1964, 57–78.
10. Lamb, S. M., "The Nature of the Machine Translation Problem," *J. Verbal Learning and Verbal Behavior*, **4**, 1965, 196–210.
11. Lyons, J., *Structural Semantics*, Basil Blackwell, Oxford, 1963.
12. Menyuk, P., "Alternation of Rules in Children's Grammar," *J. Verbal Learning and Verbal Behavior*, **3**, 1964, 480–488.
13. Ogden, C. K., and I. A. Richards, *The Meaning of Meaning*, K. Paul, French, Trubner & Co., London, 1923.
14. Quine, W. V., *Word and Object*, Wiley, New York, 1960.
15. Schützenberger, M. P., "A Remark on Finite Transducers," *Info. Contr.*, **4**, 1961, 185–196.
16. Schützenberger, M. P., "On Context-Free Languages and Push-Down Automata," *Info. Contr.*, **6**, 1963, 246–264.
17. Wells, R. S., "Immediate Constituents," *Language*, **23**, 1954, 81–117.

FURTHER READINGS

1. Chafe, W. L., *Meaning and the Structure of Language*, University of Chicago Press, Chicago, 1970.

2. Chomsky, N., *Aspects of the Theory of Syntax*, The M.I.T. Press, Cambridge, 1965.
3. Friedman, J., *A Computer Model of Transformational Grammar*, American Elsevier, New York, 1971.
4. Garvin, Paul L., and H. Von Forester (editors), *Cognition: A Multiple View*, Spartan, Washington, 1971.
5. Lyons, J., *Introduction to Theoretical Linguistics*, Cambridge Universtiy Press, New York, 1969.
6. Minsky, M. (editor), *Semantic Information Processing*, The M.I.T. Press, Cambridge, 1968.
7. Sebeok, T. (editor), *Current Trends in Linguistics*, Vol. 3, *Theoretical Foundations*, Mouton and Co., The Hague, 1966.

CHAPTER 4

Mathematical and Computational Linguistics

H. P. EDMUNDSON

Professor of Computer Science and Mathematics, University of Maryland, College Park

Contents

4.1 INTRODUCTION

In examining the conceptual bases and applications of the communication sciences, it becomes clear that the new fields of mathematical and computational linguistics occupy a fundamental role (see Chapters 2 and 3). This role has both theoretical and applied aspects since the theory has provided new concepts regarding human communication, and these have suggested interesting applications.

In this chapter the background, scope, problem areas, methods, results, unsolved problems, and outlook of these fields will be considered. Moreover, their interdisciplinary nature will be stressed. Mathematical and computational linguistics are not solely the province of mathematicians and linguists since philosophers, psychologists, computer scientists, and engineers have contributed in important ways. Of course, these new lines of investigation have deepened and broadened traditional linguistics. As the title suggests, the emphasis here will fall upon the formal and quantitative aspects of language, both in its theories and in the application of these theories by means of computers and computer programs. Also, the interplay between theoretical models and empirical data will be shown to be of paramount importance.

BACKGROUND

4.2 SCIENCE

It is instructive to start with the conceptual origins of these new fields. First, the separate natures of the disciplines of linguistics and mathematics are examined to circumscribe mathematical and computational linguistics.

4.3 LINGUISTICS

Natural languages (principally spoken) are those that have evolved as man has sought to communicate verbally. They may be grouped into major language families such as Indo-European (English, French, German, etc.) and Semitic (Hebrew, Arabic, etc.). In contrast to natural languages are *artificial languages* (principally written), which have been created by man to fill specific communication needs. For example, mathematical languages (logic, algebra, etc.) and programming languages (ALGOL, FORTRAN, etc.) are artificial languages since they were invented to serve particular scientific functions. One way of classifying languages is shown in Figure 4.1.

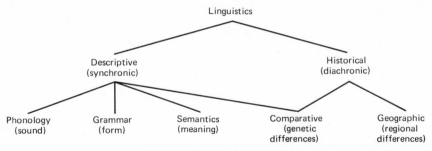

Fig. 4.1   Types of languages.

For the linguist, spoken language is the principal object of study since he regards written forms as derivatives of less theoretical interest than spoken forms. This may seem strange to the nonlinguist, but it is so because the linguist is also concerned with the anthropological, sociological, and psychological aspects of language. In the fields of mathematical and computational linguistics, however, the opposite position is often taken for technical reasons. Written text can be processed, using digital computers, more readily than can a speech stream, since the former is discrete whereas the latter is continuous. This position is taken not because of disagreement with the linguist, but because the simpler task has received more attention. For both spoken and written language, the fundamental theories involve linguistic units called *words*. The intuitive notion of a word will suffice here.

To emphasize human communication, *linguistics* is regarded here as the study of the structure and behavior of natural languages. Like all conventions, this restriction to natural languages is arbitrary and is occasionally relaxed since many of the notions of linguistics can be applied to the analysis of artificial languages such as logic and programming languages. In this chapter, however, such artificial languages will not be examined.

Figure 4.2 presents one possible view of the branches of traditional linguistics (see Gleason [16]; Hockett [21]). Here, the words in parentheses indicate the principal topic of study of that branch. It is convenient to divide the science of linguistics into two main branches: descriptive linguistics and historical linguistics. *Descriptive* or *synchronic linguistics* is concerned with language structure and behavior at a particular point in time— for example, the structure of contemporary Russian. In the field of descriptive linguistics, it is customary to recognize three subbranches: phonology, grammar, and semantics. *Phonology* is the study of speech sounds and has two subbranches: *phonetics* and *phonemics*. *Grammar* is the study of meaningful forms, that is, the forms of words, phrases, clauses, and sentences in both spoken and written languages. Grammar has two sub-

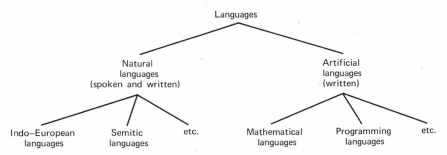

Fig. 4.2 Branches of traditional linguistics.

branches, *morphology* and *syntax,* which are the study of the structure of words and sentences, respectively. *Semantics* is the study of meaning. A theory of semantics therefore must give a meaning for "meaning" and yet avoid a logically circular definition. Until recently, many linguistic phenomena that were not understood in terms of phonology or grammar were swept under the rug of semantics. It is interesting that the traditional European school of linguistics has always regarded semantics as a proper part of descriptive linguistics, although the early American school did not regard semantic criteria as proper for syntactic analysis. In fact, the American school has been called the "structuralist" school since criteria of meaning were outlawed in favor of criteria of form. Fortunately, this is not the current American view.

The other main branch of linguistics is *historical* or *diachronic linguistics,* which is concerned with language structure and behavior in terms of its evolutionary or temporal aspects—for example, the influence of Anglo-Saxon on modern English. *Comparative linguistics* is concerned with the differences between two or more languages or language families, while *geographic linguistics* is concerned with regional differences such as dialects.

4.4 MATHEMATICS

Mathematics is regarded here as the study of abstract objects and their abstract properties and relations. This definition is intended to dispel any notion that mathematics is concerned with numbers only. This point is vital because the scientist, who is fearful of the intrusion of mathematics into his province, should understand that the mathematician is really concerned with abstract operations of a general nature and is not constrained to calculating with numbers—either on paper or in a computer.

The major branches of mathematics of particular interest in the study of mathematical linguistics are logic, analysis, algebra, geometry, prob-

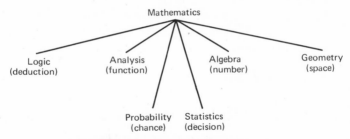

Fig. 4.3   Branches of mathematics.

ability, and statistics. The branches under consideration may be sche-matized as in Figure 4.3, where, as before, the words in parentheses denote the principal object of study of that branch. Different branches of mathematics arise because of different kinds of mathematical objects studied. *Logic* is the study of deduction and its properties such as truth, validity, and provability. Hence logic occupies a unique role in mathematics since it is fundamental to all the other branches. *Analysis* is the study of functions and their properties such as existence, continuity, and differenti-ability. *Algebra* is the study of numbers (both classical and generalized) and their properties such as magnitude, arrangement, and composition. *Geometry* is the study of spaces consisting of points, lines, and surfaces and their properties such as distance, intersection, and connectivity. *Probability* is the study of chance events and their properties such as likelihood, independence, and randomness. *Statistics* is the study of decision making in the face of uncertainty and its properties such as acceptance, bias, and significance. Although there are other branches—for example, number theory, numerical analysis, and topology—and more connections among branches, the diagram shown in Figure 4.3 is sufficient for the present treatment of mathematical linguistics.

4.5   ENGINEERING

In support of the disciplines just described, the engineering arts have played a critical role in the development of computational linguistics. For this reason, the importance of two engineering contributions—computers and communication systems—is noted (see Borko [3]; Garvin [14]).

4.6 COMPUTERS

Since their advent in 1950, scientific computers have been employed principally to solve mathematical problems by means of numerical analysis. In addition to major engineering contributions regarding the use of binary computers and stored programs, the mathematician John von Neumann made a critical educational contribution by leading the way in their application. By using computers to solve difficult problems, he made this subject more respectable to many "pure" mathematicians who previously had been uninterested in such tools and their associated techniques.

Since scientific computers were originally designed for numerical analysis, there are presently some inherent problems concerning their use in linguistic analysis even though words can be stored as well as numbers. Nevertheless, computers have permitted advances in linguistic analysis as far-reaching as those in numerical analysis. The major role has been played by general-purpose digital computers rather than analog computers since written-language data are discrete rather than continuous. Pioneering applications have been made in linguistic analysis during the decade 1960–1970, which are comparable to those that occurred in the first era (1950–1960) of computers in which they were used in numerical analysis. Research in the field of linguistic analysis may have greater consequences for mankind than has numerical analysis. Naturally, the results of such research are more meaningful to the layman who, for example, has a feeling for the importance of automatic translation of languages, but is unmoved by a computer solution of systems of equations.

4.7 COMMUNICATION SYSTEMS

Communication theory and techniques have permitted the rapid, remote, and reliable transmission of human intelligence (see Cherry [4]; Shannon and Weaver [33]). The more obvious examples concern the telegraph, telephone, and television, but it is now possible to establish communication between man and computer, and also between computers. This means that linguistic analysis need not be constrained by proximity in time or space as long as consoles for control and display are available and communication systems are integrated with computer systems. For example, the recent development of both on-line and time-shared computer systems permits the more efficient utilization of human intellect. In an *on-line system* the user interacts directly with the computer via a control and display console, and in a *time-sharing system* many users "simultaneously" use a single computer without interfering with one another.

SCOPE

Some definitions concerning mathematical and computational linguistics are now given.

4.8   MATHEMATICAL LINGUISTICS

Mathematical linguistics is regarded here as the study of linguistic structure and behavior by means of mathematical theories and methods. Here, methods and theories are accorded equal weight. Mathematical linguistics has two principal branches: algebraic and statistical. Of course, there are mixed cases, but this bifurcation, which was proposed initially by Bar-Hillel [1], is a useful one. *Algebraic linguistics* is the study of the deterministic properties of language. Here, the deterministic branches of mathematics such as logic, analysis, algebra, and geometry form the foundation. *Statistical linguistics* is the study of the nondeterministic properties of language. Here, the stochastic branches of mathematics, such as probability and statistics, are fundamental (see Plath [32]; Edmundson [10, 11]). Mathematical linguistics has also been called *theoretical linguistics* and even *computational linguistics*. It is best, however, not to confuse matters by using the term "theoretical linguistics" since there are portions of linguistic theory that are theoretical but nonmathematical.

4.9   COMPUTATIONAL LINGUISTICS

For similar reasons, it is preferable to reserve the term "computational linguistics" for the new field that depends inherently on the use of the computer as a tool. *Computational linguistics* is regarded here as the study of linguistic data and mathematical linguistics by means of computers and computer programs. It originated around 1950 with the initiation of research on automatic translation (see Hays [18, 19]). Computational linguistics involves two processes: analysis and synthesis. There are other possible views, but this one is appropriate for present purposes. *Analysis* is the reduction of natural language (as input) to data by a computer program. *Synthesis* is the production of natural language (as output) from data by a computer program. As will be seen, there are cases of computer processes that involve only analysis, others that involve only synthesis, but the most important ones involve both. For example, automatic translation requires both analysis and synthesis programs.

Mathematics can aid in the analysis of a corpus of natural-language text by means of computer programs that produce the data necessary for the formulation of mathematical models, such as those of Chomsky, Zipf, Shannon, Markov, Carnap and Bar-Hillel, and Yngve. Further, mathematics can aid in the synthesis of natural-language text by means of computer programs that represent mathematical models of language processes, such as automatic translating, indexing, classifying, abstracting, parsing, generating, retrieving, querying, and editing. The interrelations of models and processes may be depicted as shown in Figure 4.4.

Mathematical and computational linguistics have had their greatest impact in descriptive linguistics rather than in historical linguistics. With the acceptance of mathematical and computational linguistics as recognized disciplines, the branches of modern linguistics may be viewed as indicated in Figure 4.5 (see Edmundson [10, 11]).

If linguistics is separated into theoretical and applied branches, then the theoretical branch has both mathematical and nonmathematical sub-branches. Nonmathematical theoretical linguistics deals with *linguistic metatheory*, which is the study of the theories of the universal properties of natural languages. The notion of the syntactic structure of a sentence is an old one which was studied even before linguistics came to be regarded as a science. For example, the sentence structure of German is known to differ

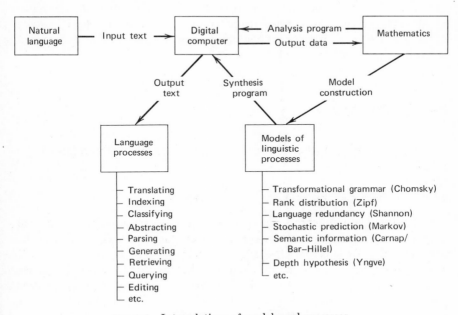

Fig. 4.4 Interrelations of models and processes.

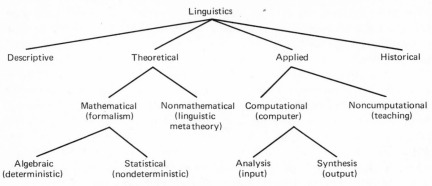

Fig. 4.5 Branches of modern linguistics.

from that of English, especially in connection with word order; and the sentence structure of Chinese differs from that of German, especially with regard to word formation. A linguistic metatheory must be general enough to account for the structure of all natural languages; simultaneously, it must be specific enough to provide individual linguistic theories that account for the particular behavior of each natural language. As yet, however, a linguistic metatheory of such generality and specificity has not been developed. Applied linguistics has both computational and noncomputational subbranches. The computational subbranch is covered here in some detail, but the noncomputational subbranch, which covers language teaching and related activities, is not treated.

PROBLEM AREAS

Next, the major problem areas in mathematical and computational linguistics are discussed.

4.10 THEORETICAL PROBLEMS

The concept of modeling is well understood in the physical and biological sciences, and much has been written recently in the field of operations research about what a model is and what it is not. The term *model* is used here in the sense of a model of a physical entity in science, not in the sense of a model of an axiom system in mathematics. Models of physical entities are abstractions of more concrete entities, whereas models of axiom systems are usually more concrete than the systems they model.

The mathematical models that have been proposed in linguistics range from very elementary to highly formal ones. Whether a language is considered to be an object or a process, it is to be modeled in the way all physical entities are modeled. There are five basic theoretical problem areas or steps that arise in the mathematical modeling of any linguistic entity (that is, object or process). The first step is the collection or observation of physical data. Second is the analysis of the data. The third, and crucial, step is the formulation of a model. Clearly, the formulation of a model of a linguistic entity is an inductive step. The fourth step is the derivation of mathematical consequences of the model, and this is strictly deductive. Finally, the fifth step or problem area is the interpretation of the implications derived deductively. The real-world interpretation of the conclusions amounts to a reinterpretation, and this is an inductive step.

4.11 PRACTICAL PROBLEMS

In addition to these five basic theoretical problem areas in mathematical linguistics, there are four basic practical or empirical problem areas that arise in computational linguistics. The first of these is the *input* problem. Clearly, for any such investigation, the text must be put in machine-readable form. This step may seem trivial; actually, though, it is not, since present methods are economically unsatisfactory. Second, once the text or corpus to be studied is in machine-readable form, there is the problem of *processing*, which involves time and cost constraints. For example, the decision of whether to use data-generation routines or table-lookup routines must be made. The third practical problem concerns the *output*. The computer output must be properly formatted and sufficiently brief so that it is of use to the linguist or mathematical linguist. This problem is not a new one; it also occurs in numerical analysis, but it is more aggravating in linguistic analysis since examining voluminous data requires much time and effort. *Evaluation* is the final step or problem. This problem arose first in the field of information storage and retrieval. At present, far too little is known about criteria for evaluating the quality of a computational linguistic method or result. For example, in the case of automatic translation the computer output is subjectively compared with human translation.

Next, some of the subproblems in each of these four practical problem areas will be examined in more detail. They may be grouped as shown in Figure 4.6 (see Borko [3]; Garvin [14]).

The first input problem is the *selection* of the corpus of text. A corpus that is appropriate, both in quality and quantity, for the research must be selected. It is clear that attempting too much at once must be avoided, and that sufficient flexibility to modify this decision should be afforded.

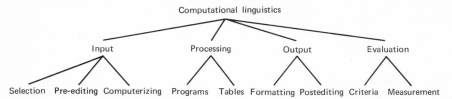

Fig. 4.6   Problem areas in computational linguistics.

In most cases, after selection, the text is *pre-edited*. This usually means that the corpus, whether it be the Dead Sea Scrolls or newspaper text, has to be photographed (usually magnified) and pre-edited by linguistic clerks. For example, chemical equations, astronomical symbols, or mathematical expressions either may be deleted, since they cannot be keypunched because of the limited character set of the input device, or else may be replaced by conventional symbols to retain as much of the linguistic environment as possible. The pre-editing step almost invariably requires that the linguist prepare a list of pre-edit instructions that the pre-editors are to follow. Usually such a set of instructions is modified after each trial run.

Next, the text must be *computerized*, that is, put in machine-readable form. The term "computerized" is used since the word "keypunched" is too specialized. At present, however, keypunching dominates other available methods. Before keypunching, a set of keypunch instructions is prepared for the keypunch operators. Of course, it would be faster to use an artificial-intelligence device that automatically reads characters, but no inexpensive optical character reader is currently available. Fortunately, a recent innovation, affording less dependence on optical character readers, is the process developed in the printing and publishing industry by which books are composed by a computer that drives a printer. For example, if the corpus is modern English, keypunching can sometimes be avoided by obtaining from the publisher the tapes that controlled the printing press and that can be reformatted by an edit routine. Of course, this cannot be done for something like the Dead Sea Scrolls.

In the processing step the problem arises about whether to use stored *programs* or stored *tables* to carry out the computer processing. Sometimes the method of stored programs, with routines embedded within routines, is sufficient. On the other hand, the expediency of table-lookup routines and list-processing languages sometimes makes the stored-table method preferable. In any case, this problem in linguistic analysis is no different from the one encountered in numerical analysis. Methodologically, a pure strategy is not indicated here since it is clear that the more efficient strategy should be used for the problem at hand.

In the output step there are formatting and postediting problems. *Formatting* involves the presentation of results (machine listings, if paper is used, or cathode-ray tube displays, if not) to the linguist so that the data can be read and studied. It is discouraging if, after the investment of considerable time and money, the linguist does not want the information displayed just that way. Hence these matters must be resolved in advance, or trial runs must be made. The *postediting* step of examining and editing the output comes next. Since the computer output is often not the final product in this kind of research, the task of postediting must be faced, usually by linguistic clerks.

Finally, in the evaluation step there are two principal problems. The first concerns the *criteria* to be adopted for judging the quality of the output. The evaluation of a computational method should be effective and should rely on predetermined criteria. Of course, numerical functions are preferred as criteria. This is much more difficult in the field of linguistic analysis than in numerical analysis because the objects being studied are words, sentences, meanings, etc., rather than numbers and functions. This is not to say that functions cannot be devised to measure linguistic objects and properties, but the solution is not as immediate as it is in numerical analysis where figures of merit easily come to mind. The second problem concerns the precision and accuracy of *measurement* and the statistical techniques to be used to analyze the data. For the former the investigator may consult the engineer or numerical analyst, while for the latter the investigator usually turns to the statistician for guidance in designing an evaluation experiment, estimating the parameters, testing the hypotheses, etc.

METHODS

The methods available are now discussed, first with respect to mathematical linguistics and then with respect to computational linguistics.

4.12 METHODS IN MATHEMATICAL LINGUISTICS

In mathematical linguistics the methods are a mixture of those from both mathematics and linguistics. In every case, reliance must be placed on two features: a mathematical model and the research cycle. As indicated previously, a mathematical model may be a very informal mathematical description—for example, a descriptive paragraph of a semantic theory. At the other extreme, a mathematical model may be formal or semiformal —for example, a semiformal axiom system for a grammar.

The research cycle is that of the scientific or hypothetico-deductive method: collect, analyze, hypothesize, test, and decide. Figure 4.7 depicts the typical research cycle (see Edmundson [11]).

The items in the top row denote the empirical aspects, and those in the bottom row denote the theoretical ones. First, a corpus of text is collected for study. Next, it is analyzed to yield linguistic data of interest. This may be done either by the linguist alone or in concert with a mathematician or statistician. Then, typically, a mathematical theory such as the theory of matrices, the theory of graphs or trees, or probability theory is selected. After an apparently appropriate theory is chosen, a model is hypothesized or conjectured. The model is formulated on the basis of the nature of the linguistic data and the existence of available mathematical theories. It may be that there is no appropriate mathematical theory; in this case, either such a theory must be created or a compromise must be made using current theories. In this connection, a model may be based on one or more theories, but each such theory is regarded as more embracing than the model.

Once the model that is to mirror the linguistic entity has been hypothesized or conjectured, an attempt is made to derive, in a strictly deductive way, its mathematical consequences. These consequences must then be interpreted in linguistic terms. If the linguistic implications are unsatisfactory, then the research must be modified. The modification of the research may involve selecting and analyzing another corpus of text, examining only a subset of the original corpus, selecting another mathematical theory, or all of these. This, in turn, entails remodeling or recon-

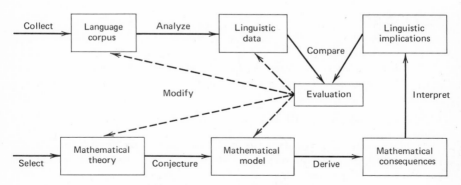

Fig. 4.7 Research cycle in mathematical linguistics.

structing the model and repeating the research cycle. Ideally, the sequence of models formulated in this iterative process converges to one deemed adequate. Thus, models proposed in mathematical linguistics, like those in the physical sciences, are tentative and must be continually replaced by newer ones.

4.13   METHODS IN COMPUTATIONAL LINGUISTICS

Methods in computational linguistics are a mixture of those from computer programming and experimental design. The variety of computational techniques ranges from standard subroutines to nonstandard stored tables. When there is access to a large-scale general-purpose digital computer system, a considerable library of routines can be used. If these are not sufficient, then special-purpose routines must be written. One of the most salient features of linguistic analysis is that it typically involves a large amount of input. For example, to construct a grammar of the Russian language, a million running words might be regarded as a small sample.

In computational linguistics involving analysis, there is an *experimental cycle*, which involves the following phases: input, processing, output, and evaluation (see Edmundson and Hays in [18]). This is indicated in Figure 4.8.

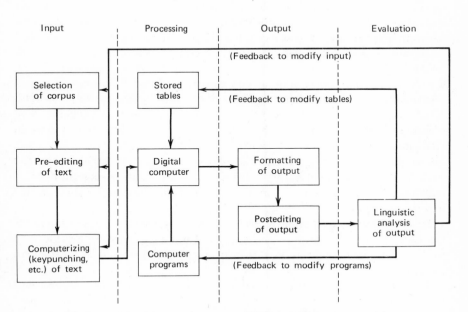

Fig. 4.8   Experimental cycle in computational linguistics—analysis.

In the input or data phase a corpus is selected, pre-edited, and key-punched. In the processing phase the data customarily enter the computer by means of an edit routine, which stores the data on tape, drum, or disk so that tables or programs (stored externally or internally) can perform the processing. The output phase necessitates a formatting step, and a post-editing step may follow. Finally, in the evaluation or test phase the linguistic analysis is performed, customarily by the linguist.

The most important features are the feedback loops. Here, as a result of the linguistic analysis, the programs, tables, corpus, formatting routines, pre-edit rules, keypunch rules, postedit rules, etc., may be modified. For example, in research on automatic translation, some linguists believed that once adequate linguistic theories had been developed, a complete theoretical solution could be found which, when programmed, would immediately translate automatically and accurately. To some nonlinguists, however, this seemed unlikely and certainly not in accord with scientific method or experience. For this reason, a methodology founded on the principles of empiricism and iteration was proposed (see Edmundson and Hays in [18]). First, research in automatic translation was to be empirically, not theoretically, based. For example, since existing grammars of Russian and English would not handle the eccentricities of these languages, a large volume of Russian text was collected to see how it actually behaved. Second, attempts at a first-time ideal solution were rejected and a cyclic or iterative approach was adopted. The processing of the first sample of Russian text gave an English output that could hardly be called a translation, but that nevertheless provided a list of errors. Of course, errors were anticipated, but only the most glaring ones were studied in the second iteration. Next, the dictionary and the grammar codes were modified to correct the most critical errors, a second corpus was examined, and the process was repeated. Most computational linguistic research projects have adopted this iterative technique without ignoring the information and codification found in traditional linguistic studies, since it would be foolish in any linguistic investigation to disregard past scholarly results. Nevertheless, in the computer processing of large volumes of text, a surprising number of features of a natural language may be exposed that have not been recorded in grammar books.

It is instructive to examine a few examples of automated processing other than automatic translation. The various kinds of processing are grouped into four major categories as shown in Figure 4.9 (see Borko [3]; Garvin [14]; Hays [19]).

In *lexical processing* the principal objects of interest are the textual items themselves. Two typical examples are indexes and concordances. In an *index*, lexical items are listed in some specified order. In a simple *concord-*

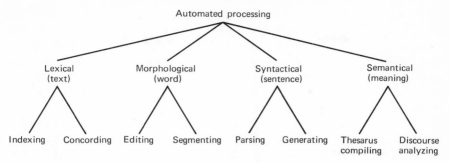

Fig. 4.9 Examples of automated processing.

ance, all occurrences of each word are listed together with their locations. A more complete concordance of a text gives for each item its frequency, context, and locations in the text. In fact, as a standard research tool, concordances have been prepared by computer for the Dead Sea Scrolls, the writings of St. Thomas Aquinas, and a variety of other corpora.

Morphological processing is concerned with words. For written languages in which the notion of "word" is clear, editing and segmenting are typical examples. *Editing* is the organizing and storing of text in a standardized machine format. For example, the text may be put in machine-readable form with all capital letters tagged, sentence and paragraph boundaries noted, and nontypewriter symbols deleted. *Segmenting* is the splitting of each word into its stem and affixes (prefixes and suffixes). For example, it might be desirable in English to separate the suffix from the stem or the root, and in German to detach the suffixes and the separable prefixes. As another example, it might be desirable to have two dictionaries, one a stem dictionary and the other an affix dictionary. This is often advantageous in automatic translation since it is inefficient to store in computer memory a dictionary of all fully inflected forms and to use a table-lookup routine on this list.

In *syntactical processing* two dual aspects of sentence structure are of interest: parsing and generation. *Parsing* is the determination of sentence structure, that is, the structural analysis of a given sentence into its grammatical components. *Generation,* which is the inverse syntactical task, is the production of grammatically correct sentences, that is, the production of sentences from a given set of grammar rules.

In *semantical processing* far less is known, but many syntactic features are carriers of meaning. Two typical examples of semantical processing are automatic thesaurus compilation and discourse analysis. A *thesaurus* is a hierarchical organization of meanings that points from a given meaning to a restricted set of words. This is to be contrasted with a *dictionary*, which is a linear list that points from a given word to a set of meanings. It is interesting to see to what extent a thesaurus of a language or a thesaurus of a subject field can be compiled automatically. One example is to instruct a computer to compile a thesaurus of psychological terms in which the concepts have a useful hierarchical structure. *Discourse analysis* is the study of the semantic content of a text. Here, the problem is how to instruct a computer to analyze discourse. For example, it might be of interest to analyze political speeches or to contrast the works of two poets of a given literary period. In the special case of discourse analysis called *content analysis*, it is necessary to look beyond the words themselves and to examine their meanings. Far less is known about discourse analysis than about indexing, and in general the progression, represented in Figure 4.9, from lexical to semantical processing reflects decreasing understanding of the fundamentals.

As a final consideration concerning computational methods, it is necessary to make the following points. First, any computational linguistic routine involves transformations between at most two natural languages L_1' and L_2' and several artificial languages $L_1, \ldots, L_n$. Typically, a natural language L_1' is transformed into a programming language L_1, which in turn is transformed into a machine language L_2, and then these steps are reversed—the sequence of transformations is inverted. Any transformation between two formal languages is relatively easy because both can be altered, whereas a transformation between a natural language and a formal language is difficult because a natural language is not subject to arbitrary alteration.

Second, most current work in computational linguistics involves off-line programming in which the linguist communicates the problem to a programmer, and the programmer analyzes the problem, draws a flow chart, codes the instructions, debugs the programs, and finally processes the data. The elapsed time in off-line programming is sometimes so long as to seriously delay the research.

RESULTS

It is now appropriate to examine some results, first in mathematical and then in computational linguistics.

4.14 SOME RESULTS IN MATHEMATICAL LINGUISTICS

Progress in mathematical linguistics has been very rapid, but the integration of separate theories has not yet been attempted. Several accomplishments can be noted as milestones, but it will suffice to mention one result in the field of algebraic linguistics and one in statistical linguistics.

In algebraic linguistics the theory of *formal grammars* has been established and related to *automata theory*, principally by the American linguist Chomsky [5, 6, 7, and in 23] (see also Bar-Hillel [1]). The implications of these results are far-reaching. The role of a formal grammar is shown in Figure 4.10.

A careful distinction must be made between the natural language L' being modeled and the formal language L that models it. Similarly, a corresponding distinction must be made between the natural grammar G' and the formal grammar G that models it. Traditionally, the linguists' objective was to discover a natural grammar G' for a given natural language L', that is, to study a natural language L' and ultimately to find its grammar G'. It turns out that a direct solution of this discovery problem is difficult practically, if not impossible theoretically, to attain. In fact, it has not been done for any natural language; no wholly adequate grammar G' has been found for any natural language L'. In the modern approach, mathematical linguists use the technique of modeling whereby intuition about the natural language L' leads to the conjecture of a formal grammar G, then the formal grammar G generates a formal language L, and finally the formal language L serves as a model of the natural language L'. Discrepancies between L' and its model L are corrected by repeating this cycle. When L is judged an adequate model of L', the natural grammar G' is said to be modeled by the formal grammar G. Hence the path of reasoning from L' to G' has the steps indicated by the arrows in Figure 4.10.

Chomsky [5] defined a *formal grammar* G as a finite set of *rules* that rewrites *strings* of symbols. First, it is necessary to assume a finite *vocabulary* V of symbols that consists of two subvocabularies. The *terminal vocabulary* T consists of terminal symbols $a, b, c, \ldots$, which denote words or morphemes. For example, in English the words "the", "man", "hit", etc., and the morphemes represented by "-s", "-ed", "-ing", etc., are regarded as terminal symbols. The *nonterminal vocabulary* $V - T$ consists of nonterminal symbols $A, B, C, \ldots$, which denote grammatical categories (parts of speech). These are conventionally written as S, NP, VP, N, V, T, etc. (where NP

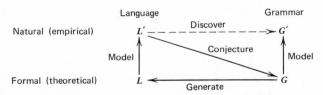

Fig. 4.10 Modeling of a natural language and grammar.

and VP are regarded as single symbols), which stand for sentence, noun phrase, verb phrase, noun, verb, article, etc., respectively. The rules are called *rewrite rules* since they rewrite strings of symbols, for example,

$$S \rightarrow NP + VP, \qquad N \rightarrow \text{man},$$

where $\rightarrow$ and $+$ are two distinguished symbols that are used to express the rules. The arrow denotes that what is on its left is to be rewritten as what is on its right, and the plus sign (sometimes omitted) denotes the concatenation or juxtaposition of vocabulary symbols.

Chomsky's main contribution was in creating a hierarchy of formal grammars in which the most general grammars are called *unrestricted rewrite grammars* since their rules permit a string of vocabulary symbols to be rewritten as a string:

$$x \rightarrow y, \qquad\qquad x,y \in V^*,$$

where $\rightarrow$ is a binary relation defined on the set V^* of all strings formed from the vocabulary V.

Within this class there is a proper subclass called *context-sensitive* (*phrase-structure*) *grammars* whose rules are restricted by conditions of context so that a nonterminal symbol is rewritten as a string in the context of specified strings:

$$xAy \rightarrow xzy, \qquad A \in V - T; \quad x,y,z \in V^*; \quad z \neq e,A,$$

where e is the empty string (of length zero). Thus $A \rightarrow z$ in the immediate context of $x \ldots y$.

Within this subclass there is a proper subclass called *context-free* (*phrase-structure*) *grammars* whose rules relax this context condition so that a nonterminal symbol is rewritten as a string, ignoring context:

$$A \rightarrow z, \qquad A \in V - T; \quad z \in V^*; \quad z \neq e,A.$$

Finally, within this class there is a proper subclass called *finite-state grammars* whose rules have the simplest, but nontrivial, form in which a nonterminal symbol is rewritten either as a terminal symbol or as a terminal symbol followed by a nonterminal symbol:

$$A \rightarrow a \quad \text{or} \quad A \rightarrow aB, \qquad A,B \in V - T; \quad a \in T.$$

This hierarchy developed by Chomsky turned out to be related to another line of investigation—automata theory (see McNaughton [28]; Ginsburg [15]; Hopcroft and Ullman [22]). An *automaton* will be regarded as an abstract machine—not a real computer—that consists of a control unit which scans via one or more heads one or more linear tapes, each of which may contain a finite string of symbols. The theory of abstract machines began with an interest in questions of effective calculability, decidability, and recursive functions. Instead of giving precise definitions of the pertinent automata, their structure (but not their behavior) can be described roughly as follows. A *finite-state automaton* has a one-way tape and a writing head, a *pushdown automaton* has a one-way tape with a reading head and a two-way tape with a reading-writing-erasing head, a *linear-bounded automaton* has a two-way tape and a reading-writing head, a *Turing machine* (named after the English mathematician A. M. Turing) has a two-way tape with a reading-writing head, and a *universal Turing machine* is one that can simulate an arbitrary Turing machine. Behaviorally (that is, as a black box), it turns out that finite-state grammars correspond to finite-state automata, context-free grammars to push-down automata, context-sensitive grammars to linear-bounded automata, and unrestricted grammars to Turing machines. It was not until 1955 that this connection was established between the theory of formal grammars and the theory of automata. Since then, the two fields have cross-fertilized one another. This is an outstanding theoretical achievement, which also has applications to programming languages. For example, it is of interest to know whether or not certain programming languages, such as ALGOL, are context-free, whether or not their syntactic structure is changed by certain computer operations, and whether or not they are syntactically ambiguous. With regard to the modeling of natural languages, finite-state and context-free grammars are thought to be inadequate, whereas unrestricted grammars are too powerful.

Next, Chomsky [5] defined a *formal language* as the set of all and only those strings of symbols generated (enumerated) by a formal grammar. This notion entails the principle that formal languages are defined in terms of formal grammars, not conversely. The hierarchy of grammars leads to a corresponding hierarchy of formal languages, as depicted in Figure 4.11.

Chomsky [5] came to believe that *generative grammars* that rewrite strings are inherently inadequate to model a natural language. So he created the notion of a *transformational grammar* (which is also generative) by extending the definition of a formal grammar to permit the transformation of structural descriptions, called *phrase-markers*, of strings into phrase-markers of other strings. The resulting theory is perhaps the most interesting and controversial topic in modern linguistics, but it will not be pursued further here. Unfortunately, its mathematical foundations are not yet well understood.

The notion of generative grammars entails a second principle that is often misunderstood or forgotten, concerning Chomsky's distinction between a person's knowledge and his behavior. *Linguistic competence* is what a native speaker knows, whereas *linguistic performance* is what he

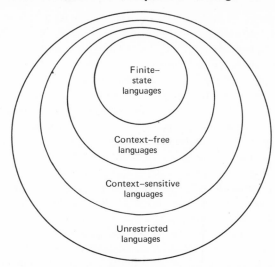

Fig. 4.11 Chomsky hierarchy of formal languages.

says. Chomsky holds that a formal grammar must account for linguistic competence but not for linguistic performance. This distinction is analogous to the distinction between a person's competence (that is to say, his knowledge of the arthmetic rules) to multiply two six-digit numbers and his inability to perform this multiplication without the use of external aids. Similarly, in language a person somehow learns the system of rules of a natural grammar, but this does not mean that he can utter or understand a sentence of arbitary length without additional aids such as paper and pencil (see Miller [29]; Miller and Chomsky [30]). Thus a generative grammar is a way of describing the structure of a language, not the human mechanism for speaking or understanding.

In statistical linguistics one of the most interesting and controversial investigations has to do with the rank-frequency relation or model, often attributed to the American philologist Zipf [36, 37]. The rank of a word in a corpus is obtained by computing the absolute frequencies of all distinct words and listing them in decreasing frequency order so that the word of rank 1 is the first on the list, the word of rank 2 is the second on the list, and so on (with a suitable convention for ties). Let f_r denote the relative frequency of occurrence of a word of rank r in a body of text. If the ranks are compared with the relative frequencies of occurrence for those ranks, then the product of the relative frequency f_r and the rank r is very nearly constant for all words, that is, independent of the word selected. This was observed empirically by Zipf, but was reported some years earlier by the

American physicist Condon [8], and even earlier by the French stenographer Estoup [13] and hence is sometimes called the Estoup-Condon-Zipf law. It is better, however, not to call it a "law" even though some mathematicians so regard it because they believe it to be linguistically true—and so do some linguists because they believe it to be mathematically true (see Cherry [4]; Herdan [20]).

By examining corpora in several languages and plotting values of f_r and r, Zipf conjectured that the constant $c = 0.1$ gave a good fit, that is, $f_r r = 0.1$. There is no question that frequency must be inversely related to rank because that is how rank is defined, but it was surprising that this particular form held reasonably well for a large class of linguistic phenomena and was also encountered in a large variety of socioeconomic phenomena —for example, the distribution of wealth and the distribution of populations of cities. However, the American linguist Joos [24] felt that the Zipf model did not express a sufficiently close fit, so he modified it by adding a second parameter, the exponent b. Later the French mathematician Mandelbrot [27] derived a new model, which contained a third parameter, the term a. With p_r denoting the probability of a symbol of rank r, these three models of rank-frequency distribution are:

Zipf	$p_r = cr^{-1}$	$c = 0.1$
Joos	$p_r = cr^{-b}$	$b \geq 1, c > 0$
Mandelbrot	$p_r = c(r + a)^{-b}$	$0 \leq a \leq 1, b > 1, c > 0$

There has been a great deal of controversy over the adequacy and generality of the rank hypothesis; that is, does it provide a good fit and does it apply to, say, Chinese ideographs was well as to English words?

Some of the most interesting recent investigations have been attempts to derive the relation from more primitive theoretical linguistic considerations instead of trying to justify it from empirical evidence. Starting from information theory, Mandelbrot ([27] and in [23]) gave a derivation of this expression by minimizing the expected cost of symbol transmission

$$E(C) = \sum_{r=1}^{v} p_r c_r,$$

where v is the size of the vocabulary, p_r is the probability of a symbol of rank r, and c_r is its cost, while holding the entropy

$$H(X) = - \sum_{r=1}^{v} p_r \log p_r$$

constant. Simon [34] gave another derivation by assuming a birth-and-death stochastic process in which the use of words in the text is subject to probabilistic factors that cause words to be born (that is, to be selected from the vocabulary as the next text word) and a death process in which words die (that is, they are not selected again). Mandelbrot and Simon disagree over which approach is better, and so this matter has not been satisfactorily settled. However, they both derived models after assuming basic theories, rather than simply observing and plotting word data.

4.15 SOME RESULTS IN COMPUTATIONAL LINGUISTICS

In computational linguistics it will suffice to mention one result in analysis, one in synthesis, and one involving both.

As an example of analysis, the automatic *parsing* of sentences has been accomplished with a phrase-structure grammar by Kuno [25] and others, and with a dependency grammar by Hays [17] and others. Figure 4.12 depicts the operation of a recognition grammar. Here each input is a terminal string. The rules of a recognition grammar and the vocabulary are stored in computer memory, and the computer produces as output a "yes" or "no" decision about the grammaticality of that string.

If a phrase-structure grammar is used, then the structure of a grammatical string can be mathematically represented by a tree. For example, if the string "the man hit the ball" is the input and the recognition grammar consists of the following simple context-free phrase-structure rules, then the output of the computer is the symbol S for sentence. The left-hand column in Figure 4.13 gives the recognition rules, which may be used in any order. The center column lists the successive steps in the *recognition* of a string that is said to be *grammatical* with respect to the given grammar. The right-hand column shows the recognition in terms of a labeled directed tree, called a *phrase-structure tree*, which is implicitly constructed by the grammar. With these rules, a computer program will attempt to recognize by starting with the terminal string. Then the computer searches its memory and rewrites one terminal symbol to give the second step of the recognition. Next, it searches for another rule to see if any symbol can be

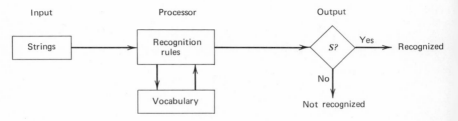

Fig. 4.12 Recognition grammar.

Recognition rules   Recognition steps   Phrase–structure tree

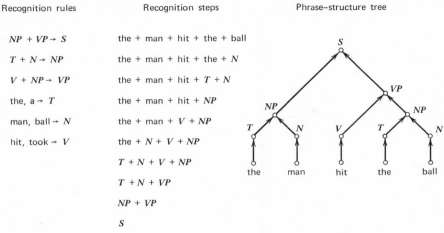

Recognition rules	Recognition steps
$NP + VP \rightarrow S$	the + man + hit + the + ball
$T + N \rightarrow NP$	the + man + hit + the + N
$V + NP \rightarrow VP$	the + man + hit + T + N
the, a $\rightarrow$ T	the + man + hit + NP
man, ball $\rightarrow$ N	the + man + V + NP
hit, took $\rightarrow$ V	the + N + V + NP
	T + N + V + NP
	T + N + VP
	NP + VP
	S

Fig. 4.13   Sentence recognition.

rewritten, and so on. Finally, if the string is grammatical according to this grammar, then the recognition ends with the nonterminal symbol S for sentence since further rewriting is impossible. Notice that this program will also recognize "the ball took the man", "a man hit a ball", and so forth, which are regarded as grammatical with respect to this grammar. This situation could be corrected by using a more realistic grammar, which might contain several hundred detailed rules rather than six simple ones. The computer program need not produce a picture of a tree but may give a table or list that is mathematically equivalent to the tree.

If a dependency grammar is used instead, the resulting tree is called a *dependency tree*. In a *dependency grammar*, the rules specify that the main verb is the only independent element of the sentence, the words that depend most immediately on the verb are the subject noun and object noun, the word that depends most immediately on a noun is the adjective or article that modifies the noun, and so on. The same string "the man hit the ball" has as output the dependency tree shown in Figure 4.14. Notice that dependency trees are different from phrase-structure trees. It is not a question of which is correct, since each reveals certain aspects of syntactic structure. In any case, computer programs have been written for both types of grammars.

As an example of synthesis, the automatic *generation* of sentences has been accomplished with a context-free phrase-structure grammar by Yngve [35] and others. Figure 4.15 depicts the operation of a generative grammar. Here each input is the symbol S, which denotes "sentence". The

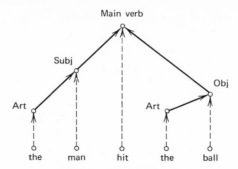

Fig. 4.14 Dependency tree.

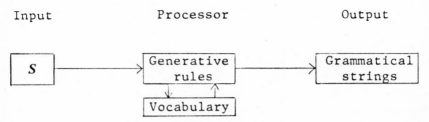

Fig. 4.15 Generative grammar.

computer stores in its memory the generation rules and the vocabulary and produces as output a grammatical string, that is, a sentence.

For example, by using the dual of the foregoing simple phrase-structure grammar, the string "the man hit the ball" can be generated. The left-hand column in Figure 4.16 gives the generation rules, which may be used in any order. The center column lists the successive steps in the *generation* of a string that is said to be *grammatical* with respect to the given grammar. The right-hand column shows the corresponding structural description in terms of a labeled directed tree, called a *phrase-structure tree*, which is implicitly generated by the grammar. With these rules, a computer program will generate strings by starting with S. Then the computer searches its memory and rewrites S as $NP + VP$ to give the second step of the generation. Next, NP is expanded to $T + N$, and so on. Finally, the generation may end with "the man hit the ball", since further expansion is not possible with these rules. Notice that the program will also generate "the ball took the man", "a man hit a ball", and so forth, which are regarded as grammatical with respect to this grammar. Although this result is to be expected of a grammar with only six simple rules, it exemplifies the outputting of English sentences using a generative grammar.

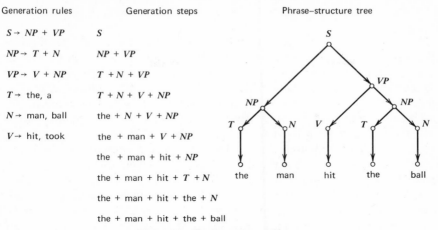

Generation rules	Generation steps
$S \rightarrow NP + VP$	S
$NP \rightarrow T + N$	$NP + VP$
$VP \rightarrow V + NP$	$T + N + VP$
$T \rightarrow$ the, a	$T + N + V + NP$
$N \rightarrow$ man, ball	the $+ N + V + NP$
$V \rightarrow$ hit, took	the $+$ man $+ V + NP$
	the $+$ man $+$ hit $+ NP$
	the $+$ man $+$ hit $+ T + N$
	the $+$ man $+$ hit $+$ the $+ N$
	the $+$ man $+$ hit $+$ the $+$ ball

Fig. 4.16 Sentence generation.

The strings that Yngve produced by computer were encouraging even though some were ungrammatical by present intuitive notions of grammaticality. For example, it is possible to generate strings such as "colorless green ideas sleep furiously". Whether or not this string is regarded as grammatical by a naive native speaker, it nevertheless is a possible output of the type of grammar that Yngve used. In fact, another such computer program, called Auto-poet, has generated poetry that was very much like "beatnik" poetry. What matters is that the structural markers are correct: adverbs occur in the right places with the "-ly" ending, adjectives premodify the nouns, and so on. The role of structural markers is more obvious in the nonsense poem "Jabberwocky" by Lewis Carroll (the English mathematician C. L. Dodgson):

Jabberwocky

'Twas brillig, and the slithy toves
Did gyre and gimble in the wabe;
All mimsy were the borogoves,
And the mome raths outgrabe.

Programming a computer to find the structural markers in this poem is a nice exercise because it illustrates that sentences contain many clues that are latent to the native speaker, but which must be made evident for computer processing. Some of these markers are suffixes, adjective-noun agreement, and word order, but they are not as prevalent in English as in highly inflected languages such as German and Russian. The study of syntactic structure concerns the determination of these clues and their relative roles.

Syntactic structure is of fundamental interest in computational linguistics because it reveals the deeper semantic structure, which is critical to many information-retrieval systems and query systems. For example, the string "they are flying planes" is seen to be *semantically ambiguous;* that is, it has more than one meaning. Interestingly, this string is semantically ambiguous because it is *syntactically ambiguous*; that is, it has more than one structural description or tree (see Figure 4.17). By using a parsing program, it is possible to see the exact cause of such semantic ambiguities. Other examples are the strings "the man turned on the barbecue spit" and "little boys shrink from washing". Such expressions are often spoken and heard, but they are usually embedded in sufficient context and accompanied by enough pragmatic clues for their semantic ambiguities to be easily resolved. The computer resolution of semantic ambiguity is often dependent on the computer resolution of syntactic ambiguity which may, in turn, depend on that of *morphological ambiguity*, that is, words with more than one meaning. Hence such data must be stored in computer memory.

As an example of analysis and synthesis, results can be cited in research on automatic *abstracting* and automatic *translation*. Automatic abstracting research was started in 1959 (see Luhn [26]; Edmundson [12]) and has remained a relatively minor effort. Programs have been written to produce an automatic *extract* of an English or Russian document, which consists of a set of selected sentences to serve as an automatic abstract suitable for screening purposes. Automatic translation research has been conducted in this country since 1949 (see Bar-Hillel [1]; Edmundson [9]; Booth [2]). The first public demonstration was in 1954, and by 1965 some six centers in this country were engaged in automatic translation research on Russian to English, German to English, French to English, and more recently on Chinese to English. It has been found, both empirically and theoretically, that it is easier to translate from a highly inflected language to a less in-

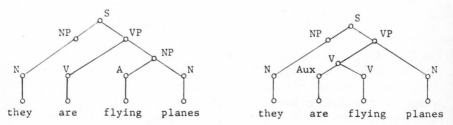

Fig. 4.17 Syntactic ambiguity.

flected language because the former has an abundance of clues, for example, cases for nouns and adjective-noun agreements. Present systems produce one English equivalent for a given source-language word, handle idioms rather effectively as complete semantic units, and correctly rearrange word order. Interestingly, the rank-frequency relation has practical uses in computational linguistics since in building an automatic translation system it is helpful to know how large an initial corpus should be to assure that the glossary compiled from it will contain a given percentage of the words of any future corpus.

UNSOLVED PROBLEMS

The results cited in the preceding section should not obscure the existence of numerous unsolved problems. Some will be mentioned in mathematical linguistics followed by some in computational linguistics.

4.16 SOME UNSOLVED PROBLEMS IN MATHEMATICAL LINGUISTICS

Mathematical linguistics contains a variety of unsolved problems that are due largely to their intrinsic mathematical difficulty. Some problems are known to be solvable but have resisted attack, whereas others are known to be unsolvable in the sense that there is no general algorithm (effective procedure) for solving them. Of course, the unsolvable problems involve deep mathematical questions of decidability, but the unsolved problems also require considerable mathematical sophistication.

In algebraic linguistics a good case in point is the theory of context-sensitive grammars, about which relatively little is known. For example, it is not known whether the set of all strings that are not in a context-sensitive language (the complement) forms a context-sensitive language, or even whether this problem is solvable. The theory of context-free grammars also contains both unsolved and unsolvable problems (see Ginsburg [15]; Hopcroft and Ullman [22]). Finally, a major unsolved problem is the formulation of an adequate mathematical foundation for transformational grammars. One formulation has been achieved that makes variable the position of a transformational grammar relative to the Chomsky hierarchy (see Peters and Ritchie, below).

In statistical linguistics an unsolved problem concerns finding an adequate model for the rank-frequency relation (see Edmundson [10]). One defect of the Joos model, and hence of the Zipf model, is that if v is the number of distinct words in the vocabulary, so that

$$\sum_{r=1}^{v} p_r = 1,$$

then

$$1 = \sum_{r=1}^{v} p_r = \sum_{r=1}^{v} \frac{1}{10r^b} = \frac{1}{10} \sum_{r=1}^{v} \frac{1}{r^b} = \frac{1}{10}\left(1 + \frac{1}{2^b} + \frac{1}{3^b} + \ldots + \frac{1}{v^b}\right).$$

This implies that v and b are functionally related; in fact, it follows that if $b = 1.000$, then $v = 12{,}367$, and if $b = 1.106$, then $v = \infty$. Both of these mathematical conclusions are linguistically untenable.

As with all such models, several statistical problems remain. Since the theoretical models are expressed in terms of the corresponding population variables p_r and r, one important class of problems is the estimation of the parameters a, b, and c. A second class of problems is the testing of the hypothesis $H_1{:}c = 1/10$ and the hypothesis $H_2{:}b = 1$. In both these problems the sample relative frequency f_r could be used as the estimator of p_r.

4.17 SOME UNSOLVED PROBLEMS IN COMPUTATIONAL LINGUISTICS

In computational linguistics many data-processing systems have not passed from the research to the operational stage. Since few of the systems that have been developed can be said to be operational, many computational linguistics problems must be regarded as presently unsolved.

In analysis all present computer programs for parsing often yield multiple parsings, even for intuitively unambiguous sentences. For example, sentence-parsing programs produce in some cases as many as one hundred different trees for a single sentence. Clearly, it is wrong to expect always to produce a unique tree (a unique syntactic structure) for every input string since some, like "they are flying planes", have more than one structure. Nevertheless, the outputting of too many trees for a given input string indicates that the grammar used is inadequate. Considerable programming effort is being expended to eliminate ungrammatical structures and reduce computer time (see Kuno [25]).

In synthesis the computer generation of sentences by present programs still produces a large number of intuitively ungrammatical strings, and, of course, only a finite number of intuitively grammatical strings are generated. However, only the first of these phenomena indicates the linguistic inadequacy of present generative grammars.

The more complicated programs involve both analysis and synthesis. Examples are processes such as automatic abstracting and automatic translating. In both cases the subjective quality of the output ranges from poor to medium. Unfortunately, engineering and programming problems often have been confused with linguistic and mathematical problems attendant to this research. One of the problems in automatic abstracting research is that of specifying the form and length of a computer abstract; but this is not the case in automatic translation, where form and quality may be more easily specified. The production of informative abstracts is more difficult than that of indicative ones, and the production of true abstracts (generated sentences) remains unsolved (see Edmundson [12]). As discussed earlier, the problem of automatic translation from English to Russian is more difficult than from Russian to English. Even more difficult is translation from Chinese to English since Chinese is not inflected at all, and there is the added practical problem of getting Chinese ideographs into computer memory. Automatic translation remains a research-and-development effort; and although considerable strides have been made, especially in the last few years, the problems cannot be considered solved, either linguistically or computationally (see Booth [2]; Borko [3]).

Information storage-and-retrieval research has been very active since 1950, but many problems remain. Indexes and dictionaries now can be compiled automatically, but the automatic compilation of thesauri is little understood. Automatic segmentation routines that hyphenate words with a tolerable error rate have been developed for book and newspaper publishing. Numerous automatic question-answering systems have been constructed that rely on syntactic and semantic analysis of both the query and the answers (see Borko [3]); but the types of questions and answers allowed are limited, and success is highly subjective.

OUTLOOK

Although it is risky to speculate on the future developments of these expanding fields, some events are foreseeable.

4.18 OUTLOOK FOR MATHEMATICAL LINGUISTICS

Mathematical linguistics will likely become a permanent part of the university curriculum, and will probably continue to use those mathematical theories that have been proved to be applicable in the past.

In algebraic linguistics the theories of semigroups, graphs, and trees will continue to be the most fruitful since they are discrete mathematics. Automata theory will continue to interact with the theory of formal grammars to their mutual benefit. It is clear that certain machines, such as finite-state automata, pushdown automata, and Turing machines, are either too special or too general for linguistic purposes. New automata will be conceived to perform functions not covered by the automata previously mentioned. The study of semantics has received a tremendous impetus in the past two years, since many researchers are now applying their knowledge about syntactic structures to the study of semantic structures. Research will go slowly here, however, because of basic philosophical, logical, and psychological difficulties.

In statistical linguistics the existing theories of statistical inference will be routinely applied to the estimation of linguistic parameters and the testing of linguistic hypotheses. Non-Markov chains will replace simple Markov chains as models of linguistic processes, and nonstationary stochastic processes will replace stationary ones since adequate models must reflect the evolutionary aspects of language. New and more powerful statistics and methods of inference will be employed to solve problems in stylostatistics, such as the determination of authorship (see Mosteller and Wallace [31]); in lexicostatistics, such as the dating of unknown texts; and in the decipherment of the Mayan and Etruscan languages.

4.19 OUTLOOK FOR COMPUTATIONAL LINGUISTICS

Computational linguistics also promises to become a permanent part of the university curriculum, most likely in departments of computer or information science.

Computer hardware will become more suitable for linguistic analysis because of increased capacity, speed, and efficiency. Hardware plays an important role because it determines the upper and lower bounds within which theories may be applied in practice. It is likely that computers used in the analysis of speech will be *hybrid* computers, that is, a mixture of digital and analog. It is more difficult to foresee whether they will be mostly general- or special-purpose computers. Up to now, special-purpose computers have not been needed since general-purpose computers have been adequate for a wide variety of special problems. The development of parallel-search memories would have an important impact on information storage-and-retrieval systems. Very large memories will be used in linguistic analysis to permit the storage of more complex techniques and of considerably larger corpora. Print readers and other input devices will substantially replace keypunching, thereby allowing the use of larger character sets having upper and lower cases in numerous fonts. Similarly, at the output end, an expanded character set will be available on new high-speed printers and composing devices to assist the linguistic analysis.

Programming software will become more useful for linguistic analysis because of increased simplicity, power, and machine-independence. It is clear that programming languages play an important role, but this is not peculiar to linguistic analysis. Some programming languages will approach natural languages in their ease of learning and use. The shift away from the machinelike languages to the problem-oriented and procedure-oriented languages will continue. On-line programming, both with and without time-sharing systems, will substantially replace off-line programming to allow the linguist to use heuristics in solving his problems. There is no reason why on-line techniques cannot be applied in the field of linguistic analysis as has been done in mathematical analysis. For example, heuristic methods have been used in the solution of integral equations and differential equations, whereby the mathematician, who can recognize a solution once he sees it on a display console, can heuristically search for a solution without knowing an algorithm in advance. The same thing will be done in linguistic analysis so that the linguist at a console can build a language processor, run it on a corpus, and study the output. If the results are unsatisfactory, the system can be modified by altering some rules and parameters, and then run on the next test corpus to see the effect. Of course, this will require a close working arrangement between on-line techniques and heuristics.

4.20 SUMMARY

The properties of natural language are encountered everywhere in the study of communication systems, information-retrieval systems, and language-data processing systems. Hence the study of natural languages is central to the study of the communication process.

Mathematical linguistics is the study of linguistic structure and behavior by means of mathematical theories and methods, and its scope covers both algebraic and statistical linguistics. Computational linguistics is the study of linguistic data and mathematical linguistics by means of computers and computer programs, and it involves the analysis of natural-language text, its synthesis, or both. Thus the core of these fields concerns the quantitative and formal aspects of language, both in theories and in their application.

Research in mathematical and computational linguistics is vital because it affords powerful methods for the study of natural languages, about which relatively little is known. Pioneering applications of computers in linguistic analysis during the decade 1960–1970 are comparable to those that occurred in the first era (1950–1960) of computers in which they were applied in numerical analysis.

In mathematical linguistics the methods rely on the use of mathematical models and a research cycle, which is that of the scientific method. Methods in computational linguistics are a mixture of those from computer programming and experimental design, whose experimental cycle involves input, processing, output, and evaluation. Thus the research methods rest on algebraic and statistical theories and require continued experimentation involving computers and communication systems.

Outstanding examples of results in mathematical linguistics are the theory of formal grammars and its relation to automata theory and the modeling of the rank-frequency relation. Corresponding examples of results in computational linguistics are the automatic parsing and generation of sentences, automatic extracting and translating of documents, and query systems for information retrieval. There remain, however, numerous open problems, some unsolved but known to be solvable, and others whose solvability remains undertermined.

The outlook is that both mathematical and computational linguistics will become permanent parts of university curricula, that new mathematical techniques will be fashioned to attack difficult theoretical problems, and that new computer systems will be developed that are more appropriate for linguistic analysis.

This research is exciting and interdisciplinary, but is in its infancy.

REFERENCES

1. Bar-Hillel, Y., *Language and Information*, Addison-Wesley, Reading, Mass., 1964.
2. Booth, A. D. (editor), *Machine Translation*, Wiley, New York, 1967.
3. Borko, H. (editor), *Automated Language Processing: The State of the Art*, Wiley, New York, 1967.
4. Cherry, C., *On Human Communication*, Wiley, New York, 1957.
5. Chomsky, N., *Syntactic Structures*, Mouton and Co., The Hague, 1957.
6. Chomsky, N., "Formal Properties of Grammars," in Luce, R., R. Bush, and E. Galanter (editors), *Handbook of Mathematical Psychology*, Vol. II, Wiley, New York, 1963, pp. 323–418.
7. Chomsky, N., and G. A. Miller, "Introduction to the Formal Analysis of Natural Languages," in Luce, R. Bush, and E. Galanter (editors), *Handbook of Mathematical Psychology* Vol. II, Wiley, NewYork, 1963, pp. 269–321.
8. Condon, E. U., "Statistics of Vocabulary," *Science*, **67**, 1928, 300.
9. Edmundson, H. P. (editor), *Proceedings of the National Symposium on Machine Translation*, Prentice-Hall, Englewood Cliffs, N. J., 1961.
10. Edmundson, H. P., "A Statistician's View of Linguistic Models and Language Data Processing," in Garvin, P. (editor), *Natural Language and the Computer*, McGraw-Hill, New York, 1963, pp. 151–179.

11. Edmundson, H. P., "Mathematical Models in Linguistics and Language Processing," in Borko, H. (editor), *Automated Language Processing: The State of the Art*, Wiley, New York, 1967, pp. 33–96.

12. Edmundson, H. P., "New Methods in Automatic Extracting," *Journal of the Association for Computing Machinery*, **16**, No. 2, April, 1969, pp. 264–285.

13. Estoup, J., *Gammes sténographiques*, 4th ed., Paris, 1916.

14. Garvin, P. (editor), *Natural Language and the Computer*, McGraw-Hill, New York, 1963.

15. Ginsburg, S., *Mathematical Theory of Context-Free Languages*, McGraw-Hill, New York, 1966.

16. Gleason, H. A., *Linguistics and English Grammar*, Holt, Rinehart and Winston, New York, 1965.

17. Hays, D. G., "Automatic Language-Data Processing," in Borko, H. (editor), *Computer Applications in the Behavorial Sciences*, Prentice-Hall, Englewood Cliffs, N. J., 1962, pp. 394–423.

18. Hays, D. G. (editor), *Readings in Automatic Language Processing*, American Elsevier, New York, 1966.

19. Hays, D. G., *Introduction to Computational Linguistics*, American Elsevier, New York, 1967.

20. Herdan, G., *The Calculus of Linguistic Observations*, Mouton and Co., The Hague, 1962.

21. Hockett, C. F., *A Course in Modern Linguistics*, Macmillan, New York, 1958.

22. Hopcroft, J., and J. Ullman, *Formal Languages and Their Relation to Automata*, Addison-Wesley, Reading, Mass., 1969.

23. Jakobson, R. (editor), *Structure of Language and Its Mathematical Aspects, Proceedings of Symposia in Applied Mathematics*, Vol. XII, American Mathematical Society, Providence, R. I., 1961.

24. Joos, M., "Review of Zipf's *The Psycho-Biology of Language*," *Language*, **12**, 1936, 196–210.

25. Kuno, S., "Computer Analysis of Natural Languages," in Schwartz, J. (editor), *Mathematical Aspects of Computer Science, Proceedings of Symposia in Applied Mathematics*, Vol. XIX, American Mathematical Society, Providence, R. I., 1967, pp. 52–110.

26. Luhn, H. P., "The Automatic Creation of Literature Abstracts," *IBM Journal of Research and Development*, **2**, 1958, 159–165.

27. Mandelbrot, B., "An Informational Theory of the Structure of Language Based upon the Theory of the Statistical Matching of Messages and Coding," in Jackson, W. (editor), *Proceedings of a Symposium on Applications of Communication Theory*, Butterworths, London, 1953, pp. 486–502.

28. McNaughton, R., "The Theory of Automata, A Survey," in Alt, F. (editor), *Advances in Computers*, Vol. **2**, Academic Press, New York, 1961, pp. 379–432.

29. Miller, G. A., *Language and Communication*, McGraw-Hill, New York, 1951, reprinted 1963.

30. Miller, G. A., and N. Chomsky, "Finitary Models of Language Users," in Luce, R., R. Bush, and E. Galanter (editors), *Handbook of Mathematical Psychology*, Vol. **2**, Wiley, New York, 1963, pp. 419–491.

31. Mosteller, F., and D. Wallace, *Inference and Disputed Authorship: The Federalist*, Addison-Wesley, Reading, Mass., 1964.

32. Plath, W., "Mathematical Linguistics," in Mohrmann, C., A. Sommerfelt, and J. Whatmough (editors), *Trends in European and American Linguistics, 1930–1960*, Spectrum Publishers, Utrecht, 1961, pp. 21–57.

33. Shannon, C., and W. Weaver, *The Mathematical Theory of Communication*, University of Illinois Press, Urbana, 1949.
34. Simon, H., "On a Class of Skew Distribution Functions," *Biometrika*, **42**, Parts 3–4, 1955, 425–440.
35. Yngve, V., "Random Generation of English Sentences," in *1961 International Conference on Machine Translation of Languages and Applied Language Analysis*, Vol. 1, Her Majesty's Stationery Office, London, 1962, pp. 65–80.
36. Zipf, G. K., *Human Behavior and the Principle of Least Effort*, Addison-Wesley, Reading, Mass., 1949.
37. Zipf, G. K., *The Psycho-Biology of Language*, Houghton Mifflin, New York, 1935, reprinted MIT Press, Cambridge, 1965.

FURTHER READINGS

1. Akhmanova, O., I. Mel'chuk, R. Frumkina, and E. Paducheva (editors), *Exact Methods in Linguistic Research*, D. G. Hays and D. Mohr (translators), University of California Press, Berkeley and Los Angeles, 1963.
2. Bach, E., *An Introduction to Transformation Grammars*, Holt, Rinehart and Winston, New York, 1964.
3. Booth, A. D., L. Brandwood, and J. Cleave, *Mechanical Resolution of Linguistic Problems*, Butterworths, London, 1958.
4. Chomsky, N., *Aspects of the Theory of Syntax*, M.I.T. Press, Cambridge, 1965.
5. Delavenay, E., *An Introduction to Machine Translation*, Praeger, New York, 1960.
6. Doležel, L., and R. Bailey, *Statistics and Style*, American Elsevier, New York, 1969.
7. Doležel, L., P. Sgall, and J. Vachek (editors), *Prague Studies in Mathematical Linguistics*, Vol. 1 and 2, University of Alabama Press, University, Ala., 1966 and 1967.
8. Friedman, J., *A Computer Model of Transformational Grammar*, American Elsevier, New York, 1971.
9. Fodor, J., and J. Katz (editors), *The Structure of Language: Readings in the Philosophy of Language*, Prentice-Hall, Englewood Cliffs, N. J., 1964.
10. Garvin, P., and B. Spolsky (editors), *Computation in Linguistics: A Case Book*, Indiana University Press, Bloomington, 1966.
11. Gross, M., and A. Lentin, *Introduction to Formal Grammars*, M. Salkoff (translator), Springer-Verlag, New York, 1970.
12. Hockett, C. F., *Language, Mathematics, and Linguistics*, Mouton, The Hague, 1967.
13. Katz, J., *The Philosophy of Language*, Harper and Row, New York, 1966.
14. Keifer, F., *Mathematical Linguistics in Eastern Europe*, American Elsevier, New York, 1968.
15. Koutsoudas, A., *Writing Transformational Grammars: An Introduction*, McGraw-Hill, New York, 1966.
16. Langendoen, D. T., *The Study of Syntax: The Generative-Transformational Approach to the Structure of American English*, Holt, Rinehart and Winston, New York, 1969.
17. Locke, W., and A. D. Booth (editors), *Machine Translation of Languages*, M.I.T. Press, Cambridge, 1955.
18. Marcus, S., *Algebraic Linguistics: Analytical Models*, Academic Press, New York, 1967.
19. Minsky, M. (editor), *Semantic Information Processing*, M.I.T. Press, Cambridge, 1968.

20. Oettinger, A., *Automatic Language Translation*, Harvard University Press, Cambridge, 1960.
21. Papp, F., *Mathematical Linguistics in the Soviet Union*, Mouton, The Hague, 1966.
22. Peters, P. S., "Mathematical Linguistics," in G. Dantzig and A. Veinott (editors), *Mathematics of the Decision Sciences, Part 2*, Lectures in Applied Mathematics, Vol. 12, American Mathematical Society, Providence, R. I., 1968, pp. 353–368.
23. Peters, P. S., and R. W. Ritchie, "A Note on the Universal Base Hypothesis," *Journal of Linguistics*, **5,** No. 1, 1969, 150–152.
24. Revzin, I. I., *Models of Language*, N. Owen and A. Ross (translators), Methuen, London, 1966.
25. Sgall, P., L. Nebeský, A. Goralčíková, and E. Hajičová, *A Functional Approach to Syntax: In Generative Description of Language*, American Elsevier, New York, 1969.

PART 2

INTRAPERSONAL COMMUNICATION SYSTEMS

We do not consider the center of laughter to be located in the sole of the foot, because tickling the sole causes laughter.

George Henry Lewes
Nature, **15,** 1876

CHAPTER 5

Neurons as Biological Transducers and Communication Channels

THEODORE H. BULLOCK[1]

Professor of Neurosciences, University of California, San Diego

Contents

[1] Original observations herein were aided by grants from the National Institutes of Health, the Office of Naval Research, the National Science Foundation, and the Air Force Office of Scientific Reserarch.

5.1 INTRODUCTION

Neurons are the nervous units of nervous systems. A nervous system is a highly organized assemblage of special components in animals, so arranged as to mediate prompt or complex responses. The human nervous system is far and away the most complex system that we know, apart from assemblages of such systems as universities, corporations, or congresses.

We can distinguish the functions of the nervous systems in different ways. One dimension is simply the time scale of the responses of protoplasm to stimuli. The nervous system helps to achieve a high rapidity of reaction because the components of the system are specialized, among other ways, in rapidity of transduction and of propagation of excitation. This in turn permits the coming together of excitation from many different sources, such as eye and ear, to be evaluated, to be summed, and in predetermined ways to be weighted so as to control the initiation of commands for the response of the organism. The rapidity is also necessary for the other achievement of the system, the complexity. This means that many steps intervene between stimulus and response, but all are accomplished rapidly enough that the response is still relevant to the stimulus; for example, the victim reacts before the predator has pounced.

Along another dimension, we can distinguish those functions of the nervous system that are regulatory or reactive from those that are initiative. The nervous system mediates compensatory responses to environmental events or states that tend to displace it from desired (adaptive) conditions; this kind of reaction we call *regulatory*. Many of the functions of the nervous system are of this kind. When one works in a cold room or becomes thirsty or steps onto a stone that suddenly tilts, regulatory reflexes are initiated. But apart from these, there is also a major function of the nervous system that is less understood, in which it initiates *spontaneous departure* from the status quo (for example, change of mood, appetitive behavior, and sleep). It is sometimes not obvious, in the short range, at any rate, what the adaptive value of each of these spontaneous actions is, but we can explain them or rationalize them in the long term on evolutionary grounds.

FUNCTIONAL COMPONENTS

In the frame of reference of communication aspects, some things need to be said about the kinds of components of the system. Here we refer to their properties, not their chemical constitution, since it is another question whether or not a particular "hardware" is the only one that could exhibit the required properties. Quite often the same function can be achieved by components made of different materials, and so the basic fields of biochemistry, molecular biology, and brain chemistry are outside the present considerations.

5.2 TRANSDUCERS

In the first place, it is necessary for the system somehow to be coupled to the environment. One of the great achievements of evolution is to multiply and diversify the types of transducers, that is, of sense organs and modalities with which we can detect interesting environmental events and states. Beyond the major modalities of sight, hearing, smell, taste, touch, position, pain, temperature, and the rest, there are submodalities that analyze colors, pitches of sound, the myriad odors, and so on; this means not only transducer differentiation, but all the machinery in the brain that handles and sorts the information from the transducers.

One of the areas of most active and difficult investigation concerns the question of how specific or nonspecific these modalities actually are. It is clear that the modalities of photic sensitivity and of acoustic sensitivity are separate, and that the transducers and central pathways are distinct. But this is not so true of many of the others, such as pain, temperature, vibration, touch, or the submodalities within smell, taste, sight, and hearing.

The finer discriminations are made by higher-level processing of information from ambiguous detectors with overlapping sensitivity. As a principle of operation of a truly complex system depending on exceedingly numerous, accurate, and delicate discriminations, this is a very ingenious method. It works both for localizing within one modality, as in detecting the spot on the skin experiencing a tactile stimulation, and for qualitative distinctions, as in analyzing smells and tastes. It calls for only modest specificity or narrowness of the receptive field of each unit transducer— what we call a *receptor*. But it requires that the central processing system in the brain "know" the receptive field or range of ambiguity of each line.

Transducer physiology is curious. On the one hand it is presently frustrating with respect to understanding the actual mechanism of transduction. Our knowledge of molecular biology is not yet up to an explanation of the conversion of touch, vibration, odor, temperature—or in fact any normal stimulus except light—into a physiological event. Even the advanced knowledge of visual pigment reactions leaves a complete gap between the alterations of those molecules by light and the next step in the chain of communication. On the other hand, sensory physiology is one of the most exciting fronts of physiology, because every year there are discovered new sense organs capable of transducing forms of environmental stimuli that we did not even realize animals are sensitive to. And this is not by any means finished. We are now aware, for example, that organisms are sensitive to weak magnetic fields of the order of that of the Earth, to far sublethal X-radiation, and to small hydrostatic pressures even in the absence of any gas spaces; but we do not know whether these are accomplished by true sense organs or by less specialized cells. It remains to be found where the transducers are situated in the body.

5.3 NEURONS

The nervous cells of the nervous system (including those sensory cells which are nerve cells) we call *neurons*. Neurons are cells specialized for the manipulation of signals, including the receipt, some degree of integration or/and conduction over a distance, and the delivery to other neurons or to effector cells of physiological events representing excitation or inhibition. Specialization for these functions and connections to other neurons are the key features. Every nerve fiber, nerve ending, and dendrite is part of a neuron.

The concept we have just defined is the conclusion of a traumatic chapter in scientific history, with furious debates, sudden turns with technical developments, colorful personalities, and the rest. We call it the *neuron doctrine*. It does not settle all the problems. We are still altering our ideas about just what a synapse (functional junction between neurons), a dendrite, and an axon (see below) are. We are still learning what contribution to nervous functions a cell can make without being a nerve cell, especially the abundant and sometimes specialized nonnervous glial cells of the nervous system. There are still borderline cases where we have to ask just when a cell is a nerve cell; for example, usage about rods and cones of the retina is still divided.

Figure 5.1 shows a representative neuron. Generally, it is more or less easy to distinguish the branching processes that are receptive for the neuron, called *dendrites*, from the longer, less arborizing, fiber that propagates nerve impulses away from the integrative and decision-making parts of the neuron, called the *axon*. There must be a nucleus and a certain amount of cytoplasm around it, and these together form the *cell body* or *soma*, which may occupy various positions on or off the main stream of signal spread from dendrites to axon (Figure 5.2)

Since nerves are bundles of axons, they carry many independent signals in as many separate neurons. *Tracts* (white matter) are similar bundles inside the brain or spinal cord. In higher animals including man, the dendrites and the beginnings and endings of axons, and therefore the

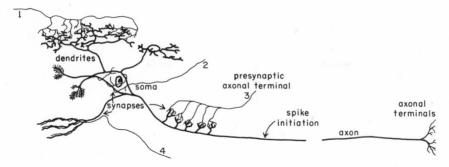

Fig. 5.1 Diagram of a neuron, based on the cardiac ganglion cell of a crab. Four types of arriving presynaptic axonal terminals and synaptic relations are shown. The axon is interrupted to indicate a long segment omitted. A scale is omitted, but the soma of most neurons is between 10 and 50 microns across; the axon is usually between 0.2 and 20 microns in diameter and from 2 millimeters to 2 meters or more in length.

synapses connecting neurons, are concentrated into certain areas of the brain and spinal cord and some ganglia. This is chiefly gray matter in vertebrates, and it contains also the nerve cell bodies; in insects and other invertebrates and in some places in ourselves, it is called *neuropile* and is more concentrated, lacking the cell bodies.

Figure 5.3 shows various ways of recording the activity of neurons. The activity is caused mainly by changes in permeability, therefore in conductance across the surface membrane bounding the neuron. Cytoplasm is low in resistance, the neuronal surface membrane is generally very high, and the external milieu between the cells is again low. This means that an electrode inserted inside a neuron and referred to another electrode in the external milieu furnishes the best method for revealing neuronal activity; that is, we place our high-resistance voltmeter (wide-frequency oscilloscope) across the main voltage drop. Not only is the recorded voltage at its maximum, but we see virtually only the activity of this one neuron. Although the cell contents are of high conductance and the internal electrode therefore sees a large area of the surface membrane, it is not isopotential throughout the neuron, and the electrode can fail to see significant events occurring far out the dendrites or axon. The parts of a neuron accessible to a penetrating microelectrode are the soma, axon, and large dendrites, provided the diameter is at least several microns; hence most of the tree of dendrites and the terminal arbors of axons are still out of reach—a very significant portion of the whole. External electrodes deal with severely shunted voltage drops, but they are useful because these electrodes can be much lower in resistance; together with a low-resistance path through the

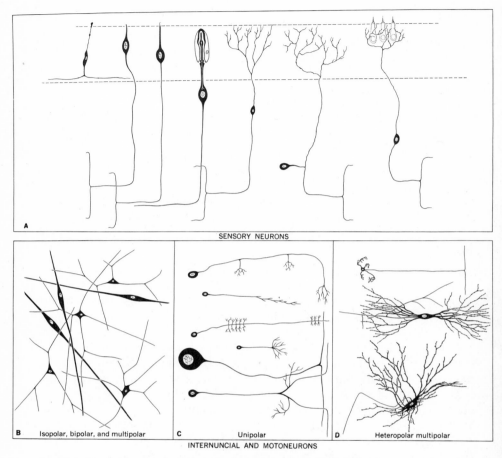

A — SENSORY NEURONS

B — Isopolar, bipolar, and multipolar
C — Unipolar
D — Heteropolar multipolar

INTERNUNCIAL AND MOTONEURONS

Fig. 5.2 Types of neurons based on the number and differentiation of processes. (A) Sensory neurons. The most primitive (left) send axons into a superficial plexus. In animals with a central nervous system, the commonest type is a similar bipolar cell in the epithelium with a short, simple of slightly elaborated (arthropod scolopale) distal process and an axon entering the central nervous system and generally bifurcating into ascending and descending branches. A presumably more derived form is that with a deep-lying cell body and long branching distal process with free nerve endings. In vertebrates, such cells secondarily become unipolar and grouped into the dorsal root ganglia. The figure on the right represents a vertebrate vestibular or acoustic sensory neuron that has retained the primitive bipolar form but has adopted (presumably secondarily) a specialized nonnervous epithelial cell as the actual receptor element. (B) Isopolar, bipolar, and multipolar neurons in the nerve net of medusa. These may be either or both interneurons and motoneurons; differentiated dendrites cannot be recognized. (C) Unipolar neurons representative of the dominant type of all higher invertebrates. Both interneurons and motoneurons have this form. The upper four are examples

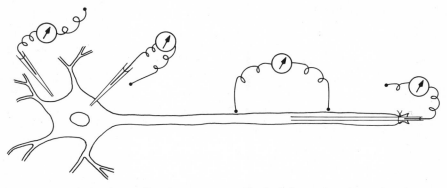

Fig. 5.3 Methods of recording from neurons. On the left are fine glass micropipettes fitted with salt solution, and on the right inserted into the axon is a similar but larger pipette. The cell lies in a saline medium of relatively high conductance. The second and fourth methods are spoken of as intracellular or transmembrane recording; the others as extracellular—monopolar or bipolar.

tissue, the inherent noise level in the observed voltage is much less, so that higher amplification can be used. Still, in general, we do not regain on this account as much as we lose, so that the weaker types of neuronal events are rarely "visible" with extracellular recording. Extracellular electrodes see the activity of one or several or many units, depending on the effective size of the tip of the electrode as well as on geometric factors and inhomogeneities of tissue conductance (glial or other membranes, infoldings of cell surface, etc.).

Neurons are the common basis of all nervous systems. Lower animals (simple polyps, *Hydra*, small jellyfish, small worms) may have as few as a thousand neurons. In higher animals like ourselves, there are approximately 10^{10} of these neurons; and as we shall see shortly, they are connected with each other in ways that make it impossible for us to say how many permutations of connections there are. A typical neuron receives from many others and delivers its output signals to many others.

Fig. 5.2 *(cont.)*

of interneurons, and the lower two of motoneurons. Dendrites may be elaborate but are not readily distinguished from branching axonal terminals. The number and exact disposition of these two forms of endings and of major branches and collaterals are highly variable. (D) Heteropolar, multipolar neurons. These are the dominant type in the central nervous system of vertebrates. The upper two represent interneurons, and the lower a motoneuron.

5.4 NONNERVOUS ELEMENTS

In higher animals particularly, a large fraction of the bulk of the brain and spinal cord, and of the ganglia and nerves, is composed of nonnervous cells. There are several kinds, collectively called *neuroglia* or *glial* cells. The microscopic anatomy is highly specialized in each of three main types, suggesting more involved functions than simply filling in between nerve cells. The question is actively debated today whether glial cells may play some role in handling signals, predisposing neurons, or storing information, or whether they are solely vegetative and essential to the maintenance of healthy neurons. There is not yet a consensus, but new developments are coming in almost monthly.

FORMS OF ACTIVITY OF NEURONS

5.5 TYPES OF POTENTIALS ACROSS NEURON CELL MEMBRANE

It used to be thought, for decades after the first application of electrophysiological methods and the discovery of the nerve impulse, that the nerve impulse was synonymous with the activity of nerve cells, that is, this was the one and only form of nervous activity of neurons. We know better today; the present status can be summarized in the following outline of types of potentials across neuronal cell membrane:

  I. Resting potential (maintained by metabolism, inside negative by ca. 50–70 millivolts).

 II. Electrotonic potential (passive displacement, maintained or transient, due to imposed current; size, form, and distribution determined by conductances and capacitance of neuron).

III. Potentials of active response.

    A. Exogenic or transducer potentials (change in membrane conductance triggered by impinging adequate stimulus).

       1. Receptor potentials (specific for each sensory receptor).
          a. Depolarizing (increasing probability of excitatory response).
          b. Hyperpolarizing (decreasing probability of neuron activity).
       2. Synaptic potentials.
          a. Depolarizing or excitatory postsynaptic potential (e.p.s.p.).
          b. Hyperpolarizing or inhibitory postsynaptic potential (i.p.s.p.).

B. Endogenic potentials (increment of response to antecedent activity within the same neuron).
   1. Local potential.
   2. Spike potential (= nerve impulse; all or none).
   3. Afterpotentials.
      a. Depolarizing.
      b. Hyperpolarizing.

C. Autogenic potentials (true spontaneity, that is, self-triggered, under suitable steady-state conditions).
   1. Relaxation-oscillator type of pacemaker activity (rhythm depends on triggering endogenic activity).
   2. Sinusoidal pacemaker potential (rhythm independent of its consequences).
   3. Quantal miniature, random, spontaneous potentials.

The list is not necessarily complete. It may be that some of the categories here are in fact heterogeneous, and we shall have to subdivide them. Or it may be that there are other forms of activity not presently recognized. Note the three major classes of active response that we know of; they can be called exogenic, endogenic, and autogenic (Figure 5.4).

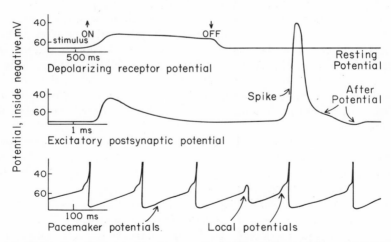

Fig. 5.4 Examples of some types of neuronal potentials. The receptor potential comes from a record of a stretch receptor response. The e.p.s.p. is a fast type; in other cells it may be much slower. After-potentials are different in different cells. The spikes in the lower record have been cut off.

5.6 EXOGENIC, ENDOGENIC, AND AUTOGENIC RESPONSES

Exogenic refers to those forms of activity of nerve cells which are due to events impinging from the environment of the cell. External events that have an effect are called *stimuli*. They may come from the outer world, as do light and sound, or from other nerve cells impinging on the one under consideration. We speak of *receptor* potentials for the changes in neuronal membrane potential that are found in the sensory transducers following a stimulating event, and we speak of *synaptic* potentials for those that occur in neurons following arrival of a presynaptic event.

This is the place for an aside on the power and the limitations of our methods of detecting these forms of activity. It is found that in all nerve cells, indeed in all excitable cells and in fact probably in all cells, there is a difference in potential between the inside and the outside of the cell across its surface membrane. The direction of polarization is usually such that the inside has a collection of negative charges and the outside a concentration of positive charges, with a difference in potential in a steady state at "rest" (excitatory, not metabolic, rest) of the order of 50 or 100 millivolts. By suitable penetrating probes (glass ultramicropipettes), we can record this resting potential and any changes in it.

Most of the forms of activity that we know about are measured as changes in potential. Electrical activity is recorded rather faithfully because the instrumentation available draws negligible current from the system and can show steady potentials or rapid changes. We cannot say this for the chemical events, so that we do not know whether there are in fact forms of activity or stages of response not reflected in parallel electrical changes, unappreciated because of the lack of rapid enough and sensitive enough chemical methods. The selective permeability changes, together with recordable changes in physical properties, such as size, opacity, ultraviolet absorption, heat production, and some detectable chemical changes, all indicate that important chemical events are associated with neuronal activity.

An important caution, often overlooked, is this. We should not assume that our electrical record of membrane potential and impedance accurately tells us when the neuron has restored a given condition with respect to excitability or responsiveness.

The formulation we have presented emphasizes the similarity or equivalence of the receptor potentials and the synaptic potentials. But there are in fact several varieties of each. In the first place, they can be either in the direction of decreasing membrane polarization or in the direction of increasing this polarization (hyperpolarization), and these will have quite different effects on the overall output of the neuron. Depolarization tends in general to excite or to make more probable the occurrence of impulses, and hyperpolarization tends to inhibit or to make less probable the occurrence of impulses. Each of these in turn exists in various forms, that is, with different time course and different degrees of effectiveness, according to the presynaptic pathway involved. So much for a very abbreviated account of this cluster of forms of activity, the exogenic responses of neurons.

The next group of activities we call *endogenic*, meaning that they are activities resulting from antecedent events in the same neuron. If, for example, a synaptic potential of sufficient magnitude has taken place, then there may in consequence arise an increment of activity which can be at first local and graded, that is to say, confined to a limited region of the neuron and existing in all intermediate levels of amplitude. This we call the *local response* or *local potential*. If this in turn rises to a sufficient amplitude (a critical level of depolarization), then a threshold is reached and a new process is initiated which is regenerative, that is, a chain reaction, an explosive all-or-none event that always goes to completion; this is a nerve impulse. A nerve impulse is not only all-or-none and rapidly developing; it is also brief, that is, rapidly recovering. It is commonly abbreviated the *spike* or *spike potential* because of its brief, sharp form as seen in records of voltage against time.

Finally, we have the class of activity which is dependent neither on imping events of the environment nor on antecedent activity of the cell, but is truly *autogenic* or *spontaneous*. Of course, it is not independent of the environment. Like a spring-wound clock or any other spontaneous system, it requires appropriate steady-state or permissive conditions of the environment. There must be an energy store; there must be proper temperature and milieu around the outside of the cell. Under suitable steady-state conditions, the cell ticks, as it were, or undergoes fluctuating change timed by its own mechanism, not timed by events of the environment. This is what we mean by spontaneity. It is an important property in many nerve cells. Some show it constantly or importantly in normal life; others do not show it under normal conditions but can be made to do so under slightly altered conditions of the cell environment.

These autogenic forms of activity are probably several in type. It is not clear to us whether these are fundamentally different in mechanism and principle or are different manifestations of some common mechanism. There is a sinusoidal type in which the potential of the membrane goes up and down more or less sinusoidally without caring, as it were, what happens in consequence, that is, whether or not impulses are initiated. There is the relaxation-oscillator type in which the membrane slowly and steadily depolarizes more and more until it reaches a critical level which may trigger an impulse. The impulse, whatever it does down the axon, has the important effect of restoring the membrane to its highly polarized condition, so that another cycle can begin. The third type is very curious. Very small, so-called *miniature* potential changes having a quantal amplitude (of a fixed size or multiples of it) occur at intervals that obey several criteria for random determination. Any given interval between these quantal, miniature events is unpredictable from the preceding intervals. Changes in the probability of occurrence of the underlying event, that is, in the average frequency, can be caused by steady-state or other conditions, and by summation of coincident miniature potentials can alter the likelihood of impulses or other activity of endogenic and exogenic sorts.

In addition to these forms of activity manifested by electrical signs, there must be forms of activity of neurons which are chemical. The release of specific substances at the endings of the axons is believed to occur at least in some and maybe in most neurons. In addition, there is a special class of cells showing a form of activity called *neurosecretion* [1], but neither of these topics will be developed here.

IMPLICATIONS OF NEURONAL CONCEPT

Let us look now at some of the consequences of this series of discoveries of the last decade or two, that is, at these diverse forms of activity of neurons.

5.7   THE LOCUS CONCEPT

These discoveries have led us to realize what we call here the *locus concept:* the neuron is made up of an assemblage of quite heterogenous patches of excitable membrane. Some patches have properties that permit them to transduce specifically impinging events such as presynaptic impulses of an excitory sort or of an inhibitory sort. These different forms of reaction are thought to require different forms of membrane. Other regions of the neuron are capable of spontaneous autogenic events. Limited parts of the neuron, basically the axon, are capable of the regenerative, all-or-none nerve impulse. The graded, subthreshold forms of activity are numerous and diverse; the all-or-none impulse is but one of the eight or ten forms of activity. The graded forms are perforce confined to limited regions, where they furthermore must be within a limited distance of each other to permit useful interaction. These interactions must in each case be strongly dependent on their spatial arrangement, on their geometry, on whether there is convergence, and on the extent of the membrane. The tremendous role of anatomy, microanatomy, and micromicroanatomy in determining what kinds of interaction and summation will be automatically provided among these various forms of synaptic potential, pacemaker potential, and eventually to spikes, will therefore be appreciated.

Although the graded forms of activity occur within limited radius, they are the important events for nervous integration; they involve enormous areas of neuronal membrane, namely, the ramifying dendrites, hence the gray matter and neuropile. The nerve impulse is not essential to nervous function. We are sure only that nerve impulses occur where they are found. We are not sure that they occur everywhere. We have been able to sample only certain neurons, those which are amenable to electrodes. It is quite possible, and there are good arguments to suggest, that many neurons do much of what they do normally in life without any impulses, whether or not they are capable of them and occasionally use them. This would require, of course, that everything be done within a short distance, because without spikes we do not have undecremented propagation. The other forms of activity do spread for distances significant in terms of the microanatomy of the nervous system—that is, hundreds of microns or even a millimeter or two. This is enough to permit them to encounter many other neurons and to exert significant influence. We need the decrementless propagation of the spike only for those cases where we have to go a long way, for example, from the eye to the brain or from the brain to the hand.

5.8 SEVERAL FORMS OF EXCITABILITY

Notice another consequence of this series of findings. We now can distinguish several forms of excitability. The classical excitability is measured *in the axon* when one stimulates it with stronger and stronger electric shocks until a threshold is found. This threshold is very nice; it is easily measured; it is precisely reproducible. But it is only the threshold of the spike, and that is only one form of activity. Normally it is significant at only one place of the neuron, namely, that spot where the impulse is initiated. At earlier stages in the neuron, this threshold does not exist; at later stages, it does not matter because the spike propagates with a sufficient safety factor that the threshold can vary a bit without much consequence.

Another form of excitability is the *local response*. It is quite different in that it does not have a threshold, but gradually develops out of the purely passive displacement of the membrane potential caused by weak electric currents, as the intensity is increased in the depolarizing direction. The response grows nonlinearly in such a way that more depolarization results with additional increments of applied voltage, becoming quite steep just before spike threshold. This curve of active response, that is, depolarization, above that expected from the passive electrotonic displacement, is due to changing membrane conductance, is different from cell to cell, and is labile from moment to moment. It is an important form of excitability in determining what is going to happen next.

Similarly, we have an excitability for each of the forms of *synaptic potential*. Not only do we have excitatory and inhibitory synaptic potentials, but each of these occurs in different varieties and subspecies depending on the presynaptic and postsynaptic cell. In this case, the stimulus will be the amplitude of the presynaptic spike as it impinges on the synapse, a variable which is difficult to record as well as to control, except in specially favorable animals and sites. What has been found is very interesting, that over a large range of presynaptic spike amplitude—up to 80% of full normal height, in the giant synapse of the squid—nothing whatsoever comes out postsynaptically, and then at about 80% we begin to have a tiny postsynaptic potential. This grows very steeply with further increase in the prespike. The curve is no doubt peculiar to each instance or subspecies of synaptic potential. We have therefore a variety of excitabilities.

Still another form of excitability exists that the author thinks may be naturally even more important in the nervous system. This is what we call *pacemaker modulation*. If there is ongoing activity, exceedingly feeble events or steady states can alter this frequency. Modulation of frequency is certainly one of the principal ways the nervous system responds to input and controls output. As a form of excitability, modulation sensitivity is not automatically given or predictable from any of the others.

5.9 SEVERAL FORMS OF INTERACTION OF NEURONS

Let us turn to another area immediately consequent upon the last, the ways in which nerve cells can influence each other. Among the forms of interaction, we have spoken already of synaptic effects. This broad class generally can be subdivided into excitatory and inhibitory forms. Within these are important differences—for example, in the presence of facilitation or its opposite, antifacilitation. Facilitating synaptic interaction means that successive events each produce more response in the postsynaptic cell. Antifacilitating synapses are those where successive events cause less response. We can distinguish between synapses on other grounds, too: some employ a mechanism of transmission that is strictly electrical, some are strictly chemical, and some probably are a mixture. These differences correlate with some properties of communicative significance such as the presence or absence of a delay at the junction. Those synapses known to be electrically transmitting show a much shorter delay than those believed to be chemically transmitting.

A form of synaptic interaction that has recently come into prominence and vastly increases the degrees of freedom possible in the nervous system is the *presynaptic synapse* or *serial synapse* (Figure 5.5). In this interaction, upon the ending of an axon just before it makes a synapse with a post-synaptic cell or dendrite there terminates another axon capable of enhancing or throttling the transmission, by acting presynaptically.

Besides the synaptic form of interaction, we can recognize as a result of recent findings that there exist interactions between specific cells which do not require synaptic potentials or even presynaptic impulses, but are direct electrical effects. These effects and the connections we infer to account for them are called *electrotonic*. They may turn out to be equivalent to electrical synapses, though often favoring slow events and filtering out spikes. Or there may be a low-resistance bridge between the cells. (Figure 5.6). Such connections with their special properties are distributed here and there in many groups of animals in characteristic places, but we do not yet know where to expect them or what correlates are meaningful.

Another general form of interaction is what we call *field effects*. This means that nonspecifically, in a mass of tissue, current flowing in the mass may exert effects on any nerve cells in the mass. We are in an even poorer position in this case to estimate the normal importance. It nevertheless appears to be worth mentioning, because it is quite conceivable that this is one of the importances of brain waves (EEG, electroencephalogram) which represent a field of current and therefore potential change possibly synchronized over a significant volume involving thousands or millions of neurons.

Fig. 5.5 Diagram of arrangement presumed to exist to account for presynaptic inhibition or facilitation. The presynaptic axon (a) terminating on postsynaptic neuron (b) receives the ending of an axon (c) which can throttle or enhance transmission from a to b.

Fig. 5.6 Diagram of low-resistance electrotonic connection between neurons. The connection shown by dashed lines is inferred from measurements of spread of potential from one cell to the other. It is probably situated differently in different cases, perhaps often between dendrites. It may be a true anastomosis (continuous protoplasimic bridge) in some, but in others there may be a cell membrane of low resistance forming an electrical synapse between the two neurons.

The evidence indicates that at least sometimes the synchronization is not due to following a common driving center, but to a local interaction not requiring spikes.

Still more diffuse effects exist—for example, hormonally mediated changes in nerve-cell activity, growth changes, or changes that might occur with use or disuse or developmental factors [11].

INTEGRATION AT THE LEVEL OF GROUPS OF NEURONS

We turn now to some principles that operate at the level of a few neurons, taking off from the neuronal properties previously discussed but looking at the *system* aspects. The first principle, and one of particular interest for communication science, is what we call the *principle of labeled lines*. This principle is that, barring exceptions, the nervous system generally operates with lines (nerve fibers) that carry coded information whose meaning for the system depends on the anatomical connections. Only in consequence of quasi-stable connections, the lines have (innately or by acquisition) labels representing the properties of the sense organs or of the effectors or the pathways they connect. The principle is the opposite of one where the message itself carries full information about the stimulus but the qualifications and reliability of the observer are unknown. ("Oh, I think there are enemy troops to the north.") The brain must know that a certain line comes from the eye and from a certain part of the retina and fires at ON of fairly strong light unless certain other lines are firing, and so on.

5.10 LABELED LINES

Clearly it is crucial how fixed the intimate connections are. Recalling the extreme fineness and complexity of the structure of synaptic regions in the electron micrograph, we can ask how characteristic of the species or even of the individual over time the connections, including their properties, are. That is, if we discover with an electron micrograph that there exists a synapse at a certain place and with a certain size and shape between cell A and cell B, we can ask whether or not we can take it as given that there is always that connection, and that its size and place are determined and consistent throughout the life of that individual or among all individuals of the species. Of course, this information is not immediately available from the anatomical finding, which is like a snapshot of a dance floor. From many such snapshots we can nevertheless infer constancies, and positions between partners, that tend to be maintained; we do have this kind of indication of stability of connections and transfer functions over long periods for some identifiable junctions.

With respect to connections, there are many parts of the brain where microscopic examination of section after section, in hosts of individuals, in different views, and in scores of laboratories has revealed characteristic features of fine structure and of connectivity. Figure 5.7 gives some impression of the kind of feature that is consistent in a given part of the brain in every specimen and throughout adult life. So, broadly speaking, we have the impression that many of the connections at least are stable and therefore that the lines are labeled. Of course there is a spectrum of justifiable degrees of confidence. In many animals, we can identify individuals cells. ("Ah yes, this is the same one that I've seen time and time again in different specimens; it's a trifle to the left from the usual in this individual, but it's in the characteristic region and it sends its axon in a characteristic way. It doesn't go over here and it doesn't go down here, but it turns in about here and makes its connections in the first layer, and in the third layer, and in the fourth layer, but not in the others; and it spreads this far to the side as usual, and so on.") When we get down to finer details at the level of electron microscopy, we can thus far say the same in only a few cases. There *are* some—for instance, in the Mauthner cell of the goldfish and the giant synapses in the crayfish, earthworm, and squid, and to a considerable degree also in the complex visual centers of flies [10]. In mammals, for the retina, the cerebellar cortex, and each of the better-studied regions, much the same is true, though individually identifiable cells are not yet known.

It is unfortunate that space does not permit us to illustrate this point further, because it is a rapidly growing, fascinating area of advancing anatomical science. To establish the degree and the features of stability leads to the ability to recognize departures correlated with use or disuse or other functional or abnormal states. The problem is much like learning to recognize faces. Most of us are probably not skillful in recognizing differences in faces among chimpanzees or among crows; but if we can learn to recognize these, then we can establish what degree of stability, and what degree of lability, exists, and perhaps we can associate these with events in the life of the individual. So the principle of labeled lines, and with it therefore of built-in circuits, is one in which we have some confidence; but we are still curious about how far it extends.

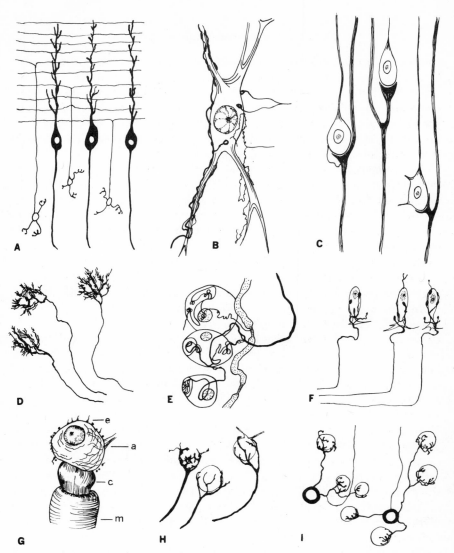

Fig. 5.7 Examples of characteristic relations between neurons. Several types of synaptic anatomy, each a consistent feature of the respective cells. (A) Parallel fibers of cerebellar cortex making right-angle synapses with heavy dendrites of Purkinje cells. (B) Cell of Clarke's column of spinal cord with its three types of synapse: fine fiber, coarse twining, and buttons on soma. (C) Cell of the tangential nucleus of a bird receiving branches from vestibular nerve. (D) Terminal tufts of presynaptic fibers in lateral nucleus of the thalamus enclosing cell bodies (not shown). (E) Endings on intraparietal neurons of auricle of heart of a fish. (F) Nests formed by centrifugal fibers in retina surrounding amacrine cells. (G) Cell of reticular formation of goldfish which besides small end bulbs (e) receives a large club shaped ending (c) of myelinated fiber (m); (a) is axon of postsynaptic cell. (H) Chalices of Held in nucleus of trapezoid body. (I) Claw endings on granule cells for cerebellar cortex. (For further details and sources, see [3], p. 66).

5.11 CODING PARAMETERS IN IMPULSE TRAINS

The principles of coding in nerve fibers form a topic, indeed a whole problem area, of utmost interest [9]. We have seen that the "language of the nerves" is the train of nerve impulses, although we have emphasized that there may be other forms of language, too—of the dendrites and the neuropile. But insofar as nerves are made up of long cables of axons, their language consists of trains of impulses which are essentially alike (there are certain differences, but they are probably of little communicative signifiance), so that we now ask the question, "What are the parameters of the code of these trains of nerve impulses?" This is an area of considerable activity today, full of ferment and constantly changing in aspect and direction.

In a minority of cases, a single impulse can be a normal, adequate signal, controlling a motor response to a train of arriving impulses in sensory receptors or in spontaneous loci. Usually, however, we have to deal with sequences of spikes. The principal variables obviously are the number and spacing of the spikes. This is not a digital code, because the intervals between the spikes are infinitely gradable; hence noise can enter during propagation down a nerve fiber—for example, due to the velocity of propagation not being absolutely constant. The nerve-impulse code operates in fact as a pulse-coded analog system. In order to find out what parameters of the code are significant for the system, that is to say, for the next nerve cell, we have to think up candidate parameters. First, we try to demonstrate that naturally occurring trains vary in ways not completely without rule. Then we can test the candidate parameter to see whether or not it matters in the system, as distinguished from, let us say, the noise of a Model-T Ford, an inevitable consequence of the working of the system but without causal significance for the operation.

Let us look at a naturally occurring sequence of impulses (Figure 5.8). In the top line are some impulses occurring in a nerve cell in the heart ganglion of a lobster. To the eye, there is obviously some structure in this sequence of impulses. Is there significance in the fact that these appear in five clumps, or does the system simply look at the overall average in a long time? In other words, what is the time constant of the integration? Is it significant that the last impulse is spaced out at some distance from the next to the last, or is there a time constant of integration shorter than that? Is it significant that the second interval is longer then the first? Is there a time constant that short? We chose this example because the repetitive character of the heartbeats tells us that the fine structure—short interval, intermediate interval, long interval, still longer interval—is systematic, within some range of variation, and not chaotic. It is still necessary to test whether or not the system cares about or can detect the

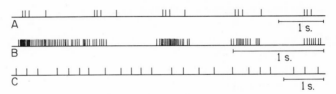

Fig. 5.8 Examples of natural impulse sequences in single axons. (A) From a cell in the lobster cardiac ganglion firing neurogenically, that is, due to spontaneous activity of the ganglion; recorded by A. Watanabe. (B) From a tactile fiber in the infraorbital nerve of the face in a cat, firing in response to four touch stimuli; recorded by Y. Zotterman. (C) From an abdominal ganglion cell of the sea hare showing a mixture of spontaneity, excitatory synaptic input, and inhibitory synaptic input, these inputs from independent sources; recorded by J. P. Segundo.

feature we have noticed. The answer seems to be that in some parts of the nervous system it cares and in some it does not; sometimes the integration-time constant is very short, and sometimes it is very long. There is no one answer that holds for all parts of the system.

The best-known parameter is spike frequency. It is available to and may be used by many nerve cells, averaged over some time, which may be shorter or longer.

Another feature that is inherent in a train of impulses can be brought out by an interval histogram (Figure 5.9). This is simply a plot of the

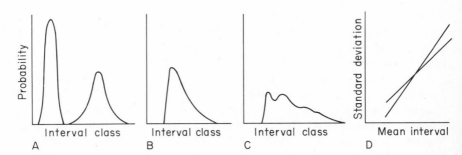

Fig. 5.9 Some statistical properties of trains of impulses. (A) Two examples of inter-spike interval histograms of symmetrical type, one with more scatter of interval length and higher mean interval (low frequency), the other faster and more rhythmic. Approximately the same number of impulses in each sample of these and the next two. (B) The same from a neuron which tends to fire close to some limiting interval so that its mode is smaller than the mean; the right-hand side approaches a Poisson distribution declining logarithmically. (C) Some neurons have complex histogram, with more than one mode or/and a long tail. (D) Standard deviation of interval is often a linear function of the mean, and the slope is likely to be characteristic for the type of neuron.

number of instances of each interspike-interval class occurring in a chosen sample. This is now a popular way of analyzing interval distribution. It has been found, in looking at many cases, that some impulse trains have a symmetrical distribution of intervals about a mean, that is, a bell-shaped curve. It is furthermore found that if the train has a longer average interval (lower frequency of firing), then there is commonly a broader curve, that is, a greater standard deviation. Some trains are asymmetrical, and the mean is a longer interval than the mode. Some have very long tails to the right; this means occasional very long intervals are observed.

Looking at such interval histograms, we can immediately recognize some other parameters worth measuring. (It should be clear that the purpose here is to show the natural-history stage that we are still in, with respect to kinds of spike signals. We are searching through the jungle to see what sorts of species occur and then asking ourselves whether the differences found are trivial or whether they are species, generic, or class differences.) For example, we can look at the relation between the standard deviation and the mean interval (Figure 5.9D). If it turns out that the standard deviation gets longer exactly in proportion to the mean interval, that is, if it is a constant fraction of the interval, we would have a curve like the dashed line. We find, in fact, that this is only occasionally the case. More often, the standard deviation gets proportionately greater as the intervals get longer, and the slope of this dependency varies, being apparently characteristic for the type of neuron. Every time we go into certain cells, we know that we are going to get a certain relation; in other places, we know that we are going to get a different kind of relation. We have thus satisfied two stages in our inquiry. We have recognized a parameter of potential significance for communication, and we have found that it is not perfectly chaotic but obeys certain rules of distribution. That makes it worthwhile to go on and ask whether or not there is causal significance.

Another way of looking at naturally occurring trains of intervals, to bring out features that are inherent but not obvious to our eye, is the plot called the joint-interval scatter diagram in which each interval is plotted on the abscissa against the next interval on the ordinate (Figure 5.10). It is a way of examining for positive or negative correlation between the magnitude of each interval and the magnitude of the next. If the system is highly rhythmic, then we expect to see a tight cluster of points centered on the mean lying on the 45° line (Figure 5.10C). If, however, there is a tendency, let us say, for strong negative correlation (short interval, long, short, long, . . .), then we expect to have two clusters symmetrically placed around the 45° line. If there is a slight tendency toward negative correlation, then we see a record like that in Figure 5.10D, where intermediate intervals are followed by intermediate intervals but whenever

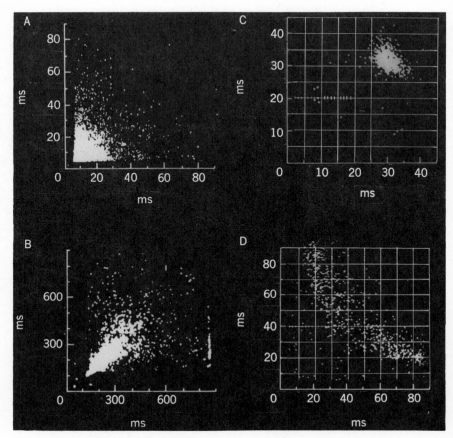

Fig. 5.10 Joint-interval histograms. (A) From Geiger counter neat luminous watch dial. (B) From moderately regular rhythm of a crayfish abdominal ganglion interneuron firing spontaneously. (C) From an intact mormyrid fish electric organ discharge starting at low irregular frequency and changing to high, regular firing. (D) From a crayfish interneuron with different firing pattern, tending toward alternately long and short intervals. Courtesy of J. Schulman and M. B. Thorson.

there happens to be a short interval it is followed by a long one and vice versa. The plot is one measure of the degree of negative correlation. If there is no correlation at all and intervals are entirely Poisson-distributed, as in the radioactive decay recorded with a Geiger counter from a luminous-dial wristwatch, then the record looks like that in Figure 5.10A.

In each of the forms of analysis so far mentioned, it is a rule that we have to pretend or defend that the sample represents a stationary state, that is, that during the series of intervals that we are observing, the animal is not running down or getting excited or significantly changing its state. In Figure 5.10B, it is extremely likely that we had a nonstationary state. The firing pattern was either regular and high in frequency to begin with, becoming slower and irregular, or vice versa; we cannot tell from the graph in which direction the change went. The joint-interval scatter diagram also reveals clearly the presence of two or more rhythms mixed, of the same or of different frequencies. It is also useful in special cases for plotting interval n against interval $n + 2$ or interval $n + 3$ or some later interval.

There still is limited experience with this form of analysis. The general result appears to be that the form of the joint-interval scatter diagram is characteristic of each type of neuron and functional state.

5.12 PATTERN SENSITIVITY

Now coming to the question whether or not these features have any significance for the animal, one form of experiment is shown in Figure 5.11. This is a joint-interval scatter diagram of a series of synaptic potentials recorded in a certain cell in a ganglion of *Aplysia*, a gastropod mollusc commonly called a "sea hare" which has very large cells, easy to see and

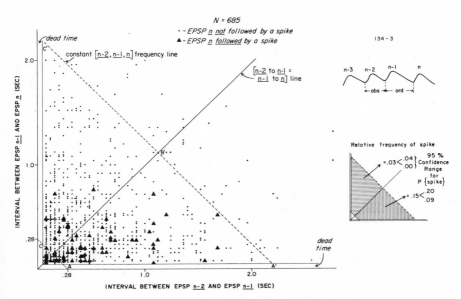

Fig. 5.11 Example of use of joint-interval histogram for test of significance of interval sequence on probability of spikes. Courtesy of J. P. Segundo.

penetrate, and showing all the integrative properties typical of nerve cells generally. The synaptic potentials in this case were caused by applying a sequence of electric shocks to a presynaptic pathway, the sequence being determined by a quasi-random process. The overall pattern is therefore that of a Poisson distribution.

The main feature of this experiment is that those intervals ending in a spike are indicated by triangles; all others failed to cause spikes. It will be noted that the occurrence of spikes is very uneven. The great majority are in a limited region below the 45° line. If the intervals are very short (below AC), then there is a high probability of a spike, no matter what the sequence was, whether a short interval preceded a still shorter one or the other way around. We can infer summation. If either interval preceding a synaptic potential is longer than some value (negative 45° slope $A'C'$), then there is never a spike; the intervals are too long for sufficient summation. But in an intermediate region, it looks as though the sequence of intervals is important; at least it correlates. There is a five-times greater probability of spikes in the area representing longer followed by shorter interval than in the reverse. Clearly, interval distribution and sequential correlation can be causally significant in determining the likelihood of a spike.

Another and more direct experiment leading to the same conclusion is the following. Instead of a random sequence of stimuli, an ordered series is applied to the presynaptic pathway and the response observed, again with an intracellular electrode in the postsynaptic cell. Figure 5.12 shows the resulting excitatory postsynaptic potentials to three stimuli with different spacing. Note that the overall time is the same: the average frequency is the same; only the middle stimulus is earlier or later. The records show that a short interval followed by a long one is quite ineffective, whereas a long interval followed by a short one causes a spike about ten times as often. This result is not trivial or predictable from the behavior of any given synaptic potential or from the recovery curve after a single synaptic potential, in other words, from a full knowledge of the behavior after two shocks. There is, as it were, a facilitation of facilitation. So, in this case, we can give an affirmative answer to the question: Is there significance to the microstructure of impulse trains or the pattern and timing of impulses?

Studying such cells stimulated over long periods of time with the same average frequency in different patterns, we found that uniform intervals under given conditions were absolutely ineffective and never caused an impulse to come out in the postsynaptic axon (Figure 5.13). Pairs (same average frequency) were also ineffective. Trios of shocks with first a short and then a long interval, followed by the still longer interval between

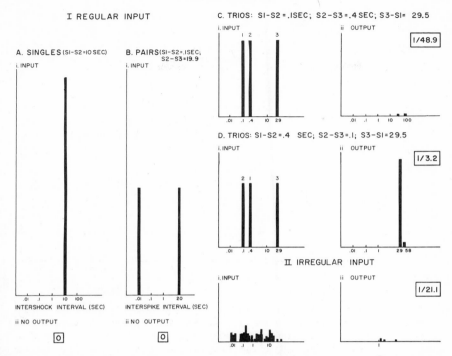

Fig. 5.12 The output in spikes from an abdominal ganglion cell of *Aplysia* (like that of Figure 5.11) which had no spontaneity and was under prolonged bombardment, at a constant frequency, by presynaptic impulses individually subthreshold for a spike in this cell. The graphs are interval histograms. In each case, both input (shocks to presynaptic nerve) and output are graphed, except where there is no output (A and B). The results of uniform intervals (A, "singles"), alternately long and short intervals (B, "pairs"), two patterns of trios and quasi-Poisson distribution of intervals between shocks ($S_1S_2S_3$) are compared. Scores in boxes are overall number of spikes per number of shocks. Courtesy of J. P. Segundo.

trios, were slightly effective, causing one spike approximately every 49 shocks. Trios, however, with first a long and then a short interval, were maximally effective, and gave one spike every 3.2 shocks; that is, almost every trio caused a spike. The quasi-random sequence of shocks gave an intermediate result, about one spike every 21 shocks. In this instance, at least, there is pattern sensitivity, and it can therefore be regarded as a usable principle for integrative purposes in the nervous system. But we now realize from experience that we have to show, in each part of the nervous system in which we are interested, whether or not pattern sen-

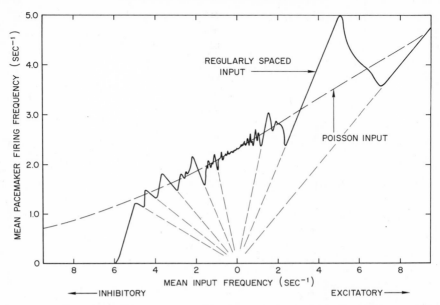

Fig. 5.13 The effect of excitatory and inhibitory input to a unit which has a spontaneous rhythm. The input events are more effective in modulating the ongoing firing the later they arrive in the interval between output spikes; the degree of this phase dependence as well as the intensity of the excitatory and inhibitory effect determine the shape of the complex curve. The one presented is from a digital-computer model which imitates closely the observed behavior of crayfish receptor and *Aplysia* abdominal ganglion cells. Note that the segments of paradoxical slope, especially on the inhibitory side, are clearest where there is a simple ratio between input and output frequency (2:1, 3:1, 5:1, 10:1). The phenomenon is a case of loose one-way coupling between oscillators and is therefore sensitive to irergularity in either rhythm. Courtesy of D. H. Perkel.

sitivity obtains there, because it is not necessarily the same everywhere as it is in *Aplysia*.

There is another consequence of this kind of analysis that is amusing and may have general significance. Consider the case where the ongoing rhythm of impulses in a cell due to its own spontaneity is modified by an extrinsic rhythm of impulses in a presynaptic path impinging upon this cell, either excitatory or inhibitory in effect. Both are rather pure rhythms with little scatter of intervals. We now examine the output over some range of input frequencies from zero to a maximum excitatory or inhibitory frequency. In the favorable cases of the *Aplysia* ganglion cell and the crayfish stretch receptor cells, the result is a striking and curious curve (Figure 5.13). As we increase the *inhibitory* frequency, we accelerate instead of inhibiting over considerable portions of the range between zero and maximal inhibition. The output shows an accelerating slope to a critical point, where with a sharp corner it plunges to a dramatic inhibition. Once more it comes to a critical point, turns the corner, and begins to accelerate again. The condition that is necessary for this to happen is that there be a significant effect of each arriving inhibitory impulse—in other words, not too much dependence on integration over considerable time. Another condition is that both output and input be rhythms with little scatter of intervals. If either one is too noisy, the curve is smoothed out. These two conditions may or may not mean that this phenomenon is rare in our brains; but it does happen, and it happens normally. These results are not anomalous or inexplicable; they are the automatic result of phase-locking between the two rhythms. We cannot predict them until we know how the effectiveness of each individual incoming event depends on its phase of arrival; but having measured that, we can predict the whole curve quantitatively. There are other curious and interesting automatic consequences of mixing oscillators with different degrees of coupling, not too tight and not too loose [3, Chapter 5].

Notice that the last few examples, as well as the next, complement our earlier conclusion of a high degree of stable anatomical connectivity, since they constitute physiological evidence of a high degree of consistent functional properties. The transfer functions within and between neurons give highly characteristic responses to input. Neuronal circuitry, where best known, is reproducible and systematic in both structure and process.

5.13 LATERAL INHIBITION

One more example of simple neuronal circuitry is the phenomenon called *lateral inhibition,* a shorthand term for an inhibition by one element of the other parallel elements in its immediate neighborhood. Consider a line going in from a visual receptor in the eye toward the brain and carrying impulses which increase in frequency with an increase in light intensity. In a parallel, adjacent receptor axon we find an inhibitory effect since its response to a standard light is less, the greater the activity of the first axon. The lateral inhibition is reciprocal and declines with distance. This means that if A receives more light and is therefore more excited, it inhibits B more than B inhibits A, thus exaggerating the difference in their stimulation. C, some distance away, has less effect on A than on B and is less inhibited by A, so that light falling on C can, by inhibiting B, reduce its inhibition of A. The consequences for information processing are considerable. If therefore becomes a matter of interest that new instances or places in the nervous system showing lateral inhibition are now cropping up right and left.

The most immediate consequence is that lateral inhibition will automatically result in sharpening contrast. If there is a slight difference between the inputs of light to A and to B, then the higher frequency of impulses in A will exert more inhibitory effect on B than B exerts back on A. With reasonable transfer functions, the result will be a marked enhancement of the difference. Further than this, there is available a still more interesting and complex consequence. If the visual fields of A and B are largely overlapping, the presence of lateral inhibition of the right degree will automatically result in a restoration of the precision of the image of the outer world upon the center, which seemed to have been lost by the overlap. The image as coded in the brain will be as good as it would be if the receptors had nonoverlapping receptive fields, that is, as good as the grain of the eye. This is a demonstration based on theory made by Reichardt in Germany. We do not yet know whether it is in fact happening, but it is just the kind of interaction between the mathematician and the physiologist that is particularly promising and exciting.

5.14 NERVE NETS

Under the same general heading of simple neuronal circuity, we now refer briefly to the most elementary case of circuity and at the same time the elementary case of organization in a large number of neurons. In general, we confine our attention in this chapter to small numbers of cells, but we allow ourselves an exception in the following case because the level of specification is low. We consider here the case of *nerve nets*, by which we mean a collection of equivalent cells connected with a minimum of specification. This is a domain of problems of great interest to many people. It has been dealt with from a purely theoretical extreme over to the physiological and anatomical extreme. My own interest started from the properties of real nerve nets in jellyfish, corals, and the like, and has moved to embrace experimental modelling with the digital computer. The subject is introduced here mainly to illustrate a domain of research which has some power for insight into the possibilities of explaining moderately complex behavior with a system of minimum specification. These animals are not utterly simple in what they do; they have quite a repertoire of activity, but we ought to be able to come closer to explaining behavior in such forms than in any other!

We deal here only with modelling, not with the whole subject of nerve net physiology, and with only one model [7] as recently enlarged. We instruct the computer to generate so many neurons, several thousand, and we specify the mean size in terms of the number of synapses with others, and the distribution around the mean. The computer connects them at random.

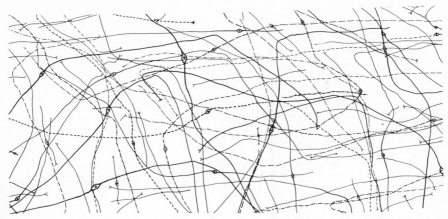

Fig. 5.14 Structure of a natural nerve net. A real net in the sea anemone consistnig of unbranching bipolar neurons that make contacts with each other presumed to form synapses. Based on work of Batham, Pantin, and Robson.

Our simulated neurons are modelled after certain real ones (Figure 5.14) in being simple linear elements, like straws, that make synapses where they touch each other (Figure 5.15). We deal usually with a mean size described as four to six synapses in length. Of the junctions so created, we instruct the computer to make a specified percentage, randomly distributed, "transmitting," that is, ready to transmit any impulse that arrives. The rest are facilitating—they require repetition of arriving impulses. Of these we specify a percentage in each of several classes of rate of decay of facilitation, again to be distributed at random. So each net created is unique, and we have to repeat the whole process on many nets in order to learn any rules that are characteristic of nets of a certain specification. Then we stimulate this net at some place and observe the spread of response. The response measured is simply the degree of spread, and the parameters can be area stimulated, timing of stimuli, and net specifications. In Figure 5.16 the stimulation is in a central patch of 16, and the excitation found transmitting junctions out only to the distance shown. Repeated stimulation at a suitable frequency causes further spread (Figure 5.17), but this soon reaches a limit if it has not already occupied the whole available net. This plateau effect is of interest theoretically and also in comparison with similar behavior in corals. The effects of structure of the net, of dynamic properties of the junctions, of frequency, of stimulation, and of temporal pattern of stimulation are neither intuitively obvious nor derivable by analytical means—so we are told. Simulation is an ideal tool here, and it

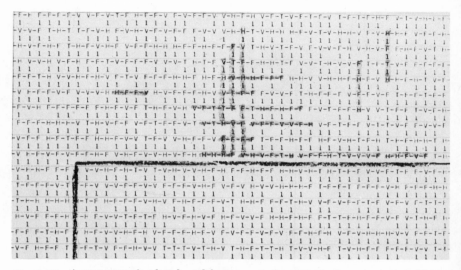

Fig. 5.15 A computer-simulated model nerve net. A printout of a net generated by a computer according to specifications as outlined in the text. This is one from an experiment testing effects of simulated cuts, narrowing the path for spread. Some of the "neurons" are brought out by ink. The letters designate some of the properties of each junction.

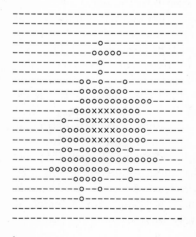

A

Fig. 5.16 Responses of a computer-simulated coral nerve net. Example of spread of excitation (O) after a stimulus applied to 16 junctions (X). Junctions marked (–) were not reached. The same answer can be read out in different ways; this printout shows graphically the odd forms due to the unique structure of each net.

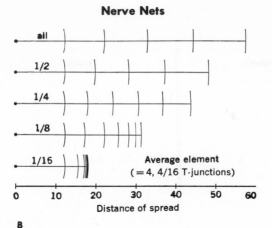

Fig. 5.17 Responses to a computer-simulated coral nerve network. The spread following repeated stimuli averaged from 15 nets of median 4-junction-long neurons with 25 per cent of junctions ready to transmit. The fractions ($\frac{1}{2}$–$\frac{1}{16}$) are the proportion of junctions that would, if reached by an impulse, remain facilitated until arrival of the next impulse at this frequency. Arcs show the distance of spread of successive stimuli. Note that a limit is soon reached if adequate facilitation is scarce [7].

gradually gives us a feeling for the behavior and possibilities inherent in so simple a system. The spread around corners, the effect of adding electrotonic spread of subthreshold excitation at junctions, the degree of temporal pattern sensitivity in the sense we used it above, besides the permutations of net specification, are now available, thanks to Mr. Shiang Fan Liu [8], with the results displayed on a cathode-ray oscilloscope on line. It is particularly noteworthy that the results give us new reason to go back to the corals and make new observations—which requires excursions onto the tropical reef!

THE MEANING OF MESSAGES

The last topic we refer to is the most complicated and will establish contact with subjects in other chapters of this book. There is quite a great fascination in the indications that as impulse trains pass successive synapses they are not just relayed or stepped down in average frequency or algebraically summed, but they change meaning. Given a coded stream of impulses, what message is it effectively carrying? It is patent that the processes of integration in the nervous system must continually be transforming the meaning of messages as impulse trains proceed, converge, diverge, and feedback.

5.15 ABSTRACTION

Suppose we find that a photoreceptor axon responds to light with a sequence of impulses having a certain dependency of frequency on intensity. When this axon carries a train of spikes, does it mean to the brain: "A light has abruptly appeared in such and such part of the visual field, of such and such intensity and time course"? Perhaps so; at least, it contains that information. But in some cases it may mean only "Hey, alarm from in front," or it may mean anything between these extremes. In others, it may mean nothing whatever above threshold reliability, unless there occur similar messages in many neighboring fibers. Furthermore, somewhere between this stage and the formulation of motor command, there must be one or more transformations. Unless the stimulus was quite unnatural, there must be a decision among alternatives that the system recognizes: friend or foe, cloud or leaf, movement within range, and so on. Here is where recent work gives promise of new insight or at least cracks for leverage. The problem is very general, not confined to sensory pathways. Every stage in information processing that is not a pure 1:1 relay, therefore virtually every junction, is performing a transformation.

The accumulated experiments taken together with an important amount of anatomical data bring us to a certain concept of this processing. Nearly always there must be a convergence or spatial summation of several or many incoming lines; the crux of the thing is a dependence of the meaning of messages in one line on what is coming in over the others. Generally, it seems, not a great number of lines converge on one cell. Successive stages of convergence occur, and useful transformations—let us call them *recognitions*—take place in steps. Hence there is a hierarchy of integrative summations, all perhaps equivalent in mechanism but each receiving impulse trains more derived and abstracted in meaning and hence more important than the preceding.

5.16 TRANSFORMATIONS OF MEANING

It is quite likely that there are many varieties of transformation of meaning in different subsystems. Probably they are often going on in parallel in separate pathways beginning with the same input. The photorecepter axon spike train referred to in Section 5.15 perhaps means only "alarm" to one central pathway, but to another tickled by the same sequence of spikes, "moving object going leftward," if certain other sequences arrive from other receptors. Still another central pathway may be concerned only with integrating the average intensity over many receptors. In another system the somatic afferent input from the skin in mammals (the input in nerve fibers from sense organs for touch, temperature, pain and pressure) bifurcates into parallel pathways. One of these goes to the higher centers for specific analysis of modality, intensity, skin locus, and time course; and one goes to the lower reticular formation, where it virtually loses all specificity, mixes with other inputs, and becomes essentially a message of alerting or arousal.

The story of what the frog's eye tells the frog's brain gives an excellent glimpse into the future of a key branch of communication neurobiology. Several laboratories have now confirmed it. Besides the classical types of nerve fibers in the optic nerve of the frog which respond to ON, or to OFF, or to ON and OFF, of a diffuse light, there are a small number of additional types which prefer, that is, respond well only to, or "recognize," more complex stimuli. Remember, the optic nerve fibers come from the third layer of cells in the retina, so that plenty of mixing and comparing of receptor messages has already taken place. To mention one example, there is a group of optic nerve fibers that does not respond to ON or OFF of the room light. Moreover, when it is adequately stimulated the overall level of illumination is quite unimportant. These fibers require not only light but a light-dark contrast, such as an object or edge. Also, it must be sufficiently sharp and focused, and it must not be too large an object or too straight or gently curved an edge. A small, dark, sharply focused object is best. Furthermore, it must be moving or have recently moved within the 3–5° excitatory receptive field of that particular retinal ganglion cell, not too rapidly and not too slowly. There must not be at the same time movement of objects in the near surround, congruent or even contrary in direction. This seems to be quite a feat of specification for a unit so early in the system, but others like it are known in arthropod visual ganglia, cat visual cortex, bat auditory cortex, electric fish cerebellar lateral lobe, and elsewhere. In the cat visual cortex, the literature speaks of "complex" neurons, "lower-order hypercomplex" and "higher-order hypercomplex" neurons! It appears that we should regard the typical central neuron as firing to a constellation of permissive and triggering inputs, thus carrying a highly sophisticated message, and that we are on the verge of finding nerve cells that respond to no pure tones but only to clucking in chickens, or to chirping in crickets, or to hawklike silhouettes in certain birds, and to sea-gull bill-like silhouettes in others. How far this will go is a prime question in the machinery of behavior. Not only innate but learned constellations of stimuli must eventually focus on a recognition unit that has a decisive threshold.

5.17 MODALITIES

With the background of this improved insight, as we suppose, into subdivisions of one modality such as vision, we can reach perhaps a better understanding of the thorny old question of modalities. What is the structural or functional basis of the several senses? We have to explain not only the human sense modalities of touch, cold, heat, pain, taste, smell, vision, and hearing, but also vibration, pressure, tickle, qualities of pain, sense organs that do not reach consciousness for muscle stretch, joint position, blood pressure, blood CO_2, and so on and on. Are these distinct modalities equivalent to the first named, or subdivisions, or combinations, or tangential entities that do not belong in the same list? Given whatever list of sensory qualities, are there separate sets of nerve fibers for each, permanantly labeled lines unambiguously signaling their respective forms of stimulation? On the evidence from visual, auditory, and some other pathways we can answer "Yes," even to the fourth- or fifth-order neuron from the sensory cell. Of course, modality is lost at some level when integration between modalities for higher associations takes place.

The interesting newer view is that some sensory influx is not so arranged, and may, to a certain degree, be ambiguous from the outset. Just as the smallest discriminable locus of touch on the skin is less than the area of sensibility of a single afferent fiber but is served by several overlapping receptors, and pitch discrimination is accomplished via input from auditory fibers of wide and overlapping frequency range, it seems clear that some sensory fibers overlap in the quality of stimulus to which they are usefully sensitive. Nevertheless, this does not necessarily mean central confusion, since by comparison of many fibers overlapping differently, the brain apparently can sort out the meaning of the combined signals. This requires that the overlapping receptivities of the units be fairly stable and that they be "known" to the analyzer. There can thus be more qualities than there are separate sets of fibers, a fact that answers to an approximation the old riddle. Our interest here is in the organizational principle illustrated, central "recovery" of apparently lost information in overlapping input lines.

This assemblage of specific experimental results and of inferences, hypotheses, and inductions should give the reader some feeling for the excitement of the field, the opportunity for basic discoveries of working principles of living beings as complex systems, the fluidity, and the ferment. Clearly in many problems we are in a natural-history phase, trying

to notice what kinds of creatures there are in the jungle and what correlates of distribution of activity and interrelations may be meaningful. For
this reason there is room and an urgent need for imaginative thinking,
new ways of looking, and even more sophisticated interdisciplinary cooperation between engineer, mathematician, physicist, and biologist.

REFERENCES

1. Bern, H., and I. Hagadorn, "Neurosecretion," in Bullock, T. H., and G. A. Harridge, *Structure and Function in the Nervous Systems of Invertebrates*, W. H. Freeman, San Francisco, 1965, pp. 353–439.
2. Brazier, M. A. B., *The Electrical Activity of the Nervous System*, Macmillan, New York, 1960.
3. Bullock, T. H., and G. A. Horridge, *Structure and Function in the Nervous Systems of Invertebrates*, W. H. Freeman, San Francisco, 1965.
4. Galambos, R., *Nerves and Muscles*, Doubleday, New York, 1962.
5. Galambos, R. (Chm.), "Glial Cells," *Bull. Neurosci. Res. Progr., Brookline*, **2** (6), 1964, 1–63.
6. *Handbook of Physiology. Section 1: Neurophysiology*, Vols. I, II, III, Field, J., H. W. Magoun, and V. E. Hall (editors), American Physiological Society, Washington, D. C., 1959.
7. Josephson, R. K., R. F. Reiss, and R. F. Worthy, "A Simulation Study of a Diffuse Conducting System Based on Coelenterate Nerve Nets," *J. Theoret. Biol.*, **1**, 1961, 460–487.
8. Liu, S. F., "Digital Computer Simulation of a Simplified Nerve Net," University of California, Los Angeles, Department of Engineering, Report No. 66-30, 1966.
9. Perkel, D. H., and T. H. Bullock, "Neural Coding," *Neurosciences Research Program Bulletin*, **6**, 1969, 221–348.
10. Trujillo-Cenoz, O., "Some Aspects of the Structural Organization of the Intermediate Retina of Dipterans," *J. Ultrastructure Res.*, **13**, 1965, 1–33.
11. Wiesel, T. N., and D. H. Hubel, "Single-Cell Responses in Striate Cortex of Kittens Deprived of Vision in One Eye," *J. Neurophysiol.*, **26**, 1963, 1003–1017.
12. Wooldridge, D. E., *The Machinery of the Brain*, McGraw-Hill, New York, 1963.

FURTHER READINGS

1. Bullock, T. H., "Reliability in Neurons," *J. Gen. Physiol.*, **55**, 1970, 565–584.
2. Gaze, R. M., *The Formation of Nerve Connections*, Academic Press, London, 1970.
3. Jacobson, M., *Developmental Neurobiology*, Holt, Rinehart and Winston, New York, 1970.
4. Schmitt, F. U., *The Neurosciences, Second Study Program*, Rockefeller University Press, New York, 1970.

CHAPTER 6

Neural Information Processing; Windows Without and the Citadel Within[1]

W. ROSS ADEY[2]

Professor of Anatomy and Professor of Physiology, Space Biology Laboratory, Brain Research Institute, University of California, Los Angeles

Contents

6.1 INTRODUCTION

To the biologist, information processing in living systems is concerned with phenomena that, in their very nature, beget paradox on paradox. Ours is an earnest search for elements of order in ceaselessly changing environ-

[1] This chapter first appeared in *The Proceedings of an International Symposium on Biocybernetics of the Central Nervous System*, edited by L. D. Proctor, M.D. Boston: Little Brown, 1969. Courtesy of Little, Brown and Company.

[2] Studies from the author's laboratory described here were supported by grants NB–01883 and MH–03708 from the National Institutes of Health, by contract AF(49) 638–1387 with the U.S. Air Force Office of Scientific Research, by Contract NONR 233(19) with the Office of Naval Research, and Contracts NsG 237–62, NsG 502, NsG 505, and NsG 1970 with the National Aeronautics and Space Administration.

ments—for elements that may be sensed, by the talismans they bear, and transformed for an eventual place in equally ordered, but subtly changed, structure and function in living tissue; these latter are the final measures of transaction and storage of information therein.

Pursued with rigorous logic, such a sequence of events clearly implies that recognition of pattern, and thus of informational content, resides with the observer, whether natural or artificial. It is in this most elemental concept that we are so fundamentally challenged. Even in the simplest situations, requirements in signal sensing, in the development of coded transforms for onward transmission in our pattern recognizer, and in the very processes of transaction and storage of information, there is an implication of selective evaluation of the signal. Thus, signal evaluation is at best a partial transform of events outside the observer, never complete and always involving a degree of degradation in the full gamut of signal processes.

The engineer is very familiar with this concept, and with its almost universal concomitant, the signal in noise. He is much less familiar with a pattern recognizer having a high level of intrinsic functional activity, to be viewed as a "housekeeping" process, rather than as a noise, and meriting our most serious consideration in any attempt realistically to model the central processor of the living nervous system. Here is the first and perhaps the most significant difference between the natural brain and the current generation of computing devices. The arrival of sensory volleys of any kind occurs in systems already engaged in a vast series of integrative processes, whether the brain be sleeping or waking. The arriving volley thus occupies the residue of a multidimensional signal space; or, at best, it can only secondarily modify activity in logical elements already engaged in processes to which the arriving volley bears only an indeterminate temporal relationship, by the very nature of their separate and unrelated origins.

The differences between the living brain and the typical artificial processor run yet deeper. Granted that both can exhibit adaptive responses based on previous experience, the natural system is also characterized by a tremendous capacity in parallel processing not currently within the capability of the artificial automaton. We shall concern ourselves very much with this aspect of the natural organism in the ensuing discussion, for it appears to lie at the core of some quite remarkable qualities of the living brain. It is a capacity found at the level of the single logical element and as a function of populations of elements. It will require consideration of redundancy and stochastic modes of operation as essential features of the living brain, concepts that render trivial any hopeful notions that mere possession of an adequate wiring diagram of cortical connections would suffice for a comprehensive understanding of those qualities unique to cerebral function.

6.2 WINDOWS WITHOUT; ESSENTIAL ASPECTS OF NERVOUS PROCESSING

Chapter 5 of this book was concerned in elegant detail with the essential phenomena in the transducing and transformation of stimuli by sensory receptors. We shall review here only those aspects which have provided useful clues to the sequence of steps leading from transducing and transmission in the peripheral nervous system, to transactional mechanisms in cerebral nuclei, where we also now see in shadowy outline certain substrates of storage processes. Evaluation of storage no longer rests exclusively on a behavioral end point. Computer analysis of electrophysiological patterns has revealed much about altered states accompanying fixation of experience [16], and further alterations in more subtle processes of conditional storage, extinction, and retraining [2, 11, 35, 41].

Studies in peripheral nervous functions continue to provide a crucible for critical testing of the most fundamental parameters determining neuronal excitability [15]. Here, the relative isolation of neuronal elements from each other has allowed accurate determination of thresholds and local interactions in ways that often can only be inferred in the more densely packed and less accessible elements in cerebral structures. These structural characteristics of cerebral tissue appear to relate to the uniqueness of its functions in storage of information, as opposed to its transmission or transaction, and are discussed further in [3]. From these studies in receptor mechanisms, and with due regard for specializations that characterize so many regional functions in the nervous system (a point often overlooked in a compulsive desire to press the universality of the neuronal doctrine and interactions confined to synaptic events), we may make cautious extrapolations to possible modes of interaction between brain cells.

Establishment of excitability threshold in sensory neurons

Since we shall consider later the presence of fixed negative charges on large molecules on the membrane surface, their role in excitation processes, and their possible role in information storage, we shall consider here only observations relating to system sensitivities, as determined at least partly by subjective tests in man.

Sensory thresholds in olfactory, auditory, and visual systems are all characterized by surprisingly low input-energy levels. We can detect odorous substances in concentrations of 10^{-13} molar [14]. This is 10^4 times more dilute than the effective threshold concentration of any known enzyme system [53], so that the effective stimulus apparently is not dependent on energy released by interaction with an enzyme. Similarly, auditory thresholds are only an order of magnitude above Brownian movements in fluid molecules of endolymph bathing the inner ear [19]. The eye can apparently detect as little as one photon of light falling upon a receptor [31].

These findings may not be directly extrapolated to thresholds for neurons in the central nervous system, since they may represent specialized sensitivities in the peripheral transducer. Nevertheless, there is increasing evidence that central neurons do indeed respond to changes in their environment which arise in the concurrent activity of other neurons, but for which synaptic connections are not essential. This "whispering together," as it was described by Young [59], on the one hand suggests a capacity in parallel processing in neurons of central nuclei that may characterize them uniquely, and on the other is an immediate deterrent to simple analogies with nerve nets having binary elements that are activated solely by a "wiring diagram" of synaptic connections.

The shift in coding patterns at central levels in the nervous system

The essential quality of coding in neural transmission is a patterning in space and time. Without exception, transmission to a distance in the nervous system appears to involve a pulse-coded series of transients. It should be added that the ubiquity of this phenomenon—indeed, its very obviousness—should not obscure our search locally in cerebral nuclei for electric processes that are not pulse-coded, and that appear to relate closely, even uniquely, to transaction and perhaps to storage of information in the tissue. The latter will be discussed below, but here we shall emphasize that, in the very nature of these central transactional processes, we can discern transforms of the peripheral neural coding that clearly imply substantially modified temporal as well as spatial codes in the conveyance of the sensory volley centrally.

Our understanding of this modification in the neural code remains incomplete, but its most characteristic aspect is an expanded time scale. Let us take an example from auditory neurophysiology. It is our common experience that an auditory source may be localized in space by the difference in time of arrival of sound waves at our two ears and requires recognition of intervals as short as one-tenth millisecond. There is no evidence that firing patterns in neurons sustain a comparable fine temporal resolution at any level in the hierarchy of auditory nuclei leading to cortical structures that are specifically concerned in this spatial localization [39, 43, 51].

Yet the sustenance of the original coding through these ill-understood transforms is equally explicit. In our search for keys to informational coding at higher levels, two phenomena invite attention. Firing in individual neurons in unanesthetized brain, in cortical and subcortical structures, occurs in a fashion best described as "spontaneous"; changes in firing patterns induced by extrinsic stimuli thus occur most frequently in windows that are already smeared and blurred in varying degrees by this ongoing activity. Moreover, the induced patterns of discharge characteristically exhibit a "jitter" in latency of both initial and subsequent impulses of the induced pattern that transcends by an order of magnitude the exceedingly fine differentials in temporal excitation patterns induced in peripheral receptors. There is, then, no rigorous one-to-one relationship between peripheral events in the auditory mechanism and the firing pattern in intermediate relays, nor in cortical structures. Central neurons rarely exceed firing rates of 100 per second in transaction of sensory information involving frequencies of thousands of cycles per second. Time, therefore, has no absolute representation in sensory transaction in the nervous system. Very obviously, environmental space likewise can have no direct counterpart in brain structure. It may be further argued that the firing of a single impulse by a neuron can have no information content *per se*. It requires consideration in terms of numerous impulses that both precede and follow it, if we are to understand the elements of this interval-based code.

Discussion of the shift to slower transactional parameters at higher neural levels must necessarily take account of wave processes mentioned above and to be discussed in detail below. In summary, they are seen in brain tissue in the most intimate aspects of membrane potential fluctuations in each neuron. In particular, they appear closely involved in information transaction, and their spectral span lies effectively between 1 and 100 hertz. The bulk of their energy is below 10 hertz. Here, also, we are confronted with a processing system with a time base vastly slower than the pulse-coded building blocks occurring in the periphery, yet apparently capable of retaining initimate details of more rapid peripheral influxes. Lest it be assumed too hastily that the essential phenomena involve a simple band-width compression, it should be emphasized that brain tissue has immense capability in parallel processing. This, too, may sustain vital aspects of phase and frequency information in the summed activity of a neuronal population.

We shall not consider centrifugal control of sensory inputs, a phenomenon in both vertebrate and invertebrate nervous systems, but shall now pass directly to a review of cerebral organization at the level of the single neuron.

6.3   THE CITADEL WITHIN; SINGLE NEURONS AS MEMBERS OF AN ENSEMBLE OF ELEMENTS

We may consider the neuron in brain as a component in a multicompartmental neuronal system that has two cellular compartments, neuronal and neuroglial, and an extracellular space (Figure 6.1). All three are functionally interdependent, forming a micrometabolic module. We must necessarily consider an even finer image of cerebral transaction, taking account of the anatomically separate and functionally distinct portions of each neuron that form its body, a greatly branched dendritic tree and an axon process by which nerve impulses are conducted away from the cell body.

A tricompartmental model of cerebral tissue

Throughout the central nervous system, nerve cells are separated in varying degree by other tissue, even though portions of one neuron, such as the dendritic tree, may come into intimate contact with the dendrites of another neuron, as discussed below. Special satellite cells, the neuroglia,

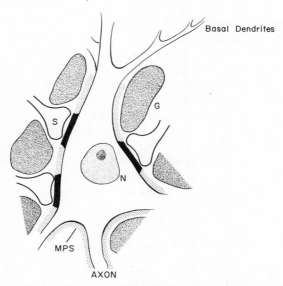

Fig. 6.1   Schematic arrangement of nerve-cell body, with surface coats of macromolecular material that is typically more dense in the zones between synaptic terminals and the cell membrane. This material also intervenes between nerve cells and neuroglial cells. Recent electron-microscopy studies have emphasized this tricompartmental arrangement in cerebral tissue.

form a substantial envelope around the neuron, and there is evidence that they form an "insulating" packet around synaptic terminals [46]. In its aggregated distribution, the neuroglial tissue intervenes between the neuron and its blood supply. Briefly, neuroglial cells may modulate transfer of metabolic substrates to the neuron and the removal of respiratory products. Enzyme granules are closely packed at the interface between neuronal and neuroglial membranes and suggest "picket fences" opposed to each other across the narrow cleft of the intercellular space [13].

The intercellular space in brain tissue has received scant attention until recently. Classic electron micrographs prepared with osmic acid fixation had suggested that it did not exceed about 4 per cent of the tissue volume. However, more recent electron micrographs prepared by very rapid cooling of the tissue indicate an extracellular space as large as 20 per cent [30].

The intercellular space will concern us in this discussion for several reasons. A substantial content of mucoproteins and mucopolysaccharides has been shown to permeate this space [45]. We do not yet know in detail the significance of these intercellular macromolecules; but as the picture unfolds, it is becoming apparent that they are far from passive structural elements at the cell surface and in intercellular fluid. Indeed, they are at the very core of processes controlling neuronal excitability. Even more important, they appear susceptible to change as the result of previous experience in the neuronal elements of this tricompartmental system.

In short, no longer can neuronal elements be considered the sole repository of information in brain tissue. The paths of present and future research require earnest pursuit of the trinity of neurons, neuroglia, and intercellular material as a functional entity in processes that lead to storage of information. We have carried our thesis to an explicit postulate that mere possession of a "wiring diagram" of synaptic connections in brain tissue would be neither adequate nor necessary for an understanding of that most unique quality of brain tissue, the laying down of a malleable memory trace, fragile indeed in both acquisition and susceptibility to extinction.

The functional role of perineuronal tissue

Neuroglial cells have been investigated extensively in the surroundings of renal receptors [54], in the invertebrate nervous system [44], in cortical tissue, and in tissue culture [33]. The majority of the evidence shows that, although possessing a membrane potential of the same order as neuronal cells, they are unexcitable to electrical stimuli. On the other hand, there is evidence that they may respond to neuronal activity in their vicinity with a slow change in membrane potential [37]. In invertebrates, the neuroglial cells show low resistance pathways from one cell to another [40].

If the neuroglial cells are electrically inexcitable, what is the basis for their interaction with neuronal elements? A clue has been provided from studies of ionic mechanisms. It was first suggested by Green, Maxwell, and Petsche [29] that modification of the shape of the action potential during a train of recurring action potentials in the cat's brain (hippocampal formation) might arise in the accumulation of potassium ions extruded from the interior of the neuron into the perineuronal environment. Recent studies in the leech by Kuffler and his colleagues have indicated that the neuroglial cell is sensitive to potassium-ion concentrations in its environment, and that it depolarizes with raised extracellular potassium [40]. Moreover, despite significant technical difficulties, neuroglial cells dissected from fresh brain have shown a sharply raised metabolism in the presence of potassium ions, an effect not detectable in neurons similarly isolated [32].

Interaction between nerve cells and neuroglial cells occurs across an intercellular fluid matrix. We have emphasized ionic messengers as the basis of interaction. It should be made clear at this point that this fluid is not a mere bucket of saline; it contains considerable amounts of macromolecules, mainly mucoproteins and mucopolysaccharides, which blend with coats of comparable material at the cell surface [45, 50]. Ionic exchanges are influenced in great degree by ionic binding characteristics of these macromolecules. This will be considered in detail below, but just now it is apposite to consider empiric evidence pointing to altered states in this macromolecular material as the result of previous experience in cerebral tissue. Briefly, the evidence suggests that information may be stored in these macromolecules lying at the surface of, and between, cerebral neurons, and that they can control fundamental aspects of neuronal excitability.

Impedance measurements in assessment of states of cerebral tissue

How may the state of macromolecular intercellular material be assessed, in relation to changing physiological activity in the cellular elements which it encloses? Obviously, any technique for such an evaluation should be capable of selective and differential measurement of ionic and/or molecular phenomena.

Our own studies have been directed to conductance changes in cerebral tissue accompanying a variety of physiological states. Most of our measurements have been made at frequencies of 1.0 kilohertz, using small measuring currents of the order of 10^{-13} amperes per square micron of electrode surface [7]. They have been made in focal volumes of cerebral tissue of about 1.0 cubic millimeter with chronically implanted coaxial electrodes in the brains of man [47] and animals. We have excluded as far as possible direct contributions to the impedance responses by altered physiological states from such factors as blood pressure, blood flow, and brain temperature [9]. We have concluded that the changes in electrical conductance accompanying physiological responses arise in cerebral tissue elements.

Through what tissue paths do these impedance-measuring currents flow? The membrane resistance of neurons is many hundreds of times higher than that of intercellular fluid. Neuroglial membrane resistance has been variously estimated in the range from slightly higher than intercellular fluid to values of the same order as in neurons. At all events, the evidence favors the view that preferred current pathways lie outside the neurons, and that they pass substantially through the extracellular spaces. This view gains support from manipulation of the ionic environment of neurons with divalent cations, as described below. Moreover, selective removal of the neurons (by retrograde degeneration) from a cerebral nucleus abolishes impedance responses to drugs (Figure 6.2). A normal neuronal population thus is essential for the impedance response, even though the bulk of the impedance-measuring current flows outside the neurons. The neurons accordingly appear to modulate conductivity of structures in their environment [8].

These impedance measurements have shown shifts closely correlated with general states of sleep and wakefulness [7, 47]. Impedance falls with behavioral arousal and in alerting responses but rises in drowsy states and actual sleep. Much finer correlates are possible, however, and these have been shown to have a regional basis.

We have examined impedance responses in different cerebral structures (hippocampus, amygdala, and midbrain reticular formation) during alerting, orienting, and discriminative responses (Figure 6.3), at different levels of training and during extinction and retraining [8]. Briefly, there is a differential regional distribution of the impedance responses to the three types of behavioral stimuli. Their magnitude increases at high levels of training, and they disappear during extinction of the response. Moreover, statistical variance in these impedance responses declines at high performance levels; but it increases temporarily on cue reversal in behavioral tasks until the new cues are learned, and it declines progressively with retraining.

In summary, the evidence is strong that evoked transients in impedance accompanying retrieval of learned behavioral responses provide a measure of information storage in perineuronal tissue, although no baseline changes

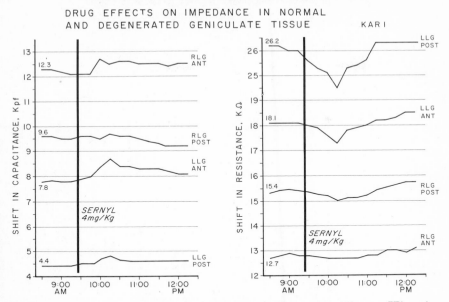

Fig. 6.2 Effects of cyclohexamine drug Sernyl (4 milligrams per kilogram IP) on impedance of normal (left, LLG) and degenerated (right, RLG) lateral geniculate tissue. The drug induced a large shift in posterior, cellular zones of normal left lateral geniculate and a smaller shift in anterior regions. Only small changes in capacitance or resistance occurred in degenerated right nucleus. Figures at commencement of each tracing show baseline values in kilopicofarads and kilohms for each lead. (From [8].)

have been detected in the tissue in the quiescent state. The findings thus suggest a change in dynamic interactions between the neuron and its surround [3], a point considered below in a review of intimate surface phenomena in nerve cells.

Electrokinetic and other phenomena at the neuronal membrane surface

The model discussed here thus emphasizes mucoproteins and mucopolysaccharides at the neuron surface and in adjoining intercellular fluid as the site of changing impedance during physiological responses. Schmitt and Davison [52] have also suggested that these macromolecules may play a direct role in processes of excitation, and they have emphasized the importance of recognition of an "electrogenic protein." The corollaries to such hypotheses have far-reaching consequences to classic models of the neuron and require specific consideration.

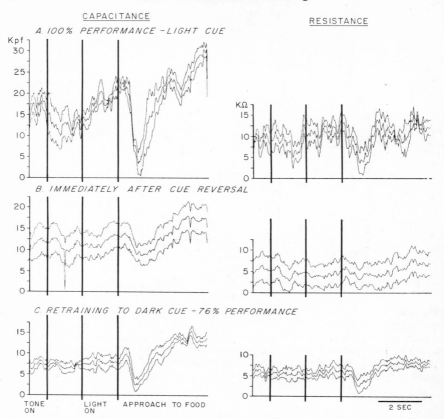

Fig. 6.3 Calculations of means and variability in hippocampal impedance over 5-day periods at various levels of training, with successive presentations of alerting, orienting, and discriminative stimuli. In each graph, middle trace indicates mean, with upper and lower traces showing one standard deviation from the mean. Calibrations indicate 50 picofarads, with mean baseline at 11.1 kilopicofarads throughout the training maneuvers; and 100 ohms, against a mean baseline of 16.0 kilohms for the same period. Variabliity was low at 100 per cent performance (*A*), increased substantially immediately after cue reversal (*B*), but decreased again after retraining (*C*). (From [8].)

Mucoproteins and mucopolysaccharides have two outstanding chemical characteristics. They bear numerous negative charges at fixed locations in the molecule, and they are capable of binding water and ions reversibly, with substantial volume changes accompanying their attachment to or removal from the molecule (Figure 6.4). Both points are of considerable significance to our membrane model.

CELL MOVEMENT INDUCED BY ELECTRIC CURRENT

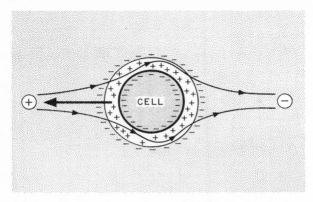

Fig. 6.4 Induction of movement in a body having net fixed surface charge in the presence of a nonuniform electric field. (From [24].)

Studies in our laboratory by Elul [23, 24] have indicated that positive external fields applied through a fine microelectrode in the vicinity of neurons in tissue culture visibly deform the membrane and also displace intracellular structures, such as the nucleus and nucleolus. The effect is not confined to nerve cells, and it can be elicited from cell fragments and in cultures killed with potassium cyanide. Origins of these movements in electroosmotic and electrophoretic effects have been considered and precluded, and the phenomenon appears to arise in fixed negative charges in the membrane. The findings raise questions of electrokinetic displacement as a phenomenon in physiological neural excitation, since the current density at the membrane surface due to the applied 5.0-millisecond pulses (10^{-6} to 10^{-8} angstroms at the electrode tip, lying 5 to 20 microns from the cell surface) is within an order of magnitude of synaptic currents. Elul has considered these phenomena in terms of physical displacements between synaptic terminal and neural membrane as a possible basis for modified neuronal excitability arising in the previous experience of the cell.

These fixed negative charges on surface macromolecules bind selectively with cations, particularly divalent cations, and have a particular affinity for calcium ions. Katchalsky [38] has pointed out that in aqueous solutions these molecules will increase their dispersed volume up to 100,000 times by binding with water in the absence of calcium. Addition of calcium reverses the process. Recent studies have exemplified the fundamental role of calcium in neuronal excitability in ways of suggesting interaction with surface macromolecules.

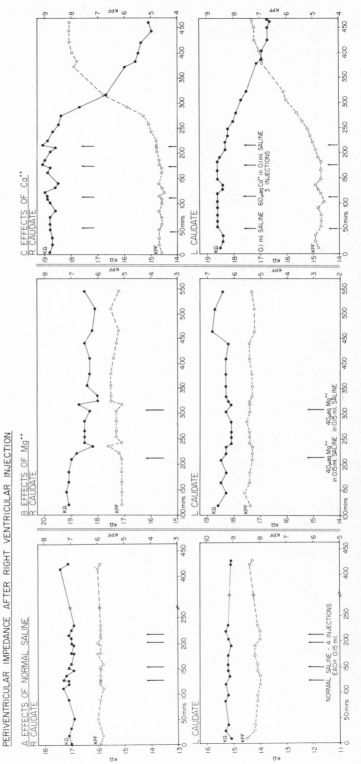

Fig. 6.5 Impedance in focal volumes (approximately 1.0 cubic millimeter) of left and right caudate nuclei following injections into the lateral ventricle of normal saline (0.15 milliliter), magnesium chloride (40 microequivalents in 0.1 milliliter), and calcium chloride (60 microequivalents in 0.1 milliliter). Major impedance changes occurred only with calcium solutions. (From [57].)

If 40 to 80 microequivalents of calcium solution are injected into the ventricular cavity of the cat's brain (Figure 6.5), impedance changes up to 30 per cent of baseline values occur within 30 to 60 minutes in tissue surrounding the ventricle, and last 24 hours [57]. The injected calcium raises the ventricular fluid concentration 10 to 20 times, and a smaller rise by diffusion would be expected in the environment of neurons near the ventricular wall. Epileptiform seizure discharges accompany the impedance changes in the hippocampus and amygdala lying in the ventricular wall. Other divalent cations, such as magnesium, are without comparable effects, and it was shown that mere concentration effects of other ions, including chloride ions, were not responsible. Repetition of these injections at bi-weekly intervals led to status epilepticus and death after three or four injections.

In the light of these findings, it seems reasonable to suggest that calcium plays a primary and intimate role in initiation of excitation, and that the classic phenomena of ionic fluxes of sodium and potassium across the membrane, to which so much attention has been paid hitherto, are probably quite secondary to processes involving calcium and its competitive binding with surface macromolecules. In even broader perspective, Kanno and Loewenstein [36] have found that large molecules, of the same magnitude as the nucleic acids DNA and RNA concerned with genetic information coding, pass freely across the cell membrane in reduced calcium environments. This suggests wide cellular interactions within a domain or gestalt of tissue, and as has been repeatedly emphasized, interactions so based give little support to models in which "wiring diagrams" of neural connections provide the sole or even the dominant scheme of functional relationships.

6.4 PATTERNS OF ELECTRICAL ACTIVITY IN CEREBRAL TISSUE; NEURONAL WAVES AND THE GROSS ELECTROENCEPHALOGRAM

Almost 100 years have elapsed since the first detection by Caton of cerebral electric waves. It is only in the last few years that penetrating studies have revealed the probable origin of the EEG, not in the ensemble of neuronal impulse firing, but in a quite different slow-wave process occurring within single cerebral neurons [18, 22, 27, 34]. These waves are of high amplitude, 5 to 15 millivolts (Figure 6.6).

Neuronal wave generators

How do these intracellular waves contribute to the gross EEG recorded on the scalp or at the brain surface? They are reduced in amplitude about

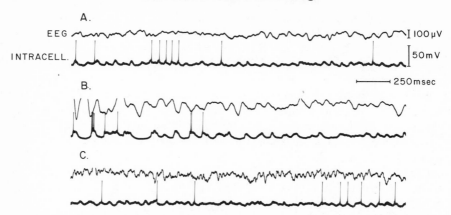

Fig. 6.6 Typical examples of cortical surface (top trace) and intracellular (lower trace) records in the same domain of tissue. Initiation of action potentials in the intracellular records occurs on the depolarizing phase of the concurrent wave process, but not necessarily on the largest waves. Calibrations for EEG channel, 50 microvolts; for intracellular records, 50 millivolts. (From [22].)

100 times between the internal and external surface of the membrane, so that the contribution of the individual generator to the waves in intercellular fluid is of the order of 50 to 100 microvolts. This is the magnitude of the gross EEG. It would be easy to consider the gross EEG as a simple sum of the synchronized wave activity of many neuronal generators. This, however, is not the case.

We have a particularly sensitive measure of the phase relations between an individual neuronal-wave generator and the gross EEG in the calculation of spectral density distributions and coherence functions. Intracellular waves and the gross EEG from the same domain of tissue have quite similar spectral density contours. On the other hand, coherence calculations, which provide a statistical measure of the predictability of linear interrelations between the two wave trains at each frequency across the spectrum, show extremely low values over long periods (Figure 6.7). The cortical generators appear to meet the requirements of the central limit theorem of Cramer [17], exhibiting individual amplitude distributions, which are not linearly related, and possessing a mean finite standard deviation. Elul has concluded that the contributions from the intracellular generator occur on a statistical basis and that the EEG may be accounted for as the normal distribution occurring from a combination of activity of nonlinearly related neuronal generators, with constantly varying coupling to other generators in the system [6,25].

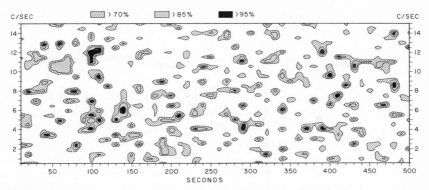

Fig. 6.7 Plot of coherence over a 500-second epoch between intracellular wave records and EEG from cortical surface in same domain of tissue. Coherence levels are below statistically significant levels at all frequencies for the major part of the analysis epoch, and the incidence of significant levels of coherence (shown in black) remains around chance levels throughout the analysis. The findings are interpreted as indicating origins of the EEG in a population of independent neuronal generators [22].

Our studies have indicated, therefore, that there are strong relations between the gross EEG and wave events in individual neurons. Certainly, the EEG does not constitute a mere "noise" in the cerebral system. Indeed, as will be described, precise and consistent patterns can be detected in surface and deep recordings in man and animals as concomitants of perceptual and learned performances. Additional emphasis is necessary, however, on the neuronal wave as a process concerned with information processing in cerebral tissue, from which the propagated nerve impulse arises only secondarily as a complex and nonlinear transform [5, 26]. We have observed that the threshold for cell firing has no fixed relationship to the level attained in the depolarizing phase of the neuronal wave. The latter may exceed the firing threshold without impulse initiation, and spike initiation may occur at multiple thresholds.

This evidence, and data presented below, suggest that great significance attaches to waves in cerebral neurons in the processing of information in cerebral tissue. Cerebral neurons are capable of parallel processing of information by a primary system of wave events, and the concurrent genesis of a secondary series of pulse-coded impulses propagated to remote locations.

The question thus arises as to whether interactions may occur between neurons in a cerebral domain on the basis of such graded wave processes. Although long discounted, such nonsynaptic interaction has been investigated by Nelson [42] in spinal motoneurons. He concluded that as much as

10 per cent of threshold excitation may be so caused, and his findings in the spinal cord may be of special significance to a cerebral model.

Anatomical and physiological models of cerebral neuron organization

Neurons in the spinal cord are relatively widely separated. On the other hand, it is characteristic of all cerebral ganglia, from ant to man, that neurons are arranged in a palisade of cells, with substantial and intimate overlap in the large dendritic fields, or "trees," which may form dendrodendritic connections between adjacent neurons, only a few hundred Angstroms apart [49]. In such a scheme, interaction by graded wave processes would be even more likely than in sparsely distributed spinal neurons [1, 11]. Moreover, wave processes characterize the intrinsic electric activity of all cerebral ganglia capable of "memory" in the usual sense of plastic information storage; they are absent, however, in "nonlearning," but nevertheless complex, systems such as the spinal cord.

At this time, we do not know the phenomena by which a neuron may be influenced by such small, graded events occurring in its environment. It is conceivable that the membrane may act as an amplifier for these extra-synaptic influences, based on longitudinal, rather than transverse, membrane current flow. A model, based on semiconductor aspects of membrane organization, that takes account of some of these parameters has been proposed by Wei [58]. Longitudinal organization of the neuron, in terms of its separate components of dendritic tree, cell body, and proximal axon segment must be determined if we are to understand its differential organization. Our studies have indicated that a "remote inhibition" may occur in cortical neurons, as previously described in spinal motoneurons by Granit, Kellerth, and Williams [28], and possibly arising in remote portions of the dendritic tree [26].

6.5 EEG CORRELATES OF BEHAVIORAL PROCESSES

We have considered a hierarchical scheme of cerebral organization, from subcellular events to integrated behavior of neuronal populations. The most compelling arguments in favor of the informational significance of wave processes in cerebral tissue must rest on detection of their necessary and consistent relationships to overt and rigorously defined behavioral processes. One would also anticipate that their dynamic distribution and patterning would be compatible with classical neurophysiology of cerebral systems. Our studies in man and animals support the view that well-defined EEG patterns accompany a wide repertoire of behavioral states, both within and between individual subjects.

Detection of these patterns has required elaborate computational procedures, and only a brief summary will be presented here. It has been possible to show that, beginning in the temporal lobe (hippocampal system) of the cat, there are distinctively different wave patterns accompanying alerting, orienting, and discriminative behavior, characterized by dominant frequencies at 4, 5, and 6 hertz, respectively [4, 20, 48]. Within the hippocampal system, phase relations, as determined by correlation analysis [12] and spectral analysis [11, 20], are consistently related to the correctness of decisions in a visual discriminative task. Cross-spectral analyses of data from surface and deep brain structures in the cat [21] have indicated high coherences (in narrow frequency bands around 6 hertz) between the hippocampus and subcortical regions (subthalamus and midbrain reticular formation) and visual and sensorimotor cortical areas during correct visual performances in the cat, but not in incorrect responses. Pattern recognition techniques applied to surface and deep EEG records in chimpanzees playing tic-tac-toe have also clearly separated EEG patterns accompanying correct and incorrect performances (see Hanley, Walter, Rhodes, and Adey, below). Pattern recognition was based on a multivariate matrix of output parameters from spectral analysis.

Phase relations and amplitude-transfer functions in these waves have suggested a stochastic patterning, with recall of previously learned information associated with reestablishment of wave patterns closely resembling, but not necessarily identical with, those associated with initial deposition of the memory trace [11].

Encouraged by these findings in animals, we have completed an analysis of scalp EEG data from 50 astronaut candidates [55]. These data covered one hour of perceptual and learning tasks presented from a master magnetic tape, and also included representative sleep records. Records were taken on magnetic tape by Drs. P. Kellaway and R. Maulsby, at the Houston Methodist Hospital. Collective "heads" for all 50 subjects in each behavioral test situation were prepared by averaging special outputs at each scalp electrode location, and comparing spectral density at each frequency with a mean covering all situations (Figure 6.8). The special analyses required more than 1400 hours of computation on an IBM 7094 computer, apart from plotting of automated displays.

It is abundantly clear from this study that, despite apparent wide individual differences in basic EEG patterns, spectral density patterns have characteristic features in a wide gamut of waking and sleeping states, ranging from simple wakefulness to performance of progressively more difficult (and ultimately challenging) visual discriminations. These baselines have proved valuable not only in relation to population characteristics, but in stimulating our use of multivariate pattern recognition (Figure 6.9)

TOPO-SPECTROGRAPHIC VARIATIONS OF
AVERAGES OVER FIFTY ASTRONAUT CANDIDATES

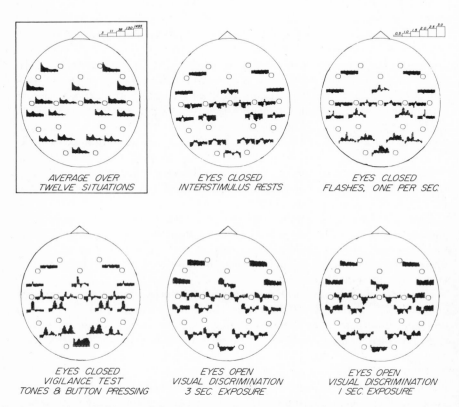

Fig. 6.8 Averaged spectral densities over the range 0 to 25 hertz for a population of 50 subjects, with each spectrum presented as a series of bars at 1-hertz intervals, and placed at the appropriate location on the scalp. The top left-hand figure is an average for all subjects across 12 situations. The contour of this average was then used as the mean against which to measure deviations in the succeeding 5 situations, with powers above the mean at any frequency shown as a bar above the baseline and vice versa. Calibrations for average over 12 situations in microvolts squared per second per cycle; for the separate situations, in standard deviations. (From [55].)

of the EEG signatures in separate individuals performing these same tasks [56] and in evaluation of the EEG of man in the highly specialized environment of space flight [9].

Thus it has been possible not only to turn our gaze inward to the microcosm of the single cell and to consider its individual contributions to wave processes of the aggregated population, but also to characterize those gross processes in man and animals that relate consistently to finely graded levels of alertness, focused attention, and discriminative performances. It would be difficult to conclude that there are not strong links between cellular events in the transaction of information and those regular waves which are recorded in all cerebral ganglia and which appear to characterize them uniquely.

6.6 UNIFYING HYPOTHESES; A SUMMARY

Recent studies in cerebral neurons have directed attention to their transaction of information on the basis of intracellular waves, as well as by pulse-coded, propagated spikes (or nerve impulses). Spectral analyses show that the electroencephalogram recorded from scalp or brain surface may arise from the separate contributions of a population of these wave generators. The evidence, however, is against a simple synchronization of the cellular generators, which appear to be independent of each other but to fit models based on the central limit theorem. At the same time, the propagated nerve impulse arises on the depolarizing phase of intracellular waves, but is a complex and nonlinear transform of the wave process. There is also evidence that in spinal motoneurons, where such interactions would be less likely than in the closely spaced neurons of cerebral structures, thresholds for neuronal firing are significantly modified by perineuronal electric fields, due to activity in adjacent neurons.

These structural and functional considerations invite development of a model of cerebral organization. It would emphasize unique features of cerebral tissue, particularly in structural aspects that might underlie both transaction and storage of information. Wave processes arise in considerable degree in dendritic structures. Dendrites of adjacent neurons are closely grouped in cerebral nuclei, with closely interwoven dendritic fields or "trees" from adjacent neurons. This "palisade" arrangement of cells characterizes the ganglia associated with learning in invertebrates and vertebrates alike. Equally general in these ganglia is the occurrence of regular electric waves, the EEG, not seen in quite complex but "non-learning" neural structures such as the mammalian spinal cord.

Cerebral neurons thus appear to process information in a parallel fashion by waves and also by pulse-coded phenomena. This has directed attention

ACCURACY OF AUTOMATIC CLASSIFICATION

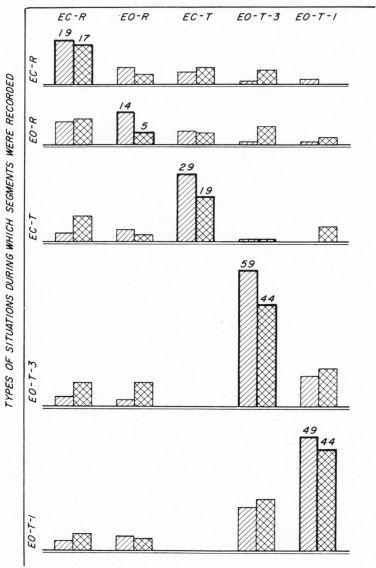

TYPE OF SITUATION INTO WHICH SEGMENTS WERE CLASSIFIED
BY BEST* COMBINATION OF 4 BEST* PARAMETERS

EC-R   EO-R   EC-T   EO-T-3   EO-T-1

TYPES OF SITUATIONS DURING WHICH SEGMENTS WERE RECORDED

EC-R

19 17

EO-R

14
5

EC-T

29
19

EO-T-3

59
44

EO-T-1

49
44

*BEST BY CRITERIA FOR STEP-WISE DISCRIMINANT ANALYSIS

SUM OF FOUR SOLO STUDIES

RESULT OF ENSEMBLE STUDY

to the separate functional components of the cerebral neuron, including a large dendritic tree, the cell body, and the axon hillock from which the axonal fiber arises. Whereas the nerve impulse appears to originate in the vicinity of the axon hillock in most adult cerebral neurons, it is equally clear that in laminarly organized structures (such as the hippocampus), wave processes arise in large measure in dendrites. These and other data point to a longitudinal organization of the cell, with different membrane characteristics in soma and dendrites.

Relationship of firing by the neuron to the genesis of intracellular waves clearly suggests nonlinearities, with absence of firing in many instances where membrane depolarization in waves exceeded levels at which firing could occur, and conversely, with evidence of multiple thresholds in the genesis of a rapid sequence of impulses. These findings may relate to a limited window on intracellular events provided by an intracellular electrode, but this would not dispose of a very evident lack of homogeneity in intracellular zones, as, for example, between cell body and dendrites.

Turning from the single cell to patterning in the gross EEG as a concomitant of behavioral processes, we find that there is a striking consistency in patterns accompanying specified behavioral states and ever-finer degrees of discriminative task performances in man and animals, down to the level of correctness or incorrectness of performance in a visual discrimination. Briefly, these findings lend striking support to data relating the gross EEG to cellular waves and, in turn, would assign a fundamental role to these waves in transaction of information in cerebral tissue.

Do these wave processes also relate to the storage and retrieval of information? There is growing evidence to warrant their further investigation in this context. They are uniquely developed in central nervous structures participating in learned responses. There is dramatic interference with

---

Fig. 6.9 Distribution of EEG segments by an automatic discrimination program. Segments were recorded in 5 situations: *EC-R*, eyes closed resting (34 segments); *EO-R*, eyes open resting (32 segments); *EC-T*, eyes closed performing auditory vigilance task (40 segments); *EO-T-3*, performing a visual discrimination on materal presented for 3 seconds for each situation (80 segments); *EO-T-1*, the same visual task with only 1 second exposure (78 segments). Five related studies are summarized: in 4 "solo" studies, each subject's records were evaluated separately, and the 4 parameters which would best categorize his records were selected; in the other "ensemble" study, records from all subjects were treated as if for a single subject. The rows of bars indicate the situations from which the records were taken, and the columns indicate categorizations by selected parameters. Bars on the diagonal (heavily outlined) represent correct categorizations. Single shading marks summed categorizations in the 4 solo studies, and cross shading indicates ensemble study. After 15 measurements were selected, the records from individual subjects were correctly classified on 95, 93, 96, and 90 per cent of the tests, compared with only 60 per cent for the group as a whole. (From [56].)

retrieval of such stored information by procedures that modify normal wave patterns, but that have relatively little effect on simpler tissue responses, such as evoked potentials. We have shown that there is a progressive decrease in the scatter of phase relations in these wave trains at progressively higher levels of performance. Within probability bounds, in wave processes at high levels of discriminative performances we may discern elements of a "stochastic" or best-fit pattern, where wave relations in the cerebral systems involved may closely resemble, but not necessarily be identical with, those present during initial laying down of the memory trace. Such wave phenomena would be associated with both "write" and "read" phases of storage. Neuronal excitability would then be determined by previous experience of these particular patterns of waves.

We come now to the final bridge in our modeling hypothesis. It must cover a substantial gap, a veritable "gulf fixed between." How do these wave trains lead to long-term changes of a chemical, structural nature, such as would be assumed to underlie a memory trace? The evidence is sparse, and any scheme highly tentative. Nevertheless, disclosure of electrical conductance changes in cerebral tissue in the course of a learned performance, and dependence of these impedance changes on the presence of an intact neuronal population, and the caveat that the impedance shifts probably reflect altered conductance in perineuronal elements, rather than through neuronal membranes, all invite consideration of large mucopolysaccharide and mucoprotein molecules at the neuronal surface as significant elements in information storage. The ion-binding characteristics of these surface molecules, particularly for divalent cations such as calcium, suggest, on the one hand, a susceptibility to electric fields in their vicinity, such as those accompanying the spread of electrotonic waves in the membrane; and, on the other, that the selective binding of calcium might thereafter modulate the flux of sodium and potassium ions across the membrane. Of itself, such a mechanism would probably not account for consolidation of the memory trace in a scheme lasting three score years and ten. It is here that more subtle mechanisms that determine location of protein building blocks at the membrane surface, perhaps in the realm of genetic and immune mechanisms, will await our evaluation.

We have come progressively from schemes of information processing in peripheral sensory mechanisms, where determinism is high and transforms of sensory information relatively simple, to the complexities of central nervous processing. Here the high level of intrinsic activity, the enormous redundancy in many functions, the capacity for parallel processing in wave and pulse-coded data in each logical element, and the subtleties of storage and retrieval mechanisms as yet unsolved, all challenge physiologist and communication scientist alike. Let us then have due regard for the uniqueness of such a processor. Let us rigorously avoid simple analogies with pulse-coded nerve nets, or worse still, with the current generation of computing devices characterized by limited parallel access and by logical elements having only a binary function. We may then hopefully aspire to a realistic model of this most complex of all living organs.

REFERENCES

1. Adey, W. R., "Brain Mechansims and the Learning Process," *Federation Proc.*, 1961, 617–627.
2. Adey, W. R., "Electrophysiological Patterns and Cerebral Impedance Characteristics in Orienting and Discriminative Behavior," *Proc. XXIII Internat. Cong. Physiol. Sci., Tokyo*, Excepta Medica International Congress Series No. 87, **4**, 1965, 324–339.
3. Adey, W. R., "Intrinsic Organization of Cerebral Tissue in Alerting, Orienting and Discriminative Responses," in Quarton, G. C., T. Melnechuk, and F. O. Schmitt (editors), *The Neurosciences: A Study Program*, Rockefeller University Press, New York, 1967, pp. 615–633.
4. Adey, W. R., C. W. Dunlop, and C. E. Hendrix, "Hippocampal Slow Waves; Distribution and Phase Relations in the Course of Approach Learning," *Amer. Med. Assoc. Arch. Neurol.*, **3**, 1960, 74–90.
5. Adey, W. R., and R. Elul, "Non-Linear Relationship of Spike and Waves in Cortical Neurons," *The Physiologist*, **8**, 1965, 98.
6. Adey, W. R., R. Elul, R. D. Walter, and P. H. Crandall, "The Cooperative Behavior of Neuronal Populations during Sleep and Mental Tasks," *Proc. Amer. Electroenceph. Soc.*, October 1966, 86.
7. Adey, W. R., R. T. Kado, and J. Didio, "Impedance Measurements in the Brain Tissue of Chronic Animals Using Microvolt Signals," *Exper. Neurol.*, **5**, 1962, 47–66.
8. Adey, W. R., R. T. Kado, J. M. McIlwain, and D. O. Walter, "Regional Cerebral Impedance Changes in Alerting, Orienting and Discriminative Responses; the Role of Neuronal Elements in These Phenomena," *Exper. Neurol.*, **15**, 1966, 490–510.
9. Adey, W. R., R. T. Kado, and D. O. Walter, "Impedance Characteristics of Cortical and Subcortical Structures; Evaluation of Regional Specificity in Hypercapnea and Hypothermia," *Exper. Neurol.*, **11**, 1965, 190–216.
10. Adey, W. R., R. T. Kado, and D. O. Walter, "Computer Analysis of EEG Data from Gemini GT-7 Flight," *Aerospace Med.*, **38**, 1967, 345–359.
11. Adey, W. R., and D. O. Walter, "Application of Phase Detection and Averaging Techniques in Computer Analysis of EEG Records in the Cat,. *"Exper. Neurol.*, **7**, 1963, 186–209.
12. Adey, W. R., D. O. Walter, and C. E. Hendrix, "Computer Techniques in Correlation and Spectral Analyses of Cerebral Slow Waves during Discriminative Behavior," *Exper. Neurol.*, **3**, 1961, 501–524.
13. Barnett, R. J., "Fine Structural Basis of Enzymatic Activity in Neurons," *Trans. Amer. Neurol. Assoc.*, **88**, 1963, 123–126.
14. Beidler, L. M., "Physiological Problems in Odor Research," *Ann. New York Acad. Sci.*, **58**, 1953, article 2, 52–57.
15. Bullock, T. H., "Neuron Doctrine and Electrophysiology," *Science*, **129**, 1959, 997–1002.

16. Chamberlain, T. J., P. Halick, and R. W. Gerard, "Fixation of Experience in the Rat Spinal Cord," *J. Neurophysiol.*, **26**, 1963, 662–673.
17. Cramer, H., *The Elements of Probability Theory*, Wiley, New York, 1962.
18. Creutzfeldt, O. D., J. M. Fuster, H. D. Lux, and A. Nacimiento, "Experimenteller Nachweis von Beziehungen zwischen EEG-wellen und Activität corticaler Nervenzellen," *Naturwissenschaft.*, **51**, 1964, 166–167.
19. Davis, H., "Excitation of Auditory Receptors," in Field, J., V. E. Hall, and H. W. Magoun (editors), *Handbook of Physiology*. Section I, Vol. 1, Neurophysiology. American Physiol. Society, Washington, D. C., 1959, pp 565–584.
20. Elazar, Z., and W. R. Adey, "Spectral Analysis of Low Frequency Components in the Hippocampal Electroencephalogram during Learning," *Electroenceph. Clin. Neurophysiol.*, **23**, 1967, 225–240.
21. Elazar, Z., and W. R. Adey, "Electroencephalographic Correlates of Learning in Subcortical and Cortical Structures," *Electroenceph. Clin. Neurophysiol.*, **23**, 1967, 306–319.
22. Elul, R., "Specific Site of Generation of Brain Waves," *The Physiologist*, **7**, 1964, 125.
23. Elul, R., "Dependence of Synaptic Transmission on Protein Metabolism of Nerve Cells: A Possible Electrokinetic Mechanism of Learning?," *Nature*, **210**, 1966, 1127–1131.
24. Elul, R., "Use of Non-Uniform Electric Fields for Evaluation of the Potential Difference between Two Phases," *Trans. Faraday Soc.*, **62**, 1966, 3484–3492.
25. Elul, R., "Amplitude Histograms of the EEG as an Indicator of the Cooperative Behavior of Neuron Populations," *Proc. Amer. Electroenceph. Soc.*, October, 1966, 80–81.
26. Elul, R., and W. R. Adey, "Instability of Firing Threshold and Remote Activation in Cortical Neurones," *Nature*, **212**, 1966, 1422–1425.
27. Fujita, Y., and T. Sato, "Intracellular Records from Hippocampal Pyramidal Cells in Rabbit during Theta Rhythm Activity, "*J. Neurophysiol.*, **27**, 1964, 1011–1025.
28. Granit, R., J. O. Kellerth, and T. D. Williams, "'Adjacent' and 'Remote' Post-synaptic Inhibition in Motoneurones Stimulated by Muscle Sretch," *J. Physiol.*, **174**, 1964, 453–472.
29. Green, J. D., D. S. Maxwell, and H. Petsche, "Hippocampal Electrical Activity. III. Unitary Events and Genesis of Slow Waves," *Electroenceph. Clin. Neurophysiol.*, **13**, 1961, 854–867.
30. Harreveld, A. van, J. Crowell, and S. K. Malhotra, "A Study of Extracellular Space in Central Nervous Tissue by Freeze-Substitution," *J. Cell. Biol.*, **25**, 1965, 117–138.
31. Hecht, S., S. Shlaer, and M. H. Pirenne, "Energy, Quanta, and Vision," *J. Gen. Physiol.*, **25**, 1941, 819–840.
32. Hertz, L., "A Possible Role of Neuroglia: A Potassium Mediated Neuronal-Neuroglial-Neuronal Impulse Transmission System," *Proc. XXIII Internat. Cong. Physiol. Sci., Tokyo*, 1965, 408.
33. Hild, W., and I. Tasaki, "Morphological and Physiological Properties of Neurons and Glial Cells in Tissue Culture," *J. Neurophysiol.*, **25**, 1962, 277–304.
34. Jasper, H. H., and C. Stefanis, "Intracellular Oscillatory Rhythms in Pyramidal Cells of the Cat," *Electroenceph. Clin. Neurophysiol.*, **18**, 1965, 541–553.
35. John, E. R., and K. F. Killam, "Electrophysiological Correlates of Avoidance Conditioning in the Cat," *J. Pharmacol. Exper. Therap.*, **125**, 1959, 252–274.

36. Kanno, Y., and W. R. Loewenstein, "Cell-to-Cell Passage of Large Molecules," *Nature*, **212**, 1966, 629–630.
37. Karahashi, Y., and S. Goldring, "Intracellular Potentials from Idle Cells in Cerebral Cortex of Cat," *Electroenceph. Clin. Neurophysiol.*, **20**, 1966, 600–607.
38. Katchalsky, A., "Polyelectrolytes and Their Biological Interactions," in Symposium, *Connective Tissue: Intercellular Macromolecules*. New York Heart Association. Little, Brown, Boston, 1964, pp. 9–42.
39. Kiang, N. W., "The Use of Computers in Studies of Auditory Neurophysiology," *Trans. Amer. Acad. Ophthal. and Otorhinolaryng.*, **65**, 1961, 735–747.
40. Kuffler, S. W., J. G. Nicholls, and R. K. Orkand, "Physiological Properties of Glial Cells in the Central Nervous System of Amphibia," *J. Neurophysiol.*, **29**, 1966, 768–787.
41. Morrell, F., "Electrophysiological Contributions to the Neural Basis of Learning," *Physiol. Rev.*, **41**, 1961, 443–494.
42. Nelson, P. G., "Interaction between Spinal Motoneurons of the Cat," *J. Neurophysiol.*, **29**, 1966, 275–287.
43. Nelson, P. G., and S. D. Erulkar, "Synaptic Mechansims of Excitation and Inhibition in the Central Auditory Pathway," *J. Neurophysiol.*, **26**, 1963, 908–923.
44. Nicholls, J. G., and S. W. Kuffler, "Na and K Content of Glial Cells and Neurons Determined by Flame Photometry in the Nervous System of the Leech," *J. Neurophysiol.*, **28**, 1965, 519–525.
45. Pease, D. C., "Polysaccharides Associated with the Exterior Surface of Epithelial Cells: Kidney, Intestine, Brain," *J. Ultrastruc. Res.*, **15**, 1966, 555–583.
46. Peters, A., and S. L. Palay, "An Electron Microscope Study of the Distribution and Patterns of Astroglial Processes in the Central Nervous System," *Proc. Anat. Soc. Great Britain and Ireland*, Nov. 1964, 17.
47. Porter, R., W. R. Adey, and R. T. Kado, "Measurement of Electrical Impedance in the Human Brain," *Neurology*, **14**, 1964, 1002–1012.
48. Radulovacki, M., and W. R. Adey, "The Hippocampus and the Orienting Reflex," *Exper. Neurol.*, **12**, 1965, 68–83.
49. Rall, W., G. M. Shepherd, T. S. Reese, and M. W. Brightman, "Dendro-dendritic Synaptic Pathway for Inhibition in the Olfactory Bulb," *Exper. Neurol.*, **14**, 1966, 44–56.
50. Rambourg, A., and C. P. Leblond, "Electron Microscope Observations on the Carbohydrate-Rich Cell Coat Present at the Surface of Cells in the Rat," *J. Cell. Biol.*, **32**, 1967, 27–54.
51. Rupert, A., G. Moushegian, and R. Galambos, "Unit Responses to Sound from Auditory Nerve of the Cat," *J. Neurophysiol.*, **26**, 1963, 449–465.
52. Schmitt, F. O., and P. F. Davison, "Role of Protein in Neural Function," *Neurosciences Research Program Bulletin*, **3**, Part 6, 1965, 55–76.
53. Sumner, J. B., "Problems in Odor Research from the Viewpoint of the Chemist," *Ann. New York Acad. Sci.*, **58**, 1953, article 2, 68–72.
54. Svaetechin, G., R. Fatehchand, M. Laufer, P. Witkovsky, K. Negishi, and A. Selvin de Testa, "Glial-Neuronal Interaction and Its Metabolic Dependence. A New Theory of Nerve Function," *Acta Cientifico Venezolano*, **14**, Suppl. 1, 1963, 135–153.
55. Walter, D. O., R. T. Kado, J. M. Rhodes, and W. R. Adey. "Establishment of Electroencephalographic Baselines in Astronaut Candidates with Computed Analyses and Pattern Recognition," *Aerospace Med.*, **38**, 1967, 371–379.

56. Walter, D. O., J. M. Rhodes, and W. R. Adey, "Discriminating among States of Consciousness by EEG Measurements. A Study of Four Subjects," *Electroenceph. Clin. Neurophysiol.*, **22**, 1967, 22–29.
57. Wang, H. H., T. J. Tarby, R. T. Kado, and W. R. Adey, "Periventricular Cerebral Impedance after Intraventricular Calcium Injection," *Science*, **154**, 1966, 1183–1184.
58. Wei, L. Y., "A New Theory of Nerve Conduction," *Inst. Electrical and Electronics Engineers, Spectrum*, **3**, Part 9, 1966, 123–127.
59. Young, J. Z. *Doubt and Certainty in Science: A Biologist's Reflections on the Brain.* Oxford University Press, New York, 1951.

FURTHER READINGS

1. Adey, W. R., "Spectral Analysis of EEG Data from Animals and Man during Altering, Orienting, and Discriminative Responses," in Mulholland, T., and C. Evans (editors), *Attention in Neurophysiology*, Butterworth, London, 1969, pp. 194–229.
2. Adey, W. R., "Spontaneous Electrical Brain Rhythms Accompanying Learned Responses," in Schmitt, F. O. (editor), *The Neurosciences*, Rockefeller University Press, New York, 1970, pp. 224–243.
3. Adey, W. R., "Evidence for Cerebral Membrane Effects of Calcium, Derived from DC Gradient, Impedance, and Intracellular Records," *Exper. Neurol.*, **30**, 1971, 78–102.
4. Berkhout, J., D. O. Walter, and W. R. Adey, "Alterations of the Human Encephalogram Induced by Stressful Verbal Activity," *Electroenceph. Clin. Neurophysiol.*, **27**, 1969, 457–469.
5. Hanley, J., D. O. Walter, J. M. Rhodes, and W. R. Adey, "Chimpanzee Performance: Computer Analysis of Electroencephalograms," *Nature*, **220**, 1968, 879–881.
6. Heimer, Lennart, "Pathways in the Brain," *Scientific American*, **225**, 1971, 48–60.
7. Noda, H., and W. R. Adey, "Firing of Neuron Pairs in Cat Association Cortex during Sleep and Wakefulness," *J. Neurophysiol.*, **33**, 1970, 672–684.

CHAPTER 7

Information Storage in the Brain

E. ROY JOHN

Professor of Psychiatry, Director, Brain Research Laboratories, New York Medical College, New York City

Contents

7.1 INTRODUCTION

The problem of mechanisms of learning and memory has interested psychologists and neurophysiologists for a long while. The approach followed early in the history of this field reflected the heritage of the early anatomical and physiological studies of the brain. Such studies, particularly anatomical studies concerned with the tracing of pathways, almost inevitably focused on the attempt to assign discrete functions to particular structures. The connection of a region in the brain to peripheral receptors led early workers to conclude that the structure mediated the function implied by such a connection.

Similar reasoning was applied to the problem of learning. The first investigations of this problem used classical conditioning methods. This technique basically involves establishment of functional equivalence between two more or less arbitrarily selected stimuli. One of these, the *unconditioned stimulus* (US), initially is capable of producing some autonomic or motor response. The other, the *conditioned stimulus* (CS), does not normally elicit this response but acquires the capacity to do so after systematic association with the US.

The picture of learning developed by these early workers was one in which connections were made between input regions receiving the CS and output regions controlled by the US and mediating the unconditioned response. Their reasoning, which intuitively still seems feasible, was: "There is an input region activated by the CS and an output region which produces the response. During learning, this input somehow comes to produce that output as a conditioned response. Therefore, there must be a connection established between the CS and US regions; some kind of pathway is built." This line of thinking led to the belief that there must be certain cells which form a definite pathway from the sensory input to the motor output region. The responsiveness of neurons in the pathway constituted the memory. Training wore a "groove" of increased excitability or new connections along certain neural paths from input to output, and the existence of that groove was the memory of the experience. Remembering, in such a picture, involved the discharge of the cells that constituted the pathway.

7.2   THE DILEMMA OF THE PHYSIOLOGICAL PSYCHOLOGIST

Following along the directions dictated by the logic just indicated, generations of physiological psychologists and neurophysiologists attempted to localize memory, that is, to identify these pathways by destroying localized regions of the brain. Perhaps surprisingly, the results of such endeavors were fairly negative. Although it was sometimes possible to demonstrate deterioration in the performance of some previously learned response as a consequence of injury to a specified part of the brain, a number of difficulties developed in the attempt to pursue this rather simplistic approach. First, great damage could frequently be wrought with surprisingly little effect on the ability of an animal to perform previously established conditioned responses or to acquire new responses. Further, in cases where deterioration of performance was observed, it was quite perplexing to find that after a period of time with no further training, frequently the ability to perform the disturbed function returned to the same level as before the operation.

A particularly poignant example of the dilemma of the physiological psychologist was provided not too long ago by a classical experiment performed by Heinrich Klüver at the University of Chicago [18]. Klüver trained monkeys to perform a number of different kinds of discriminations.

The animals were taught visual discriminations on the basis of brightness or pattern, auditory discriminations on the basis of loudness or pitch, and weight discrimination. After all these discriminations had been acquired by the animals, they were subjected to surgical removal of all cortical association areas. Klüver found, as had other workers before, that after this operation the animals were unable to perform any of the discriminations that they had been taught. Previous workers who found such results had concluded that the memories were localized in the regions that had been removed. After the demonstration that performance was no longer elicited from these animals, Klüver retrained them to perform one of the discriminations which they had learned—for example, the discrimination between two weights. During the retraining period none of the other problems was presented to these animals. *After the ability to discriminate weights had been re-established, testing showed that all the other discriminations were again performed perfectly.* The apparently ablated memories had been restored.

Karl Lashley, perhaps the best-known American investigator in this genre of experiments, in a brilliant article called "In Search of the Engram" [19], summarized the feelings of frustration of that whole school of investigators. He wrote that the only conclusion that one could reach from the failure to demonstrate memory deficit after local lesions was that it was really impossible for the brain to accomplish what it did. It could not learn. He formulated two generalizations, sometimes called "laws," which are still widely accepted by workers in this field. The first was the *law of mass action:* The deficit in the performance of an animal after a brain lesion is a function of the total volume of tissue damage and is relatively independent of its location. Implicit in that formulation is the second generalization, the *law of equipotentiality:* There are regions of the brain which become primarily responsible for the performance of a given function; under appropriate circumstances, however, it can be demonstrated that other regions are equally capable of performing the same role. An example may be useful here. Surgical removal of all regions of the visual cortex might be expected to result in a blind animal. Yet if kittens are thus operated on shortly after birth, when these animals grow up they can see perfectly well. They can be taught complex visual pattern discriminations, and they learn as readily as normal animals [5]. Adult animals with such lesions can learn, can use visual cues in their environment, and display remarkable visual motor coordination [2, 29].

A recent experiment illustrates some facts that are highly relevant to hypotheses about brain mechanisms of information storage and retrieval. It was performed by Burns and Smith, who studied the activity of single nerve cells in curarized and retrained animals [1]. These workers reached two conclusions of fundamental significance. First, all cells observed were in incessant activity. Second, each cell was affected by every stimulus. Every cell which was monitored could be demonstrated to alter its firing pattern as a consequence of any arbitrary stimulus presented. Such observations raise a perplexing question: What distinguishes neuronal events related to the input of information or the retrieval of previously stored information, if the nerve cells discharge spontaneously with relatively high incidence and if these nerve cells also respond to most events effusively and indiscriminately with a change in their activity pattern?

It is unrealistic to think in terms of a pathway between two places in which cells sit quietly until a specific event occurs, whereupon they burst into activity which "stands for" that event to some detector in the nervous system. If cells discharge spontaneously at a significant rate, how can the brain discriminate the discharge of cells due to spontaneous influences from discharge due to the occurrence of a significant event in the surround? Further, if cells discharge when arbitrarily selected events are presented to the animal, how can the discharge of a cell due to the reoccurrence of a previous experience be discriminated from the discharge of a cell due to the occurrence of a novel event which has not been previously experienced? Thus *it seems highly unlikely that single cells become labeled by experience so that their discharge will subsequently represent that experience.* The "filing card" conception of memory, in which the discharge of a cell represents the selection of the card and the tuning of that cell for discharge represents the information written on it, seems implausible. It is a simple and attractive way to think about information storage in the brain, but it is most probably incorrect.

7.3 ELECTROPHYSIOLOGICAL STUDIES OF BRAIN PROCESSES

Some notion of alternative formulations is provided by the electrophysiological study of brain processes during learning and the retrieval of information, which permits more direct observation of neural activity as these functions are performed by nervous systems. Phenomena observed in such studies suggest significant changes in our formulations of learning mechanisms. In this presentation, we shall outline certain of these alternatives. A major purpose, however, is to illustrate various experimental strategies now being used and to indicate the nature of the results forthcoming from the application of these approaches.

Numerous electrophysiological studies have examined the changes in gross electrical activity, usually from externally located electrodes, as animals or men were exposed to certain learning experiences [8, 24]. Such studies, which began in the early 1930s, led to a relatively small number of generalized conclusions, based on the overall characteristics of the electrical activity. For example, because the reaction of an organism to the initial occurrence of an event was fairly global, with widespread distribution of electrical reaction throughout the nervous system, the so-called mesencephalic reticular formation was assumed to be involved. With further training, this global response was replaced by a more differentiated, more highly localized electrical reaction, which was interpreted to indicate a shift in the mediating structures from the mesencephalic reticular formation to the so-called thalamic reticular formation.

In recent years, a variety of electrophysiological approaches have evolved from these beginnings. A particularly fruitful group of electrophysiological studies is characterized by the use of intermittent stimuli, to which significance is attached by conditioning methods. We call the intermittent event a *tracer stimulus*, and search the electrical activity of various brain regions for rhythms at the frequency of the tracer stimulus. Such electrical events are called *labeled responses*. In this fashion, the response of the brain to the stimulus is made appreciably easier to detect. Changes in the distribution and amplitude of labeled responses during conditioning are assumed to reflect changes in the processing of information about the stimulus by the various brain regions or to indicate local changes in excitability.

In the usual application of these techniques, animals are permanently implanted with multiple cortical and subcortical electrodes. We use 34 electrodes per animal. These electrodes are relatively fine wires, about .005 inch in diameter, yet they monitor the activity of large groups of cells, perhaps as many as 100,000. The EEG activity which is observed by such a large electrode is correlated with the potentials appearing across the membrane of single nerve cells in the region, if pierced with microelectrodes. EEG potentials probably represent the integrated fluctuation of postsynaptic potentials in a large population of cells around the tip of the recording electrode. These membrane potentials are not to be confused with the action potentials resulting from actual discharge of nerve cells. Rather, membrane potentials constitute regulatory mechanisms which influence the *probability* of cell discharge. Given an extremely large sample of discharges from nerve cells in a region as stimuli are repeatedly applied, the frequency distribution of such a population of cellular discharges correlates extremely well with the evoked potential waveshape from the region [6]. These electrical events are related to the probability of *coherent* activity in a large population of cells in the vicinity of the electrode tip [13].

The tracer method previously described was applied first in the Soviet Union toward the end of World War II by Livanov, who still is extremely active in this field [21]. Many of the phenomena which are described in that initial study are still of extreme interest to those who pursue this line of investigation. First, marked changes are seen in the distribution of labeled potentials as an animal acquires experience about his environment. For example, Killam and the present author studied the effects of conditioning an animal to perform an avoidance response consisting of jumping over a hurdle within 15 seconds after the onset of a flickering light [11]. Before training began, the cats were familiarized with the flicker. The stimulus was presented about 20 times a day, for about 15 seconds at a time. Presentations were about one minute apart. Between sessions, each animal was returned to his home cage. As familiarization proceeded, the electrical responses displayed by various brain regions to the stimulus gradually diminished and disappeared. When avoidance training began, and shock was paired with flicker presentation, there was a dramatic reappearance of labeled responses in most but not all of the structures initially responsive to the novel stimulus, and also in structures previously nonreactive. Thus it was apparent that the response of the brain could be strongly inhibited to a familiar and inconsequential stimulus. Further, external events could markedly alter the inhibited response. Response inhibition can be differential, with certain responses suppressed while others are not affected. It has been shown that the effect of a stimulus on the nervous system can be either enhanced or diminished by simultaneous presentation of a second stimulus. For example, the responses evoked in the cochlear nucleus of a cat by presentation of clicks are very strongly inhibited by presentation of a mouse to the cat [7]. When the mouse is taken away and the cat settles down, the click response returns to its previous amplitude. There is a dynamic interplay between ongoing events in the nervous system. The effect of a stimulus on the nervous system is not invariant. The nervous system exerts a great deal of regulation upon its input. That regulation is strongly dependent on the effect of past experience. Afferent control mechanisms may reflect the influence of memory on brain activity.

In our work, as avoidance training proceeded, the reaction of the nervous system to the light changed markedly. Some of these changes were probably due to generalized aspects of the situation, and some may be due to the specific informational significance attached to the stimulus by the learning experience. McAdam has shown that some of the changes which occur are consequences of the general training situation, whereas others seem to be related to the specific informational significance which has been attached to a certain aspect of the environment [22]. It has been noticed that with overtraining of a given response, the widespread reactivity to the stimulus gradually diminishes [8]. One possible explanation is that it is no longer necessary for the animal to attend to the quality of the event. It suffices merely to detect the occurrence of stimulus in the environment; since no differential evaluation is necessary, adequate response can be performed by reaction to *the* ON *of an event*. For this reason, we became interested in the study of differential conditioned responses in which animals were trained to perform one response to one stimulus and an incompatible response to a second stimulus. Since stimuli are presented in random sequence, correct performance requires that the animal monitor the *quality* of each event. The present stimulus must be referred to some internal representation of the alternatives in order to decide which of the two possible responses is appropriate. Since the arousal level of an animal can be held relatively constant in such a situation, the contribution of arousal can be parceled out by studying the *difference* in the configuration of electrical activity when the animal performs correctly and when a mistake occurs. It is extremely informative to compare electrical responses during correct and incorrect decisions in a differential response situation.

As differential training is carried out, labeled responses become very much more marked and widely distributed through the nervous system. During correct behavioral performance, labeled responses correspond well to the stimulus frequency. During incorrect performance or failures to respond, however, labeled responses in certain structures are in poor agreement with the frequency of the stimulus but correspond well to the frequency that would be appropriate to the cue for behavior which is actually performed. Data of this sort led Killam and the present author to the formulation of a coincidence detector scheme [12]. We observed that in such decision-making situations, certain structures of the brain tend to show activity which is stimulus bound. These structures are called *sensory specific*, because their input is more or less localized to a particular sensory modality. There are other structures which are *nonsensory specific*. In such situations, nonsensory specific structures do not show activity which is stimulus bound. They may or may not display rhythms corresponding to the stimulus, but it is noteworthy that their activity is highly related to the behavior displayed by the animal. Such observations led us to suggest that discrimination behavior involved the comparison of input related to reality, transmitted via sensory-specific pathways, with *released* patterns established by past experience, propagated via nonsensory-specific pathways to the cortex. The reaction of the cortex seemed to be determined by the congruence between these two patterns.

This is an extremely difficult hypothesis to test, and we cannot claim that our subsequent work has validated it. We can, however, provide further data compatible with that hypothesis. One piece of evidence comes from the known fact that sensory-specific influences reach the cortex somewhat earlier than nonsensory-specific influences. We explored the relative role of early and late processes in the performance of responses requiring the identification of an input, by using electrical stimulation delivered bilaterally to the visual cortex with varying time delays after the presentation of a peripheral flicker CS. We studied the behavioral consequences when electrical disturbance of the cortex coincided with the arrival of the early sensory-specific influences versus the effect of delaying that disrupting input so as to coincide with the late-arriving nonsensory-specific influences [9].

The results showed that the delivery of central electrical stimulation shortly after a peripheral signal (15 milliseconds) had relatively little effect on conditioned response. When that same electrical perturbation was shifted in time so as to coincide with arrival of the nonsensory-specific influences on cortex (80–110 milliseconds), the behavior was severely disrupted. The animal sat and looked about as though it did not perceive the peripheral signal as meaningful. When the stimulus was presented, the animal alerted and stared at the source of the stimulus but gave no indication of knowing what was to be done. This evidence, together with the reasoning presented earlier, suggested that the temporal pattern of events at a place rather than their spatial distribution might constitute information for the brain.

We conducted experiments to explore whether this was a reasonable proposition. Those experiments investigated whether it was possible to train an animal to perform differentiated conditioned responses to two electrical patterns delivered to a *single* pair of electrodes [9]. The two stimulus patterns were equated for energy, differing only in their temporal distribution. We found that cats could be trained readily to discriminate between such electrical patterns.

These findings show that the temporal sequence of events at a particular place can constitute information for the brain, whether or not information is normally processed in this fashion. A given electrode site in the brain constitutes an information channel of capacity yet to be evaluated. As a consequence of that realization, we and other laboratories are engaged in exploring the possibility of sensory prosthetic devices using direct electrical input into the brain as a source of information.

7.4 COMPUTER ANALYSIS OF ELECTRICAL DATA

The discussion thus far has been based on data examined only by inspection. At this stage we began to apply computer analysis to electrical data elicited from studies of this sort. In such studies, a large number of electrodes are chronically implanted into a nervous system. Therefore, information is available about the events going on in a large number of brain regions simultaneously. At any given site, we can distinguish several kinds of activity: processes relating to the ongoing functions of the nervous system in which the observed region is participating, and processes relating to the response of that region to specific stimuli which the experimenter presents to the animal. Although the ongoing activity is by no means functionless, it is not related to the processing of the information about the stimuli with which we are primarily concerned. Let us call it "noise," with the proviso that it is not random activity. It is desirable to enhance the signal-to-noise ratio, in order to observe that portion of the neural activity in a brain region which is due to the response to a particular experimental manipulation. Relatively inexpensive average-response computers to do this are now commercially available and have been used extensively in studies of this sort. In average response computation, samples of electrophysiological responses to a stimulus are summed. The contribution of unrelated processes going on in the system will randomize out during such repetition, while the responses to the stimulus will summate to the extent that they are time-locked. Average-response computation enhances that portion of the response of a system consisting of time-locked coherent reactions to a perturbation.

Consider an average-response waveform over some analysis epoch of duration T. Let us divide that epoch into a number of intervals ΔT. The waveshape can be digitalized as a series of numbers corresponding to the value of the voltage at each interval of time. By the appropriate operations upon these series, the correlation coefficient between two average response waveshapes can be computed. The correlation coefficient is equal to the expression

$$\frac{\int_0^T F(t) \cdot G(t)\, dt}{f \cdot g},$$

where

$$f = \sqrt{\int_0^T [F(t)]^2\, dt} \quad \text{and} \quad g = \sqrt{\int_0^T [G(t)]^2\, dt}\,,$$

and where $F(t)$ equals the first waveshape, $G(t)$ equals the second waveshape, and T is the integration epoch over which the correlation is to be determined. This corresponds to the Pearson-product moment correlation coefficient, which varies from -1 to $+1$ and has been well studied.

Our laboratory and the laboratory of Livanov in the Soviet Union reported the same conclusion almost simultaneously [16, 20]. *As an animal is taught that a given event has meaning, the average correlation coefficient between various brain regions increases.*

Consider some hypothetical average waveshape. Imagine for the sake of simplicity that it consists only of measurements at three points in time, T_1, T_2, and T_3, and that the corresponding voltages are V_1, V_2, and V_3. Define a three-dimensional space X,Y,Z, and adopt the convention that X stands for T_1, Y stands for T_2, and Z stands for T_3. The numbers V_1,V_2,V_3 are then the direction numbers of a signal vector. The successive translations V_1 in the direction X, V_2 in the direction Y, and V_3 in the direction Z define a point such that a line from the origin to that point is a *signal vector* representing the initial waveshape. An analogous operation could be performed in N-dimensional space, if the average-response waveshape were divided into N time intervals. The correlation coefficient between two waveshapes is analogous to the cosine of the angle between the two signal vectors and therefore is a measure of the relative orientation of two signal vectors thus defined. The matrix of correlations between each waveshape and every other waveshape defines the relative orientation of the set of signal vectors in the hyperspace. Using techniques of signal analysis, we can ascertain the dimensionality of the space in which these signal vectors exist. The dimensionality corresponds to the *minimum* number of orthonormal vectors which will span the space. Principal-component analysis imposes a further constraint: the orientation of the orthonormal vector set which is selected must maximize the rate of reduction of residual variance in the set of signals. The set of basis vectors is oriented in this space so that each vector accounts for more of the total energy of the space than *any* other possible vector. That contribution is then subtracted from all the signal vectors, and a similar procedure is iterated for the residuals.

In this way, a set of vectors is constructed which corresponds to a set of hypothetical generators capable of reproducing the original set of signals by *linear* interaction. The constraints of linear interaction intuitively seem so unreasonable as to make the procedure inapplicable to analysis of brain activity. Surprisingly, the linear assumption seems to be applicable to the nervous system. It is possible to account for 97 per cent of the communality of a set of 30 to 35 signals with as few as 9 to 10 factors. Therefore, there is a great amount of linear dependence among the signals. The reconstruction could be carried beyond the 97 per cent point, save for the fact that our original data vectors are not reliable beyond that point. We must acknowledge that these hypothetical generators correspond to nothing at all in reality. Vectors defined in this arbitrary fashion are idealizations to which it is almost impossible to attach a physical significance. Second, was it possible to make it less abstract? By comparing the reconstruction equations which reproduce the initial signal vectors as a linear combination of this orthonormal vector set *before* a signal has been established as meaningful for the animal, and again *after* that same signal has been established as meaningful, a very striking difference can be discerned. The coefficients necessary to reconstruct the electrical activity of different anatomical regions before the stimulus has been made meaningful differ greatly from structure to structure. That is, the composition of electrical activity in these various sites differs from region to region. After training, when the stimulus has been made meaningful, computation of regression equations reveals that in various anatomical regions of the brain the regression equations now contain essentially identical terms. In other words, certain components of the electrical activity in different places appear to be made homogeneous by attaching *significance* to the stimulus evoking the electrical activity [16].

In recent studies [13, 14], the neural concomitants of these similarities in evoked potential waveshapes were studied, using chronically implanted movable microelectrodes. The post-stimulus histograms describing the probability of firing in neural ensembles in response to differential conditioned stimuli were recorded throughout extensive regions of the thalamus, by mapping with these movable probes. The results showed unequivocally that responsive neural ensembles in many different brain regions displayed essentially identical patterns of firing upon the presentation of conditioned stimuli. Great differences in firing patterns were observed from region to region in untrained animals. These data provide evidence that an extensively distributed neural system displays a characteristic mode of activity when a familiar stimulus is presented to a trained animal.

7.5 ANATOMICAL AND PHYSIOLOGICAL IMPLICATIONS

Turning to the question of the anatomical and physiological significance of such an analysis, we used the following stratagem to try to rotate the initial orthonormal set into a set of vectors that would span the space but that would now be oriented to correspond to some definable anatomical or physiological entity. The procedure which was followed began with a principal-component analysis. Consider the coefficients representing the contribution of the first principal component to each signal vector. That signal vector which requires the greatest loading coefficient for the first component in its regression equation is the signal vector which lies closest to the first principal axis in the hyperspace. Define that signal as the first physiological factor. Then use the least-mean-square techniques (see Chapter 9) to subtract the contribution of that first physiological factor from all other waveshapes. Deal now with the residuals in the same fashion. Simply repeat this operation, and thus construct that set of physiological processes which is the best possible approximation to the mathematical idealization represented by the principal-component solution. This procedure results in a somewhat increased residual error, but it provides a description of the activity in each place in the brain as the result of the linear interaction of a specified set of anatomical influences.

Using this convention to re-examine the data before and after a given stimulus acquires meaning, we observe a very interesting fact: the dominant influence on most brain regions when a visual stimulus without informational significance is presented to an animal is the sensory-specific thalamic nucleus corresponding to that modality of input, that is, the lateral geniculate body in the case of vision. If the same computation is repeated after the visual input is made meaningful, the dominant influence on various brain regions comes from the nonsensory-specific system, particularly the so-called midline thalamic nuclei. These are the structures where previously cited data indicated that activity was not stimulus bound. These findings indicate that a portion of the activity observed in the brain when a stimulus is presented arises from the action of the stimulus itself. However, a portion presumably originating in nonsensory-specific regions of the brain is not directly produced by the action of the stimulus but represents the *release* of stored patterns of activity, *established by previous experience*. When an animal makes a mistake, whether he makes it spontaneously or because a drug has interfered with the performance of the response, this similarity in regression equations deteriorates. Certain structures, usually in the thalamic reticular system, depart from adherence to this common set of rules and display idiosyncratic behavior. They depart from membership in a tightly organized system with *common* processes and display characteristic *individual* process. Where do these common components come from?

7.6 CHARACTERISTICS OF ENDOGENOUSLY GENERATED ACTIVITY

The remainder of this discussion examines the characteristics of endogenously generated activity (see [8] for a documented review of this topic). The first description of such activity was reported by Livanov [21], as a phenomenon which he called "assimilation of the rhythm." If some frequency of repetition is selected for the intermittent conditioned stimulus used in a training situation, as the animal begins to learn the significance of that stimulus, electrical rhythms at the fundamental, the first subharmonic, or the first harmonic of that frequency come to dominate the resting activity during the intertrial interval. If the animal at that stage is returned to his home environment and recordings are taken there, no such activity can be seen. When the animal is brought back into the training situation, this assimilated rhythm is reactivated. Assimilated rhythms have been seen in rat, cat, dog, rabbit, monkey, and man in a wide variety of experimental situations and over a range of frequencies from 3 to around 30 per second. Assimilation is a fairly widespread phenomenon. Assimilated rhythms can be seen in many regions of the brain, but they tend to arise first, are most marked, and persist longest in nonsensory-specific regions [8].

Studying the patterns of discharge displayed by single units, Morrell has shown that single units display a phenomenon like assimilated rhythms [23]. If a nervous system is stimulated with a rhythmic stimulus, single neuron responses can be organized so that they regularly follow the stimulus, if local DC polarization is applied to alter the reactivity of the cell. After a period of such rhythmic stimulation, if the stimulus frequency is changed, the response of the unit to the new stimulus frequency persists at the old rhythm. In recent work, Morrell has shifted to syncopated patterns instead of regular rhythms and found that the cells can also reproduce syncopated patterns [25]. Working on the chronically isolated cortical slab, Dewson and Chow have shown a very similar phenomenon. Under certain experimental conditions, the chronically isolated cortical slab is capable of displaying a previously experienced pattern of discharge in response to a new pattern of stimulation [4].

The question of the possible functional nature of these assimilated rhythms was raised first about 1956 by Chow, Dement, and the present author at the University of Chicago [3]. We took advantage of a procedure devised by Morrell and Jasper, which they called cortical conditioning [26]. Cortical conditioning is a sensory-sensory conditioning procedure in which two sensory stimuli are systematically paired. In a typical experiment, one stimulus is a steady tone, whereas the other stimulus is a rhythmic flicker. After a certain amount of such pairing, an interesting phenomenon is observed. On presentation of the steady tone, a rhythmic discharge *at the frequency of the flicker* appears in visual regions of the brain. Steady tone comes to elicit rhythmic discharge in the visual areas. First, we trained a cat to perform an avoidance response to a flickering light. Second, we paired steady tone with flickering lights until steady tone elicited frequency-specific response in visual cortex. That frequency-specific response was the release of a stored pattern acquired by experience and therefore represents an assimilated process. When assimilated visual rhythms came to be elicited by the tone, the animal was returned to the avoidance apparatus in which flicker had been used to establish an avoidance response, and steady tone was presented. Recording from the animal's brain showed that the steady tone elicited frequency-specific response at the flicker frequency in the visual cortex, but the animal did *not* perform the conditioned response. We concluded that the mere occurrence of assimilated rhythm in the cortex was not sufficient to release a functional behavior established by a peripheral stimulus with the same temporal characteristics.

Schuckman and Battersby [28] repeated the experiment just described, with one minor change: the sequence of steps was reversed. The animal was first subjected to cortical conditioning. After the tone came to elicit frequency-specific response in visual cortex, the animal was trained to avoidance of flicker. After the avoidance response was established to flicker, steady tone was presented. Recordings showed frequency-specific response in visual cortex accompanied quite often by performance of the avoidance behavior learned to the flicker. For some reason, probably related to the extinction of a generalization gradient resulting from the interspersing of the sensory conditioning procedure after the original avoidance training, in our procedure this result was not forthcoming. Under appropriate circumstances, however, the release of assimilated rhythms can be accompanied by the performance of a learned behavior initially acquired to stimuli at that frequency. This suggestion that assimilated rhythms represent potentially functional processes received support from the data on noncorrespondence of rhythms between specific and nonspecific regions of the brain in erroneous performance, which we described earlier.

7.7 ELECTROPHYSIOLOGICAL STUDY OF ANIMAL GENERALIZATION

The bulk of the evidence that assimilated rhythms are functionally relevant comes from studies of generalization. By *generalization* we mean the tendency of an animal to perform a previously established learned response when presented with a stimulus with characteristics similar to the stimulus actually used during training. Under such circumstances, the animal will perform the previously learned response with a probability which diminishes as the similarity between the two stimuli decreases. The "generalization gradient" is the decreasing probability of such performance as a function of increasing difference between stimuli. Let us examine the electrophysiological events observed when an animal generalizes and performs a previously learned response upon the presentation of a neutral stimulus.

The top portion of Figure 7.1 illustrates the intertrial activity in an animal at the beginning of avoidance training with a 10-per-second flicker; there is relatively little rhythmicity to be seen in any leads. In contrast, the middle portion of the figure shows the electrical rhythms in the animal while resting between trials, at about the 25-per cent performance level. In the top two leads is seen a 20-per-second bursting, while the third, fifth, and sixth channels show a 5-per-second subharmonic. At this stage, such rhythmic activity often dominates the intertrial record. If, however, the

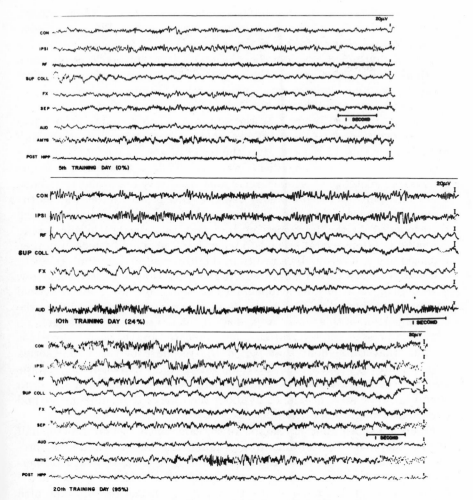

Fig. 7.1 CON: bipolar transcortical (visual) derivation; IPSI: bipolar derivation from the same optic gyrus; RF: midbrain reticular formation; SUIP COLL: superior colliculus; FX: fornix; SEP: septum; AUD: auditory cortex; AMYG: lateral amygdaloid complex; POST HIPP: dorsal hippocampus. Spontaneous activity at different stages of training. "Assimilation of rhythm" during avoidance training using ten-per-second flicker as conditioned stimulus. (From [11].)

animal is returned to his home cage, then these rhythms vanish, to reappear if he is reintroduced into the training apparatus. When an animal reaches 100-per cent performance levels, as seen in the bottom records, such intertrial rhythmicity cannot be observed. If a mistake occurs, such rhythmic activity returns to the intertrial record for a period of time shortly after the inappropriate reenforcement (from the animal's viewpoint), and then again diminishes [11].

The next records (Figure 7.2) were obtained when an animal which had been trained to perform an avoidance response, pressing a lever in the wall of his cage within 15 seconds after the onset of a *4-per-second* flicker, was exposed to a *10-per-second* flickering light. The bottom channel is the lateral geniculate, the "primary relay nucleus" for vision, which responded quite faithfully to the peripheral visual event. Flicker onset was at the first arrow. The initial response of the visual cortex, seen in the top channel, corresponded to the frequency of the light as indicated in the lateral geniculate. After several seconds, a slow wave appeared which was then replaced in a half second by a return to the 10-per-second rhythm. In about a second, the slow wave reappeared. At about the time of the second arrow, a second or so after the reappearance of that slow wave in the visual cortex, the animal displayed a startle response, stood up, and during the ensuing portion of this record walked slowly across the cage to the far wall, where he pressed the lever at the time indicated by the last arrow. It is obvious that throughout that period the response of the visual cortex approximates a 4-per-second rhythm, rather than corresponding to the 10-per-second flicker. In the mesencephalic reticular formation, the sixth channel, a slow wave developed at about the time of the middle arrow and persisted through this period [9].

Figure 7.3 shows another example of the same phenomenon. The top half of this figure shows recordings from a number of structures in a cat previously trained to a 4-per-second flicker, while generalizing to a 10-per-second flicker. (These records come from work by Mark Weiss, in the Center for Brain Research at the University of Rochester [9].) The fifth channel is the response of the lateral geniculate, which corresponds to the flicker frequency. The third and fourth channels are from the visual cortex. In the middle portion of the visual-cortex record, a very clear slow activity at 4-per-second can be observed. Simultaneously, on the upper contour of the slow wave a faster component appears, at a 10-per-second frequency. In contrast, the bottom half of this figure was recorded after differentiation, during which the animal was punished for performing the avoidance response to the 10-per-second flicker. It is apparent that the slow rhythm is now essentially absent from the visual cortex, exhibiting a one-to-one correspondence in frequency with the lateral geniculate, which follows the

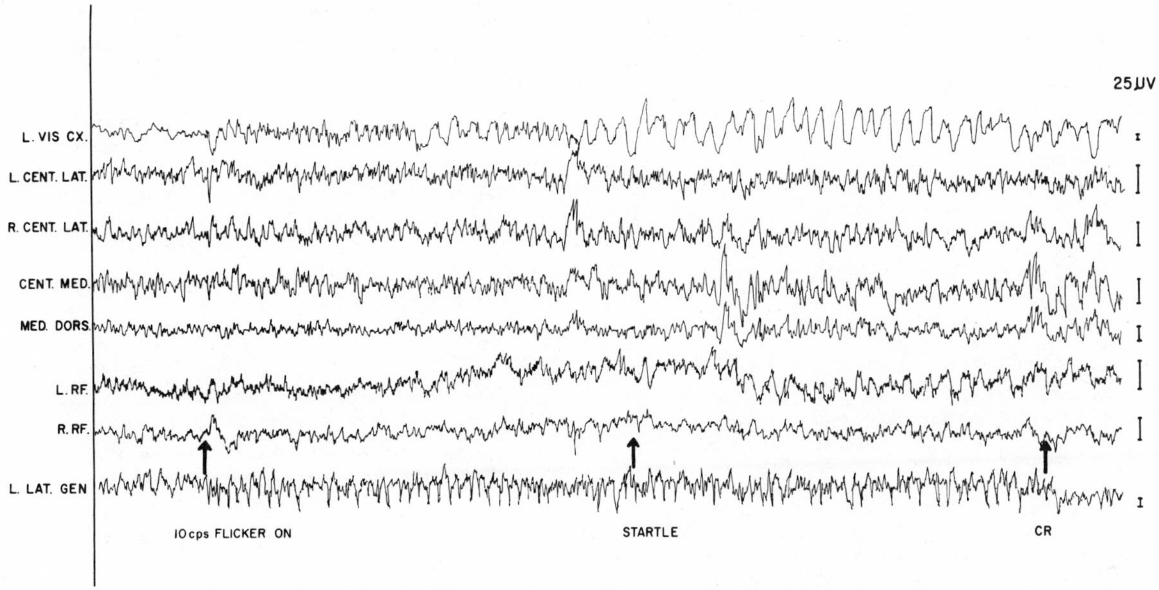

Fig. 7.2 L. VIS. CX.: left visual cortex; L. CENT. LAT.: left centralis lateralis; R. CENT. LAT.: Right centralis lateralis; CENT. MED.: center median; MED. DORS.: medialis dorsalis; L. RF.: left mesencephalic reticular formation; R. RF.: right mesencephalic reticular formation; L. LAT. GEN.: left lateral geniculate. Generalization to 10 cps flicker after training to 4 cps. All leads bipolar. (Histological verification not available.) Electrical responses to ten-per-second flicker during generalization of the conditioned avoidance response after avoidance training with a four-per-second flicker-tracer-conditioned stimulus.

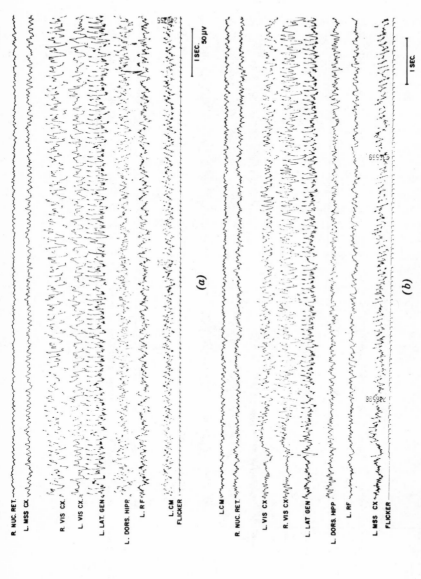

Fig. 7.3 R. NUC. RET.: right nucleus reticularis; L. MSS CX.: left medial suprasylvian cortex; R. VIS CX.: right visual cortex; L. VIS CX.: left visual cortex; L. LAT. GEN.: left lateral geniculate; L. DORS. HIPP.: left dorsal hippocampus; L. FR: left mesencephalic reticular formation; L. CM: left center median. (Histological verification not available.) (a) Electrical responses to ten-per-second flicker during generalization, after avoidance training using a four-per-second flicker-tracer-conditioned stimulus. (b) Electrical responses to ten-per-second flicker following differentiation of avoidance response. (From [30].)

198

flicker. An average-response computer was in parallel with the EEG pre-amplifiers while the records in Figure 7.3 were obtained.

Figure 7.4 illustrates the average response computation from the lateral geniculate during generalization to 10-per-second flicker. A rhythmic process appears in the lateral geniculate, with a periodicity of 100 millliseconds. In other words, the lateral geniculate is responding accurately to the 10-per-second flicker stimulus. This and the subsequent averages are each based on 100 repetitions of the flicker during numerous behavioral trials.

Figure 7.5 represents a number of averages taken from the visual cortex. The top waveshape is the average response of the visual cortex to the 4-per-second conditioned stimulus which was actually used during avoidance training. The second tracing shows the waveshape elicited in the visual cortex by the 10-per-second flicker during generalization. There is a 10-per-second spike visible on the upward aspect of that tracing, but that waveshape clearly is not periodic at 100-millisecond intervals. In contrast, the third tracing illustrates the effect of the 10-per-second flicker after differentiation. The animal has been punished for lever pressing during 10-per-second flicker, and it now reacts to that frequency as if it were informationally different from what it was during generalization.

There is now a clear periodic response at the actual stimulus frequency, similar to the response in the previous geniculate average. Thus the second waveshape shows the average response of the visual cortex when an animal treats a new event as if it were functionally equivalent to a previously experienced event. In order to explain his behavior, we argued that the new stimulus released previously stored information. These data thus represent

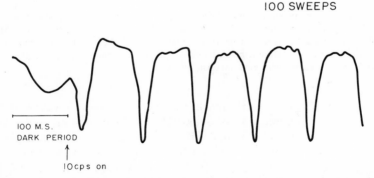

IOO SWEEPS

IOO M.S.
DARK PERIOD

IOcps on

Fig. 7.4 Average response computed from lateral geniculate during generalization to ten-per-second flicker, after avoidance training using a four-per-second flicker-tracer-conditioned stimulus. (From [30].)

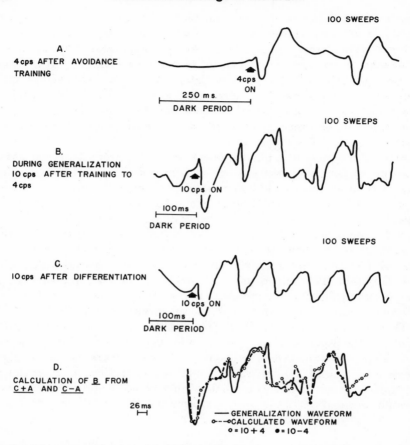

Fig. 7.5 Average response computed from visual cortex. (A) In response to four-per-second flicker after avoidance training using a four-per-second flicker-tracer-conditioned stimulus. (B) During generalization to ten-per-second flicker. (C) In response to ten-per-second flicker after differentiation training. (D) Comparison of generalization waveform with calculated interference pattern. (From [30].)

an interaction between neural mechanisms responsive to a new event and stored information about a prior event. How might incoming and released information interact? What happens if we assume a one-to-one mix between the release of stored information and the input of new information?

We digitized the upper tracing as a series of voltage values through time, $A(t)$. The second tracing was digitized as the series $B(t)$, the third tracing as the series $C(t)$. Is it possible to produce the series $B(t)$ by an algebraic manipulation of the two waveshapes, $A(t)$ and $C(t)$? In that algebraic manipulation, $C(t)$ retained its actual sign, and $A(t)$ was added or subtracted to produce the best possible approximation to $B(t)$. Figure 7.5D shows the best approximation produced by such an arbitrary manipulation. The solid line is the actual data, $B(t)$; the dotted line is the best reconstruction obtained by either adding or subtracting the value of $A(t)$ from $C(t)$. That reconstruction is reasonably good. It is difficult to evaluate the statistical significance of this fit, considering the arbitrary procedure which was carried out. The open and closed circles indicate the optimal operation. In general, if the two waveshapes were in phase, they were added; and if they were out of phase, $A(t)$ was subtracted from $C(t)$. These results suggest that one way to look at the electrical activity during generalization is as if it were composed of two components, one of which reflects the physical event and one of which reasonably well seems to reconstruct the prior event. Presumably the latter component is released "memory."

Figure 7.6 indicates comparable data from the reticular formation. Similarly, the first tracing shows the effect of the 4-per-second stimulus after training, the second shows the interference pattern during generalization, the third shows the pattern after differentiation, and the fourth shows the adequacy of the fit resulting from the assumption that it is an interference pattern. Again, a stored pattern seems to be released during generalization.

Subsequently, we carried out a detailed analysis [15, 27] of a body of data provided from animals trained by my colleague Dr. Arnold Leiman, now at the University of California, Berkeley. This particular body of data consisted of a group of 30 generalization trials. Those 30 trials were distributed throughout a fairly long recording session, in which the stimulus most frequently presented to the animal was the 10-per-second flicker CS which had been used during training. Thirty times during that session, however, a 7.7-per-second flicker was introduced instead of the 10-per-second stimulus which had actually been used to establish the response. The animal's reactions to those 30 test presentations were so nicely distributed as to provide an ideal body of data for intensive analysis. In six trials, CR_1, the animal performed generalization of the conditioned response with a latency slightly more than 2 seconds. In six trials, CR_2, he generalized with a latency slightly over 3 seconds. In six trials, CR_3, he generalized with a latency slightly over 4 seconds. In six trials, CR_4, generalization occurred with a latency slightly over 5 seconds. Finally, in six of those trials, NR, the cat failed to respond, although the stimulus remained on over 30 seconds.

The data in Figure 7.7 are taken from the lateral geniculate body, and represent average responses from those different groups of trials, ranged from top to bottom in order of increasing latency. The averages in the

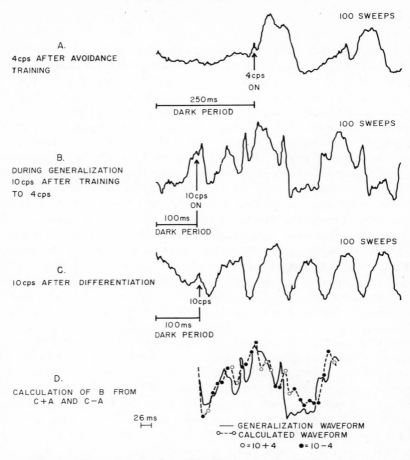

Fig. 7.6 Same as Figure 7.5, but data derived from mesencephalic reticular formation.

left-hand column summate the initial evoked potentials in the six trials of each group. That average is based on an N of 6 in the left-hand column. The purpose of that initial average is simply to show that *the reactivity of the animal was quite the same in all these trials*, as evidenced by the similar amplitude and shape of the initial response in the lateral geniculate body. The remaining averages are based on an N of 48 samples each and are, second by second, the average response summed across the six trials in each of those five latency groups—again arranged from top to bottom. The most striking feature of these data can be seen by comparing the tracings in the bottom row, coming from trials in which no generalization occurred, with

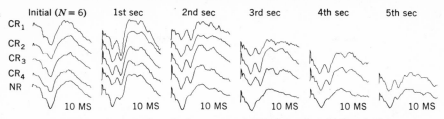

Fig. 7.7   Averaged evoked responses in the lateral geniculate body.

the tracings in any of the rows above. Note that in the bottom row the process can be described as essentially *unimodal*, with one large deflection. We consider this process to be "evoked." In all of the averages obtained from the cases where generalization occurred, the wave shape is *bimodal*. There is a pronounced late process, of size equal to or larger than the early neural process, which appears when the previously established behavior is released by this neutral stimulus.

It is extremely informative to compare the waveshapes evoked by a neutral stimulus during generalization, when it elicits no behavioral response, with the waveshape elicited by the conditioned stimulus during performance of the conditioned response. Examples of such waveshapes, from two different brain regions, are provided in Figure 7.8. Note that during generalization (middle row of waveshapes), the neutral stimulus elicits an evoked response essentially identical with the response to the conditioned stimulus (top waveshapes). During trials resulting in no behavioral generalization, however, the neutral stimulus elicits responses which seem to lack some of the later components (bottom waveshapes). We suggested that the earlier components might largely reflect afferent input, whereas the later components (II and III) might reflect *readout* processes released by that input [27].

By subtracting the average response waveshape when generalization fails to occur (input alone) from the average-response waveshape when the same stimulus results in the performance of generalization (input plus readout), it is possible to parcel out the common "evoked" component and obtain a clear sample of the *difference* process (readout alone), that is, the *endogenous* process which takes place in a neuronal population when stored information is released by a neutral stimulus. This operation has been performed in the structures in the animal for which recordings were obtained during this set of trials. A similar operation, but in less detail, has been carried out on three other animals trained similarly and generalizing under similar circumstances. Basically similar difference processes have

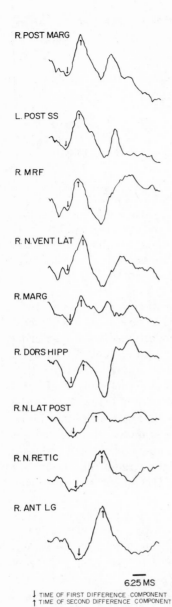

R. POST MARG

L. POST SS

R. MRF

R. N. VENT LAT

R. MARG

R. DORS HIPP

R. N. LAT POST

R. N. RETIC

R. ANT LG

6.25 MS

↓ TIME OF FIRST DIFFERENCE COMPONENT
↑ TIME OF SECOND DIFFERENCE COMPONENT

Fig. 7.8 Comparison of waveshapes evolved by neutral stimulus with those elicited by conditioned stimulus.

been seen in the visual cortex and the reticular formation of three animals in addition to the one here presented [10].

Figure 7.9 illustrates the difference between the neural events which occur when a neutral stimulus releases a previously learned behavior and when that same stimulus fails to elicit any learned performance [15]. The figure contains a number of tracings, arranged from top to bottom in order

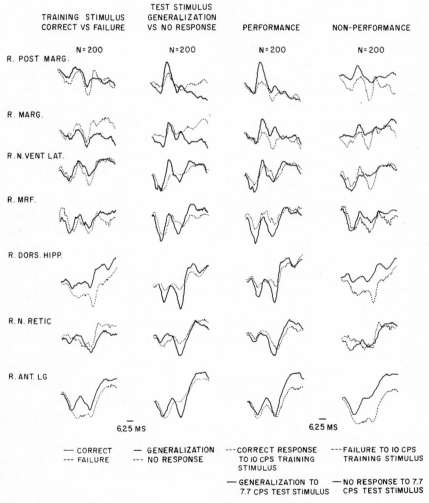

Fig. 7.9 Comparison of average evoked responses to training and test stimuli during performance and nonperformance.

of the latency of onset of the difference process. It is striking that a set of structures which lie quite far apart show extremely small latency differences. The distances between these structures are such that neural propagation of this process in so short a time is highly implausible. It seems more probable that this difference process is released independently but simultaneously in these various structures, as the result of a perturbation impinging on these various populations of cells from the peripheral event. Some other structures, however, show a physiologically reasonable difference in latency, that is, a longer latency for the difference process. It is interesting that the structure with longest latency is the anterior lateral geniculate, nearest to the periphery of the animal.

It appears as though several regions of the brain release the difference process with apparent simultaneity. This neural event appears to be related to the release of stored information. The consequence of this activation is exerted in a corticofugal direction to alter the responsiveness of the more peripheral structures. Further, the basic characteristics of the difference processes are quite the same from structure to structure.

If we consider the released difference process as a reflection of the readout of a stored memory, then the place where this process appears earliest would be a logical candidate for the site of the engram. These and more recent data, however, indicate that there is no anatomical region where this process appears first; rather it occurs simultaneously in anatomically extensive regions [10, 13, 14]. These findings indicate that memory is mediated by an anatomically distributed representational system.

These data show that when a learned behavior is released by a neutral event, there appears a readout or difference process in the evoked potential which does not appear when that behavior is not released. The *effect* of the difference process is to make the physiological response to the neutral stimulus correspond well to the actual effect of the conditioned stimulus used in training. The extent of such correspondence has been quantitatively assessed in our recent experiments on differential generalization [17]. Animals were trained to press a lever for food (CR) upon presentation of one frequency of flicker (V_1). They were then trained to press a second lever to avoid shock (CAR) upon presentation of a second frequency of flicker (V_2). After this discrimination had been greatly overlearned, flicker at a third frequency (V_3) was occasionally presented interspersed between random presentations of V_1 and V_2. Presentations of this neutral stimulus sometimes elicited pressing of the lever appropriate for food $(V_3 \, CR)$ and sometimes of the lever appropriate for shock avoidance $(V_3 \, CAR)$.

The waveshape evoked in many brain regions during $V_3 \, CR$ was markedly different from that observed during $V_3 \, CAR$. Further, the waveshape during $V_3 CR$ closely resembled the evoked potential usually elicited during $V_1 CR$, whereas the waveshape during $V_3 CAR$ closely resembled that usually seen during $V_2 CAR$. These conclusions were based on the computation of correlation coefficients between the responses recorded under these different conditions.

Results obtained from eight cats are illustrated in Figure 7.10. The intermittent line between $V_3 CR$ and $V_3 CAR$ indicates the intervals during which the difference between these average response waveshapes was significant at better than the .01 level. Similar results were obtained from a ninth animal trained to an approach-approach discrimination. These findings demonstrate unequivocally that during differential generalization, an electrical wave is released in the brain which corresponds to the usual effect of a specific stimulus. This released process cannot be attributed to the action of the stimulus itself, since two radically different processes can be released by the same physical stimulus. The readout process appears before any overt movement of the animal. It does not depend on the position or orientation of the animal. The differential generalization experiment permits us to rule out unspecific origins for the readout process, such as arousal, attention, muscle tension, movement, and motivational level. *These data support the contention that the particular waveshape of the released process reflects the specific information about a previous experience, that is, the activation of a particular memory.* The results of related microelectrode studies [13] show that the firing patterns of neuronal ensembles during generalization to a neutral stimulus faithfully reproduce the firing patterns usually elicited by the conditioned stimulus.

These observations might explain the similarity in waveshape which appears on factor analysis of the signal set elicited by the presentation of a familiar stimulus to a trained animal. Signals in various regions contain both

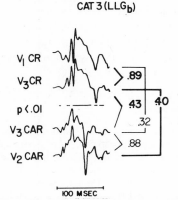

CAT 3 (LLG$_b$)

V_1 CR

V_3 CR   .89

p <.01   43   40

                        .32

V_3 CAR   .88

V_2 CAR

100 MSEC

Fig. 7.10 Comparison of waveshapes during conditioned response with those during conditioned avoidance response.

evoked and endogenous components in varying ratio. The composite waveshape approaches a constant form in all places. *These potentials represent similarities in the probability of coherence in the activity of large populations of neurons through time.*

7.8 CONCLUSION

Training seems to accomplish stabilization of the transition probabilities of similar stochastic processes in different neural networks. Consider the population of neurons in a structure to be a network capable of assuming a number of states. The averaged evoked potentials under specified conditions represent the time course of coherence in that state. During conditioning, the transition probabilities of these Markov processes have been constrained to follow similar rules in different cellular populations. Subsequently, a neutral event releases a behavior which logically requires utilization of stored information about a prior event. When this happens, these various neural populations are driven into a mode of oscillation which follows those same transition rules.

This is quite different from the picture of memory as mediated by the discharge of specific cells constituting a specific pathway between an input region and an output region. The present picture attributes memory to the stabilization of certain modes of oscillation in a neural population. A specific item of information corresponds to a given mode of oscillation in a network. Neural populations in different regions involved in a common mode of response apparently have the ability to transfer neural activity from one system to another in a fashion which selects certain response patterns, almost as if resonance were involved. *The transmission of information in a scheme of this sort involves the coupling of common modes rather than the traversal of a specific pathway.*

Although further work is needed to evaluate the relative merits of the connectionistic formulation and the statistical model which has been presented, our purpose will have been accomplished if the existence of these two alternative ways of viewing the problem has been clearly established.

REFERENCES

1. Burns, B. D., and G. K. Smith, "Transmission of Information in the Unanesthetized Cat's Isolated Forebrain," *J. Physiol.* (*London*), **164**, 1962, 238–251.
2. Chow, K. L., "Visual Discriminations after Extensive Ablation of Optic Tract and Visual Cortex," *Brain Research*, **9**, 1968, 363–366.
3. Chow, K. L., W. C. Dement, and E. R. John, "Conditioned Electrocortical Graphic Potentials and Behavioral Avoidance Response in Cat," *J. Neurophysiol.*, **20**, 1957, 482–493.

4. Dewson, J. H., III, K. L. Chow, and J. Engel, Jr., "Bioelectrical Activity of Isolated Cortex. II. Steady Potentials and Induced Surface-Negative Cortical Responses," *Neuropsychologia*, **2**, 1964, 167–174.

5. Doty, R. W., "Functional Significance of the Topographical Aspects of the Retino-Cortical Projection," in Jung, R., and H. Kornhuber (editors), *The Visual System: Neurophysiology and Psychophysics*, Springer, Berlin, 1961, pp. 228–245.

6. Fox, S. S., and J. H. O'Brien, "Duplication of Evoked Potential Waveform by Curve of Probability of Firing of a Single Cell," *Science*, **147**, 1965, 888–890.

7. Hernandez-Peon, R., H. Scherrer, and M. Jouvet, "Modification of Electrical Activity in Cochlear Nucleus During 'Attention' in Unanesthetized Cats," *Science*, **123**, 1956, 331–332.

8. John, E. R., "Higher Nervous Functions: Brain Functions and Learning," *Ann. Rev. Physiol.*, **23**, 1961, 451.

9. John, E. R., "Neural Mechanisms of Decision Making," in Fields, W. S., and W. Abbot (editors), *Information Storage and Neural Control*, Charles C. Thomas, Springfield, Ill., 1963, pp. 243–282.

10. John, E. R., *Mechanisms of Memory*, Academic Press, New York, 1967.

11. John, E. R., and K. F. Killam, "Electrophysiological Correlates of Avoidance Conditioning in the Cat," *J. Pharm. Exptl. Therap.*, **125**, 1959, 252.

12. John, E. R., and K. F. Killam, "Electrophysiological Correlates of Differential Approach-Avoidance Conditioning in the Cat," *J. Nerv. Mental Dis.*, **131**, 1960, 183.

13. John, E. R., and P. P. Morgades, "Neural Correlates of Conditioned Responses Studied with Multiple Chronically Implanted Moving Microelectrodes," *Exptl. Neurol.*, **23**, 1969, 412–425.

14. John, E. R., and P. P. Morgades, "The Pattern and Anatomical Distribution of Evoked Potentials and Multiple Unit Activity Elicited by Conditional Stimuli in Trained Cats," *Communications Behav. Biol.*, **3**, 1969, 181–207.

15. John, E. R., D. S. Ruchkin, A. Leiman, E. Sachs, and H. Ahn, "Electrophysiological Studies of Generalization Using Both Peripheral and Central Conditioned Stimuli," *Proc. XXIII Int. Cong. Physiol. Sciences, Tokyo*, **87**, 1965, 618–627.

16. John, E. R., D. S. Ruchkin, and J. Villegas, "Signal Analysis and Behavioral Correlates of Evoked Potential Configurations in Cats," *Ann. N. Y. Acad. Sci.*, **112**, 1964, 362–420.

17. John, E. R., M. Shimokochi, and F. Bartlett, "Neural Readout from Memory in Generalization," *Science*, **164**, 1969, 1534–1536.

18. Klüver, H., "Functional Significance of the Geniculostriate System," *Biol. Symp.*, **7**, 1942, 263–264.

19. Lashley, K. S., "In Search of the Engram," *Symp. Soc. Exptl. Biol.*, **4**, 1950, 454–482.

20. Livanov, M. N., *Proc. XXII Intern. Congr. Physiol., Leiden*, 1962, 899.

21. Livanov, M. N., and K. L. Poliakov, "The Electrical Reactions of the Cerebral Cortex of a Rabbit During the Formation of a Conditioned Defense Reflex by Means of Rhythmic Stimulation," *Izv. Akad. Nauk. USSR. Ser. Biol.*, **3**, 1945, 286.

22. McAdam, D. W., "Electroencephalographic Changes and Classical Aversive Conditioning in the Cat," *Exptl. Neurol.*, **6**, 1962, 357.

23. Morrell, F., "Effect of Anodal Polarization on the Firing Pattern of Single Cortical Cells," *Ann. N. Y. Acad. Sci.*, **92**, 1961, 860–876.

24. Morrell, F., "Electrophysiological Contributions to the Neural Basis of Learning," *Physiol. Rev.*, **41**, 1961, 443.

25. Morrell, F., J. Engel, and W. Bouris, *Neurosciences Research Program*, Boulder, Colo., 1966.

26. Morrell, F., and H. Jasper, "Electrographic Studies of the Formation of Temporary Connections in the Brain," *Electroenceph. Clin. Neurophysiol.*, **8**, 1956, 201–215.

27. Ruchkin, D. S., and E. R. John, "Evoked Potential Correlates of Generalization," *Science*, **153**, 1966, 209–211.

28. Schuckman, H., and W. S. Battersby, "Frequency Specific Mechanisms in Learning, I. Occipital Activity during Sensory Pre-Conditioning," *Electroenceph. Clin. Neurophysiol.*, **18**, 1965, 44–55.

29. Winans, S. S., "Visual Form Discrimination after Removal of the Visual Cortex in Cats," *Science*, **158**, 1967, 944–946.

30. Weiss, Marc, *Unpublished Master's Thesis*, University of Rochester, 1962. Data included in E. R. John, "Neural Mechanisms of Decision Making," in Fields, W. S., and W. Abbot (editors), *Information Storage and Neural Control*, Charles C. Thomas, Springfield, Ill., 1963, pp. 243–282.

FURTHER READINGS

1. Hammond, Kenneth R., "Computer Graphics as an Aid to Learning," *Science*, **172**, 1971, 903–908.

2. Neff, William D., *Contributions to Sensory Physiology*, Vol. 1, Academic Press, New York, 1965.

3. Neff, William D., *Contributions to Sensory Physiology*, Vol. 2, Academic Press, New York, 1967.

4. Russell, Roger W., *Frontiers in Physiological Psychology*, Academic Press, New York, 1966.

5. Talland, George A., *Deranged Memory, A Psychonomic Study of the Amnesic Syndrome*, Academic Press, New York, 1965.

CHAPTER 8

Manifestations of Structural Defects of the Nervous System

RICHARD L. MASLAND

Chairman, Department of Neurology, Columbia University Neurological Institute, New York, New York

Contents

8.1   INTRODUCTION

The nervous system represents a communications network of the utmost complexity. Our knowledge of its mechanisms is derived from an analysis of the function and structure of its elementary units, the neuron and the synapse; from the responses derived from standardized "natural" stimuli; from "artificial" stimulation of the nervous system or its parts; and finally from disorders of function observed to result from demonstrable injury of its parts. Such functional disorders are reviewed in the present chapter, with particular emphasis on the effect of the nature, location, duration, and extent of the injury upon the symptomatology which it produces.

Our concern here is not so much with communications as with the communicator, for in every communication process there exists at some point the human mechanism of communication. We propose in this chapter to review current knowledge regarding the nature of this mechanism, with emphasis on the underlying processes and structures on which its function depends. In doing so, we can envisage three possible gains from such a review: This mechanism must be taken into account in any communication process; it represents a model system, certain aspects of which may have implications for other systems; and, finally, information derived from other approaches to communication may enhance our understanding of the operation and breakdown of the human.

8.2 METHODS OF STUDYING THE HUMAN MECHANISM OF COMMUNICATION

Our knowledge of the workings of this mechanism is derived from several methods of study, each with certain important limitations. Much regarding structure has been learned from actual dissection, and more recently by special microscopic staining techniques capable of demonstrating throughout its length a nerve pathway which has been experimentally injured at any point. Such techniques are valuable for demonstrating the origin and destination of the interconnecting nerve pathways within the brain. A second method of study is by electrical recording of nervous activity. This method is still in its infancy and suffers serious limitations. Recording from the surface of the skull reveals fluctuations of electrical potential where there exists synchronous activity of large groups of nerve cells. Recording by microelectrode reveals the activity of single neurons or of very limited groups. Our present methods provide only partial information regarding the patterns of simultaneous activation of widely separated neurons within the brain—patterns which must underlie its normal activity.

Electrical stimulation of the brain has similar limitations, but it has provided important information regarding the results of activation of circumscribed regions on the surface or in the depths of the brain. Such activation, since it must be of the grossest pattern, is more likely actually to lead to inhibition of ongoing activity than to its duplication.

Possibly the most revealing method for the study of the nervous system has been the observation of the results of naturally occurring or experimental destruction of areas or pathways within the system.

It must be noted that loss of a function following removal of some circumscribed area does not necessarily indicate that that function is subserved exclusively by the area removed. We may merely have interrupted an important inflow or outflow channel, or more likely destroyed one component of a complex mechanism whose other elements extend much more widely throughout the nervous system.

8.3 AREAS OF THE BRAIN AND ASSOCIATED ACTIVITIES

In spite of the foregoing limitations, we do have considerable information regarding those areas of the brain which are involved in certain definable activities, and of the types of deficit that follow their removal.

Figure 8.1 [21] shows four areas of the surface of the brain having the most direct relations with the major channels of inflow and outflow of external information. Connections are crossed—the left hemisphere relating to the right side of the body and vice versa. Area 17 is the primary vision receptor area. The visual field is projected in a maplike fashion on the visual cortex. Areas 1, 2, and 3 receive sensation from the skin. Here, also, there is in general a point-to-point relationship, information from the face being projected to the lower margin of the area and that from the foot to the upper. This type of spatial array appears ideally designed for the maintenance of spatial orientation—the individual evidently carrying on his cortex a map upon which objects and events in the surroundings may be projected. Just anterior to this "somesthetic" area 1, 2, and 3 is a motor area, stimulation of which leads to rather discrete movements of the opposite parts of the body. Here, also, a similar spatial array is

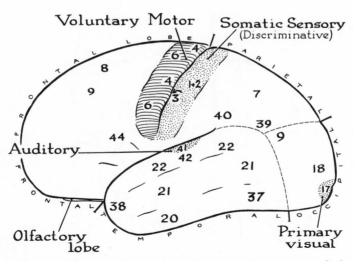

Fig. 8.1   Primary areas of information input to human cortex [21].

preserved. Note, however, that there appears to be considerable plasticity of these responses— the nature of the response and the ease of its production may be considerably modified by previous activity and other ongoing events in the brain.

The fourth shaded area, 41, is the primary auditory receiving area. Although the right ear appears to relate primarily to the left hemisphere, deafness will occur in either ear only if both sides of the brain are destroyed. Furthermore, the spatial array on the cortex relates to pitch and not to environmental spatial relationships. In fact, one must emphasize a fundamental difference in the type of orientation involved in respect to sound as compared with the other senses. The major element of significance in sound relates to its *temporal* sequencing. It is indeed likely that whereas the major emphasis of the other senses relates to orientation in *space*, the emphasis for hearing relates to orientation in *time*.

Figure 8.2 [21] is a cross-sectional diagram of the brain indicating the major inflow and outflow channels. Note that in each instance (except

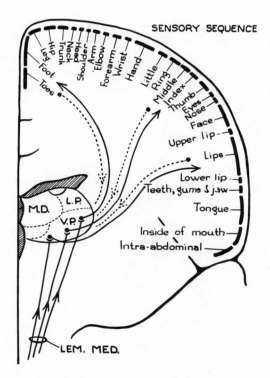

Fig. 8.2 Spatial display of somesthetic data on human cortex [21].

possibly a portion of the motor outflow) there is a "way station" at the base of the brain. Here within the structure labeled V.P. and others exist important gating mechanisms, through which there can be exerted considerable control over inflow to the cortex. Consciousness, awareness, and attention focusing depend on the integrity of this system, referred to by Penfield and Jasper [19] as "centrencephalic." Viewed in this light, the major controlling functions may be subserved in these central regions, the cortex serving as areas to which information is relayed for correlation and evaluation. In recognition of this concept, members of the Pavlovian school often refer to the cortical areas as the "analyzers." Certainly the organization of the cortex is suitable to extensive intermodality correlation and analysis.

Surrounding each of the primary receptor areas is an "association area." Simple functions are apparently analyzed in areas immediately surrounding those points where the primary information is received. In Figure 8.1, for example, area 18 is spoken of as a *visual association area*. If we should excise area 17, the individual becomes, in essence, blind—at least in the field of vision for the opposite side of the body. If, on the other hand, we excise area 18 and leave area 17, the individual will not become blind. He will still recognize the presence of an object and have some crude notion of its location, brightness and existence, but he will not be able to evaluate the quality of the object—its size, shape, form, or meaning. These functions require an interaction between the input—the arriving information and some previous experience—and some information which has been derived from other structures within the nervous system. Similar association areas are presumed to lie behind the somatic sensory area in the areas 40 and 7, or, at least, somewhat anterior to those. Recent investigations suggest that the association area for sensation is not as precisely mapped out as is that for vision. Presumably, areas 42 and 22 are association areas in the auditory sphere. When we consider language, it will be evident that these subserve a most critical function in relation to that activity.

Figure 8.3 depicts an experiment demonstrating the results of injury to one of the primary receptive areas. An animal which has had this area removed has difficulty in learning new patterns of behavior involving the use of the hand for recognition of the quality of objects in his hand. He probably will still retain a sense of touch and certainly will respond to pain, but, when it comes to judging the nature of the object he is feeling, that ability is lost. Interestingly enough, previously retained information may still be present, even when interhemispheric connections have been severed.

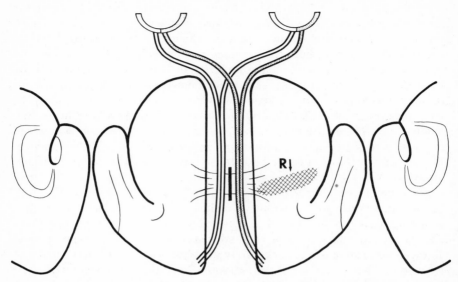

Fig. 8.3 Location of lesions producing loss of tactile learning in left hand; previously learned skill retained.

On Figure 8.4 [17, 3] are depicted several more complicated experiments to demonstrate the way in which information patterns are laid down in the brain. An animal is blindfolded and trained to recognize different shaped objects with his right hand [3]. Information on this skill is presumably laid down in the left side of his brain. This animal will subsequently learn the same task with his left hand in a very brief period of time. In other words, there is a transfer of this skill from one side to the other. If we now train an animal to use his right hand in this fashion, and after he has learned the trick, we then make the section indicated by (2), severing the connections between the left side of the brain and the right, the animal will still demonstrate a capability to learn more quickly with the left hand than he did with the right. In other words, the information which he obtained when he learned with his right hand was transferred across to the other hemisphere at the same time.

If, however, we make section (2) first, and subsequently train the animal to learn a trick with his right hand, we now find that if we wish to train with the left hand we must start from scratch. The information coming in from the right hand into the left hemisphere has not been transferred to the right side, and the right side is on its own. This means that the memory trace of this skill has been laid down in both sides of the brain, even though it was learned on only one side.

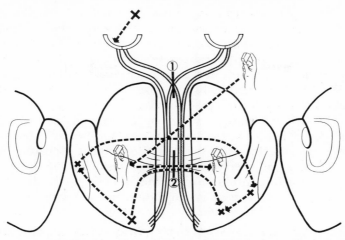

Fig. 8.4 Interhemispheric transfer of learned task. Visual or tactile skill learned with one eye or hand will be transferred readily to the other side unless the interhemispheric pathway has been cut (2) *before* the task is learned. If it is cut *after*, the skill will be found already transferred [3, 18].

The same principle applies for visual information [18]. Thus a similar experiment can be performed by making section (1), which cuts the pathways from the right eye to the left hemisphere and from the left eye to the right hemisphere. Under these circumstances, information coming into the left eye comes only to the left side of the brain. This animal, incidentally, will be able to see with his left eye only those objects which are to the right, as indicated by the cross. If, however, we train an animal to recognize and distinguish objects with his left eye, we then find he knows that trick with his right eye. But if, before we teach him this trick we make the section at point (2), we find that he has to learn it all over with his right eye.

Again, the information from one side coming into one hemisphere is conveyed across the connecting pathway and is laid down on the other side of the brain. These experiments indicate that memory patterns are laid down at least bilaterally and probably rather diffusively within the nervous system. Simple functions such as brightness discrimination, weight, texture, and two-point discrimination apparently can be accomplished adequately within the primary association areas which we have described. But more complicated functions such as the understanding of the significance of an object and finer interpretations probably require the interrelationship of several different sense modalities. For example, an animal may have to see and feel an object to understand what its meaning is and may have to relate this to complex prior experiences to make a judgment about it. For such complex integrations, certain areas of the hemisphere have assumed specialized functions. These functions generally are bilaterally represented, and either side of the brain can subserve them; but they are at the same time rather sharply localized. In Figure 8.5 [22], we have indicated the location of a crucial area in the posterior portion of the temporal lobe. Excision of this area bilaterally will lead to an inability to distinguish minor differences in pairs of visual stimuli.

Figure 8.6 [27, 28] shows a rather similar area but somewhat anterior and more closely related to the auditory area. Following bilateral removal of this area, an animal will lose the ability to differentiate pairs of auditory stimuli—again, a more critical, analytical task. The temporal lobe is apparently a structure within which certain complex tasks, which probably require utilization of intersensory modalities, are accomplished.

8.4 ELECTRICAL RESPONSES ACCOMPANYING ESTABLISHMENT OF INTERSENSORY ASSOCIATIONS

There are some interesting experiments regarding the electrical responses which accompany the establishment of intersensory associations within the brain. These experiments suggest that complex learning processes are associated with the occurence of patterns of activity within the involved areas of the brain. These patterns may be reactivated by subsequent activation of some fragment of the whole. For example, Dr. Frank Morrell [15] at Stanford University has recently described a study of the human electroencephalogram during response to photic and auditory stimulation.

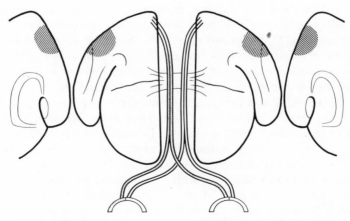

Fig. 8.5 Bilateral posterior temporal lobe lesion causing impaired visual discrimination [22].

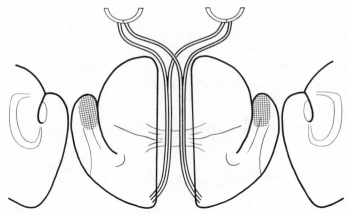

Fig. 8.6   Bilateral superior temporal lobe lesion causing inability to differentiate pairs of auditory stimuli [27, 28].

Recordings were made from the temporal (auditory) area, and from the occipital (visual) area during the presentation of rhythmic tones and/or flashes of light. Responses were averaged to permit recognition of the specific cortical responses elicited. When auditory stimuli were presented, a response was recorded from the auditory area only. When visual stimuli were presented, a response was recorded from the visual area only. When both stimuli were presented simultaneously, responses were recorded from both areas. Most significant, however, was a change which occurred after the subject had been subjected to a long series of the paired stimuli. Under these circumstances, an auditory stimulus which previously produced a response only in the auditory area now produces responses of both auditory and visual areas. As a result of the continued association over a period of time of these two events, a change has occurred in the nervous system such that when one of the events takes place the brain responds as though to their combined occurrence.

A similar series of experiments was done in animals some time ago by Morrell and Jasper [16]—an experiment of conditioned reflexes in monkeys. For this experiment, the animal was subjected to a rhythmic flashing light (Figure 8.7). Under these circumstances in any individual man or animal, we can record a rhythmic response of the occipital rhythm roughly corresponding to the rhythm of the applied flash. This flash was used as a conditioning stimulus. Subsequent to each such exposure, the animal received a shock in his right front paw, as a result of which he jerked it away. This was carried out for a number of trials until the animal had developed a conditioned reflex so that when the light was shined he would himself

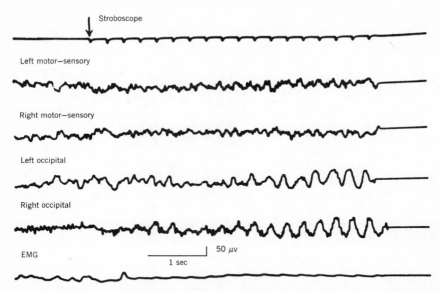

Fig. 8.7 Electroencephalographic tracings from occipital and central areas during the establishment of a conditioned reflex. Upper two tracings: left and right central areas, respectively. Lower two lines: left and right occipital [10].

withdraw his paw (see Figure 8.8). As the conditioned response develops, the electroencephalographic pattern undergoes an interesting alteration. Here again the activity which normally takes place only in the occipital area has in some fashion been linked to the activity of the motor area where this input ordinarily has no effect. Now we see that as the animal prepares to respond, the corresponding area of the brain is activated. Indeed, we might say that this light flash has now developed meaning for the animal in terms of movement and sensation in his paw.

As this experiment is continued and continually reinforced over a period of time, another rather interesting change takes place (Figure 8.9). The area of activation becomes even more sharply circumscribed to the part of the brain which is in fact to be activated in response to the light. Now we see that the rhythmic response to a flashing light appears primarily in the left sensory-motor area—that area which is involved with movement of the right paw. It seems safe to assume that mechanisms such as these underlie the establishment of memory patterns, of patterns of association through which the occurrence of a stimulus that represents only a part of a total picture will in fact activate within the brain the totality of that picture. Clearly, the process of association, which is what this represents, is one of the most fundamental functions of the nervous system. The actual

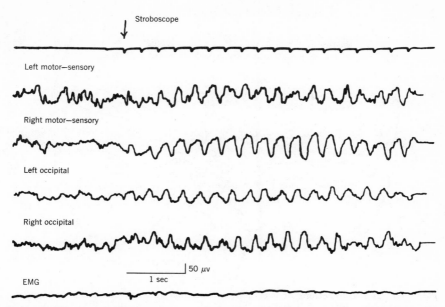

Fig. 8.8 Electroencephalographic tracings from occipital and central areas during the establishment of a conditioned reflex. Upper two tracings: left and right central areas, respectively. Lower two lines: left and right occipital [10].

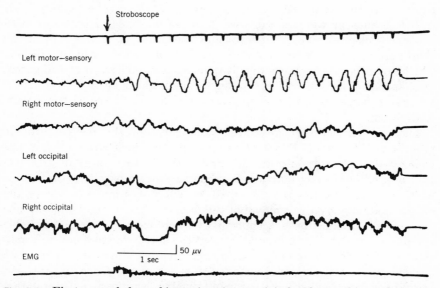

Fig. 8.9 Electroencephalographic tracings from occipital and central areas during the establishment of a conditioned reflex. Upper two tracings: left and right central areas, respectively. Lower two lines: left and right occipital [10].

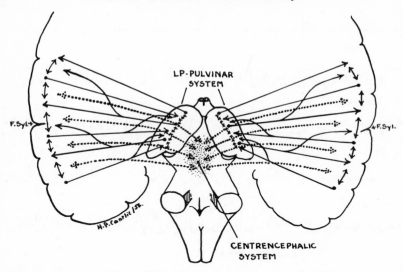

Fig. 8.10 Interconnections of cortex with thalamus and reticular areas of "centren-cephalic" system [21].

neural mechanisms underlying these changes are uncertain (Figure 8.10) [21]. It is unclear whether this association of one area of the brain with another transpires across the surface of the brain along the lines of the short arrows (and certainly there are plenty of pathways in this fashion which could be used) or whether it involves a modification of the gating mechanism at the base of the brain through which an input ordinarily going to one area is in fact displayed widely in other areas on the surface of the brain.

There is another very interesting component of the memory-storage process. On Figure 8.11 [11, 20] we have indicated the location of an injury which, when it occurs in both temporal lobes, is particularly destructive. In a limited number of individuals subject to severe psychotic disease for which radical measures were required, an effort was made to relieve the symptomatology by the removal of the undersurface of the temporal lobe on each side. Under those circumstances, there ensues a very remarkable symptom complex. These individuals lost the ability to store new information. They could retain an item of information only during the immediate period during which they continued to "keep it in mind." Once the attention was diverted, no further recollection of that item was possible. Information which had been stored before the operation was retained. The picture resembled that of old people who lose their memory.

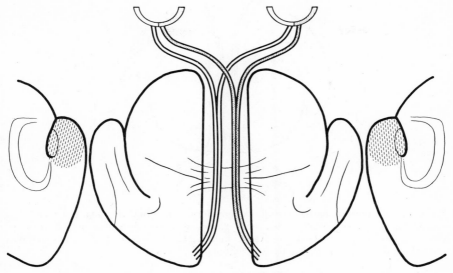

Fig. 8.11   Location of lesion causing loss of recent memory [13, 20].

Figure 8.12 [4] suggests in a little more detail the pathways that might be involved in evaluation and learning in the visual modality. The information comes into the occipital area; some evaluation and integration takes place in the auditory association area. A further interpretation involves the lateral temporal lobe. From here, the information goes through to the crucial area in the undersurface of the temporal lobe. From there, there are channels which lead directly to the basal areas of the nervous system (Figure 8.13). These areas in turn project to the thalamus and other basal ganglia, and from there there is the potential at least for influencing widely the cortex over the surface of the brain. We assume then that through some such reverberating circuit as this there occurs a process through which the memory trace is eventually laid down in those areas of the brain where it is ultimately stored. As mentioned earlier, these storage areas are probably related to the input areas, but certainly they are by no means limited to them. The following quotation from Russell and Espir [23] states their view of this process. Memory represents ". . . the capacity of the central nervous system to make use of its storage systems for repetitive action . . . . repetitive activity leads to the establishment of storehouses of neuronal patterns which are used with ever-increasing confidence as the individual matures . . . . the fornix-hippocampal system seems to facilitate storage of current happenings in whatever part of the brain is appropriate." For

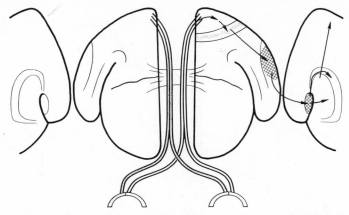

Fig. 8.12   Theoretical pathway required for storage of visual learning and memory. Input to occipital pole, crude evaluation in visual association area. Interpretive evaluation in lateral temporal region. Integration in amygdala to thalamus and hypothalamic central regulatory areas, thence back to cortex [4].

example, a "patient who cannot remember the previous pages he has read might have a wound either of the hippocampal system or of the storage mechanisms in the posterior parietal lobes."

Possibly, whereas other areas of the hemispheres are concerned with orientation in space, the memory mechanism of the temporal-lobe system is essential for orientation in time. Obviously the memory process is an absolute essential for temporal orientation. As such, its function assumes special significance in relation to the language function within which patterning in time is an important element.

In summary, animal experiments indicate that with increasing complexities of perceptual tasks, functions tend to become dependent on areas of interaction within which intersensory modality integration transpires. The temporal lobe appears to play a very important role in such complex perceptual tasks. These functions in animals appear to be represented equally in the two hemispheres. In fact, in a majority of instances, the unilateral destruction of one of these highly specialized areas leads to little or no deficit as long as connections with the corresponding area in the remaining hemisphere are intact. A different situation appears to exist in the human, as we shall see in the next section. Here, there are evidences that in certain highly complex perceptual tasks the integrated functions have become centered in one or the other hemisphere. Within this "dominant" hemisphere, information is integrated from both hemispheres. Destruction of this area leads to global deficits.

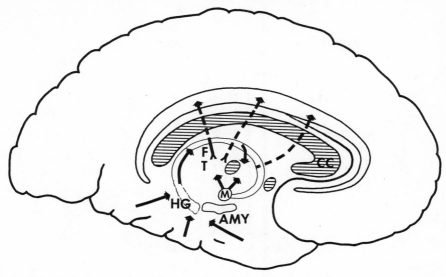

Fig. 8.13 General relationships of structures involved in memory storage on medial and inferior surface of cerebral hemisphere.

8.5 INTERACTIONS WITHIN A SINGLE HEMISPHERE

The localization of highly complex interactions within a single hemisphere may result from the fact that intersensory integration occurs more readily within a single hemisphere than between hemispheres. Thus Mishkin [14] cites the following experiment to indicate that integration accomplished within a single hemisphere is more effective than is integration which requires interaction between the two hemispheres.

A series of rhesus monkeys were subjected to unilateral temporal lobe removal (Figure 8.14) [14]. Upon recovery, some of these animals were subjected to a second removal (2) within the same hemisphere as that previously subjected to temporal-lobe operation. In these animals, no demonstrable impairment of visual discrimination occurred. In those animals in which both eyes were open and utilized, it is assumed that the visual discrimination task was effectively accomplished within the un-impaired left hemisphere. Within this hemisphere, correlation between the unimpaired occiput and the ipselateral temporal lobe was adequate for the task.

In a second group of animals, the *right* temporal lobectomy was followed by a *left* occipital lobectomy (2A). Under these circumstances, a significant impairment in the ability to complete the visual discrimination task

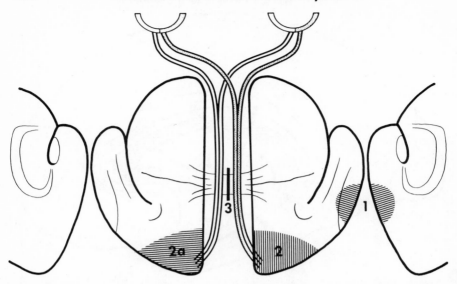

Fig. 8.14 Experiment to demonstrate interdependence of occipital and temporal lobe for visual discrimination [14].

occurred. The accomplishment of the task required the interaction of the right occipital area and the left unimpaired temporal region. When this interhemispheric reaction was required, there was a demonstrable deficit of the performance of the task.

As further evidence that this latter task required interhemispheric interaction, in some of these animals a third procedure was carried out and the corpus callosum was sectioned (3). As a result of these three lesions, the animal was completely deprived of any opportunity to interrelate the incoming visual signal with a functioning temporal lobe. A severe deficit resulted.

Only recently have serious efforts been made to define with precision those functions for which one or the other hemisphere appears to be "dominant." The more conventional data regarding the functions of the cerebral hemispheres in man are portrayed on Figures 8.15 [21] and 8.16 [21]. A number of recent studies of more subtle differences might be mentioned. Mishkin (cited by Milner in [13]) has demonstrated that tachistoscopically presented words and letters tend to be preceived more accurately in the right than in the left visual field (Figure 8.17) [14]. This superiority of the right visual field applies, however, only to alphabetical (symbolic) material. Under similar circumstances, geometric forms and nonsense figures are recognized equally well in both right and left fields (see also

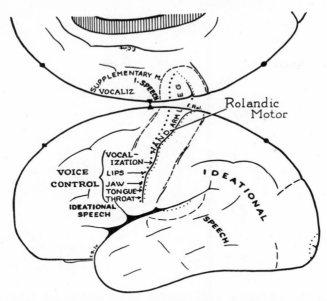

Fig. 8.15   Speech mechanisms in the dominant hemisphere. Three areas are devoted to the ideational elaboration of speech; two areas are devoted to vocalization. The principal area devoted to motor control of articulation, or voice control, is located in lower precentral gyrus. Evidence for these localizations is summarized from the analysis of cortical stimulation and cortical excision [21].

[1], [6], and [30]). The tachistoscopic test is accomplished as the subject fixes his central vision on an object directly in front. We then flash a picture or an object in one side or the other of his field of vision. In this way, we can test the relative competence of the two sides of his brain to interpret such a signal. Under those circumstances, if words or letters are used as a test object, the individual will recognize these more effectively when they are to his right, and he is using the left side of his brain, than he will when they are to his left. If, on the other hand, we use geometrical figures, there seems to be no difference. Similarly in the auditory sphere, if we use words and sudden brief exposure to spoken digits in the right ear, the person will do better than if he hears these digits with his left ear—suggesting that the left hemisphere is better than the right for the interpretation of words. But if we use a pattern of clicks, there seems to be a slight difference in favor of the left ear as opposed to the right. There is further evidence derived from the effects of removal of the temporal lobe for surgical relief of epilepsy. If the right temporal lobe is removed, there is a more serious impairment of nonverbal, visual, and auditory function—such as music.

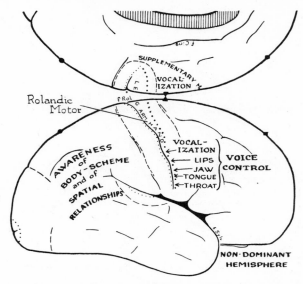

Fig. 8.16 Area of right hemisphere, injury of which impairs body image and spatial orientation [21].

On the other hand, when the left temporal lobe is removed, the impairment is more serious in the verbal sphere. Another piece of evidence—there are certain individuals who suffer from epileptic seizures originating in one or the other temporal lobe. Such seizures are quite bizarre in that as the seizure begins the individual will have a peculiar memory or a dream or a recollection, or a strange feeling of unreality or a distortion of his time sense. This is exactly the type of thing that one would anticipate in relation to the complex functions of the temporal lobe we have been describing. There is a suggestion that when these seizures originate in the *right* temporal lobe, this pattern is likely to involve pictures and visual illusions, but when the seizure originates in the left temporal lobe, the effect is one of auditory illusions and speech [31]. This needs further confirmation.

There are at least two possible interpretations of these phenomena. One group of investigators contend that the difference between the right and left hemisphere has to do with the use of symbols—that the left hemisphere has developed a function specifically related to intersensory correlations involving the use of symbols [12], whereas the right hemisphere is more involved in the analysis of certain nonsymbolic relationships. Another interpretation, which the author personally tends to favor, is that the difference has to do with the emphasis on time relationships versus

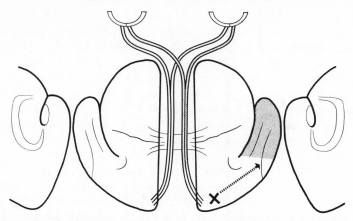

Fig. 8.17 Temporal lobectomy in humans impairs visual discrimination in contralateral visual field [14].

spatial relationships—that the activity of the left hemisphere seems to concentrate much more precisely on time relationships which are fundamental for language and auditory input, whereas the right hemisphere might be the focal point or the major patterning area for spatial relationships, body image, and similar functions.

Figure 8.18 [29] presents evidence which tends to support the thesis just mentioned. War injuries of the left hemisphere which destroyed the

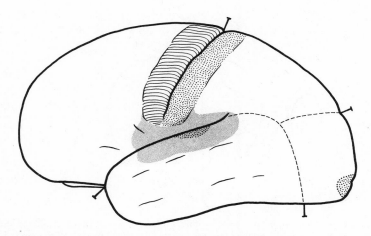

Fig. 8.18 Locus of lesions producing loss of discrimination of rhythms [29].

shaded portion of the brain were characterized by a loss of appreciation of rhythm. A typical example is that of a man who had been an excellent guitar player. Subsequent to his injury, he was aphasic. There was no impairment of his hearing. His appreciation of pitch was preserved: he could tune his guitar with great precision. However, when he attempted to play a sequence—a tone sequence, a pattern of sound, or a rhythm—he was completely lost. This has been described as "amusia," lack of musical skill, and is actually a loss of the ability to retain the auditory patterns underlying musical rhythms. It seems obvious how essential this is for speech function.

Aside from the somewhat controversial hemispheric differences already described, there are certain well-established asymmetries of considerable significance. Figure 8.16 shows an area marked "awareness of body-scheme and of spatial relationships." This area is appropriately located for interaction of visual, auditory, and sensory information. This temporo-parietooccipital area is undoubtedly the most crucial of any part of the surface of the brain from that point of view. Destruction of this area of the right hemisphere leads to peculiar disturbances of sensation or awareness of body-scheme, particularly on the left side of the body. Individuals with damage in this area behave as though their left arm and leg simply were not there at all and appear not to know that there is anything wrong with them [5]. This has led to the belief that the right hemisphere is dominant for spatial relationship and for the integration of simple visual cues as well.

An alternative explanation is presented (Figure 8.19) by Geschwind [4]. He assumes that the injury on the right side of the brain is destructive

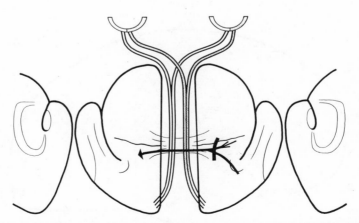

Fig. 8.19 Geschwind alternate explanation for disturbance of body image (of left side) with right parietal lesion. Left hemisphere is actually "dominant." "Disconnection" of right parietal area separates this from the integrating center of left hemisphere [4].

because it separates the right side from the left and, according to this interpretation, the overall integration and synthesis of a total body image in fact takes place within the left hemisphere. If the right hemisphere is separated through a disconnecting injury in the right side, then the individual behaves as though the left side of his body did not exist. We cite this to indicate that many of the things currently being discussed are at the moment in a very unsettled state indeed. The corresponding area of the left hemisphere (Figure 8.20)[32] has an even more vital function. Among a large series of brain-injured veterans, those whose wound was located in the shaded area had experienced a significant lowering of their Army General Classification Test (GCT) score. The unique strength of this study lay in the fact that this group of individuals had been tested before the injury and could be subjected to an almost identical test after the injury. Thus it was injury of this area that led to the impairment in their GCT score. Most intelligence tests require utilization of language; but more than this they require an integration of verbal, visual, and auditory information. The left hemisphere is essential for the accomplishment of these most complicated intellectual functions.

8.6 THE LANGUAGE FUNCTION AND INTERSENSORY INTEGRATION

The most complicated and the most human of all activities is language. Considering the complex nature of the language function, and in view of the evidences that intermodality integration can be mediated more effectively within a single hemisphere, it is understandable that the language

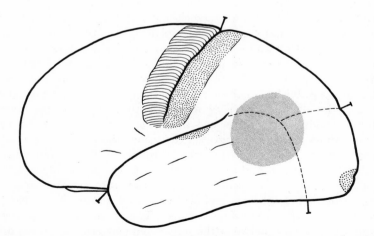

Fig. 8.20 Area of left hemisphere, injury of which impairs general intelligence [32].

function should be highly concentrated on one side. In over 95 per cent of individuals, it is the left hemisphere within which this function is centered. Thus, in over 99 per cent of right-handed individuals, the speech center will be in the left hemisphere. In the case of left-handed individuals, the speech center is located on the left about 50 per cent of the time. There is some evidence to suggest that when the speech center is in the right hemisphere, there is a greater tendency toward bilateral representation. An understanding of the nature of the language function and its breakdown is facilitated by a consideration of the steps in language development. These have been outlined by Dr. Jerzy Konorski [9] as follows.

Let us assume that the child starts out by babbling, by making sounds. Each time he makes a sound, he hears a noise and at the same time he feels the movements of his lips, tongue, larynx, and chest. This involves then a coordinated pattern of activity in area 44 (Figure 8.1) within which are integrated the motor act of speech, in area 40 which is the lower end of the areas where the sensation of movement is subserved, and in the auditory area 41, and those closely related to it, 42 and 22. Over a course of time, the child develops such integrated patterns.

In the next step of language development, the child hears spoken words in his environment and he copies those words. This activity is reinforced by the pleasure of the parent who is likely to be enthusiastic when the child tries to make a sound. Then the child hears a word and attempts to duplicate that word, again by a pattern of movement and the sensation of movement and the sound that goes with it. There must develop, then, a very strong constellation of activity patterns involving these three areas, roughly 44, 41, and 40. Now, the sound still has no meaning and at this stage we have nothing other than what we would expect from a parrot. But at some point other input clues become associated with this sound-pattern-movement constellation that we have described. This may be the vision—the picture of the object which becomes associated with the sound. For example, the mother says "spoon" and clinks the spoon in the cup, or the mother says "cup" and holds up the cup in the child's vision. A somesthetic association is established at the same time the child holds the cup. Through these activities, a correlation is established between this pattern of activity which we previously have described and the activity of areas 7, 39, 19, and 21 within which are being integrated the visual and sensory input.

These then may be the types of steps through which the ability to speak is established. Now, in addition to this, starting with simple words, it is quite likely that there are established feedback automatic cycling devises through which whole phrases and sentences and groups of words become patterned into an automatic sequence. This presumably comprises a continuing interaction between the movement patterns involving area 44 and the sensation of those movements and sound involving areas 40 and 41.

Konorski envisages that there must be four different types of conditioned connections involving these areas. *Audio-verbal* refers to the connection between area 41 and area 44 through which a sound initiates the movement to reproduce it. The *audio-visual* or *audio-somatic* is the channel through which, when an individual hears a sound, he pictures the object that the sound means. This is the ability to recognize the meaning of a sound and obviously involves connection between area 42 and those more posterior, 21, 39, and 19. The third, *visual-verbal*, is a mechanism through which the individual is able to mobilize the word that relates to a seen or felt object. This presumably involves long connections such as would connect area 19 to area 44. Finally, the *kinesthetic-verbal* connection between area 40 and 44, which involves the reverberating circuit, is described above.

8.7 LANGUAGE DEFICITS

Konorski believes that language deficits may reflect specific injury of these connections. He speaks first of those with audio-verbal deficit as depicted in Figure 8.21 [9]. This occurs if there is an interruption of the connection between the "auditory analyzer" and the motor engrams, the motor patterns for speech. Then, the individual may be able to understand what is said to him but he will not be able to reproduce a spoken word

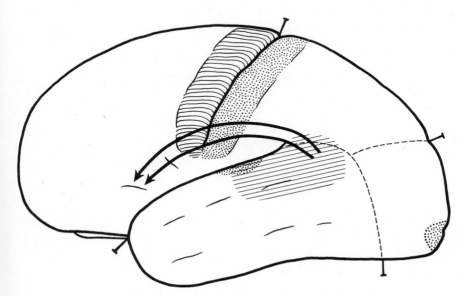

Fig. 8.21 Locus of lesions causing audio-verbal aphasia [9].

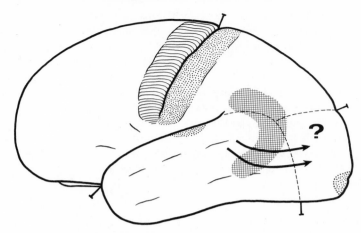

Fig. 8.22 Locus of lesions causing audio-visual aphasia [9].

which is said to him. Such an individual may be able to talk but not repeat what he has heard.

The second defect is shown on Figure 8.22 [9]. Konorski speaks of this as audio-visual or audio-somatic or even audio-gustatory. This is an impairment of the comprehension of speech. The individual hears the sound of a word but is unable to make the association of that word-sound with its meaning. He may be able to make automatic speech or even to initiate speech, but his ability to understand with accuracy what is said is impaired.

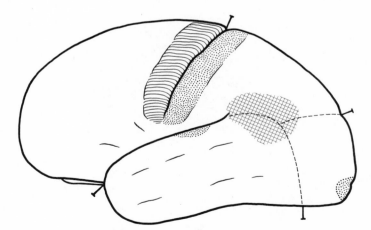

Fig. 8.23 Locus of lesion causing visuo-verbal aphasia [9].

The next type of impairment, shown in Figure 8.23 [9], is described as visual-verbal. Here the individual, upon seeing an object, is unable to express its name. He is unable to utilize the association between the seen object and the word that goes with it.

In Figure 8.24 [9], the defect shown is spoken of by Konorski as kinesthetic motor aphasia. This is an inability to activate the motor pattern of movement for speech.

Under the term "disconnection syndromes," Geschwind [4] has described a variety of symptom complexes involving interruptions of pathways which relate to language functions. He describes individuals who are unable to read but who can write to dictation or who can write spontaneously (Figure 8.25) [4]. They apparently are unable to make a connection between the visual area where visual information is brought in and the writing area quite close to it through which the patterns of written words are laid down. He postulates that this occurs when both occipital lobes are cut off from the left temporo-parietal area which is involved in the writing process.

Geschwind describes a more serious deficit in individuals who are unable to write. Here, presumably, the area where these several functions involved in writing are integrated is in fact destroyed (Figure 8.26) [4].

Another unusual form of deficit is "pure-word deafness" (Figure 8.27) [4]. Here Geschwind envisages a bilateral injury such that the areas into which the word comes are separated from those areas where it is interpreted. The individual may still be able to talk, but he is not able to understand words which he hears. Such individuals also have rather serious

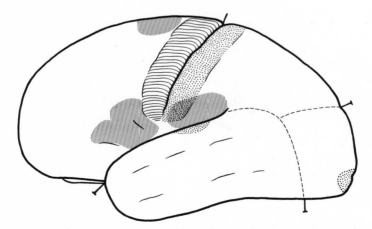

Fig. 8.24 Loci of three lesions causing kinesthetic motor aphasia [9].

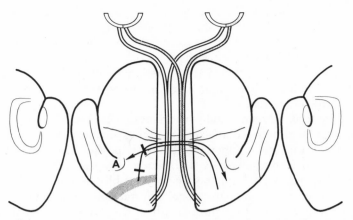

Fig. 8.25 Word blindness without agraphia. Can write and understand spelled word, but not read. Visual "analyzer" of each hemisphere has been disconnected from "word center" of left speech area [4].

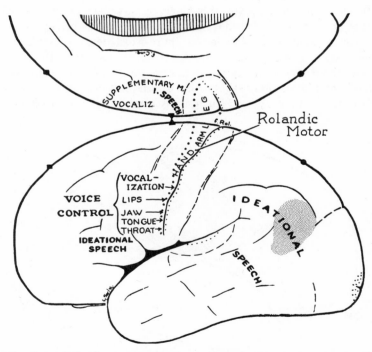

Fig. 8.26 Word blindness with agraphia. Can understand spoken word and can speak. Language area primarily concerned with storage of visual patterns is destroyed [4].

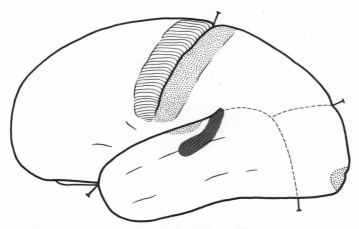

Fig. 8.27 Can read and speak but not understand spoken word. Bilateral lesion separates auditory input from word-association area [4].

disability in their own speech, in that they are not able to monitor their own speech. They are likely to make errors without recognizing them.

The most destructive type of injury is that depicted on Figure 8.28 [4]. Within this centrally located area are established the activity patterns which represent the word and its meaning. When this area is destroyed, the individual has an incapacity to recapture the words he needs to use for

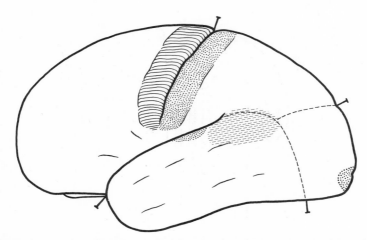

Fig. 8.28 Gross language defect: comprehension poor; syntax poor; verbose with little meaning [4].

understanding spoken words or for activating speech. Such a person has a very serious disability of language.

In Figure 8.29 [4] is another rather unusual pattern of deficit not unlike that shown earlier in some of the monkeys. If such an individual is permitted to feel different objects with his left hand, and then we place in his right hand an object similar to one of those which he has felt, he can pick out objects which are similar and distinguish them from those which are dissimilar. This means that he can demonstrate the ability to recognize objects by their feel with his left hand. If, however, you ask him to name what he has in his left hand, he cannot do it. Evidently, here there is a disconnection between the area of the brain involved in the naming of objects and the right side of his brain where the information comes in from his hand.

Figure 8.30 [4] represents Geschwind's concept of the audio-verbal deficit of Konorski previously described. This is the individual who can understand what is said but is not able to repeat the spoken word.

Finally, Figure 8.31 [4, 26] depicts a very bizarre situation which is seen not infrequently in severely handicapped children. These individuals have a rather extensive pattern of language, but it is only mimicry. We have seen children who could recite a whole poem but who have never given any indication that they understood a single word of what was said to them or that they had the capability of initiating meaningful language. This occasionally occurs in adults. In this condition, called "echolalia," the individual will repeat what is said to him without understanding it. Presumably, this represents a very extensive disconnection of the language

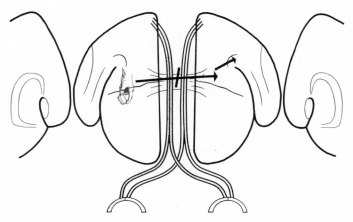

Fig. 8.29   "Tactile aphasia." Cannot name object palpated with left hand. Tract injury separates the somesthetic area of the right hemisphere from the word center of the left [4].

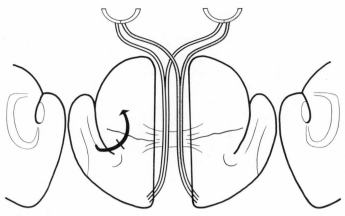

Fig. 8.30 "Conduction aphasia." Can understand but not repeat. Disconnection of auditory from motor area [4]. (Compare Konorski "audio-verbal" deficit.)

area from the posterior areas within which language is invested with meaning.

Such circumscribed deficits as those just described, of which there are many types, actually are rare. The cases described are culled from a much larger number of "aphasics." The fact is that, clinically, we rarely observe this type of discrete deficit.

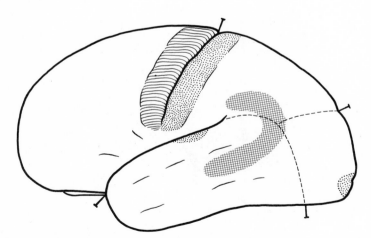

Fig. 8.31 "Echolalia." Can repeat but not understand. Bilateral large lesions separate the "audio-verbal" areas from the languate center. Language has no meaning ([4], after [26].)

8.8 BRAIN LESIONS AND APHASIA

An unusual opportunity to observe the results of discrete, carefully controlled removal of brain tissue, and the results of electrical stimulation of the human brain, has been afforded during surgical procedures for the control of epilepsy. Much of this work has been reported by Penfield [21] and his associates at the Montreal Neurological Institute. These men in the course of operations for the relief of epilepsy have stimulated the surface of the brain and excised small areas for the relief of seizures.

In Figure 8.32 [21] are shown those areas of the brain stimulation of which led to arrest of speech. One sees that these As (arrests) group themselves rather sharply in the areas which we have been discussing. Those in

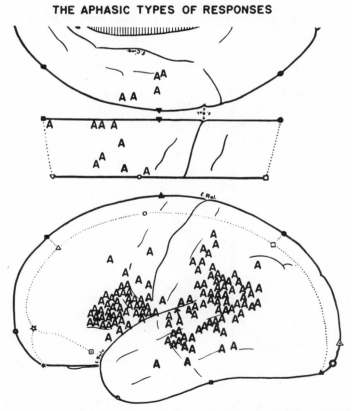

THE APHASIC TYPES OF RESPONSES

Fig. 8.32 Areas of the cortex where electrical stimulation produced "aphasic" type of response [21].

the anterior area are grouped around the place where motor patterns of speech exist. Those in the temporal and parietal area are those where the patterns for the sound and meaning of speech are laid down.

Figure 8.33 [21] shows the speech areas delineated by electrical stimulation. Almost identical results were obtained by plotting areas whose removal caused language deficit. We should mention one additional area at the very top of this picture, the so-called "superior speech·cortex," which apparently has to do with the production of speech and is involved in motor patterns of speech activation and movement. Removal of this area produces a very minor transitory disturbance.

Figure 8.34 [23] summarizes the analysis of a large number of war injuries. This is the work of Russell and Espir [23]. The upper diagram indicates injuries which did produce aphasia, and the bottom one those that did not. In these diagrams, we must recollect that some of these people probably were right-brained. Figure 8.35 [23] is a similar map of the right hemisphere. It shows that most of these injuries were not associated with loss of speech. The only ones producing loss of speech were shown in the upper part of this diagram, and we note that three of these people were

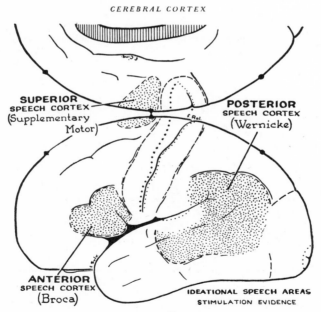

CEREBRAL CORTEX

SUPERIOR
SPEECH CORTEX
(Supplementary
Motor)

POSTERIOR
SPEECH CORTEX
(Wernicke)

ANTERIOR
SPEECH CORTEX
(Broca)

IDEATIONAL SPEECH AREAS
STIMULATION EVIDENCE

Fig. 8.33 Areas of the brain where stimulation or excision produced distrubance of language [21].

left-handed. It is interesting that three people who were right-handed also had aphasia and presumably were right-brained.

In Figure 8.36, small wounds causing aphasia are shown.

Figures 8.37, 8.38, and 8.39 demonstrate that even with the gross type of destruction occasioned by war wounds, one can demonstrate different patterns of language loss depending on the area involved. In the patients

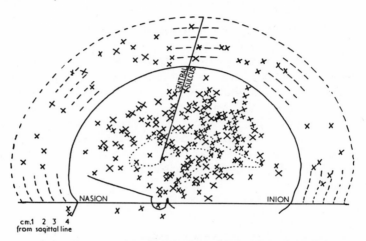

Skull outline. Each X indicates the centre of a wound in the left cerebral hemisphere causing aphasia.

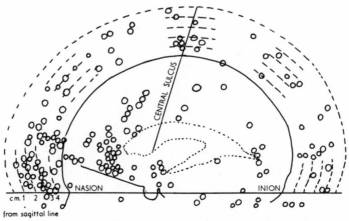

Each O indicates the centre of a wound in the left cerebral hemisphere not causing aphasia.

Fig. 8.34   Aphasia from war wounds (left hemisphere) [23].

depicted on Figure 8.37, there was very little impairment of language comprehension, but there was a serious impairment in language production. In Figure 8.38, quite a different pattern is shown. These were individuals whose ability to make speech was preserved but whose comprehension of speech was seriously impaired. These individuals are likely to exhibit serious errors of grammar and construction relating to their inability to

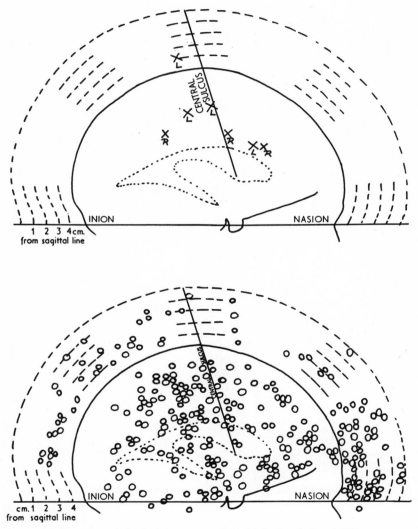

Fig. 8.35 Aphasia from war wounds (right hemisphere) [23].

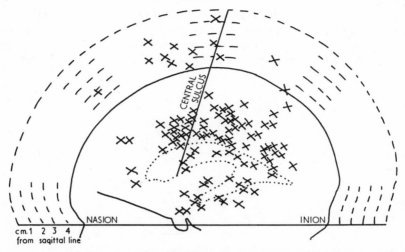

Fig. 8.36 Aphasia from small (presumably localized) wounds of the left cerebral hemisphere.   Each x indicates the center of a small wound [23].

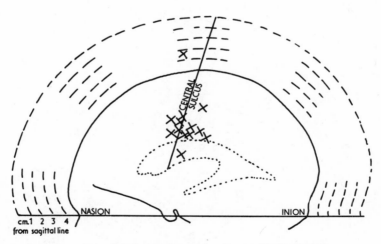

Fig. 8.37 Small wounds causing "motor" aphasia [23].

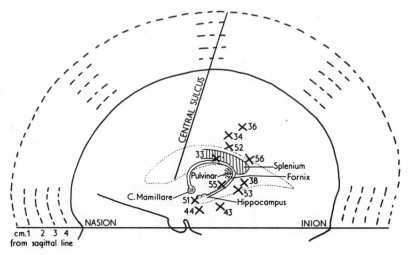

Fig. 8.38 Small wounds causing "central" aphasia [23].

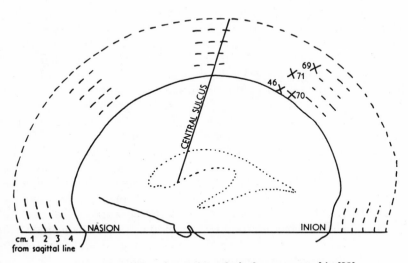

Fig. 8.39 Wounds causing relatively pure agraphia [23].

monitor their speech production. Figure 8.39 shows individuals with agraphia—that is, loss of writing without major impairments of spoken language. On the basis of these careful clinical anatomical correlations, these two sets of investigators have very much simplified the patterns described.

Penfield and Roberts [21] also describe two chief types of aphasia. They describe, for example, the results of a small removal in the region of the supramarginal gyrus and the first temporal gyrus of one patient (Figure 8.1, areas 42, 22, and 40). This patient differed from other patients because of the severity of his difficulty in understanding spoken words. One year after the operation, his only defect was reduced ability to carry out complicated oral commands. On the other hand, another patient is described as follows. After removal of the motor and sensory face area (Figure 8.1, areas 6 and 3), the aphasia which resulted brought little interference with the understanding of the spoken and written word, but this patient had marked perseveration and difficulty in naming. These findings support the conclusion that the sensory aspects of aphasia are more marked when the lesion is in the temporal region (areas 41, 42, and 22), whereas the motor aspects are more damaged by lesions in the general vicinity of Broca's area (44).

Penfield and Roberts [21] add, however, that the speech mechanism must function as a whole and is not divisible into restricted functional units. Russell and Espir [23] put it this way: "The scaffolding on which speech is developed is built up in relation to hearing, vision, and the sensori-motor skill involved in uttering words. Injury to the central part of this structure disrupts all aspects of speech, but small wounds at the periphery of the scaffolding may lead to a special disorder of one or other speech function, such as motor aphasia, agraphia, or alexia. . . . those posterior parietal wounds which cause alexia often produce severe loss of intellectual functions." This latter is the area which we described earlier, and lesions in which cause lowering of the General Classification Test scores.

There is considerable difference of opinion regarding the extent to which localized brain injury can cause partial language deficit. There are strong proponents of a holistic view that the ability to convey linguistically coded information is a single function—impairment of any part of which will damage all aspects of this function. Schuell and co-workers [25] say: "We think that aphasia is characterized by impaired retrieval of a learned code, and that this impairment is reflected in all language modalities. Involvement of specific associated sensory systems results in additonal impairment, produces identifiable patterns of aphasic deficit, and makes differential diagnosis possible."

There appears to be a very general agreement of the essential truth of these statements. We are dealing here with a highly integrated pattern of motions, sensations, and hearing and vision. When one knocks a hole in any part of that pattern, the ability to reconstruct it, which is necessary for language utilization and retrieval, is impaired. This general impairment is particularly reflected in an inability to recapture specific words—a so-called amnesic aphasia. That is to say, the person cannot remember the name of an object. This is, of course, a difficulty which we all experience under normal circumstances and which is evidently a very essential phenomenon of language patterning. This description of Schuell's bears some resemblances to a classification of Schiller [24], who emphasizes that all such patients have a common amnesic aphasia, but vary depending on specific additional deficits. He speaks of five different types of language disability (Figure 8.40) [24]. He speaks first of the results of frontal lesions (this is area 44). Individuals with defects in this area, in addition to the amnesic phenomenon, suffer from a loss of the impulse to speak. Their speech is slow. Their articulation is poor, and they are deficient in inflection. Individuals with lesions in the temporal regions (areas 41, 42, and

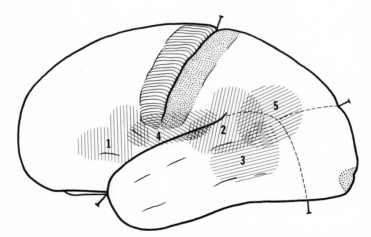

Fig. 8.40 Approximate locations of cortical areas exhibiting special aphasic features. (1) Frontal region characterized by loss of impulse to speech—slow speech and poor articulation and inflection. (2) Temporal region characterized by loss of comprehension and superior auditory control leading to paraphrasia, jargon, and agrammaticism. (3) Posterior temporal and parietal region—likely to be characterized by reading disabilities. (4) Parietal region (opercular) characterized by perseveration and stuttering. (5) Posterior Sylvian region characterized by deficiencies in abstract thinking; a lesion in any part of this area would produce some degree of amnestic aphasia [24].

22) have a loss of comprehension and of superior auditory control, as a result of which there is likely to be a jargon. They may talk a great deal, but the words are garbled and often meaningless. Lesions further back toward area 39 produce aphasic symptoms with difficulties in reading predominating. Lesions in the area between areas 40 and 44 lead to interference with the speech-control mechanism that we discussed earlier; they are manifested by perseveration of speech and stuttering as one of their important phenomena. Finally, a lesion in the posterior Sylvian area is characterized by deficiencies in abstract thinking.

The analyses of language disorders outlined here emphasize an important aspect of the language function—its dependence on intersensory integration. In general, language impairments are described in terms of interference with the interaction of the various centers within the left hemisphere required for the effective use of verbal symbols. As previously discussed, Milner and others postulate that the major difference between the two hemispheres lies in the fact that these associations relating to the use of symbols have become centered in the left hemisphere.

8.9 AN ALTERNATIVE POINT OF VIEW

A different point of view is that expressed by Efron [2]: "In order to deal appropriately with the events in its environment, an animal must perform at least two essential actions. It must be able to identify or characterize an event, and it must also be able to determine when the particular event occurred in relation to other events." He further points out that the most essential feature of verbal communication is the sequencing of auditory events. In a group of patients suffering from lesions of the dominant and nondominant hemispheres, with and without "motor" and "sensory" aphasia, Efron has tested the ability of the patient to recognize time relationship between pairs of stimuli. Two types of trials were conducted, those involving visual stimuli and those involving pairs of auditory stimuli. These studies appear to confirm his hypothesis that the ability to perform sensitive time-discrimination tasks is impaired with lesions in the left hemisphere and is unimpaired with comparable injury in the nondominant side. It is interesting that individuals demonstrating predominantly "motor" aphasia exhibited the most severe deficit in the evaluation of auditory signals—those with predominantly "sensory" aphasia were more seriously impaired in the visual sphere (Figure 8.41) [2].

Efron concludes that these experimental observations support the hypothesis that temporal analysis of sequence, interval, and simultaneity is performed in the dominant hemisphere.

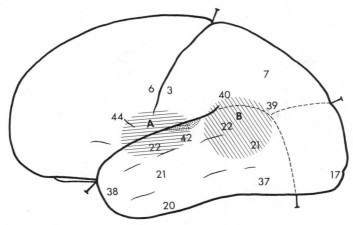

Fig. 8.41 Approximate locus of lesions producing: (A) "motor" aphasia and impairment of auditory temporal sequence; (B) "sensory" aphasia and impairment of visual temporal sequence [2].

Possibly some support for this thesis is contained in the analysis of language presented by Jakobson [8]. Within his classification, Jakobson makes a distinction between those individuals who are lacking in phonemic and grammatical units and those who appear to have command of these units but exhibit a disruption of the ability to create phonemic and/or grammatical sequences. It may be that these individuals differ primarily in the extent of their incapacity to achieve the temporal patterning of sounds required for the grammatical constructions of speech.

These views are to some extent supported by a recent paper by Luria [10]. Luria describes the following four types of aphasia.

1. Sensory aphasia. A lesion of the left temporal lobe produces a "loss of phonemic hearing." Slight injuries lead primarily to difficulty in discrimination of correlative or opposite phonemes having only one distinctive differentiating feature (such as p/n, d/t, v/w). In severe cases, however, even words cannot be distinguished from mere sounds. Loss of comprehension, loss of acoustic recall, and characteristic writing disorders are superimposed. This loss of verbal acoustic discrimination appears to center in Wernicke's area (Figure 8.42). If the upper parts of the left temporal lobe (Tl) are left intact, prosodic and melodic components of speech may be left intact. Minor confusions of similar-sounding words may occur along with loss of recall of names and uncommon words.

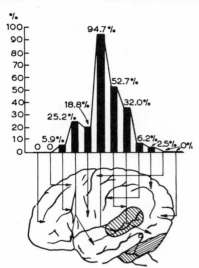

Fig. 8.42 Distribution of frequency of cases with impaired phonematic perception, according to the localization of the cerebral lesion [10].

2. Afferent (kinaesthetic) motor aphasia. Lesions of the postcentral opercular area (Figure 8.43) interfere with kinaesthetic control of speech movements. The patient is unable to produce the correct articulemes, or to produce differentially b/p/m or d/t/l. A disturbance of fine, sophisticated articulatory movements is the primary factor in this disorder. Secondary disturbances include defects of articulation, repetition, and word naming. Characteristic errors in reading, reading comprehension, and writing are observed. A transition from single words to whole-sentence propositions is, however, unimpaired.

3. Efferent or kinetic motor aphasia. Lesions of Broca's area produce a destruction of the kinetic schema, or skilled movements required for speech production. The kinetic melodies of speech are destroyed. Transition from one articuleme to a different one becomes difficult, and perseveration results. Luria says, "Inability to name an object or to pass from the expression of one word to the next, and also a loss of propositional speech as a kinetic unit, are the most significant secondary or systematic results. . . ." There is also a characteristic writing disorder—the appropriate order of letters in a word is often lost. There is a severe impairment of contextual organization of speech, with loss of melodic organization leading to telegraphic speech and "dynamic aphasia."

4. Semantic aphasia. Deterioration of the semantic organization of language, as described by Head, is a far more complex phenomenon, and the physiological factors that underlie this most complicated form of disturbance require further elucidation. Of particular interest is the fact that

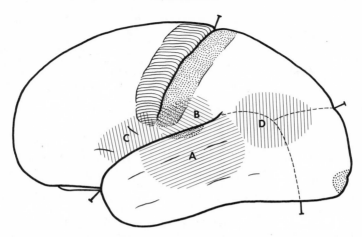

Fig. 8.43 Schema of Luria: (A) acoustic; (B) afferent; (C) efferent; (D) semantic [10].

symptoms of semantic aphasia can be observed with lesions of the left parietal or temporo-occipito-parietal regions, and they are characteristically associated with disorders of simultaneous or spatial schemata—the bringing together of separate components, and the analysis of complex spatial relationships. Right-left disorientation and spatial disorientation are prominent symptoms. Types of grammatical structure which require an analysis of asymmetrical spatial relationships (such as "father's brother" versus "brother's father"; "Jenny is older than Mary but younger than Betty") are most difficult for such patients.

Luria's interesting analysis contains many of the components of Konorski's schema. One might consider that, like Schuell, he has described a central language function (semantic aphasia and loss of word naming) of poorly defined localization, or one that requires an intact broadly represented integrated structure, with special symptoms (perceptual disorders or apraxias) relevant to the functions of more specific localized areas of damage. His observations tend to confirm those of Efron, in that he notes disturbances of temporal ordering are more prominent in frontal (motor) and superior temporal lesions than in cases with more inferior or posterior (sensory) types of aphasia.

8.10 CONCLUSION

Let us end with a comment made by Howes [7], who says, "The fact that pure aphasias have not been commonly found for any classification scheme that has been tried in a century of investigation may well signify only that none of those schemes has been appropriate to the natural lines along which the language process breaks apart."

Probably our task for the next hundred years is to try to find out what these fundamental patterns are.

REFERENCES

1. Bryden, M. P., "Tachistoscopic Recognition of Nonalphabetical Material," *Canadian J. of Psychology*, **14**, 1960, 78–86.
2. Efron, Robert, "Temporal Perception, Aphasia, Deja Vu," in Mishelevich, David J., and Richard A. Chase (editors), *Interdisciplinary Seminar Program, Temporal Lobe Function in Man, II, Language and Speech*, Part 2, Neurocommunications Laboratory, Department of Psychiatry, The Johns Hopkins University School of Medicine, Baltimore, 1965.
3. Ettlinger, George, "Interhemispheric Integration in the Somatic Sensory System," in Mountcastle, Vernon B. (editor), *Interhemispheric Relations and Cerebral Dominance*, The Johns Hopkins Press, Baltimore, 1962, pp. 75–85.
4. Geschwind, Norman, "Disconnection Syndromes in Animals and Man," *Brain*, **88**, Part II, June 1965, 237–294.
5. Hécaen, H., W. Penfield, C. Bertrand, and R. Malmo, "The Syndrome of Apractognosia Due to Lesions of the Minor Cerebral Hemisphere," *AMA Archives of Neurology and Psychiatry*, **75**, 1956, 400–434.
6. Heron, W., "Perception as a Function of Retinal Locus and Attention," *American J. of Psychology*, **70**, 1957, 38–48.
7. Howes, Davis, "Application of the Word-Frequency Concept to Aphasia," in de Reuck, A. V. S., and Maeve O'Connor (editors), Ciba Foundation Symposium, *Disorders of Language*, Little, Brown and Company, Boston, 1964, pp. 47–78.
8. Jakobson, Roman, "Towards a Linguistic Typology of Aphasic Impairments," in de Reuck, A. V. S., and Maeve O'Connor (editors), Ciba Foundation Symposium, *Disorders of Language*, Little, Brown and Company, Boston, 1964, pp. 21–46.
9. Konorski, J., "Pathophysiological Analysis of Various Forms of Speech Disorders and an Attempt of Their Classification," in Konorski, J., H. Kozniewska, L. Stapien, and J. Subczynski (editors), *Pathophysiological Mechanism of Disorders of Higher Nervous Activity after Brain Lesions in Man*, Polish Acad. of Sci. (Witold Orlowski, Director), Warsaw, 1961, pp. 1–10.
10. Luria, A. R., "Aspects of Aphasia," *J. of the Neurological Sciences*, **2**, May-June 1965, 278–287.
11. Milner, Brenda, "The Memory Defect in Bilateral Hippocampal Lesions," *Psychiatric Research Reports*, American Psychiatric Assoication, **11**, December 1959, 43–58.
12. Milner, Brenda, "Laterality Effects in Audition," in Mountcastle, Vernon B. (editor), *Interhemispheric Relations and Cerebral Dominance*, The Johns Hopkins Press, Baltimore, 1962, pp. 51–73.
13. Milner, Brenda, "Laterality Effects in Audition," in Mischelevich, David J., and Richard A. Chase (editors), *Interdisciplinary Seminar Program, Temporal Lobe Function in Man, I, Auditory Function*, Neurocommunications Laboratory, Department of Psychiatry, The Johns Hopkins University School of Medicine, Baltimore, 1965.

14. Mishkin, Mortimer, "A Possible Link between Interhemispheric Integration in Monkeys and Cerebral Dominance in Man," in Mountcastle, Vernon B. (editor), *Interhemispheric Relations and Cerebral Dominance*, The Johns Hopkins Press, Baltimore, 1962, pp. 101–107.

15. Morrell, Frank, personal communication.

16. Morrell, F., and H. Jasper, "Electrographic Studies of the Formation of Temporary Connections in the Brain," *Electroenceph. and Clin. Neurophysiol.*, **8**, 2, 1956, 201–216.

17. Myers, Ronald E., Discussion, in Mountcastle, Vernon B. (editor), *Interhemispheric Relations and Cerebral Dominance*, The Johns Hopkins Press, Baltimore, 1962, pp. 117–129.

18. Myers, Ronald E., "Transmission of Visual Information within and between the Hemispheres: A Behavioral Study," in Mountcaste, Vernon B. (editor), *Interhemispheric Relations and Cerebral Dominance*, The Johns Hopkins Press, Baltimore, 1962, pp. 51–73.

19. Penfield, W., and H. Jasper, *Epilepsy and the Functional Anatomy of the Human Brain*, Little, Brown and Company, Boston, 1954, p.896.

20. Penfield, W., and B. Milner, "The Memory Defect Produced by Bilateral Lesions of the Hippocampal Zone," *AMA Archives of Neurology and Psychiatry*, **79**, 5, May 1958, 475–497.

21. Penfield, Wilder, and Lamar Roberts, *Speech and Brain-Mechanisms*, Princeton University Press, Princeton, 1959.

22. Pribram, Karl H., Discussion in the Second Session, in Mountcastle, Vernon B. (editor), *Interhemispheric Relations and Cerebral Dominance*, The Johns Hopkins Press, Baltimore, 1962, pp. 107–111.

23. Russell, W. Ritchie, and M. L. E. Espir, *Traumatic Aphasia*, Oxford Neurological Monographs, Oxford University Press, London, 1961.

24. Schiller, F., "Aphasia Studied in Patients with Missile Wounds," *J. of Neurology, Neurosurgery, and Psychiatry*, **10**, 1947, 183–197.

25. Schuell, Hildred, James J. Jenkins, and Edward Jiminez-Pabon, *Aphasia in Adults*, Hoeber Medical Division, Harper and Row, New York, 1964.

26. Segarra, J. M., and F. A. Quadfasel, "Preserved Temporal Lobe Tips—Preserved Ability to Sing with Total Aphasia," A Clinico-Anatomical Report, in *Excerpta Medica, Int. Cong. Series, No. 38* (VII International Congress of Neurology, Rome, Sept. 10–15, 1961), 35–38.

27. Stepien, L. S., J. P. Cordeau, and Theodore Rasmussen, "The Effect of Temporal Lobe and Hippocampal Lesions on Auditory and Visual Recent Memory in Monkeys," *Brain—A Journal of Neurology*, **83**, Part III, 1960, 470–489.

28. Stepien, L., and S. Sierpinski, "The Effect of Focal Lesions of the Brain upon the Auditory and Visual Recent Memory in Man," in Konorski, J., H. Kozniewska, L. Stepien, and J. Subczynski (editors), *Pathophysiological Mechanism of Disorders of Higher Nervous Activity after Brain Lesions in Man*, Polish Acad. of Sci. (Witold Orlowski, Director), Warsaw, 1961, pp. 44–49.

29. Subczynski, J., "Disorders of Reproduction of Compound Numerical Sequences in Focal Lesions of the Brain in Man," in Konorski, J., H. Kozniewska, L. Stepien, and J. Subczynski (editors), *Pathophysiological Mechanism of Disorders of Higher Nervous Activity after Brain Lesions in Man*, Polish Acad. of Sci. (Witold Orlowski, Director), Warsaw, 1961, pp. 37–43.

30. Terrace, H. S., "The Effects of Retinal Locus and Attention on the Perception of Words," *J. of Experimental Psychology*, **58**, 1959, 382–385.

31. Teuber, Hans-Lukas, "Effects of Brain Wound Implicating Right or Left Hemispheres: Differential Effects on Certain Intellectual and Complex Perceptual Functions," in Mountcastle, Vernon B. (editor), *Interhemispheric Relations and Cerebral Dominance*, The Johns Hopkins Press, Baltimore, 1962, pp. 131–157.

32. Weinstein, Sidney, "Differences in Effects of Brain Wounds Implicating Right or Left Hemispheres: Differential Effects on Certain Intellectual and Complex Perceptual Functions," in Mountcastle, Vernon B. (editor), *Interhemispheric Relations and Cerebral Dominance*, The Johns Hopkins Press, Baltimore, 1962, pp. 159–176.

FURTHER READINGS

1. *Human Communication and Its Disorders—An Overview; A Report Prepared and Published by the Subcommittee on Human Communication and Its Disorders*, National Institute of Neurological Diseases and Stroke, United States Public Health Service, Washington, D. C., 1969.

2. Mello, Nancy K., "Concerning the Inner-Hemispheric Transfer of Mirror-Image Patterns in Pigeon," *Physiol. Behavior*, **1**, 1966, 293–300.

3. Noble, John, "Paradoxical Interocular Transfer of Mirror-Image Discrimination in the Optic Chiasm Sectioned Monkey," *Brain Research*, **10**, 1968, 127–151.

4. Penfield, W., and H. Jasper, *Epilepsy and the Functional Anatomy of the Human Brain*, Little, Brown and Company, Boston, 1954.

5. "Report of the Research Group on Aphasiology of the World Federation of Neurology Conference on May 5–7, 1966," *Cortex*, **3**, 1967, 2–156.

PART 3

MATHEMATICAL ASPECTS OF COMMUNICATION SCIENCES

Mathematics takes us into the region of absolute necessity, to which not only the actual world, but every possible world, must conform.

Bertrand Russell
The Study of Mathematics

CHAPTER 9

Poisson Counting and Detection in Sensory Systems

WILLIAM J. MC GILL

President, Columbia University, New York City

Contents

9.1 INTRODUCTION

It is not exactly newsworthy to record that the Poisson distribution now plays a vital role in our treatment of visual detection and intensity discrimination. More notable would be some indication of why this is so, but objectives of that sort pose many problems. Historically, at least, the answer is simple. The distribution describes quantum energy fluctuations in flashes of incandescent light at constant intensity. Researchers in vision noted the Poisson character of visual-threshold data and put two and two together.

The classical picture of Poisson statistics in visual psychophysics began to develop during World War II, with activity spanning both sides of the Atlantic. Hecht, Shlaer, and Pirenne [17, 18] demonstrated that quantum fluctuations in the amount of light reaching the retina could provide a complete account of the psychometric function at absolute threshold. About the same time, de Vries [48], writing in the Netherlands, outlined a theoretical argument leading to nearly the same conclusion, and suggested that visual-intensity discrimination ought to follow a square-root law (in contrast to Weber's law). Rose [35] and Van der Velden [47] offered similar analyses.

These papers recognized that the absolute threshold of human rod vision must involve a very small amount of light energy (roughly 3×10^{-10} erg, or 100 quanta). Moreover, estimates of the amount of light absorbed in the retina must also take into account losses of the order of 85–90 per cent of the incident light at peak sensitivity. Quantum statistics in the threshold stream of photons must then play an important role in determining the shape of the psychometric function, and they might indeed determine it totally.

The spirit of this early work in visual detection is perhaps best expressed by saying that it projects the whole detection problem outside the organism. Lower limits on detectability are set by the statistics of the visual stimulus. The system transmitting the message from the eye to the brain, saying that a detection has occurred, is taken to be virtually noise-free. It is not completely clear how this classical view can be made to deal with the phenomena of intensity discrimination in which incremental stimuli are detected against a background of continuous stimulation. One supposition is that a fraction of the incident light flux is transformed into an equivalent flux of nerve impulses. Limits on detectability are then interpreted as a behavioral reflection of the ebb and flow of events in the sensory channel.

Although it may be a handy explanatory device, the conjecture that Poisson statistics in visual psychophysics are literally imparted by the Poisson distribution of light quanta seems unnecessarily restrictive. Studies of renewal processes in probability theory establish that parallel channels carrying nonrandom (even periodic!) impulse sequences generate Poisson statistics when the information is brought together at a common focal point, as was indicated by Cox and Smith [10]. The Poisson limit has been demonstrated for a variety of superposed renewal processes. The essential conclusion seems to be that Poisson statistics can be injected into the flow of a sensory channel merely by removing information from a system observing the passage of events to higher centers. Thus even a stimulus with fixed energy would be mapped into a Poisson-impulse-counting distribution by a neurological monitoring system with low information about details of the flow, that is, a counting device. This is what happens when a pneumatic tube is placed across a highway to measure traffic density.

With Poisson statistics well established in visual detection, the preceding arguments might lead us to conclude that the statistics characterizing intensity discrimination are generated spontaneously in the sensory channel and have little direct connection with the statistics of the incident light. Poisson counting would then seem to have applications in sensory analysis extending considerably beyond the visual case.

Both treatments (light flux and channel flux) are energy-detection schemes resembling particle counting. Stimulus energy is mapped into a count. If the latter exceeds a *critical number*, a stimulus is detected, whether or not one is there. The critical number is a detection criterion which is normally set high enough to control false reports (or perhaps squelch them altogether). The essential differences between detection in the eye and detection in the visual channel have been developed very clearly by Barlow [2, 3]. In the channel, the critical number is a flexible criterion associated with a sensory monitoring system, whereas for detection in the eye the criterion is viewed as a fixed summation rule.

It is not generally understood but nevertheless true that rules similar to those just described in the visual case also provide an accurate account of the detectability of increments in acoustic white noise and sinusoids in white noise, when the rules are applied to the flux of information in the auditory channel. This does not mean that the auditory case is characterized by Poisson detection phenomena. The problem is more complicated. Energy distributions of short bursts of white noise, or brief sinusoids in noise, are now fairly well understood—and they are not Poisson. If these energy distributions are used to drive the mean information rate through a counting mechanism with Poisson statistics, the counting process will resemble a negative binomial distribution. This is the famous generalization of the Poisson law by Greenwood and Yule [15]. The explanation of the change (which is substantial) is found in the fact that large fluctuations of the stimulus energy are compounded with spontaneous fluctuations of the sensory-information flow, determining a new distribution in the latter.

In this chapter, we do not discuss the auditory case except by implication. Our intention is to try to draw visual and auditory detection closer together by unhitching visual detection from its strict dependence on the stimulus. We attempt to show that Poisson statistics probably characterize the mass flow of information through any sensory monitoring system with low intelligence about the "tags" on impulses that pass through it. The driving energy of flashes of light preserves the Poisson character of this information flow, whereas the energy distribution of bursts of noise transforms it. Visual and auditory detection should then be more closely allied than surface analysis would indicate.

Interaction between visual and auditory detection theories is surprisingly meager. A significant exception is the work of Barlow [2, 3], who treats visual intensity thresholds as the outcome of a noisy detection process in the sensory channel (also see Treisman [45]). The process is geared to maintain a stable false-report rate. Detection probabilities and false-report probabilities must then trade off against each other. This is just the point of view taken in audition. We now want to extend the quantitative analysis of visual detection and especially Barlow's work, in an effort to construct a bridge between the typical Poisson arguments in vision research and the somewhat better-developed detection theories of psychoacoustics and signal analysis.

Following this introduction, Section 9.2 deals with the *square-root law* of Poisson detection. Sections 9.3 and 9.4 take up two types of criteria— *least error and equalized error*—as they operate in the Poisson case. Finally, in Section 9.5, the information flow in a sensory channel is analyzed as a *stochastic process*.

The point of view presented here is more or less bounded by sensory mechanisms (see, for example, Barlow [3]; Swets, Green, and Tanner [42]). Alternative approaches to detection data couched in the framework of learning models have also been proposed (Bush, Luce, and Rose [8]; Luce [25]; Atkinson, Bower, and Crothers [1, Chapter 5]). Learned biases in responding appear to be particularly important whenever values or rewards are placed on alternative responses in psychophysical experiments. As a practical matter, most work on detection must be thought of as manifesting both sensory mechanisms and learned response biases in varying degrees. Our position here is to try to analyze the sensory mechanisms and to display great anxiety about the learned-response biases. Understanding in both cases is too primitive to tolerate mixing them up.

9.2 THE SQUARE-ROOT LAW

The most prominent feature of Poisson detection is a square-root-law detectability restriction. As the mean level of a Poisson process grows, its capacity to fluctuate also grows (although not quite as fast). This loss of resolution affects the size of the minimum detectable change in a systematic way. The point is obvious from study of the Poisson distribution (the mean and variance are equal), but it is not easy to capture in the language of detection. We first show how it is established and then discuss a number of forms of the square-root law.

Imagine a sensory channel and a continuing sequence of impulses forming an information flow, which may be thought of as being generated mainly by a background stimulus, and partly by internal, spontaneous discharges. The flux is collected at a focal point in the channel and counted. An auxiliary signal, indicating a stimulus period, starts the counting record which accumulates for a fixed (short) interval of time. The integration time is obviously a question of great importance, but it will play no significant role in the present development. It is taken to be a parameter of the detection process. We should also say that several of our stipulations on the format of detection are unnecessarily restrictive, for example, the single counting focus and the fixed integration time. Other options are available without doing serious violence to a Poisson model.

In any event, the counting scheme described above generates something close to a Poisson distribution out of the background process, if only the origins of the background are independent and sufficiently numerous. Just what this means is discussed in Section 9.5, but intuition may be satisfied with the explanation that uncertainty about when the next impulse will appear in order to be counted must become more uniform as the number of independent impulse sources builds up. Uniformity of uncertainty is the essential mark of a Poisson process.

The count on any trial is an integer j. Its expected value $E(j)$ is labeled n_0, where n_0 is taken to be the average background count. This need not be an integer. Now let a transient stimulus—for example, a flash of light—be presented on some subset of the trials. In these instances, we suppose the counting distribution to be still Poisson; but the expected value jumps to $n_s + n_0$, where n_s is the mean-stimulus count. The problem is formulated by saying that the detection mechanism must look at a particular count j and decide whether it came from a typical fluctuation of the background or from a new stimulus.

In visual psychophysics, detection is said to occur whenever the count reaches or exceeds a *critical number* k (see [18]). This is the natural criterion in an energy-detection scheme based on counting, and we adopt it here. Accordingly, when a stimulus is presented, the probability of detection will be

$$(9.1) \qquad P_s(k) = \sum_{j=k}^{j=\infty} w_{n_s+n_0}(j),$$

and the analogous probability of a false report is given by

$$(9.2) \qquad P_0(k) = \sum_{j=k}^{j=\infty} w_{n_0}(j).$$

In (9.1) and (9.2), the term $w_m(j)$ specifies a Poisson probability

$$(9.3) \qquad w_m(j) = \frac{m^j e^{-m}}{j!}.$$

Evidently the detection probability and the false-report probability are tied together as the critical number changes. Much of what we say on the subject of such changes is an effort to rationalize principles governing the selection of a critical number. Hence we are unabashedly interested in theories of the criterion, and we find ourselves deeply involved with what was once a mystical and almost forbidden topic, namely the criterion problem in psychophysics. We owe a great debt of gratitude to the last two decades of research on signal detection for making the step unnecessary to defend on grounds of propriety.

The square-root law emerges in its simplest form when the background count n_0 is allowed to change while the false-report probability remains fixed. Equation (9.2) is approximated by a unit normal integral whose lower limit is

$$(9.4) \qquad \frac{k - n_0}{n_0^{1/2}} = c,$$

where the constant c is a normal deviate that is fixed when the false-report probability is fixed. Usually a simple continuity correction is also included [k is reduced by half when (9.4) is used to estimate $P_0(k)$]. The approximation is found to be satisfactory when n_0 is moderately large. Now set the detection probability at $\frac{1}{2}$ in equation (9.1). A normal approximation will have as its lower limit

$$(9.5) \qquad \frac{k - (n_s + n_0)}{(n_s + n_0)^{1/2}} = 0,$$

and if the value for the critical number is inserted from (9.4) into (9.5), we find

$$(9.6) \qquad \frac{n_s}{n_0^{1/2}} = c.$$

In other words, the incremental count that is just detectable with the probability $P_s(k) = \frac{1}{2}$ against a given background is proportional to the square root of the background count, provided the false-report probability is fixed but independent of what that probability is. Vision research often assumes that n_s and n_0 are governed by the mean number of light quanta incident on the eye. Equation (9.6) then leads to a square-root law of intensity discrimination, as deVries [48] and Rose [35, 36] pointed out long ago. Our development thus far follows the exposition of the square-root law found in the vision literature, and is closely patterned after Barlow [3], and Triesman [45].

Next we turn to a formulation that is a bit more general and more characteristic of communication work. Figure 9.1 shows four Poisson *response operating characteristics* (ROC curves). These are graphs relating the probability of detection to the probability of a false report. The curves were obtained in each instance by plotting $P_s(k)$ in (9.1) against $P_0(k)$ in (9.2) as

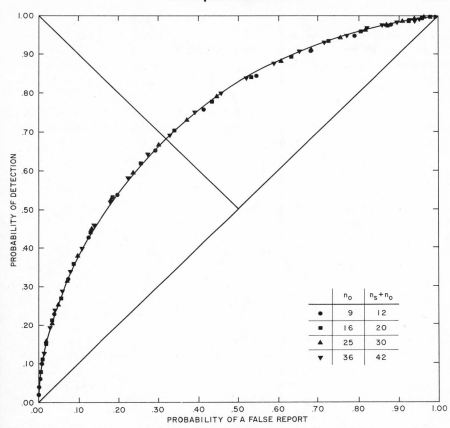

Fig. 9.1 Response operating characteristic (ROC) curves showing the square-root law in Poisson detection. A mean count n_0 (abcissa) is compared with $n_s + n_0$ (ordinate) as detection criterion changes in integral steps. Each case shows the incremental count in unit ratio to the square root of the background. Continuous curve is a normal approximation.

k changes in discrete steps. Probabilities were read from the General Electric Co. [14] tables of the Poisson distribution. The figure provides a bit of a surprise in that the four curves are hardly distinguishable over the entire range. Some correspondence was expected since each Poisson curve has the same value $c = 1$ in (9.6), but the argument we used in establishing the square-root law holds only where the detection probability is .50. Furthermore, the format of the normal approximation in (9.5) suggests a breakdown as detection probabilities depart appreciably from .50, but it does not seem to happen. Finally, the normal approximation to the Poisson curve in Figure 9.1 is determined not for $c = 1$ but for $c = .95$. These anomalies are explained as soon as it is realized that more than one normal approximation exists for the Poisson distribution. The square-root transformation of the Poisson count is a particularly strong approximation, and it appears to account for the regularities evident in Figure 9.1, as we now show.

Let $n_s/n_0^{1/2} = r$. This is not a statement of the square-root law but a choice of n_s and n_0 subject to the restriction. Generally speaking, r must be small relative to n_0. Consider

$$(n_s + n_0)^{1/2} - (n_0)^{1/2} = n_0^{1/2}\left(1 + \frac{r}{n_0^{1/2}}\right)^{1/2} - n_0^{1/2}.$$

If r is not too large, the bracketed square root on the right can be expanded in series, yielding

$$(n_s + n_0)^{1/2} - (n_0)^{1/2} = \frac{r}{2}\left(1 - \frac{r}{4n_0^{1/2}} + \frac{r^2}{8n_0} - \dots\right).$$

Hence

(9.7)
$$2[(n_s + n_0)^{1/2} - (n_0)^{1/2}] \to \frac{n_s}{n_0^{1/2}}.$$

The square-root transformation is the expression in the left-hand member of (9.7). It approaches the square-root law asymptotically from below as the level of the background count increases. Consequently, both must be normal approximations for the Poisson distribution. It appears that the square-root transformation performs somewhat better than (9.4) and (9.5) when n_0, the mean-background count, is small.

The four ROC curves in Figure 9.1 lead to the following normal deviates under the square-root transformation:

n_0	$2(n_s + n_0)^{1/2} - 2(n_0)^{1/2}$
9	.9282
16	.9443
25	.9545
36	.9615

The value of .95 drawn through the points in Figure 9.1 splits the cluster down the middle, and hence this feature of the individual Poisson curves in Figure 9.1 is handled nicely.

In view of (9.7), it follows that if $n_s/n_0^{1/2} = 1$ and n_0 is allowed to increase, the square-root transformation must also approach unity asymptotically. Accordingly, the whole range of ROC curves from $n_0 = 9$ on up generates no more than a thin shell in Figure 9.1, and the square-root law is seen to be much stronger than our original argument would seem to suggest.

Bartlett [4, p. 41] and Rao [34, pp. 209–210], as well as many other sources, show that when j is Poisson distributed with mean n_0, the square-root transform $2(j)^{1/2}$ is approximately normal with mean $2(n_0)^{1/2}$ and unit variance. This was our guide in constructing Figure 9.1. (Various authors suggest small adjustments to improve the approximation, but we have not found them particularly helpful in this context.) In any case, the detection probabilities in (9.1) and (9.2) can now be rewritten via the square-root transform:

$$(9.8a) \qquad 2(n_s + n_0)^{1/2} - 2(k)^{1/2} = d_{cs},$$

$$(9.8b) \qquad 2(k)^{1/2} - 2(n_0)^{1/2} = d_{0c},$$

where the quantities d_{0c} and d_{cs} are unit normal deviates, or Thurstone distances. The distance d_{0c} runs from the mean of the background-counting distribution to the critical number, and d_{cs} is the analogous distance from the critical number up to the mean count with stimulus-added-to-background. For comparison with Poisson sums, it is useful to make a continuity correction, replacing k in (9.8) with $k - \frac{1}{2}$. The net result is that the numbers corresponding to the background count, critical number, and stimulus count are easily converted to normal deviates via the square-root transformation. The deviates then lead directly to detection and false-report probabilities by means of the normal probability table.

Figure 9.2 illustrates these rules and displays our notation. Additional clarification may be obtained from the following example:

Let $n_0 = 16$, $n_s = 4$, $k = 17$. A table of the Poisson distribution yields $P_0(k) = .434$, $P_s(k) = .779$, as the respective false-report and detection probabilities. The square-root transformation

$$2(k)^{1/2} - 2(n_0)^{1/2} = d_{0c},$$

$$2(16.50)^{1/2} - 2(4) \quad = +.124,$$

brings us the desired false-report probability via the region in the tail of the normalized background distribution beyond the critical number. The probability is read from the normal table as $P_0(k) = .450$. Similarly,

$$2(n_s + n_0)^{1/2} - 2(k)^{1/2} \quad = d_{cs},$$

$$2(20)^{1/2} - 2(16.50)^{1/2} = +.820.$$

The detection probability is the area to the right of the critical number in the normalized stimulus distribution. A normal table shows it to be $P_s(k) = .794$.

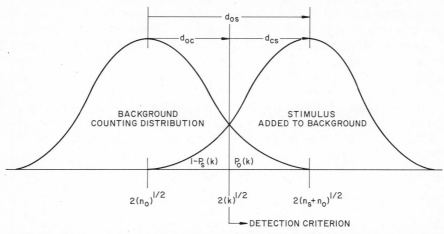

Fig. 9.2 Unit normal metric (Thurstone distances) resulting from square-root transform of Poisson count. Detection criterion is shown at locus of least error when stimulus and background conditions are equally likely.

Probabilities derived from the pair of Thurstone distances d_{oc} and d_{cs} lie on the continuous curve in Figure 9.1, while the Poisson probabilities are the coordinates of the black square plotted adjacent to the curve. Overall detectability (independent of critical number) is easily expressed as a Thurstone distance via Figure 9.2 and equations (9.8a) and (9.8b):

$$d_{0s} = d_{0c} + d_{cs},$$

(9.8c) $$d_{0s} = 2(n_s + n_0)^{1/2} - 2(n_0)^{1/2} \leq \frac{n_s}{(n_0)^{1/2}},$$

when the expansion leading to (9.7) is valid. Inserting $n_0 = 16$, $n_s = 4$, we obtain

$$d_{0s} = 2(20)^{1/2} - 2(4)$$
$$= .944.$$

This last normal deviate is the locus of the continuous curve drawn through the points of Figure 9.1. (It is ordinarily labeled d' in detection theory. We attach subscripts because there are several such distances to keep track of.) Evidently Poisson detection can be closely approximated to the gaussian case via the square-root transform, and this fact materially simplifies a detectability analysis of Poisson counting. In Figure 9.1, the normalized counting distributions are separated by about .95 standard unit, and the superposition of the ROC curves shows that both the normal approximation and the square-root law are good generalizations.

The symmetry of the Poisson ROC curve may prove to be in conflict with data on visual detection [25, p. 9; 43, p. 319]. Probably, however, it is too early to tell. Asymmetry can be generated by a variety of experimental artifices ranging from stimulus uncertainty to payoff structure, and we still lack an understanding of how these factors are reflected in the data.

9.3 LEAST-ERROR CRITERION

Visual detection ordinarily treats the criterion as a stable parameter, fixed in relation to the background and functioning to control (or perhaps squelch) false reports (see [2, p. 638], [5, pp. 380–381], [45, p. 315]). Our development adheres to this principle whenever the critical number is set at

$$(9.4a) \qquad k = n_0 + c(n_0)^{1/2}.$$

False-report probability is then determined by the constant c and is (nearly) fixed when c is fixed, provided the background level n_0 is sufficiently large. Poisson detection identifies this restriction (often called a Neyman-Pearson criterion by analogy with statistical testing) as a stable criterion.

In practice, the result might be achieved by using an undistractible subject S, a continuous background, randomized stimulus intensities, and a detection method similar to constant stimuli. A sensory-monitoring mechanism would be forced to rely entirely on the background in order to determine a stimulus, and it presumably would detect whenever the count emerged in some characteristic way out of the background level. Shades of meaning of the word "characteristic" span an equivalent range of possible false-report rates. There is no easily communicable rule rendering c constant from subject to subject or from session to session. Consequently, detection behavior will prove to be unstable unless the false-report rate can be systematically constrained. Since the typical procedures employed in the method of constant stimuli force the false-report rate to be vanishingly small, $c > 3$, stability training presents a problem. It means in practical terms that ordinary psychophysical procedures are unstable. Barlow (1956) has attempted to trace such instabilities in reported variations of the critical number of quanta at absolute threshold in vision.

Many workers in detection are prepared to sacrifice the stable criterion in order to control false reports via discrimination training. Only one intensity is compared with the background. On any trial, a single stimulus is presented. S responds with his judgment as to which it was, and the apparatus then signals back to S which stimulus it really was. This completes a cycle and the next trial begins. During a run of such trials, there are two possible stimuli: background-alone and stimulus-added-to-background. They are programmed to follow each other in random order with predetermined probabilities.

It is well known that these restrictions permit a detection model to grind out a unique criterion minimizing detection errors. We call it the *least-error criterion*. The literature on detection often labels it "Siegert's ideal observer" (see [21, pp. viii, 168], [32, p. 177], [46, p. 120]).

In Poisson detection, the least-error criterion is a straightforward problem. Call the probability of the background condition $P(O)$, and let $P(S)$ be the analogous probability of a stimulus increment. On any trial, one or the other must be presented. Hence

$$P(O) + P(S) = 1.$$

Now set up the ratio $l(k)$ of stimulus and background counting probabilities. These are joint probabilities covering the condition to be presented and the resulting count. In each instance, the latter is set at k:

(9.9)
$$l(k) = \frac{P(S) \cdot w_{n_s+n_0}(k)}{P(O) \cdot w_{n_0}(k)},$$

$$l(k) = \frac{P(S)}{P(O)} \left(1 + \frac{n_s}{n_0}\right)^k \exp(-n_s).$$

This ratio increases monotonically with k. Refer to the continuous approximation in Figure 9.2, and verify that $l(k) = 1$ at the point where the *weighted* ordinates cross. The monotone increase in $l(k)$ means that the crossover point, if it exists, is unique—no other crossing occurs. Refer again to Figure 9.2, and note that displacing the criterion to the right of the crossover point generates an increase in errors due to missed stimuli in excess of the drop in false reports. Similarly, if the criterion is displaced to the left of the crossover point, the increase in false reports exceeds the decrease in missed stimuli. Accordingly, any departure from the crossover point boosts the total errors, and the latter must be least where $l(k) = 1$. This approach is closely related to the likelihood-ratio method used by Van Meter and Middleton [46, pp. 128–129] and Peterson, Birdsall, and Fox [32, p. 175].

The critical number corresponding to the crossover point in Poisson detection is easily found by solving (9.9) with $l(k) = 1$:

(9.10)
$$k = \frac{n_s + \ln \beta}{\ln(1 + n_s/n_0)},$$

where $\beta = P(O)/P(S)$.[1]

[1] The parameter β is usually defined in terms of a weighted payoff matrix [32, p. 178]. We have retained the notation to make our presentation more intelligible for readers who work with payoff matrices. The least-error criterion occurs as a special case when the payoff matrix is symmetric.

It is not always easy, however, to see this critical number in relation to the stimulus and background distributions that determine it. A somewhat better view is obtained by going to a closely related expression. First expand the log series in the denominator in (9.10):

$$k = \frac{n_0(1 + \ln \beta/n_s)}{1 - n_s/2n_0 + n_s^2/3n_0^2 - n_s^3/4n_0^3 + \ldots}.$$

The denominator closely resembles

$$\left(1 + \frac{n_s}{n_0}\right)^{-1/2} = 1 - \frac{n_s}{2n_0} + \frac{3n_s^2}{8n_0^2} - \frac{5}{16}\frac{n_s^3}{n_0^3} + \ldots.$$

Accordingly, the least-error critical number must be approximately[2]

(9.11) $$k = n_0^{1/2}(n_s + n_0)^{1/2}(1 + \ln \beta/n_s).$$

Equation (9.11) is essentially the result found from direct analysis of the normal approximation. Marill's [26, pp. 45–46] gaussian formula for the least-error criterion is readily obtained from it by converting to normal deviates. More important, equation (9.11) is easy to study. For instance, when stimulus and background are equally likely, the critical number settles at the geometric mean of the two counts. Substituting this geometric mean into the normal approximation for the Poisson distribution shows that $d_{0c} \cong d_{cs}$: the least-error criterion is located at the midpoint of the Thurstone distance between stimulus and background. With the criterion in this location, the detection probability $P_s(k)$ and the false-report probability $P_0(k)$ must sum to unity, as depicted in Figure 9.2. Evidently as stimulus intensity increases, the criterion is pulled along, adapting to increasing differences between stimulus and background counts. Moreover, it is apparent that the least-error criterion also obeys the square-root law. The latter is a property of detection and is not limited to a specific criterion.

In case stimulus and background conditions are not equally likely (when $\ln \beta \neq 0$), (9.11) shows the critical number to be displaced up or down from the geometric mean, depending on which condition predominates. For example, let the background count be $n_0 = 16$, $n_s = 4$, $P(S) = .25$. The stimulus raises the background by four counts on the average, but it is presented on only a quarter of the trials. Where is the least-error criterion? Equation (9.10) yields $k = 22.85$ for the critical number [the approximation

---

[2] The Poisson formula in (9.10) and the approximation in (9.11) have been computed over a wide range of values of β by Lanson on the IBM 7094 at Columbia University. The error in the approximation was found to be a half count or less when $n_s/n_0 \leq 1$. Error magnitude was insensitive to changes in β. The author is grateful to Mr. R. N. Lanson for making these computations available.

in (9.11) turns out to be 22.80]. This value for k is then substituted directly into the square-root transform (see Figure 9.2) and produces

$$d_{0c} = 2(k)^{1/2} - 2(n_0)^{1/2} = 2(4.78) - 2(4.00) = +1.56,$$

$$d_{cs} = 2(n_0 + n_s)^{1/2} - 2(k)^{1/2} = 2(4.47) - 2(4.78) = -0.62,$$

$$d_{0s} = 2(n_0 + n_s)^{1/2} - 2(n_0)^{1/2} = 2(4.47) - 2(4.00) = +0.94.$$

Corrections for continuity are not applicable when the critical number is computed in (9.10) or (9.11). Our results show the Thurstone distance between stimulus and background to be unchanged (see earlier example in Section 9.2). The critical number, however, is now shifted to a location above the mean of the normalized stimulus distribution. The shift evidently protects against false reports since the background condition predominates in the experiment. Moreover, the distance d_{cs} from the criterion to the mean of the stimulus-counting distribution must be negative because of this protection. Accordingly, the detection probability is less than .50 [$P_s(k) = .27$ via the normal table]. On the other hand, the distance d_{0c} is large and the false-report probability must be small [$P_0(k) = .06$ from the normal table]. Linear interpolation in the Poisson table for $k = 23.35$ produces $P_s(k) = .26$ and $P_0(k) = .05$ as the analogous Poisson probabilities. Again the square-root transformation is seen to be an accurate guide.

We noted earlier that the geometric-mean count generates an outcome in which

(9.12) $$P_s(k) + P_0(k) = 1.$$

As the stimulus count increases in size, the least-error criterion is constrained to fall along the main diagonal, as illustrated in Figure 9.1. The intersection of the ROC curve with this diagonal [$P_0(k) = .32$, $P_s(k) = .68$, corresponding to $d_{0s}/2 = .47$] is the locus of least error when stimulus and background conditions are presented equally often. The main diagonal is called an *isocriterion contour* corresponding to $\beta = 1$, and the projection of these same points on the axis of detection probability generates the psychometric function. When $\beta \neq 1$, isocriterion contours and psychometric functions are derived via the least-error critical numbers and the square-root transform.

The upper and lower graphs on the left side of Figure 9.3 are isocriterion contours and psychometric functions, respectively, computed for Poisson detection by using (9.10) and the square-root transform (9.8a, b). These curves are very similar to the ones obtained in gaussian detection [9, p. 390; 46, p. 145, Figure 3]. Our analysis of the Poisson case is helpful, however, because it is especially easy to see what is going on. For example, the curvatures in Figure 9.3 are a consequence of the fact that a least-error criterion turns to optimum strategy when it is faced by increasingly difficult discriminations ($n_s \rightarrow 0$). Equation (9.11) then shows the critical number exhibiting three stable states as β changes:

$$(9.13) \qquad \lim_{n_s \rightarrow 0} k = \begin{cases} \infty & P(0) > P(S), \\ n_0 & P(0) = P(S), \\ 0 & P(0) < P(S). \end{cases}$$

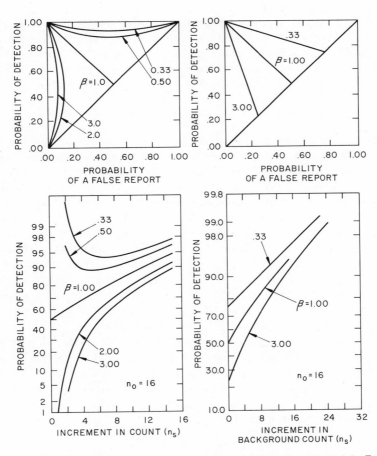

Fig. 9.3 Isocriterion contours (upper) and psychometric functions (lower) in Poisson detection. Curves on left are obtained with least-error criterion. Curves on right are generated by equalizing (instead of minimizing) error.

When the critical number is at infinity, detection never occurs; at zero, detection always occurs. Hence if $n_s = 0$, the detection probability jumps from zero to unity as the "stimulus" presentation probability sweeps through .50. Siegel [38] has discussed this outcome in the context of choice strategies. It is particularly interesting to note that detection experiments shade into choice problems as the stimulus increment moves toward zero. This delineates a vital region of overlap between research on choice and research on detection. The overlap is still largely uninvestigated except for the work of Luce [23, pp. 58–68, Chapter 3] and Norman [30].

Discrimination analysis of the visual quantum problem is unknown to the writer. A fair amount of work has been done on analogous problems in auditory detection, including several efforts to trace the shape of iso-criterion contours [20; 24, Chapter 3; 29; 30, p. 1439; 37; 41]. These studies seem to show the criterion being pulled in the direction of reduced error (in accord with theory) as stimulus intensity increases, but we still have only a vague idea of the mechanics of the process.

9.4 EQUALIZED ERROR

The least-error principle is of considerable logical and even historical significance as a way to specify a criterion, but its psychological importance is less clear. Unease is felt not so much because least-error psychometric functions and isocriterion contours look a bit unusual to the practiced eye. These aspects of detection behavior are still relatively unexplored, and some of Norman's [30] data are sufficiently unusual to make us cautious. The main difficulty is that no easy way of sensing error probabilities suggests itself, and we find it difficult to devise error-minimizing mechanisms that would be responsive to changes in short-term error rates. S might perform an intuitive operation similar in form to that of (9.11), somehow managing to minimize his errors. No one, after all, expects a spider to comprehend the geometry governing its web. But this is more of an appeal than an explanation. The need for a mechanism persists.

The issue is interesting because a principle closely related to least error leads to adjustment mechanisms that are schematically simple and be-haviorally plausible. The alternative principle operates in its most primitive form whenever the detection criterion adjusts so as to balance detection errors equally between the two kinds that can occur.[3] The adjustment then defines an equilibrium condition

$$(9.14) \qquad\qquad P_s(k) + \beta P_0(k) = 1,$$

equalizing the frequency of occurrence of missed signals and false reports.

[3] This criterion was suggested by W. K. Estes.

Isocriterion contours are now linear, as illustrated in (9.14) and the upper right-hand corner of Figure 9.3. Moreover, the equilibrium equation can be rewritten in the form

$$\Pr\{\text{Detection}\} = P(S).$$

We see that probability matching occurs along each of the contours. Evidently the slope of the linear characteristic can be modified by permitting a bias parameter to multiply β. This would put the probabilities of the two classes of errors into fixed ratio instead of equating them, but the essentials of the equilibrium condition specified in (9.14) would not be altered. A mechanism that does this kind of biasing will be discussed shortly. It is clear that we are not dealing with a single criterion but with a class of criteria.

Since k is the only unknown in (9.14), solution for the critical number is a simple matter, but no closed expression or near approximation is known (except at $\beta = 1$, where the result is identical with the least-error criterion). The square-root transformation, however, makes it relatively easy to find the incremental count corresponding to a particular critical number that equalizes error. For example, let $n_0 = 16$, $P(S) = .25$, and set the critical number at $k = 20$. What value of n_s equalizes errors with these parameters? First note via the Poisson tables that $P_0(k) = .188$, in which case (9.14) requires that $P_s(k) = .436$. The normal table then yields $d_{cs} = -.158$. We now write out the square-root transform

$$n_s + n_0 = \left[\left(20 - \frac{1}{2}\right)^{1/2} - \frac{.158}{2}\right]^2$$

$$= 18.81.$$

This increment, $n_s = 2.81$, added to a background count $n_0 = 16$ on one-quarter of the trials, equalizes the frequency of missed signals and false reports when the critical number is $k = 20$. Poisson tables show the approximation to be accurate.

The method just outlined can then be used to construct psychometric functions generated by an equalized error criterion. Typical examples are shown at the lower right of Figure 9.3. We should emphasize that these psychometric functions result when the critical number is fixed at the criterion.

Equalized error (or, more generally, a fixed error ratio) characterizes a class of short-term memory devices in which final adaptation is accomplished by repeated application of a simple corrective rule. In view of this, the equalized-error restriction is sometimes found in simple response-learning models applied to psychophysics (for example, see [1, p. 196]).

One of the most striking instances of stable adaptation achieved via repeated trial-by-trial adjustments is a feedback mechanism proposed by Sklansky [39, 40] and illustrated in Figure 9.4. Sklansky's mechanism leaves the criterion unchanged when feedback indicates a correct discrimination. When an error occurs, the critical number is immediately shifted up b counts if a false report; down b' counts if a missed signal. These two modifications work in opposite directions and eventually drive the critical number into equilibrium. At the equilibrium point, the net expected change is zero. Accordingly,

$$P(0)\ P_0(k)\cdot b\ -\ P(S)[1\ -\ P_s(k)]\cdot b'\ =\ 0,$$

(9.15)
$$P_s(k)\ +\ \left[\beta\ \frac{b}{b'}\right]P_0(k)\ =\ 1,$$

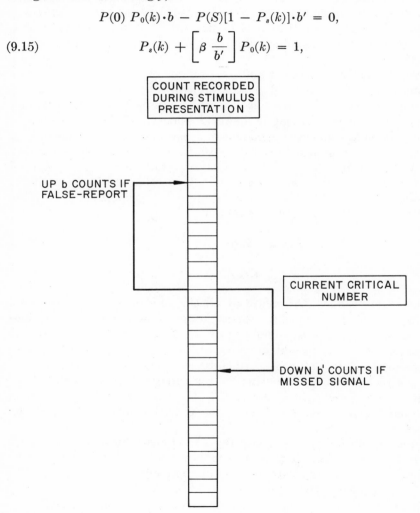

Fig. 9.4   Sklansky's feedback-adjustment mechanism for detection criterion. Asymptotic adaptation puts detection errors into the ratio b/b'.

and the expected location of the critical number equalizes error if the corrective adjustments are symmetrical. When the feedback adjustments are asymmetric, isocriterion contours are biased away from probability matching but continue to be linear. We speak of "expected" location of the critical number. This is because the critical number cannot remain fixed while the feedback corrective process is going on. Instead, the critical number walks up and down at random around its equilibrium point. If the loop is opened (that is, if feedback is stopped), the criterion remains fixed in the neighborhood of the equilibrium point. Hence the open-loop condition produces detection data similar to the functions shown on the right of Figure 9.3.

Closed-loop operation generates an asymptotic distribution of the critical number as it walks up and down at random. The transition matrix of the random walk is not difficult to work out with the aid of Figure 9.4. If the critical number is currently at k, it jumps up to $k + b$ with probability $P(0) \cdot P_0(k)$, and down to $k - b'$ with probability $P(S) \cdot [1 - P_s(k)]$; otherwise it remains where it is. This process generates what proves to be an attractive force at the expected value of the critical number. The further the current value drifts from the expected value in either direction, the stronger the pull to return. In this respect, Sklansky's feedback model in Poisson detection (when $b = b' = 1$) resembles the Ehrenfest model, for which the asymptotic distribution of the critical number is binomial (see [13, pp. 343–344; 19, pp. 380–385]). The Ehrenfest model suggests the conjecture that the asymptotic distribution of Sklansky's feedback process operating on the critical number is also approximately normal. The conjecture can be tested directly by constructing sample transition matrices and raising them to very high powers via matrix multiplication on a digital computer. Preliminary work with this approach shows it to be practical and reinforces the conjecture that small, symmetrical feedback adjustments yield asymptotic normality for the distribution of the criterion in Poisson detection.[4] But the main objective is to determine what happens when the magnitude of the feedback adjustments grows large in relation to the two counts to be discriminated. The random-walk distribution then appears to fragment, producing phenomena that are qualitatively similar to the quantal effects described by Luce [24, Chapter 3] and Norman [29, 31].

[4] The approach was suggested and programmed without difficulty by Dr. David L. Brown, Columbia University. Sample transition matrices were raised to the 320th power in order to stabilize the asymptotic distribution. Although it is a brute-force operation, computing time is very fast. Six samples (involving different feedback adjustments) were run through in 2.19 minutes.

9.5 SENSORY FLUX

A point of view that is currently well established in visual energy detection treats the eye as a quantum counter. This conception dates from the work of Hecht, Shlaer, and Pirenne [18] and van der Velden [47], although the mechanics involved are still poorly understood. It is not known, for example, whether the crucial events in detection take place in the eye itself, or further back in the visual system. In either case, the flux of photons incident on the eye is thought to be converted to a proportional neural flux. The exchange is triggered by absorption of photons in molecules of photopigment, leading eventually to nerve impulses. This idea, a neural flux reflecting the statistics of the light flux, has been stated very clearly by Bouman, Vos, and Walraven [6]. It probably also lies at the heart of the arguments offered by de Vries [48] and Rose [35, 36], leading to the square-root law of visual intensity discrimination (hence the "de Vries-Rose law").

Transduction of light flux into an equivalent sensory flux is a natural expectation, given the quantum character of light and the behavior of photopigments. Experimental support is added in studies of the limulus eye. Poisson statistics have been verified in the barrage of nerve impulses following a flash of light (see Hartline et al. [16] and Mueller [27]).

Perhaps the simplest stochastic mechanism that might govern the conversion process involves random deletions from the Poisson sequence constituting the light flux. Certain photons are earmarked at random to pass through the obstacles provided by the visual system and to be counted. The rest are lost. This is essentially what happens in a particle counter. If we label the mean light energy (quanta/flash) in the stimulus measured at the cornea, using the symbol N_s, the mean count traceable to this stimulus in the sensory channel will be

$$(9.16) \qquad\qquad n_s = aN_s.$$

The constant a is the probability of survival of an element of the light flux as an element of the counting flux. Random deletion does not affect the form of the distribution. If N_s has a Poisson distribution, so will n_s have a Poisson distribution. Thus the visual system is thought of as a proportional counting device. This point of view is discussed by Barlow [3] and Bouman et al. [5, 6]. Evidently restriction (9.16) leads directly to the de Vries-Rose square-root law governing visual intensity discrimination. The law has been established experimentally over a range of some 6 log units above absolute threshold when peripheral stimuli, small visual angles, and brief flashes are used (see [3] and [7]). Barlow's data also show a weak but measurable noise level limiting visual intensity discrimination near absolute threshold. The noise is inferred because the square-root law breaks down at roughly 10^3 quanta/second degree^2 background light intensity. Integration in the eye seems to occur over a region that is approximately 10^{-1} second degree^2. This means that the noise level of the eye estimated from the breakdown of the square-root law is the equivalent of 10^2 quanta/summation unit, and, since 90 per cent of these would be lost in transmission, there must be approximately 10 noise events in the average background count. Barlow's study [2] of the absolute threshold produces a figure of 8.9 noise events confused with the stimulus flash. This result was obtained via manipulation of the false-report rate. Accordingly, the two sets of data are in basic agreement. The absolute limit on detectability seems to derive from internal noise in the visual system, or, as Barlow puts it, from *dark light*.

Whatever the attraction and ultimate applicability of a pat and pretty scheme such as proportional counting in the visual system via random deletions from the stimulus, it is not absolutely required. Half hidden is the assumption that Poisson statistics are introduced into the sensory channel by the Poisson statistics of the visual stimulus, whereas it seems likely that Poisson-channel statistics would occur in any case.

A repetitive flow of impulses down a nerve pathway fits the definition of a renewal process, and separate nerve pathways can be taken to be independent. If this flux is collected at a focal point and counted, the outcome is equivalent to superposing the renewal processes. Superposition effectively removes the "tags" on the separate pathways and introduces spontaneous fluctuations into an observing system that cannot see the tags. There are several treatments of this important topic in stochastic processes. Cox and Smith [10] show that when independent pathways carry different and mutually indivisible periodic impulse sequences, the interresponse times in the superposed sequence nonetheless tend toward an exponential distribution (that is, Poisson statistics), as the number of separate pathways increases. Drenick [12] proves essentially the same limit for a wide class of renewal processes in the separate pathways. Cox [11, pp. 77–79] discusses the conditions under which superposition of renewal processes generates Poisson behavior.

These arguments, in fact, establish the logical basis for applying stochastic models to phenomena such as traffic flow. Traffic on a superhighway is a causal phenomenon. Each auto is tagged in the strictest sense. It comes from somewhere and is traveling to somewhere. Consequently, a high-order intelligence could in principle unscramble the flow completely and say where each vehicle was at any time. Regularities such as a military convoy would be detected easily, but a pneumatic counting device lying across the highway sees exactly the same activity as a Poisson process.

Renewal theory thus offers considerable scope to a Poisson analysis of the flux of sensory data. We can assume that a brief stimulus whose energy content is precisely fixed will nevertheless be mapped into a Poisson counting distribution in the sensory integration time. The stimulus energy is converted to a mean count through a scaling or attenuation constant a. Poisson statistics are imparted by superposed renewal processes in the sensory channel. The channel's counting statistics are thus a compound of the Poisson distribution and whatever statistics characterize the driving energy of the stimulus. If the latter has fixed energy, the counting distribution will be Poisson; otherwise, the process requires integration over the statistics of the stimulus in order to arrive at the channel statistics. The problem is formally related to Greenwood and Yule's [15] generalization of the Poisson law. Essentially the same approach can be found in an early Russian paper on auditory detection by Lifshitz [22].

We are brought around to an obvious question. Suppose N photons impinge on the cornea, and, following our rules, this event gives rise to a Poisson counting distribution in which the mean count in the sensory channel is aN. However, N photons cannot be guaranteed with each flash. The compound generating function of the stimulus fluctuations and counting fluctuations must then be

$$M_j(\theta) = \sum_{N=0}^{N=\infty} w_{N_0}(N) \cdot \exp aN(e^\theta - 1),$$

(9.17) $$M_j(\theta) = \exp \{N_0[e^{a(e^\theta-1)} - 1]\},$$

where N_0 is the mean number of quanta per flash.

It is apparent that (9.17) is not the moment-generating function of a Poisson distribution. The inversion is in fact

(9.18) $$P(j) = \sum_{N=0}^{N=\infty} w_{N_0}(N) \cdot w_{aN}(j),$$

where $P(j)$ is the probability that j impulses are counted following stimulation. The result is readily verified by going over to the moment-generating function of (9.18) and noting that it is the same as that of (9.17). Equation (9.18) is seen to be a discrete counting distribution analogous to the Poisson distribution. It is formed from products of Poisson terms using our notation in (9.3), and is identified in the literature as Neyman's Type A distribution [28].

We seem to be caught in our own web. Poisson statistics are well established in the visual case. A treatment contradicting this explanation will not be easy to swallow. Fortunately, the difficulty does not appear to be serious. The mean and variance of the counting distribution in (9.18) are found to be

$$n_0 = aN_0,$$

$$\sigma^2 = a(1 + a) N_0.$$

Applying the normal approximation to (9.18) generates a detection law analogous to the square-root law in (9.6) of Section 9.2:

(9.19) $$\left(\frac{a}{1 + a}\right)^{1/2} \cdot \frac{N_s}{N_0^{1/2}} = c.$$

If the attenuation constant a is small, as it probably is in any realistic treatment, the detection behavior of the compound counting distribution is almost indistinguishable from the Poisson case.

The importance of the approach just outlined, a Poisson channel flow combined with arbitrary stimulus energy statistics for determining the statistics of sensory detection, rests on the fact that it opens the prospect of a unified description of sensory detection. Poisson counting statistics in the auditory channel can be combined with the energy statistics of acoustic white noise to determine the detection statistics underlying threshold distributions and intensity discrimination. This compound, by the way, is a very close parallel of the Greenwood-Yule problem. It generates a form of Weber's law as the detection law for increments in acoustic white noise.

The Poisson law is seen to be a building block that is shaped into a detection law by the energy statistics of the stimulus. The whole process is much too simple to be taken at face value, but it is clearly formulated and thus capable of being wrong, which is important.

REFERENCES

1. Atkinson, R., G. Bower, and E. Crothers, *An Introduction to Mathematical Learning Theory*, Wiley, New York, 1965.
2. Barlow, H. B., "Retinal Noise and Absolute Threshold," *J. Opt. Soc. Amer.*, **46**, 1956, 634–639.
3. Barlow, H. B., "Increment Thresholds at Low Intensities Considered as Signal/Noise Discrimination," *J. Physiol.*, **136**, 1957, 469–488.
4. Bartlett, M. S., "The Use of Transformations," *Biometrics*, **3**, 1947, 39–52.
5. Bouman, M. A., "History and Present Status of Quantum Theory in Vision," in Rosenblith, W. A. (editor), *Sensory Communication*, M.I.T. Press and Wiley, Cambridge, 1961.
6. Bouman, M. A., J. J. Vos, and P. L. Walraven, "Fluctuation Theory of Luminance and Chromaticity Discrimination," *J. Opt. Soc. Amer.*, **53**, 1963, 121–128.
7. van den Brink, G., and M. A. Bouman, "Visual Contrast Thresholds for Moving Point Sources," *J. Opt. Soc. Amer.*, **47**, 1957, 612–618.

8. Bush, R. R., R. D. Luce, and R. M. Rose, "Learning Models for Psychophysics," in Atkinson, R. C. (editor), *Studies in Mathematical Psychology*, Stanford University Press, Stanford, 1961.

9. Clarke, F. R., and R. C. Bilger, "The Theory of Signal Detectability and the Measurement of Hearing," in Jerger, J. (editor), *Modern Developments in Audiology*, Academic Press, New York, 1963.

10. Cox, D. R., and W. L. Smith, "The Superposition of Several Strictly Periodic Sequences of Events," *Biometrika*, **40**, 1953, 1–11.

11. Cox, D. R., *Renewal Theory*, Methuen, London, 1962.

12. Drenick, R. F., "The Failure Law of Complex Equipment," *J. Soc. Ind. Appl. Math.*, **8**, 1960, 680–690.

13. Feller, W., *An Introduction to Probability Theory and Applications*, 3rd ed., Wiley, New York, 1968.

14. General Electric Co. (Defense Systems Dept.), *Tables of the Individual and Cumulative Terms of Poisson Distribution*, D. van Nostrand, Princeton, 1962.

15. Greenwood, M., and G. U. Yule, "An Inquiry into the Nature of Frequency Distributions Representative of Multiple Happenings with Particular Reference to the Occurrence of Multiple Attacks of Disease or of Repeated Accidents," *J. Roy. Stat. Soc.*, **83**, 1920, 255–279.

16. Hartline, H. K., L. J. Milne, and I. H. Wagman, "Fluctuations of Response of Single Visual Sense Cells," *Fed. Proc.*, **6**, 1947, 124.

17. Hecht, S., S. Shlaer, and M. H. Pirenne, "Energy at the Threshold of Vision," *Science*, **93**, 1941, 585–587.

18. Hecht, S., S. Shlaer, and M. H. Pirenne, "Energy, Quanta and Vision," *J. Gen. Physiol.*, **25**, 1942, 819–840.

19. Kac, M., "Random Walk and the Theory of Brownian Motion," *Amer. Math. Monthly*, **54**, 1947, 369–391. (Reprinted in Wax, Nelson (editor), *Selected Papers on Noise and Stochastic Processes*, Dover, New Work, 1954.)

20. Kinchla, R., and R. C. Atkinson, "The Effect of False-Information Feedback on Psychophysical Judgments," *Psychon. Sci.*, **1**, 1964, 317–318.

21. Lawson, J. L., and G. E. Uhlenback, *Threshold Signals*, McGraw-Hill, New York, 1950.

22. Lifshitz, S. J., "Sensation Elements for Hearing and Touch," *Comptes Rendus (Doklady) de l'Academie des Sciences de l'URSS*, **48**, 1945, 479–481.

23. Luce, R. D., *Individual Choice Behavior*, Wiley, New York, 1959.

24. Luce, R. D., "Detection and Recognition," in *Handbook of Mathematical Psychology*, Vol. 1, Luce, R. D., R. Bush, and E. Galanter (editors), Wiley, New York, 1963.

25. Luce, R. D., "Asymptotic Learning in Psychophysical Theories," *Brit. J. Stat. Psychol.*, **17**, 1964, 1–14.

26. Marill, T., *Detection Theory and Psychophysics*, Tech Report No. 319, M. I. T. Research Lab. of Electronics, October 30, 1956.

27. Mueller, C. G., "A Quantitative Theory of Visual Excitation for the Single Photoreceptor," *Proc. Nat. Acad. Sci.*, **40**, 1954, 853–863.

28. Neyman, J., "On a New Class of 'Contagious' Distributions, Applicable in Entomology and Bacteriology," *Ann. Math. Stat.*, **10**, 1939, 35–57.

29. Norman, D., *Sensory Thresholds and Response Biases in Detection Experiments: A Theoretical and Experimental Analysis*, Unpublished doctoral dissertation, University of Pennsylvania, 1962.

30. Norman, D., "Sensory Thresholds and Response Bias," *J. Acoust. Soc. Amer.*, **35**, 1963, 1432–1441.

31. Norman, D., "Sensory Thresholds, Response Biases, and the Neural Quantum Theory, *J. Math. Psychol.*, **1**, 1964, 88–120.
32. Peterson, W., T. Birdsall, and W. Fox, "The Theory of Signal Detectability," *Trans. Prof. Group on Information Theory* (IRE), PGIT4, 1954, 171–212.
33. Pfafflin, S., and M. Mathews, "Energy Detection Model for Monaural Auditory Detection," *J. Acoust. Soc. Amer.*, **34**, 1962, 1842–1853.
34. Rao, C. R., *Advanced Statistical Methods in Biometric Research*, Wiley, New York, 1952.
35. Rose, A., "The Relative Sensitivities of Television Pick-Up Tubes, Photographic Film, and the Human Eye," *Proc. Inst. Radio Engrs.*, **30**, 1942, 293–300.
36. Rose, A., "The Sensitivity Performance of the Human Eye on an Absolute Scale," *J. Opt. Soc. Amer.*, **38**, 1948, 196–208.
37. Shipley, E., *Detection and Recognition with Uncertainty*, unpublished doctoral dissertation, University of Pennsylvania, 1961.
38. Siegel, S., "Theoretical Models of Choice and Strategy Behavior: Stable-State Behavior in the Two-Choice Uncertain Outcome Situation," *Psychometrika*, **24**, 1959, 303–316.
39. Sklansky, J., "Markov Chain Model of Adaptive Signal Detection," *Proc. 1963 Biomics Symposium*, Air Force Systems Command, Wright Patterson A. F. B., March, 1963.
40. Slansky, J., "Threshold Training of Two Mode Signal Detection," *IEEE Trans. on Information Theory*, **IT–11**, 1965, 353–362.
41. Swets, J. A., "Indices of Signal Detectability Obtained with Various Psychophysical Procedures," *J. Acoust. Soc. Amer.*, **31**, 1959, 511–513.
42. Swets, J. A., D. Green, and W. P. Tanner, "On the Width of Critical Bands," *J. Acoust. Soc. Amer.*, **34**, 1962, 108–113.
43. Swets, J., W. P. Tanner, and T. Birdsall, "Decision Processes in Perception," *Psychol. Rev.*, **68**, 1961, 301–340.
44. Tanner, W. P., and T. Birdsall, "Definitions of d' and η as Psychological Measures," *J. Acoust. Soc. Amer.*, **30**, 1958, 922–928.
45. Treisman, M., "Noise and Weber's Law," *Psychol. Rev.*, **71**, 1964, 314–330.
46. Van Meter, D., and D. Middleton, "Modern Statistical Approaches to Reception in Communication Theory," *Trans. Prof. Group on Information Theory* (IRE), Symposium on Information Theory, PGIT4, 1954, 119–145.
47. van der Velden, H., "Over het aantal lichtquanta dat nodig is voor een lichtprikkel bij het menselijk oog," *Physica*, **11**, 1944, 179–189.
48. deVries, H. L., "The Quantum Character of Light and Its Bearing upon the Threshold of Vision, the Differential Sensitivity and Acuity of the Eye," *Physica*, **10**, 1943, 553–564.

FURTHER READINGS

1. Bartlett, M. S., *An Introduction to Stochastic Processes, with Special Reference to Methods and Applications*, Cambridge University Press, New York, 1966.
2. Birkhoff, Garrett, "Mathematics and Psychology," *SIAM Rev.*, **11**, 1969, 429–469.
3. Coleman, R., and J. L. Gastwirth, "Some Models for Interaction of Renewal Processes Related to Neuron Firing," *J. Appl. Probability*, **6**, 1969, 38–58.
4. Suppes, Patrick, *Studies in the Methodology and Foundations of Science, Selected Papers from 1951 to 1969*, Humanities Press, New York, 1969.

CHAPTER 10

Learning and Memory[1]

WILLIAM K. ESTES

Professor of Psychology, Rockefeller University, New York City

Contents

10.1 INTRODUCTION

Perhaps it is not obvious at first thought just how learning and memory should be expected to enter into a communication system. In the simplest communication system (Figure 10.1), a sender makes a choice of one from a set of possible messages and transmits it along a single channel which has capacity to transmit but one message at a time; at the other end of the channel a receiver decodes the message received, selecting from the set of possible alternative messages the one he believes to have been sent to him over the channel. A little consideration reveals at least two points at which psychological processes might play a major role in the communication process, even in this simple situation.

[1] Preparation of this chapter was supported in part by Contract Nonr–225(73) between the Office of Naval Research and Stanford University. Reproduction in whole or in part is permitted for any purpose of the United States Government.

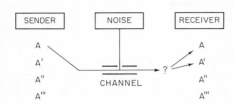

Fig. 10.1 Schematic representation of a simple communication system. Some one from a set of alternative messages (A, A', A'', A''') is chosen by the sender for transmission through the channel. Distortion of the message by noise in the channel may lead to confusion on the part of the receiver as to which of two or more similar messages was sent.

First, owing to similarities among possible messages, or noise in the communication channel, or some combination of these, there may be uncertainty on the part of the receiver as to which of the possible messages he has actually received. That is, given that the sender has actually transmitted message A, the receiver may be in some uncertainty as to whether he has received A as opposed to A' or A'', each of which resembles the true message in some respects. To the extent that these confusions are due simply to properties of the stimuli involved, for example, when messages have similarities in their physical properties, the problems arising are treated by the methods of psychophysics, which have been described in other chapters in this book. It is known, however, that an individual's perception of an uncertain event is influenced not only by the stimulus properties of the event but also by any advance expectations he may have as to the most likely event out of a set of possibilities [7]. Thus, if the receiver, through learning over a series of occasions, builds up certain expectations as to which messages are more likely and which messages less likely, then this process may come to influence his interpretations of received messages and therefore to contribute either positively or negatively to the efficiency of communication in the system. An important branch of learning theory has to do with the process of building up such expectations concerning uncertain events.

Once a message has been decoded by the receiver in the communication system, a *second* major possibility arises for processes of learning and memory to influence the outcome. During the interval between receiving the message and recording the message, carrying out an instruction, or relaying the message to another station, there is the possibility that, through some process of forgetting, the receiver might distort or lose the message that he received over the channel. Thus we must consider not only the probability that the receiver's interpretation of the message coming from the channel will correspond to the message actually initiated by the sender, but also the probability, given that the correct message is once received, that it will be preserved without error and will be available in the receiver's response repertoire at some later time when he has to make use of it. To handle the total operation of the system, we need not only a full understanding of the physical system over which the message is sent, but commensurate understanding of the processes whereby the receiver interprets the message and preserves it in memory until he in turn acts as sender in the next stage of the communication process.

In this chapter, we first present an example of the kind of learning theory involved in the building up of expectations which may modify a receiver's interpretation of messages coming over a channel. Second, we give some examples of the kinds of mathematical theories now under development to handle the process of short-term retention of received material and the conditions which make for optimal retention.

LEARNING: THE PROCESS OF ACQUIRING EXPECTATIONS OF UNCERTAIN EVENTS

Since the receiver in a communication system may be subject to errors of judgment as a function of expectations that he has built up concerning relative frequencies of possible messages, it becomes of interest to study the process whereby such expectations develop. It happens that a very active branch of learning theory during the past five to ten years has been concerned with precisely this problem in a number of contexts. The learning phenomena involved are commonly grouped under the rubric "probability learning" by psychologists (for a review of the literature on this topic, see [5]).

In the simplest probability-learning experiment, the individual whose learning is being studied (whom we shall henceforth term the *observer*) is confronted on each of a sequence of trials with a signal S, which may be followed by any one of a set of alternative events $E_1, E_2, \ldots, E_r$. On each trial, the signal is followed by exactly one of these events, and the observer's task is to respond to the signal on each trial with his best prediction of the event that will follow. The problem facing the subject depends on the experimenter's rules for generating the sequence of events which terminate successive trials. If the experimenter chose to terminate every trial with event E_1, for example, the observer would soon learn to expect this event on every trial; if events E_1 and E_2 alternated, again the learning problem would be simple for the human observer, who would soon learn to predict E_1 on odd trials and E_2 on even trials. More interesting is the case in which the events are controlled by a random device so that event E_1 occurs with some fixed probability π_1, event E_2 with probability π_2, and so on. Even under this more difficult condition we might expect that the observer's accuracy of prediction would improve with experience, but it is not intuitively obvious just how this learning should proceed or what the limits should be.

10.2 BASIC MODEL FOR PROBABILITY LEARNING

A type of mathematical model which has proved useful in analyzing this type of learning is based on the following concepts (for more detailed developments, see [2], [7], and [8]).

We shall let $p_{i,n}$ denote the probability that the observer predicts event E_i on trial n. The initial problem for the theory is to describe precisely how this probability changes on any trial. A strong simplifying assumption in the type of theory we are illustrating here is that the change in the observer's probability on any trial depends solely on the event which occurs on that trial. Specifically, if the signal S is followed by event E_1, the change in response probability is given by

$$(10.1) \qquad p_{1,n+1} = p_{1,n} + \theta(1 - p_{1,n})$$
$$= (1 - \theta)\, p_{1,n} + \theta;$$

that is, the new probability of the observer's predicting event E_1 after this trial is equal to the old probability plus a constant fraction θ of the difference between the old probability and unity. The parameter θ, which is assumed to be constant over a given experiment for a given observer and set of experimental conditions, has a value between zero and unity. Similarly, if the signal is followed by event E_2, the change in probability of predicting the second event is given by

$$(10.2) \qquad p_{2,n+1} = (1 - \theta)\, p_{2,n} + \theta.$$

It will suffice for our purposes to consider a situation in which there are only two possible events, E_1 and E_2, in which case (10.2) can be rewritten as

$$(10.3) \qquad p_{1,n+1} = (1 - \theta)\, p_{1,n}.$$

Now suppose that the probability of event E_1 on trial n is $\pi_{1,n}$. If so, it is easy to show that on the average the observer's probability at the end of the trial will be given by

$$(10.4) \qquad p_{1,n+1} = (1 - \theta)\, p_{1,n} + \theta\pi_{1,n}.$$

The last equation is basic to the generation of predictions about changes in the observer's response probability over sequences of trials, given various rules as to how $\pi_{1,n}$ changes during the series. If π_1 is a constant, the simplest case, then it is easy to verify by mathematical induction that the observer's probability of predicting the first event on any trial is given by

$$(10.5) \qquad p_{1,n} = \pi_1 - (\pi_1 - p_{1,1})(1 - \theta)^{n-1},$$

a simple exponential function approaching π_1 in the limit as n becomes large. Thus for this particular experimental routine, termed the "simple noncontingent case" in the literature, we should predict that on the average the observer's probability of predicting the first event would begin with some value $p_{1,1}$ (normally $\frac{1}{2}$, in the absence of any information to the contrary) and would change gradually over a series of trials, in the limit approaching the true probability of the first event. In numerous experiments which satisfy the simplifying conditions of our derivation (constant event probabilities over trials, no sources of information available to the observer other than his observations of the events occurring on successive trials, no complications in the way of differential rewards or punishments, and so forth), these implications of the model have been found to characterize human behavior with considerable fidelity. For example, in a half-dozen independent experiments reported between 1939 and 1956, involving 18 groups of subjects run under a variety of π values, the probabilities of occurrence of the E_1 event varied from .50 to 1.00 with an overall mean of .76. The mean of the subjects' estimated asymptotic probabilities of predicting the E_1 event (that is, the arithmetic mean of proportions of E_1 predictions in the terminal trial block of each experiment) was .76, and the standard deviation of differences between π values and mean response proportions for the various groups was .02 [4].

10.3 PROBABILITY TRACKING

The phenomenon of "probability matching," predicted for situations in which event probabilities are constant, is simply a special case of a more general phenomenon that might be termed "probability tracking," predicted for any situation in which event probabilities change in some orderly manner over trials. Suppose, for example, that the probability of an event changed linearly over a series of trials; then we could write the probability of event E_1 as

$$(10.6) \qquad \pi_{1,n} = a + bn,$$

and we could expect to generate predictions for an experiment in which the true event probability changed over trials in accordance with this relation (provided, of course, that the length of the series was so chosen that the value of $\pi_{1,n}$ would remain between 0 and 1). To develop such predictions, we need only substitute our expression from (10.6) into the right-hand side of (10.4), obtaining

$$(10.7) \qquad p_{1,n+1} = p_{1,n} + \theta(a + bn - p_{1,n}).$$

This function is to be read much like the one for the simpler case; it indicates in effect that on any trial the observer's probability of predicting event E_1 will move from its current position toward the current value of the true event probability, in this case $a + bn$. Once again the difference equation can readily be solved to obtain a formula predicting the value of $p_{1,n}$ on any trial:

$$(10.8) \qquad p_{1,n} = a + bn - \frac{b}{\theta} - \left(a + b - \frac{b}{\theta} - p_{1,1}\right)(1 - \theta)^{n-1}.$$

The precise form of this function will depend on the values of the constants a and b and on the initial response probability, but in all events one prediction is that over a series of trials, as n becomes large, the function describing the observer's response probability will have a graph approaching the straight line

$$(10.9) \qquad p_{1,n} = a - \frac{b}{\theta} + bn,$$

which has the same slope as the line represented by (10.6) giving the value of $\pi_{1,n}$, but which runs parallel to it.

An experiment was conducted to provide a test of this aspect of the theory a number of years ago by the writer in collaboration with Dr. Marcia Johns. A group of 16 subjects, undergraduate students at Indiana University, was run under the following conditions. On each trial of the experiment, a signal appeared and then the subject indicated by pressing one or the other of two response keys which of the two event lights would appear to terminate the trial. During the first 40 trials of the experiment the probability of one of the lights, the E_1 light, was .90 and the probability of the E_2 was .10. Then following the fortieth trial the subjects were shifted to a procedure in which the probability of the E_1 light changed from trial to trial in accordance with the linear function $\pi_n = .10 + .0075n$, where n varied from 0 to 119 over the remainder of the sequence. During the first 40 trials, the mean curve of estimated response probabilities (that is, probability of E_1 predictions) approached an asymptote in the neighborhood of .90 following a course approximately as prescribed by equation (10.5). With the initial response probability taken to be $\frac{1}{2}$, (10.5) was fitted to the mean learning curve of response probability versus trials for the group of subjects over the first 40 trials; the best fitting curve proved to have a θ value of .05. With this value of θ and the experimenter-prescribed values of a and b in (10.6) and (10.7), various predictions can be derived concerning the empirical curve in the right side of Figure 10.2, which exhibits the observed proportion of E_1 predictions per 10-trial block for this group of subjects.

Salient predictions entailed by the model are that the response proportions should start relatively high (having dropped during the first block of 10 trials from the value near .90 which held during the latter portion of the initial 40-trial series under the constant π value of .90), decline until the empirical curve crosses the straight line representing the probability of reinforcement, then increase along a line parallel to the function representing the changing probability of reinforcement. In engineering terminology, we might characterize the course of learning by saying that any point on the empirical curve of response probabilities tracks the corresponding point on the probability-of-reinforcement function with a lag, the lag depending on the value of the parameter θ which characterizes the observer's rate of learning in this situation.

The choice of conditions for this experiment was made not so much to represent any particular situation that might be expected to hold commonly outside of the laboratory as to illustrate the fact that the theory charac-

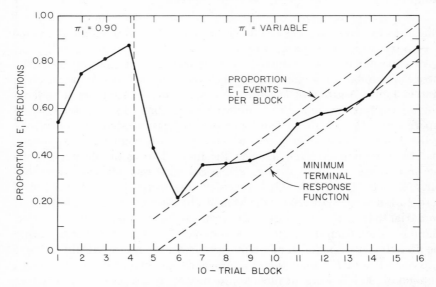

Fig. 10.2 Proportion E_1-predictions per 10-trial block by a group of observers in an experiment with changing probability of E_1-occurrence over trials. The parallel lines in the right-hand portion of the graph indicate bounds between which the terminal portion of the empirical curve is predicted to lie. The lower bound is obtained by substituting the value $\theta = .05$, estimated from the data of the first four blocks, in equation (10.9).

terizes the course of learning sufficiently well so that quantitatively accurate predictions can be generated even for rather unusual situations in which one would have little basis on intuitive grounds for any detailed predictions whatever concerning changes in response tendencies with experience. It would be reasonable to expect that in situations involving transmission and reception of messages over communication systems, where the receiver's information concerning relative frequencies of various messages builds up solely as a result of experience with past sequences of messages in the same situation, the course of learning (that is, the building up of expectations concerning relative frequencies of various messages) may be expected to conform reasonably well to the mathematical model prescribed by the theory.

10.4 INTERPRETATION OF SIGNAL DETECTION UNDER BIASED PRESENTATION SCHEDULES

The mathematical model presented in the preceding section permits us to generate quantitative predictions concerning the manner in which an operator's expectations of uncertain events will change in any situation, once we are given adequate information concerning the event probabilities. It will be recalled that our immediate interest in this type of problem arises from the observation that the judgments made by a receiver in a communication situation regarding messages arriving over a noisy channel may be influenced by his expectations with respect to relative frequencies of different possible messages. Application of the model to an experimental situation corresponding closely to the one just outlined can conveniently be accomplished in terms of a signal-detection experiment performed by Kinchla and reported by Atkinson, Carterette, and Kinchla [1]. The observer in Kinchla's situation was confronted with a milk-glass screen comprising two areas, one on the left side of the screen and one on the right, on which signals might appear. A signal was simply a temporary increase in luminosity in one area or the other. The observer was given instructions to the effect that on each trial a signal would appear in one area or the other and that his task was to make his best judgment as to the location of the signal. Actually, two types of trials were given: signal trials, on which a luminosity change actually occurred in one area or the other, and blank trials on which there was actually no luminosity change in either area. The luminosity change on signal trials was small enough, however, that the observers could not detect it with certainty; consequently, the observers were unaware that there were actually two types of trial involved in the experiment and gave their judgments on each trial under the impression that there was a signal present.

There were two principal experimental conditions, as illustrated in Table 10.1. For the equiprobable condition represented in the first column of the table, occurrence of the signal in areas A_1 and A_2 on signal trials was in a 1:1 ratio; in the bias condition, represented in the second column of the table, the relative frequencies of signals in the two areas were 1:3. The cell entries in the table give the proportions of times over the final 400 trials of an 800-trial series in which the observers judged the signal to have occurred in area A_1 under each combination of conditions. In the equiprobable condition, as might be expected, judgments of the two areas occurred equally often on signal trials; but in the bias condition, A_1 judgments were less frequent than A_2s. With regard to the latter condition, the proportion of A_1 judgments on signal trials would be expected to be .25 if detection were perfect and .50 if detection were impossible, so the observed value of .34 is an indication of the difficulty of the discrimination required.

TABLE 10.1
Influence of Expectations on Judgments of Visual Signal Locations

	$A_1:A_2 = 1:1$	$A_1:A_2 = 1:3$
Signal trials	.50	.34
Blank trials	.49	.39

Of more interest in the present context are the results for blank trials given in the bottom row. On these trials, when no signal was in fact present, relative frequencies of judgments should be expected to deviate from .50 only if these judgments were influenced by any expectations the observers had built up concerning relative frequencies of signals. We know that there was opportunity for such expectations to develop as a result of information received on the signal trials, and the model developed in the preceding section leads us to predict that the proportions of A_1 judgments should be near .50 for the equiprobable condition and should deviate below .50, and in fact approach .34, for the bias condition. These predictions seem quite well borne out by the data exhibited in the lower row of the table. The very substantial deviation of the observers' proportion of A_1 judgments below .50 on blank trials in the bias condition confirms our hypothesis that judgments regarding ambiguous messages may be determined to an important extent by expectations on the part of the observer. Consequently, a model for the learning of such expectations must be an integral part of a full description of a communication system.

SHORT-TERM MEMORY

The memory of a receiver in a communication system becomes an important factor whenever it is necessary for him to retain one or more messages in memory for an interval of time before he can record the information received, carry out prescribed operations, or relay the information through another channel. In this chapter we do not touch on the vast psychological literature concerning the conditions of retention loss for learned material, but we confine our attention to a mathematical formulation of the process. The interpretation to be developed is that associated with a more general statistical theory of learning and retention (see [3]), of which one aspect has been presented in connection with multiple-choice learning.

10.5 STATISTICAL MODEL FOR SHORT-TERM MEMORY

The theory to be presented is psychological rather than neurophysiological in character, in that the overall strategy is to set down assumptions concerning properties of the process of retention loss without hypothesizing physical loci for the events involved. Also, for the present, the merits of the theory are assessed in terms of its demonstrable potentiality for predicting phenomena observed in experiments on memory. Nonetheless, the theory is not unrelated to basic concepts of neurophysiology and neuroanatomy which have been introduced in other chapters.

On the basis of our general knowledge of the structure and operation of the nervous system, perhaps the most salient single characteristic we should expect a model for memory to exhibit is that of multiplicity, or redundancy of basic elements. The earliest work concerned with searching for the anatomical bases of memory was organized in terms of the search for an "engram," the engram being the physical trace presumably laid down somewhere in the nervous system as a result of a learning experience and serving as the carrier of memory for the experience. It was, however, one of the first major accomplishments of physiological psychology, associated primarily with the work of Lashley, to demonstrate convincingly that the engram, whatever it might be physically, was not localized in any one small region of the nervous system. Numerous studies showed that memory for a particular learning experience could not be eradicated by ablation of any one localized area of the brain, and that for the most part impairment of memory for a learning experience was roughly proportional to amount of tissue removed. Thus it seems necessary to assume that not a single engram, but a collection of them, are involved in the establishment of any particular memory. To avoid undesired connotations, we shall speak of the members of this collection simply as elements.

A second major characteristic which must be assumed to characterize the systems involved in retention is that of spontaneous variation in activity over time. Electrophysiological studies of the nervous system have shown abundantly that at all levels of the brain there is constant fluctuation in activity independent of the changes produced by incoming stimulation. Thus in the model for retention we assume that the memory elements fluctuate between an active and an inactive state, the fluctuation being random with respect to time and independent of learning experiences.

With these basic considerations in mind, we are ready to sketch more specifically the assumptions embodied in a statistical model for short-term memory. This presentation can be accomplished most conveniently with reference to the schematization shown in Figure 10.3.

We should emphasize that if the individual under study, say the receiver in a communication system, has a number of learning experiences involving different events, then the theory defines a different set of memory elements corresponding to each of these experiences. Thus in Figure 10.3 we represent the receiver's memory with respect to message 1 in a series by the rectangle labeled M_1, his memory with respect to message 2 by the rectangle labeled M_2, and so on. For an experiment involving a number of different messages, it is not necessary that the different sets of elements all

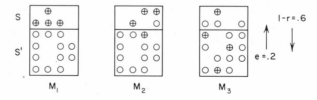

Fig. 10.3 Theoretical schema for fluctuation model. The three rectangles represent sets of memory elements, circles above and below the horizontal lines representing elements active and inactive, respectively, at the given time. An element marked with a + sign is positive relative to recall of the message. The parameters e and r determine the rate of fluctuation of elements between the active and inactive states. The diagram represents the states of the systems immediately after initial receipt of message M_1, a short time after initial receipt of message M_2, and a sufficiently long time after receipt of message M_3 for the fluctuation process to have reached the asymptotic equilibrium condition.

be of the same size or have the same fluctuation parameters, though for simplicity in the diagram all of the sets have been taken to be of the same size. Taking the set corresponding to one of the messages, say M_1, we note, first, that the system has an active and an inactive state, represented by the upper and lower parts of the rectangle, respectively. Elements above the horizontal dividing line are in the active state at the time represented, and those below the horizontal line are in the inactive state. It is assumed that constant random fluctuation occurs across the boundary, the parameter e denoting the probability that any currently inactive element enters the active state during a short interval of time Δt and the parameter r denoting the probability that any currently active element remains active during the same interval.

The second primary property of a set of memory elements is the state of the elements with respect to the learning of the item of information involved. It is assumed that at any time the elements in a given system are partitioned into those that are positive and those that are negative with respect to memory for the particular message. Positive elements are those that would contribute to a correct response if the individual were asked to recall the message, and elements which are negative are those that would not contribute to correct recall. Our assumptions concerning the way in which the state of learning changes are as follows: Stated in terms of the communication situation, upon receipt of a message, say M_1, all of the elements in the momentarily active set are turned positive for that message.

This change of state is permanent in that it does not decay or otherwise change as a function of time and can be altered only by later learning experiences. A message generally states some relationship, and one tests the individual for his memory of a message by supplying some cue to which a correct response will be taken as evidence of memory for the message. Elements that have been turned positive by an effective learning experience are said to be associated with the correct response. This association persists until and unless some later learning experience produces a change in state of these elements, again on an all-or-none basis, so that they become associated with some different response.

For example, suppose message M_1 were "The temperature is 69 degrees." Upon receipt of this message by the receiver, his currently active memory elements for this item would become associated with the response "69 degrees" and would lead him to make this response if subsequently questioned concerning the temperature. These elements would, then, remain associated with this response unless a later message concerning temperature, say "The temperature is now 75 degrees," should change the state of the currently active elements so that they become associated with the response "75 degrees" rather than the response "69 degrees."

The way in which the individual's recall response depends on the current state of his memory elements may be more fully specified as follows. We assume that when a cue for recall of a message is given, the individual selects one of the currently active memory elements at random and responds on the basis of the state of this element. If the element sampled is positive for a given response, then that response is given. If the element sampled is in the negative state, then the individual is assumed to respond at random. The sense of randomness intended is the following. For simplicity, we consider a situation in which there are N possible messages, all equally likely to be sent over the channel, with the full set known in advance to both the sender and the receiver. Under these circumstances, if the receiver is asked to recall a message and samples a negative memory element, it is assumed that he has probability $1/N$ of making each of the possible responses. Thus probability of recall of the correct response to a given cue is directly related to the proportion of memory elements that have become associated with the appropriate response.

Since the state of learning of memory elements is assumed not to change over time, it is clear that observed retention loss must be due to fluctuations over time in the proportions of positive elements which are in the active state. The way in which this fluctuation process will lead to typical functions for forgetting of learned material can readily be seen by reference to Figure 10.3. The rectangle for M_1 shows the state of a system immediately following the first receipt of the particular message. Originally all of the memory elements were negative, but upon receipt of the message all of those in the currently active subset turned positive. If the receiver were asked immediately thereafter to give the message, it is assumed that he would do so with probability 1 since any memory element he sampled would necessarily be in the positive state. Over a subsequent interval of time, however, fluctuation of elements between the active and inactive states would proceed, so that if the individual were tested for recall after an interval, the state of the system would be more like that shown for message M_2 in the figure. That is, some of the positive elements would have become inactive and some of the negative elements would have become active, so that the individual would no longer be certain to sample a positive memory element when asked to recall the message. Thus probability of correct recall would have decreased from its maximum value immediately after the learning experience. As time goes on and fluctuation continues, this "diffusion" of elements across the boundary between the active and inactive subsets continues until a statistical equilibrium is reached at a level at which the density of positive elements is the same in the active and inactive states. From this point on, on the average, no further observed retention loss should occur.

To develop some of the more detailed implications of the model, we require a difference equation expressing the probability f_{t+1} that any particular element is active at time $t + 1$ recursively in terms of the probability f_t obtaining during the preceding time interval and the parameters of the fluctuation process. The desired recursion takes the form

$$(10.10) \qquad f_{t+1} = (1 - f_t)e + f_t r.$$

This difference equation is readily solved by standard methods to obtain the following formula for probability that any given associative element is active at time t:

$$(10.11) \qquad f_t = \frac{e}{1 - r + e} - \left[\frac{e}{1 - r + e} - f_0 \right] (r - e)^t,$$

which may be written more simply

$$f_t = \lambda - (\lambda - f_0)a^t$$

where $a = r - e$ and $\lambda = e/(1 - r + e)$.

With this basic function in hand, we can readily derive the probability ϕ_t that a positive memory element will be sampled by the observer on a recall test at time t following a learning experience. We note, first, that the probability that the element sampled at time t was in the active state at time 0, and therefore necessarily positive, is $\lambda - (\lambda - 1) a^t$, whereas the probability that it was inactive at time 0 is $(1 - \lambda) (1 - a^t)$. Denoting by ϕ_0' the probability that any element inactive at time 0 was positive, we have

$$(10.12) \qquad \phi_t = \lambda - (\lambda - 1) a^t + (1 - \lambda)(1 - a^t) \phi_0'$$
$$= \lambda + (1 - \lambda) \phi_0' + (1 - \lambda)(1 - \phi_0') a^t.$$

Finally, utilizing the assumptions stated earlier regarding response determination, we can write for p_t, the probability of a correct recall at time t following receipt of a message in the communication situation with N equally likely possible messages,

$$(10.13) \qquad p_t = \phi_t + (1 - \phi_t)(1/N)$$
$$= [1 - (1/N)]\phi_t + (1/N)$$
$$= [1 - (1/N)][\lambda + (1 - \lambda)\phi_0'] + (1/N)$$
$$\qquad + [1 - (1/N)](1 - \lambda)(1 - \phi_0') a^t$$
$$= p_\infty + (1 - p_\infty) a^t,$$

where p_∞ denotes probability of a correct response after an indefinitely long time following receipt of the message. The gist of this result is that, during a period of time following receipt of a message, the probability of a correct response on the part of the receiver will decline exponentially to a limiting value which depends jointly on the parameters of the statistical diffusion process and on the proportion of elements associated with the correct response at time 0.

10.6 IMPLICATIONS OF THE FLUCTUATION MODEL FOR PHENOMENA OF SHORT-TERM MEMORY

Considering the schema of Figure 10.3, together with the functions just derived, we note first that rate of retention loss following the learning experience is predicted to depend on the parameters of the fluctuation process but to be independent of previous experiences. The fluctuation parameters e and r will be different for different situations, even in the case of the same individual, and they may be expected to be modified by such factors as drugs (for example, barbiturates) or even by variations in bodily temperature. These aspects of the theory are compatible with such well-known experimental results as that rate of retention loss for learned material is slowed if a period of sleep follows immediately upon the learning experience, in the case of human subjects, and that retention of conditioned responses in goldfish is inversely related to the temperature of the water. In particular, we have no reason to expect that rate of fluctuation of memory elements, and therefore rate of forgetting, can be modified by practice, rewards, punishments, or motivation.

The situation is quite different, however, concerning the limit of the forgetting process. Thus, in contrast to the rate of change, the asymptote of the retention curve depends not only on the fluctuation parameters but also on the state of learning. To take one extreme, suppose that all of the elements in a memory system, both those currently active and those currently inactive, were positive for a given item of information. In that event, at whatever time the individual was tested for recall, he would necessarily give the correct response and no changes in correct response probability would occur over time. Since only a portion of the elements in a memory system are active at the time of any one learning experience, it follows that improvement in retention in the sense of raising the asymptote of the retention curve can be achieved only by repetition. If a learning experience is repeated a number of times, in general different memory elements will be in the active state on different occasions, and thus the total number of positive elements in the system will increase.

It can readily be seen, further, that the temporal spacing of repeated learning experiences is of the utmost importance with respect to efficiency. Suppose, for example, at one extreme, that a second instance of message M_1 were sent immediately following the first message, thus arriving when the system was in the state shown at the left side of Figure 10.3. Since all of the currently active elements would already be positive at the time of the second occurrence of the message, no gain would result from the repetition, and the resulting course of forgetting would be precisely the same as though only one instance of the message had been received. Suppose, however, a second instance of message M_2 occurred immediately following the point illustrated in the center rectangle in Figure 10.3. At this point, some time after the first occurrence of the message, a portion of the positive elements would still be in the active state but some would have become inactive, and a second occurrence of the message would have the effect of turning positive some elements that were inactive on the first occurrence but were active at the time of the second occurrence. In general, the greatest gain from repetitions of a message will be attained if the time between repetitions is such that the system arrives at the equilibrium condition shown in the right-hand rectangle of Figure 10.3 prior to each repetition. Further increases in the intertrial interval beyond the time needed to arrive at the equilibrium state would, however, add no further advantage.

The optimal procedures are just the opposite if one's purpose is to correct errors in message transmission rather than to maximize retention on the part of the receiver. Suppose, for example, that at the point represented by the left-hand rectangle in Figure 10.3 the sender discovered that he had inadvertently sent the wrong message, say, "The temperature is 50 degrees," rather than the intended message, "The temperature is 69 degrees." The obvious remedy would be to send a correction message replacing the first one. An important implication of the model is that the time at which the correction occurs may be of major importance. If the second, correct, message were sent immediately following the first one, thus arriving at the point illustrated in the left-hand rectangle of Figure 10.3, when all of the elements which had been turned positive for the incorrect response "50 degrees" were still active, then all of these elements would have their state changed to positivity for the correct response "69 degrees," and the damage would be undone. Henceforth the receiver's memory for the correct message would be entirely unaffected by the inadvertent receipt of the erroneous message.

Suppose, however, that the situation were, instead, that illustrated in the middle rectangle of Figure 10.3. That is, some time had been allowed to elapse following receipt of the incorrect message before the correction message was sent. In this situation, the correct message, when it arrived, would produce the desired change of state of the currently active elements, but some elements which had been turned positive for the incorrect response would be inactive at the time of the correction message and thus unaffected by the correction. If the receiver were tested for recall immediately after receipt of the correction message, he would necessarily give the correct response. If, however, he were not tested until some time later, after further fluctuation of elements between the active and inactive states had occurred, his active set would now include a mixture of elements positive for the incorrect and elements positive for the correct message, and he would have some probability of making an error.

The effects of an incorrect message reception can, then, be completely undone in two quite different ways. First, by sending the correct message promptly enough so that it catches all of the elements active at the time of the incorrect message before any have escaped into the inactive state; or, second, by repeated correction messages given at spaced intervals and continuing until all elements that were active at the time of the incorrect message have been turned positive for the correct one.

10.7 IMPLICATIONS OF THE FLUCTUATION MODEL FOR INFORMATION TRANSMISSION

When there is occasion to do so, predictions from the model, in terms of response probabilities on the part of the receiver, can readily be translated into predictions about information transmitted. Consider, for example, the standard reference situation discussed in preceding sections. A set of N possible messages is known in advance to the receiver; each of the N messages is equally likely to be sent on any trial, and in the absence of any incoming information the receiver's probability of using each of the N responses is simply $1/N$. If on some trial the receiver receives a message, then at time t thereafter his probability of giving the correct response will be p_t, and the probability of giving any one incorrect response will be q_t, which is simply equal to $(1 - p_t)/(N - 1)$. For this situation, the uncertainty associated with the message set and the uncertainty associated with the set of possible responses are each equal to $\log_2 N$. The conditional uncertainty of the response, given the message, is

$$(10.14) \quad U_S(R) = -p_t \log_2 p_t - \sum q_t \log_2 q_t$$

$$= -p_t \log_2 p_t - (N - 1) \frac{(1 - p_t)}{N - 1} \log_2 \frac{(1 - p_t)}{N - 1}$$

$$= -p_t \log_2 p_t - (1 - p_t) \log_2 \frac{(1 - p_t)}{N - 1}.$$

The average amount of information transmitted per message from the sender to the receiver's response is then given by

$$(10.15) \quad I_t = U(R) - U_S(R)$$

$$= \log_2 N + p_t \log_2 p_t + (1 - p_t) \log_2 \frac{(1 - p_t)}{N - 1}.$$

Now we can substitute in this last equation the previously derived value of p_t, the recall probability as a function of time, from equation (10.13), and thus predict the course of loss of transmitted information during a period of time following the receipt of the message. The predicted curve for loss of transmitted information over time is similar in form to the classic curve of forgetting, for it can readily be shown that the measure of transmitted information is directly related to correct response probability for the types of situations we are considering.

By appropriate application of the fluctuation model for immediate memory, it is possible to generate numerous predictions concerning conditions for achieving various desired properties of information transmission. If a series of messages is being sent across a channel to a single receiver, and if some messages are particularly important so that it is desirable to maximize the probability that they will be transmitted without memory loss on the part of the receiver, then the desired objective can be obtained by introducing redundancy into the series of messages. That is, some of the messages should be repeated at the cost of reducing the total number of different messages that can be sent. Referring to Figure 10.3 and the related formal deviations, we readily see that retention loss for any particular item can be reduced by building up the store of positive elements in the temporarily inactive set S', which increases the value of ϕ_0' in the formula for p_t. With a sufficient number of repetitions of a message, ϕ_0' can be driven to unity, and memory for the item on the part of the receiver will then be perfect; that is, there will be no retention loss. Further, we can see that when redundancy is used, the repetitions of a particular item should be spaced rather than bunched in the sequence of messages. This follows from the fact (see Figure 10.3) that if a message is repeated too soon, there will be no interchange of active and inactive elements between S and S' and thus nothing will be gained by the repetition. In general, repetitions are more effective the more widely they are temporally spaced. If several messages are equally important, then maximum efficiency will be obtained if these messages are given in a repetitive sequence ($A,B,C,$ $A,B,C,$ $A,$ $B,C, \ldots$). This last result is a consequence of a general theorem to the effect that the maximum amount of information transmitted by any one message will be obtained if the message chosen is the one that will add the greatest number of positive elements. Thus if there are many possible messages, maximal information transmission will result if a different message is sent on each trial, with no repetitions. When, however, there is a large population of possible messages and many are to be sent, it would generally be useful to attempt to achieve maximum transmission only if the receiver had a perfect memory. If the receiver is a human operator with a fallible memory, then, according to the theory, it will nearly always be necessary to repeat some messages at the expense of omitting others.

In closing, let us emphasize that the particular behavioral models presented in this chapter are not the only relevant ones, and that they should not be applied uncritically since they may well be subject to revision in the course of continued research. The illustrative applications we have considered may, however, suffice to show the feasibility of including a quantitative specification of the functioning of the human operator in any mathematical description of a communication system.

REFERENCES

1. Atkinson, R. C., E. C. Carterette, and R. A. Kinchla, "Sequential Phenomena in Psychophysical Judgments: A Theoretical Analysis," in *Institute of Radio Engineers Transactions on Information Theory—Transactions of the 1962 International Symposium on Information Theory*, Vol. IT–8, Brussels, Belgium, 1962, 155–162.
2. Bush, Robert R., and Frederick Mosteller, *Stochastic Models for Learning*, Wiley, New York, 1955.
3. Estes, W. K., "The Statistical Approach to Learning Theory," in Koch, S. (editor), *Psychology: A Study of a Science*, Vol. 2, McGraw-Hill, New York, 1959, pp. 380–491.
4. Estes, W. K., "A Descriptive Approach to the Dynamics of Choice Behavior," in Nagel, E., P. Suppes, and A. Tarski (editors), *Logic, Methodology and Philosophy of Science: Proceedings of the 1960 International Congress*, Stanford University Press, Stanford, 1962, pp. 424–433. (Reprinted in *Behavioral Science*, **6**, 1961, 177–184.)
5. Estes, W. K., "Probability Learning," in Melton, A. W. (editor), *Categories of Human Learning—Proceedings of the Michigan-ONR Conference on Human Learning*, Academic Press, New York, 1964, pp. 89–128.
6. Estes, W. K., and Marcia D. Johns, "Probability-Learning with Ambiguity in the Reinforcing Stimulus," *Amer. J. Psychol.*, **71**, 1958, 219–228.
7. Estes, W. K., and J. H. Straughan, "Analysis of a Verbal Conditioning Situation in Terms of Statistical Learning Theory," *J. Exp. Psychol.*, **47**, 1954, 225–234.
8. Estes, W. K., and P. Suppes, "Foundations of Linear Models," in Bush, R. R., and W. K. Estes (editors), *Studies in Mathematical Learning Theory*, Stanford University Press, Stanford, 1959, pp. 137–179.

FURTHER READINGS

1. Estes, W. K., "Research and Theory on the Learning of Probabilities," *J. Amer. Statistical Association*, 1972, in press.
2. Kintsch, W., *Learning, Memory, and Conceptual Processes*, Wiley, New York, 1970.
3. Norman, D. A. (editor), *Models of Human Memory*, Academic Press, New York, 1970.
4. Myers, J. L., "Sequential Choice Behavior," in Bower, G. H. (editor), *The Psychology of Learning and Motivation*, Vol. 4, Academic Press, New York, 1970.

CHAPTER 11

Laplace-Fourier Transforms
and Mathematical Probability

JOHN L. BARNES

Professor of Engineering and Applied Science, University of California, Los Angeles

Contents

11.1   INTRODUCTION: SCIENTIFIC ASPECTS OF NATURAL COMMUNICATION SYSTEMS

Science is concerned with the satisfaction of man's curiosity. It is carried out by the *analysis* of the universe, through *experimentation* using *instrumentation* and the *logic* of *mathematics*. Its results are tentatively summarized by laws, which in turn are *synthesized* into (tentative) theories. On the other hand, *engineering* is concerned with the satisfaction of a certain class of man's needs by the *synthesis* of (physical) systems and their elements.

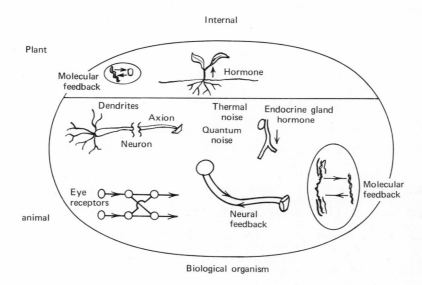

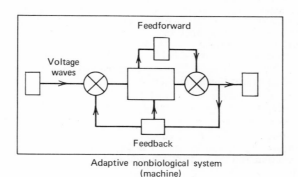

Fig. 11.1   Block-diagram classification of communication problems.

In contrast, *mathematics* is concerned with logical *methods* for deriving conclusions from hypotheses. Thus while the methods of mathematics are used in the analysis of science and in the synthesis of engineering, and while historically mathematics was in many instances abstracted from engineering and science, it is nevertheless basically not concerned with these. In the present chapter, we investigate the use of mathematical and engineering models for the scientific analysis of communication systems found in nature.

In particular, we deal with the internal and external communication systems of biological organisms (Figure 11.1). As was discussed in considerable detail in Part 2 of this book, animals have a high-speed internal

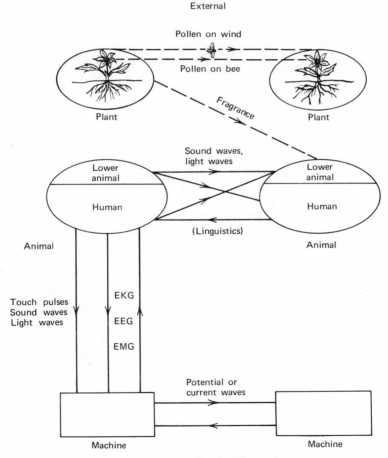

Fig. 11.1 *(continued)*

neuronal communication system, which is of increasing capability as one goes up the evolutionary scale from jellyfish neuronal nets through flat-worms with ganglia, finally to man with the most advanced brain. Animals in addition have low-speed internal communication systems using hormone molecules produced by endocrine glands; while, in the downward direction of complication, plants have a low-speed hormonal communication system. Hormone speeds are measured by using radioactive tracer atoms which replace the usual stable atoms.

What constitutes the basic characteristic of aggregates of molecules which are said to be alive? The author's belief is that it is the characteristic of *adaptivity*—for example, feedback. Thus the same tobacco virus is alive when it can adapt, and dead when it is in crystalline form and not able to adapt. Feedback is the key to life!

All biological cells and even the phage viruses contain deoxyribonucleic acid (DNA) molecules. In some cells, DNA by messenger and transfer ribo-nucleic acid (RNA) and hormone-actuated isolating (insulating) histones is believed to control the synthesis of protein enzymes. (Reference on action of histones: Dr. James Bonner, California Institute of Technology.) It appears that feedback is basic to this control in both the growth phase of a plant or animal and in the mature nongrowth operating phase. The forward and return paths of these molecular feedback processes are examples of basic communication channels.

External communications between biological organisms are carried on at the highest speeds by electromagnetic waves in the visible (eye receptors) and in the infrared (snake's receptor) parts of the frequency spectrum. The particular chemical reaction in the light-sensitive cells of a light-seeking plant is, interestingly enough, one of three found in the human eye. This is a second example of biological communication simplicity found at the molecular level. At the next descending levels of transmission speed appear water- then air-pressure waves. At the low-frequency end of air-pressure waves, the cockroach's wind-sensing tail receptor is found. For communica-tion through ground by vibration waves, an example is exhibited by a variety of African ant which comes to the surface if the surface is tapped to simulate rain. Part 1 of this book focused on linguistics, the science of acoustic communication between humans. At still lower speeds, external communication is carried on by transfer of molecules. The fragrance of flowers attracts bees. The male moth can detect a female moth at distances up to a mile (Reference: Kenneth Roder, Tufts University).

It is hoped that the concepts discussed in this chapter will be sufficiently basic to cover the whole domain of biological communication in nature, as suggested above. It is believed that they will also cover a much wider domain of communication such as the radiation from radio (including pulsars), visible (stars), infrared (stars), X-ray, and quasar sources; but these will not be explicitly discussed here.

MATHEMATICAL AND ENGINEERING MODELS OF SIGNALS, NOISE, AND LINEAR INVARIANT SYSTEMS

Important keys to top-grade science are the following:

1. The construction of models which incorporate those features of the physical world that can be measured.

2. The separation of the real-world system to be modeled into parts which may be studied individually.

Here we use sets of mathematical functions as models for *signals* (wanted information) and for *noise* (unwanted information). The block-diagram geometry of engineering enables us to show the gross connections between separated operations of a system.

11.2 SEPARATION OF AN INFORMATION SYSTEM INTO PARTS ON THE BASIS OF TYPE OF OPERATION

One example of the partition of an information system is the following:

Generating information
 • Signals and noise resulting from action, or from stored information
Processing information
 • Preparing signals for more convenient treatment
 • Encoding and decoding
 • Pre-emphasis and de-emphasis of frequency components
 • Modulating and demodulating
 • Translating from one language to another
 • Deciding between alternatives
 • Choosing states or symbols
 • Sampling and desampling (interpolation)
 • Correlating, or filtering on basis of time—or space—frequencies
 • Computing, including summing, averaging, etc.
 • Predicting and extrapolating
 • Collating and reordering
 • Reshaping deteriorated signal elements such as pulses

- Compacting and expanding
- Amplifying and attenuating
- Phase shifting

Storing information
- Remembering
- Transferring in time
- Filing: in and out
- Dynamic and static storing

Transporting information
- Transferring in space and time
- Communicating

Using information
- Converting into action

11.3 SAMPLES OF ENGINEERING AND OF INTERNAL BIOLOGICAL INFORMATION SYSTEMS

In Figure 11.2 both separated and combined information-system operations are illustrated. It has been useful to lump electrical and mechanical properties of nonbiological networks into separate "elements" with pure properties such as inductance, resistance, capacitance, mass, mechanical resistance, and elastance. In some parts of biological systems, however, it is not yet clear how to separate conveniently such combined operations as storing, processing, and transporting. This mixture is illustrated in Figure 11.2*b*.

11.4 CHOICE-INFORMATION CAPACITY AND ITS MEASUREMENT

Numerical *measurement* is carried out by counting the smallest units used. The measurement of information is no exception (see Figure 11.3). Note that in this example the cells shown along the abscissa and the states shown along the ordinate are not represented by points, but rather by one-dimensional point sets—here, line segments. The resulting state-cells which are occupied in the product space are shown by black squares. These are the product-space elements of state "channels" and cell "channels." The use of line segments rather than points for states and cells emphasizes the idea that in neither instance is the resolution complete (that is, infinite). It will be shown later that this limitation is a fundamental one for any measurement in the physical world.

Observe in Figure 11.3 that choice-message capacity,

$$M = 2^8 = 256,$$

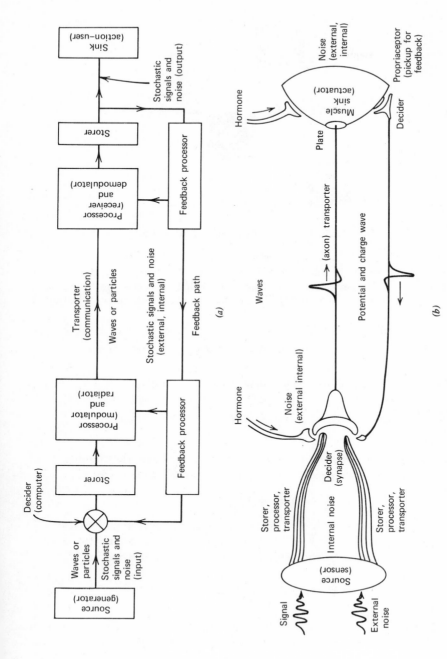

Fig. 11.2 Examples of stages in simple information systems. (*a*) Engineering system. (*b*) Biological system.

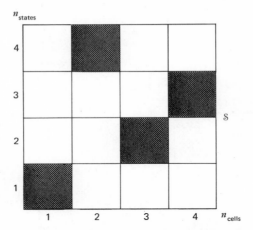

Fig. 11.3   Information carried by states in cells.

- The elementary (minimum-sized) decision, namely choice of one out of two, is the *quantum of information.* It is called one bit (one binary unit).
- Here one cell can have any one of four available independent states having equal statistical frequencies shown by the height location of black square, $n_s = 2^2$, hence 2 *state channels.*
- Here the available independent cells number n_c is $n_c = 4$, hence 4 *cell channels.*
- Here the *choice message capacity*—number of possible messages M—is

$$M = n_s^{n_c} = (2^2)^4 = 2^8.$$

- The *choice information capacity* in bits of the available state-cell space S is defined as the exponent of 2 which corresponds to the number of messages, thus $M = 2^8$. Here $g = 8$ bits.

is determined by *counting* the number n_s of states and the number n_c of cells in the available space, S, which in this example consists of

$$n_s n_c = 4(4) = 16$$

state-cells, or locations. Not all of this message capacity in either states or cells need be used for a particular message. Again, although the choice-information capacity in the available space S here is (see Section 12.5)

$$g \triangleq \log_2 M = \frac{n_s}{2} n_c = 8 \text{ bits,}$$

where $\triangleq$ means equal(s) by definition, not all of this amount of information capacity need be used by a particular message. The *efficiency* of available space usage, however, which is defined as

$$\eta \overset{\Delta}{=} \frac{(n_s n_c) \text{ used}}{(n_s n_c) \text{ available in } s},$$

is not 100 per cent if only part of the available space s is used. For example, if only two states are used (binary signal, $n_s = 2$), but all four cells are available for a particular message, then the efficiency is

$$\eta = \frac{2(4)}{4(4)} = 50\%.$$

A sample human DNA molecular string of 1000 individual molecules is estimated to have the capacity to store $s = 4000$ bits of information in its helical structural arrangement. With $M = 2^{4000}$ messages and parts of these available for control of protein synthesis, it seems quite possible to explain the growth operation and the normal operation of single biological cells and connected sets of them.

11.5 SETS, STATISTICS, PROBABILISTICS, AND STOCHASTICS

Certainly finite sets, if they are not too large for the available time, space, and cost, can be *counted* in the physicist's *operational* sense (see P. W. Bridgeman [7]). Historically, statistics began with the counting of people and animals. Relative statistical frequency is computed as a ratio of counts and can be called *relative count*.[1] Consider the binary choice-information system illustrated in Figure 11.4. Here it is assumed that at each cell a memoryless, unbiased decider, such as a tossed "fair" penny, *chooses* whether the increment in ordinate will be $+1$ or -1. The ordinate then follows a one-dimensional "random walk," while each possible path in the resulting state-cell space constitutes a possible generated message of $+1$'s and -1's. If the cells are traversed in unit intervals of time, then one possible message might consist of all $+1$'s, and this message path would move up a line of slope 1. If, however, we look at other routes which end on the axis of abscissas for any even number of cells $n_c = 0,2,4, \ldots$, it is clear that there are $n_{paths} = 1,2,6, \ldots$. Note also that this is the mode (greatest number) of the statistical count function. If for each value of n_c, that is, each stage (in time), the number of routes ending at a chosen ordinate, σ, $C(\sigma, n_c)$ is divided by the total number of routes ending at that value of n_c, then the result is a relative count $\tilde{C}(\sigma, n_c)$ at ordinate σ. Thus

$$\tilde{C}(\sigma, n_c) \overset{\Delta}{=} \frac{C(\sigma, n_c)}{2^{n_c}}.$$

---

[1] This term was suggested by Professor Frederick Mosteller of Harvard University.

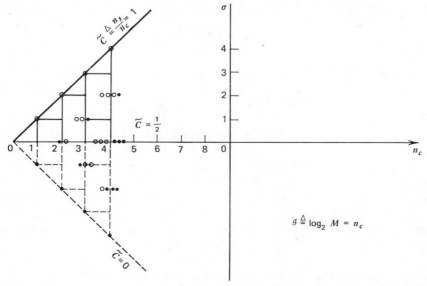

Fig. 11.4 A binary (spike or no spike) communication system as an example of statistics, probability, stochastics, and information capacity.

For $\sigma = 0$, $n_c = 4$,

$$\tilde{C}(0,4) = \frac{6}{2^4} = \frac{6}{16} = \frac{3}{8},$$

and for $\sigma = 4$, $n_c = 4$,

$$\tilde{C}(4,4) = \frac{1}{2^4} = \frac{1}{16}.$$

The choice-message capacity,

$$M(n_s, n_c) = n_s{}^n,$$

for $n_s = 2$, $n_c = 4$ is

$$M(2,4) = 2^4 = 16.$$

The choice-information capacity is

$$g(2,4) \triangleq \log_2 M(2,4) = 4 \text{ bits.}$$

With this binary communication system, in general

$$g \triangleq \log_2 2^{n_c} = n_c \text{ bits.}$$

In words, the binary choice-information capacity $\mathcal{I}$, in bits (binary decision units) of this system with increasing number of available *message states* n_{ms}, is equal to the number of available cells n_c. Thus $n_{ms} = n_c$.

Consider the effect on the relative count $\tilde{C}(\sigma, n_c)$ as n_c becomes large. This discrete function spreads out since $n_{ms} = n_c$, and its ordinates decrease since

$$\sum_{\sigma = -n_c}^{n_c} \tilde{C}(\sigma, n_c) = 1$$

for all values of n_c. Probabilists would say that its limit in probability is the normal, or gaussian, probability density function (see Chapter 1 of this book).

Also consider the effect on the choice-message and choice-information capacities as n_c becomes large: $M(2, n_c) = 2^{n_c}$ and $\mathcal{I}(2, n_c) = n_c$. After many units of time, $t = n_c$, they become very large (mathematically, for $n_c \to \infty$, they diverge to infinity).

Figure 11.5 illustrates the transition from statistics to probability in the case of the mathematician's continuous probability density function (pdf) and cumulative distribution function (cDf). Continuous models can be used as approximations for the discrete world of physical measurement

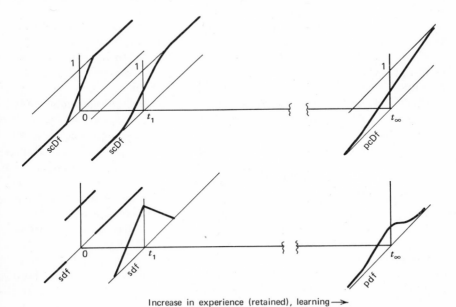

Increase in experience (retained), learning ⟶

Fig. 11.5 Example of the stochastic transition from statistics to probability.

if the number of states and the number of cells are both very large, and their separations both very small. As more data are accumulated, that is, as more experience is obtained and retained, by an organism—whether it be biological, or, say, an antimissile-weapon director—the statistical density functions (sdfs) and the cDfs evolve to the right of the previous ones in Figure 11.5. In other words, the organism is *learning* (if its memory is functioning) as the statistical experience increases. And, in the sense of probability limit explained above in Chapter 1, if we could wait long enough to go through an infinite number of changes, the sdf would approach a pdf, and the statistical cDf would approach a probabilistic cDf. Hypothetically, these would be the ultimate attainment to which learning experience would lead.

11.6 BAYES' THEOREM FOR COMMUNICATION SCIENCES

As with the application of all mathematical methods to the analysis of science, it is necessary to check that the mathematical input assumptions (axioms) and rules of procedure (mathematical logic) fit the real-world problem to which they are applied before attempting to interpret the mathematical conclusions as corresponding real-world conclusions. Engineer P. M. Woodward in his book of 1953 [19] introduced the use of inverse probability (Bayes' theorem) in communication problems. The problem is a scientific one if the subject matter is, say, aural communication between people. An extension of this Bayesian approach was developed mathematically in Chapter 1 of this book. For the method to be useful in concluding that a particular word or symbol was sent when a particular noise-corrupted word or noise-corrupted symbol is received, it is necessary first to check that probability axioms as well as the methods of reasoning apply as a model to the real situation. Specifically, it is necessary to have as preinformation the symbol probabilities and the transmission conditional (transition) probabilities which apply at the time of the communication. How does the receiving person (addressee) obtain this information? Is he given a list of the word (symbol) prior probabilities? Does he, with the cooperation of the originating person, run tests on the system to get the forward conditional probabilities? Would the sender read a list of words and the receiver determine the forward-transmission conditional probabilities by some alternative transmission means? If these inputs to the Bayes formula are not available, then how can the formula be used to obtain the inverse (backward) conditional (a posteriori) probability that a particular word (symbol) was sent? Furthermore, it is assumed in deriving the Bayes formula that the set of input signals constitutes an exhaustive partition, that is, a set of disjoint subsets which completely fill the input space. In other words, the receiver needs to know beforehand all the words the sender will use as well as the earlier-mentioned prior absolute and conditional probabilities. We shall leave the question of the practical applicability of the Bayesian approach to communication science to the reader and to Chapter 13 of this book. We suggest, however, that an approach to answering the question of how the receiver obtains the needed input probabilities is as follows: He *learns* them by continuing statistical experience with the frequency of word use and by the distorting characteristics of transmission through a similar channel *before* the particular communication to which he applies the Bayesian approach of inverse probability to deduce what the sender said.

11.7 SEMANTIC INFORMATION AND ITS MEASUREMENT

A method for measuring semantic (meaning) information has been proposed by one of the author's students, J. K. Wade [16]. This theory makes possible the development of the theory of semantic information communication along the same lines as the present well-developed choice-information theory [4]. Wade measures semantic information by measuring the statistical distribution parameters of the meaning of symbols (vocal or written words, for example). The problem is complicated by the presence of phonic or letter redundancy together with interword influence.

TRANSFORMATIONS AND THEIR INVARIANTS

11.8 GENERAL CLASSES OF TRANSFORMATIONS

There are three general classes of transformations with which we are especially concerned in the basic approach to the communication sciences. They and their invariants are discussed below.

Coordinate Transformations

The Lorentz coordinate transformations of special relativity theory are important for communication by electromagnetic waves in various frequency bands, such as the visible for animals including man, and infrared for certain snakes. Prominent invariants under these coordinate transformations are *time-distance* (the Schwarzschild metric), *momentum-spin*, *mass-energy*, *charge-magnetic flux* and *choice information*. For all but the last, one can refer to texts on modern physics and to [6].

Information Transformations

To this class belongs coding (encoding and decoding) of many varieties. The deterministic Morse telegraph code of 1838 was perhaps the first engineering use of statistics in communication. To improve the system efficiency, Samuel F. B. Morse chose shorter telegraph symbols to be used with the more frequently occurring symbols to reduce the message transmission time.

Under the title "probabilistic coding" would be listed language translation. The partially successful attempts to carry this out by automatic computers in the last 20 years have thrown much light on some difficult problems in linguistics—the principal subject of Part 1 of this book.

Another class of coding is known as modulation and demodulation. This placing of information on waves suitable for transport will be discussed in more detail later in this chapter.

The prominent invariants under proper information transformation are *choice information* and *semantic information*. As an example, it has been asserted that any idea can be expressed in any language. If this be so, then the semantic information for the idea must be invariant under translation from one language to another.

Functional Transformations

Functional transformations such as the Laplace-Fourier (L-F) transformations [2, 8, 10, 15] are used for simplifying the solution of real-world problems which fit the model of linear-invariant integrodifferential equations or sum-difference equations, convolution equations, and so on. At present this is a very large class in physics, economics, and engineering. It is a small class in biology thus far, no doubt due to the fact that, as was explained in Chapter 5 of this book, most of the material considered is still in the natural-history phase.

Other types of functional transformations simplify the solution of other classes of mathematical equations [4, 15].

Prominent invariants of the L-F transformation can be deduced by using the Rayleigh-Parseval theorem (see [6]) and are *time-distance, momentum-spin, mass-energy, charge-magnetic flux* and *choice in formation*.

11.9   TRANSFORMS OF OPERATIONS AND DETERMINISTIC FUNCTIONS

There are now many tables of Laplace-Fourier transforms [2, 8, 10] in one dimension and a few in two and three dimensions. These tables give both operation transforms and function transforms. Of great importance are the theorems which state that calculus operations such as differentiation, integration, convolution, and correlation are transformed into the simpler algebraic operations of multiplication by the variable, division by the variable, multiplication, and complex-conjugate multiplication, respectively.

Of course, a unicity theorem must hold for the transformation, with the consequence that the set of quantum states which define a system in the original domain is transformed into an equivalent set in the transform domain. (Choice information is conserved.)

11.10 TRANSFORMS OF STOCHASTIC PROCESSES

A *stochastic process* is the name given to the set of time-space functions generated by a decider controlled by a statistical or (in the probability limit by a probability) distribution function. Modern models of the real-world sets of waves which are used for communication are of this type. The importance of this was pointed out by Norbert Wiener in 1942 [18].

The operation of putting information on a set of waves is called *modulation*, that is, moulding. Taking the information off a set of waves is *demodulation*. The information can be put on the height (ordinate) or on the timing or phase angle (abscissa) or on both ordinate and abscissa, in one dimension [6]. Figure 11.6 shows a few samples of modulation of both sets of sine waves and sets of pulses. Sets of spike pulses were presented in Chapter 5 of this book, one of these sets coming from a ganglion controlling the heartbeat of a lobster.

The type of modulation in Figure 11.6a is height, or envelope, modulation. It is commonly called amplitude modulation, AM; but strictly speaking, amplitudes cannot be time modulated. Figure 11.6b shows the corresponding amplitude-versus-frequency functions obtained by L-F transformation. One is for the low-frequency base band, possibly audio-frequency band, case, while the other is for the high-frequency band carrier-modulation case.

Constant-envelope angle-modulation types and their amplitude-versus-frequency function transforms are shown in Figures 11.6c and 11.6d. Here the information may be on the instantaneous phase angle of the wave, called phase modulation (PM) or on, say, its time derivative, in which case it is called instantaneous-frequency modulation (FM).

Figures 11.6e and 11.6f show constant-envelope pulse-position modulation. Here the information may be on the instantaneous position of the pulse relative to a reference pulse, or on the time rate of change of this position. The first is called pulse-position modulation (PPM) by engineers, and the second is called pulse-frequency modulation (PFM). There are many other ways for putting information on pulses and for removing it.

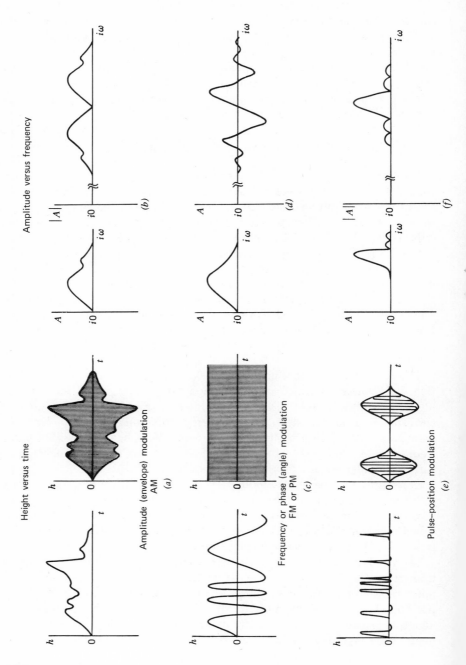

Height versus time

Amplitude versus frequency

Amplitude (envelope) modulation
AM
(a)

(b)

Frequency or phase (angle) modulation
FM or PM
(c)

(d)

Pulse-position modulation
(e)

(f)

The diagrams on the right in Figure 11.6 show the amplitude-frequency parts of the L-F transforms. The phase-frequency functions are not included.

11.11 TIME-SPACE FUNCTIONS, LAPLACE-FOURIER TRANSFORMS, METRIC SPECTRA, AND INTEGRAL SPECTRA

In Figure 11.7e a time or space or combined time-space function, say a gaussian ("normal") pulse, and its L-F amplitude-versus-frequency transform are illustrated. The theory is much more elegant if expressed in terms of angular frequency, $\omega = 2\pi f$, rather than for cyclic frequency f. The letter i (for engineers, j) is the imaginary-number unit. Figure 11.7f shows the L-F transform amplitude-versus-frequency function of the original pulse (here another gaussian pulse). It is referred to as the *amplitude spectrum*. If the original time-space function (pulse) is squared, then, as shown in Figure 11.7c, there results a function proportional to the metric (rate of change of integral) for the original pulse. Figure 11.7d shows not the L-F transform of this pulse, but rather the square of the amplitude-frequency

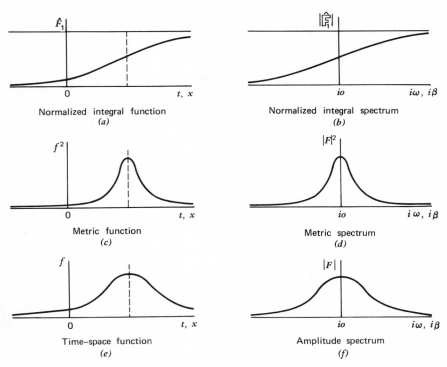

Fig. 11.7 Time-space functions, transforms, power and energy spectra.

function in the row below it. This function is called the *metric spectrum* of the original pulse. The time or space integral of the metric function below it, normalized by dividing it by the integral over all time or space, is shown in Figure 11.7*a*. This is called the *normalized integral function*. Finally, Figure 11.7*b* illustrates the normalized (by division by the integral over all frequency) integral of the metric spectrum below it. This is the *normalized integral spectrum*.

If the amplitude-frequency function of a communication system (or, say, a filter) is plotted and compared with the amplitude spectrum of an input function (or the set average of an input stochastic process), then it is possible to see (that is, pictorially multiply the two frequency functions) what the amplitude spectrum of the output function will be.

11.12 CORRELATION AND FILTERING

If a continuous function is translated (that is, if its graph is shifted) forward or backward by a fixed amount, called its period or wavelength, or any multiple of this, and then agrees identically with the original untranslated function, then the function is defined to be *periodic*. A generalization of this notion arises if a function is translated by a small amount and compared with the original function; and then this operation is repeated for translations of other size; and finally, the sum or integral of these comparisons is obtained. Such a multiple comparison generates a new function called an *autocorrelation function*. If the comparison is made for two original functions which are not necessarily the same, then the resulting new function is called the *crosscorrelation function*. The original generalization, in 1920, of an idea in statistics which constitutes correlation is due to the famous British fluid dynamicist G. I. Taylor. A later theorem named after two of its originators, the Wiener-Khinchin theorem, roughly states that the L-F transform of a correlation function is the complex-conjugate product of the L-F transforms of the two functions compared by the correlation. The transform result is the cross- or auto-power spectrum of the functions correlated: this is the transform of the correlation function. Depending on the view wanted, one may then compare functions for, say, hidden periodicities, or for separating signal from noise by crosscorrelating them in the time-space domain (correlation separation), or multiply the transform of one by the complex conjugate of the transform of the other to obtain their cross-power spectrum in the L-F transform domain (filtering).

It may be the case that in forming an image of the real world, nerve fibers from adjacent sensory cells in an insect's short-range eyes have their information functions crosscorrelated on the way to, or in, the eye ganglion. This may provide the "lateral inhibition" effect referred to in Chapter 5.

11.13 COMPOSITION OF pdfs AND OF cDfs

If two independent stochastic functions are added, then the operation by which the resulting pdf of the sum function is obtained is the well-known convolution operation of L-F transform theory. For pdfs, the Fourier transform will be adequate for converting the convolution operation into the simpler operation of multiplication of the F-transforms. An $\mathfrak{F}^{-1}$ inverse transformation will yield the pdf of the sum. For combining the cDfs of two added stochastic functions, however, the convergence factor of the Laplace transformation is required to obtain the cDf transforms. After multiplying these transforms, we obtain the cDf of the sum of stochastic functions by the $\mathcal{L}^{-1}$ inverse transformation.

These same techniques may be used to prove the central limit theorems of probability, but in this case an infinite number of convolutions appear, and an infinite product of the transforms of the pdfs or of the cDfs.

Even if calculations are made by the largest existing digital computers, L-F transformation reduces the calculation of the resulting distribution if more than four independent stochastic functions are to be added. (This was determined at the Columbus Division of North American Rockwell Corporation by a careful count.)

TRANSFER OF INFORMATION ON SIGNALS ACCOMPANIED BY NOISE THROUGH LINEAR INVARIANT COMMUNICATION SYSTEMS

Functional-transform theory is the best existing theory for treating both stochastic processes and the linear invariant systems used to transport and handle the information in them. As an example of such a system, one may recall Figure 11.2a. (In this chapter, we are discussing only the basis for this approach and will not carry it out in detail.)

11.14 MEASURES OF PERFORMANCE

In the human, we can find fantastic levels of communication performance. Thus a single quantum of light *action* (integral of energy) will actuate a rod sensor of the human eye, although several quanta are lost by the light beam on the way to the rod cell (Hecht). The human ear sensitivity is adjusted to just below the level where it would register the continual bombardment of thermal noise in the sensor cells. The energy level of actuation of a neuron in the brain is two orders of magnitude below that required by the most efficient (energywise) transistor available today. Microminiature-engineering computers are still many orders of magnitude larger than the molecular computer components of the brains of ants and of men.

In comparing communication systems of nature, measures of performance are needed. Prominent among these measures are *information-capacity efficiency, energy efficiency, symbol-, word-,* and *idea-redundancy, information capacity, information rate* and *density capacity, error statistics* and *error probability,* and *signal-to-noise power ratio.* Under the category of noise may be collected *distortion, interference from unwanted signals, thermal noise, discrete-charge noise, discrete-mass noise,* and *quantum-action noise.*

11.15   USE OF ADAPTATION BY SOPHISTICATED SYSTEMS

As remarked earlier, in the author's opinion the essence of life is adaptation [5]. A set of molecules which use adaptation is alive. Hence even the simplest biological systems are "closed loop," in engineering terminology. Prominent types of adaptation use *feedback, feedforward, parameter adaptation, connection adaptation,* and *system adaptation.* An example of the last is the metamorphosis of a caterpillar into a butterfly. Of course, the communication system is adapted along with the remainder of this change of form. Another example of adaptation, unexpected by a physicist, arose in a radiation-damage study of a DNA molecular string. Its unexpected behavior under mild radiation was finally explained by saying that for small amounts of radiation the damaged molecules were automatically repaired by enzymes which were present. (Reference: Donald Glazier, Nobel Laureate in Physics, University of California, Berkeley.) Similar results were obtained in radiation damage to trees at the Brookhaven National Laboratory. With small amounts of radiation, trees grew better than the unradiated control trees.

INFORMATION CAPACITY

11.16   SETS OF WAVES AND RELATED SPANS

The choice-information capacity of (the maximum amount of choice information which can be carried by) wave sets in the available state-cell space S is constrained by the principle of related spans. This relation is derived as follows:

Consider a set of time pulses

$$\{p(t)\} \subset \text{Lebesque class } L_2, \qquad -\infty < t < \infty,$$

and let the Fourier transform $\mathcal{F}[p(t)]$ be given by

$$\mathcal{F}[p(t)] \overset{\Delta}{=} P(i\omega).$$

Then by a theorem of Weiner [6],

$$\{|P(i\omega)|\} \subset L_2, \qquad -i\infty < i\omega < i\infty.$$

Make the following definitions:

$$e(t) \overset{\Delta}{=} \int_{t_1=-\infty}^{t} p^2(t_1) \, dt_1, \qquad e(\infty) < \infty,$$

$$E(i\omega) \overset{\Delta}{=} \int_{i\omega_1=-i\infty}^{i\omega} |P(i\omega_1)|^2 \, \frac{di\omega_1}{2\pi i},$$

where, by the Rayleigh-Parseval theorem, $e(\infty) = E(i\infty)$.

Next define relative energies:

$$e_r(t) \overset{\Delta}{=} \frac{e(t)}{e(\infty)}, \qquad \text{(first moment } \mu_t = 0).$$

Then define standard deviation σ_t:

$$\sigma_t \overset{\Delta}{=} \left[\int_{t=-\infty}^{\infty} t^2 \, de_r(t) \right]^{1/2},$$

where

$$E_r(t) \overset{\Delta}{=} \frac{e(t)}{e(\infty)}, \qquad \text{(first moment } \mu_{i\omega} = 0),$$

and define standard deviation $\sigma_{i\omega}$:

$$\sigma_{i\omega} \overset{\Delta}{=} \left[\int_{i\omega=-i\infty}^{i\infty} |i\omega|^2 \, \frac{dE(i\omega)}{2\pi i} \right]^{1/2}.$$

Also assume

$$\frac{dp(t)}{dt}, \qquad \frac{d^2p(t)}{dt^2} \subset L_2, \qquad -\infty < t < \infty.$$

Using the Cauchy-Schwartz inequality,

$$(\vec{A} \cdot \vec{B})^2 \leq A^2 B^2,$$

and treating $tp(t)$ and $i\omega P(i\omega)$ as vectors in Hilbert space, we obtain the *basic inequality*

$(U_{t,i\omega})$ $\qquad\qquad\qquad 1 \leq 2\sigma_t \cdot \sigma_{i\omega}.$

Defining the pulse spans as

$$\Delta t \triangleq 2\sigma_t \qquad \text{and} \qquad \Delta\omega \triangleq 2\sigma_\omega \equiv \sigma_{i\omega},$$

we thus have the *related-spans inequality*

$(U_{t,\omega})$ $\qquad\qquad\qquad 1 \leq \Delta t \cdot \Delta\omega.$

Multiply by Planck's quantum of action $\hbar \triangleq h/2\pi$, and use Planck's relation, $\Delta E = \hbar\Delta\omega$, to obtain

$(U_{t,E})$ $\qquad\qquad\qquad \hbar \leq \Delta t \cdot \Delta E,$

which is one of Heisenberg's two uncertainty principles.

Analogously, consider a set of space pulses

$$\{p(x)\} \subset L_2, \qquad\qquad -\infty < x < \infty,$$

and let the Fourier transform $\mathfrak{F}[p(x)]$ be given by

$$\mathfrak{F}[p(x)] \triangleq P(i\beta).$$

Then by the same type of assumptions and the same reasoning as above, there results another representation of the basic inequality $(U_{t,i\omega})$:

$(U_{x,i\beta})$ $\qquad\qquad\qquad 1 \leq 2\sigma_x \cdot \sigma_{i\beta}.$

Defining pulse spans as

$$\Delta x \triangleq 2\sigma_x$$

and

$$\Delta\beta \triangleq 2\sigma_\beta \equiv \sigma_{i\beta},$$

we thus have

$(U_{x,\beta})$ $\qquad\qquad\qquad 1 \leq \Delta x \cdot \Delta\beta.$

Multiply by $\hbar$ and use de Broglie's relation, $\Delta\breve{P} = \hbar\Delta\beta$, to obtain

$(U_x, \breve{P})$ $\qquad\qquad\qquad \hbar \leq \Delta x \cdot \Delta\breve{P},$

which is the second of Heisenberg's uncertainty principles.

It can be shown by use of the calculus of variations that for the gaussian (normal) pulse,

$$p_m(t) = \frac{e^{(-1/2)(t/\sigma_t)^2}}{(2\pi)^{1/2}\sigma_t},$$

which also has a gaussian pulse as transform, the product of the spans in the two domains is a minimum.

Many other uncertainty or related-span principles follow from the basic one $(U_{t,i\omega})$. An example is the range-and-angle sonar related-span principle used by bats in the location of insects and cave walls.

11.17 INFORMATION CAPACITIES, INFORMATION TIME-RATE CAPACITIES, AND INFORMATION SPACE-GRADIENT CAPACITIES

The question may now be asked, "How much information-carrying capacity has a set of waves?" To answer this, we must first decide how closely pulse cells may be packed and still distinguished for counting. The answer to this packing question depends in turn on how elaborate is the available separation procedure, and how long is the available solution time. As an arbitrary decision, let us assume that time metric-pulse cells, distance metric-pulse cells, and their metric-spectra pulse cells are all packed with coincident ends of spans; that is, consider gaussian metric[2] pulses packed up to their ± 1 σ points.

Figure 11.8 presents an example for time metric-pulse cells and their metric-spectra pulse cells. The number of distinguishable states is here determined by noise-power levels or their equivalent energy levels. Here $\Delta \hat{E}$ stands for the noise-energy magnitude. To avoid loss of signal information, signal-energy levels must be separated by at least this amount, $\Delta \hat{E}$. In Figure 11.8 are shown $n_s = 2^2$ energy levels, which constitute two energy channels. There are $n_t = 7$ time channels, and $n_{i\omega} = 7$ frequency channels. Altogether in the available state-cell space shown, S, the message capacity M is given by $M = 2^{98}$, so the choice-information capacity $\mathcal{I}$ is 98 bits.

Our assumptions of independence of choice and equal statistical frequency are relaxed in Chapter 12, where information theory will be discussed. With the present assumptions, however, we can obtain information capacity—the maximum ability to carry information. These assumptions lead to general capacity relations which may be derived as follows:

Message capacity: $M = n_s{}^{n_c}$.

Information capacity: $\mathcal{I} \triangleq \log_2 M = (\log_2 n_s) \, n_c$.

The distance vector for a Minkowski space is

$$\vec{x} = ict \vec{1}_0 + \underbrace{x_1 \vec{1}_1 + x_2 \vec{1}_2}_{\text{transverse space}} + \underbrace{x_3 \vec{1}_3}_{\text{longitudinal space}},$$

[2] The square of a gaussian pulse is also gaussian.

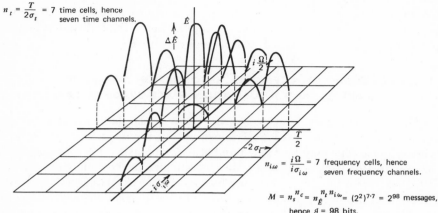

$n_s = n_E = \dfrac{\hat{E}}{\Delta \hat{E}} = 2^2$ energy states, hence two energy channels.

$n_t = \dfrac{T}{2\sigma_t} = 7$ time cells, hence seven time channels.

$n_{i\omega} = \dfrac{i\Omega}{i\sigma_{i\omega}} = 7$ frequency cells, hence seven frequency channels.

$M = n_s^{n_c} = n_{\hat{E}}^{n_t \, n_{i\omega}} = (2^2)^{7 \cdot 7} = 2^{98}$ messages, hence $\mathcal{I} = 98$ bits.

Fig. 11.8 Information carried by pulse-energy states in time (or space) and frequency cells.

in which t is time, c is the velocity of light in free space, i is the imaginary unit, and $\hat{1}_j$ are unit vectors.

The number of distinguishable states is

$$n_s = \frac{\hat{E}}{\Delta \hat{E}} + 1,$$

and the number of cells is

$$n_c = n_{ct} \cdot \frac{n_{i\omega}}{c} \cdot \prod_{d=1}^{2} n_{xd} \cdot n_{\beta d}.$$

Transmission choice-information capacity is

$(\mathcal{I}_{\hat{z}, t_r})$ $\qquad$ $\mathcal{I}_{\hat{z}, t_r} = \left[\log_2 \left(\dfrac{E}{\Delta E} + 1 \right) \right] \cdot \dfrac{T}{\Delta t} \cdot \dfrac{\Omega}{\Delta \omega} \cdot \displaystyle\prod_{d=1}^{2} n_{xd} \cdot n_{\beta xd}$ bits.

Choice-information time-rate capacity is defined as

$(R_{\hat{z}, t_r})$ $\qquad\qquad$ $R_{\hat{z}, t_r} \triangleq \dfrac{\Delta \mathcal{I}_{\hat{z} t_r}}{\Delta t}$ bits/time span.

Choice-information space-gradient capacity is defined as

(G_{xd}) $\qquad\qquad$ $G_{xd} \triangleq \dfrac{\Delta \mathcal{I}_{\hat{z}, st}}{\Delta x_d}$ bits/distance span $\qquad (d = 1, 2, 3).$

11.18 CONCLUSIONS

The conceptual bases of the communication sciences go back to counting. Statistics, probablistics, stochastics, and information capacity are all founded on counting.

It is important to formulate the communication sciences in terms of the invariants of transformations whether these transformations be coordinate transformations, coding (language) transformations, or functional transformations such as the Laplace-Fourier transformation.

REFERENCES

1. Abramson, N., *Information Theory and Coding*, McGraw-Hill, New York, 1963.
2. Aseltine, J. A., *Transform Method in Linear System Analysis*, McGraw-Hill, New York, 1958.
3. Barnes, John L., "Functional Transformations for Engineering Design," in E. F. Beckenbach (editor), *Modern Mathematics for the Engineer*, First Series, McGraw-Hill, New York, 1956, pp. 346–360.
4. Barnes, John L., "Information Theoretic Aspects of Feedback Control Systems," Inst. of Elec. and Electronic Engineers, Convention Record, Part I, March 24, 1964, 142–153. (Revised version in *Automatica*, **4**, 1968, 165–185.)
5. Barnes, John L., "Adaptive Control as the Basis of Life and Learning Systems," IFAC Tokyo Symposium on Systems Engineering for Control System Design, 1965, 187–191.
6. Barnes, John L., "Laplace-Fourier Transformation, the Foundation for Quantum Information Theory and Linear Physics," in Gunning, Robert C. (general editor), *Problems in Analysis, A Symposium in Honor of Salomon Bochner*, Princeton University Press, Princeton, N. J., 1970.
7. Bridgeman, P. W., *The Logic of Modern Physics*, Macmillan, New York, 1927.
8. Doetsch, G., *Guide to the Applications of Laplace Transforms*, Fairbairn, W. McA. (translation editor), D. Van Nostrand, Princeton, N. J., 1963.
9. Feller, W., *An Introduction to Probability Theory and Its Applications*, 3rd Ed., Vol. 1, Wiley, New York, 1968.
10. Gardner, M. F., and J. L. Barnes, *Transients in Linear Systems*, Wiley, New York, 1942.
11. Mandelbrot, B., Contribution à la théorie mathématique des jeux de communication, Ph.D. thesis, Paris, December 16, 1952; Publ. de l'Inst. de Statistique de l'Univer. de Paris, Vol. 2, facs, 1, 2, 1953, 80–102.
12. Quastler, H., *Information Theory and Biology*, University of Illinois Press, Urbana, 1953.
13. Shannon, C. E., "A Mathematical Theory of Communication," Bell Syst. Tech. J., 27, 1948, 379–423, 623–656.
14. Shannon, C. E., and W. Weaver, *The Mathematical Theory of Communication*, University of Illinois Press, Urbana, 1949.
15. Sneddon, I. N., *Fourier Transforms*, McGraw-Hill, London, 1951.
16. Wade, J. K., "Quantative Measurement of Semantic and Pragmatic Information," Master of Science thesis, UCLA, August 1964.
17. Webb, P. (editor), *Bioastronautics Data Book*, National Aeronautics and Space Adminstration, Washington, D. C., NASA SP–3006, 1964.

18. Wiener, N., *Extrapolation, Interpolation, and Smoothing of Stationary Time Series*, Wiley, New York, 1950.
19. Woodward, P. M., *Probability and Information Theory, with Applications to Radar*, Pergamon Press, London, 1953.

FURTHER READINGS

1. Arbib, M., *Brains, Machines, and Mathematics*, McGraw-Hill, New York, 1964.
2. Belevitch, V., *Classical Network Theory*, Holden-Day, San Francisco, 1968.
3. Green, C. D., *Integral Equation Methods*, Thomas Nelson and Sons, London, 1969.
4. Grenander, Ulf, *Foundations of Pattern Analysis. Technical Report GRAPHICS/ IBM-2*, Brown University, Providence, 1967.
5. Hammer, Preston C. (editor), *Advances in Mathematical Systems Theory*, The Pennsylvania State University Press, University Park, Pa., 1969.
6. Mendel, J. M., and K. S. Fu (editors), *Adaptive, Learning and Pattern Recognition Systems. Theory and Applications*, Academic Press, New York, 1970.

CHAPTER 12

Discrete Signaling and Coding Systems

LEO BREIMAN

Consultant, Topanga, California

Contents

12.1 INTRODUCTION

This chapter is concerned with an elementary exposition of Shannon's theory of information [1, 3, 4]. It is just not true that there is *a* theory of information; there are as *many* theories of information as there are different contexts containing something that can be called information. A theory is pertinent only against a backdrop of given reality boundary conditions.

There are, from the author's point of view, a variety of reasons for singling our Shannon's theory for discussion. First, the physical context from which it arises is common to many situations, and the results of the theory have many important practical applications. Second, it is exciting mathematical modeling. It is the first coherent theory that gave mathematical meaning to the difficult and vague concepts of information and communication. Some of the most significant parts of this theory, as in any good mathematical model, revolve around the symbolization, or rather the translation, of physical-world entities into mathematics. The right words here are "Let x equal . . . ," the magical words, haunting us from high school on, that herald the beginning of the translation phase.

One of our major purposes in this chapter is to communicate a sense of "Let x equal." Thus the chapter is much more involved in heuristic tracking down, formulating, and understanding, than in proofs and exact mathematical statements.

SHANNON'S FIRST THEOREM

12.2 WHAT IS INFORMATION, AND HOW MUCH DO WE HAVE?

There are essentially two important results in Shannon's theory. The first revolves around the question: What is information and how much do we have? Some attempt has to be made to find out what a thing is, before the thing can be measured.

The most important observation to start with is that there can be no information without ignorance! Information can have meaning only in a context of uncertainty and unpredictability. If there is a being that knows all and can predict everything completely, then information is entirely irrelevant to him. He cannot use it, and he does not need it. If we get a tip on the third dog race, or on the stock market, then the amount of information conveyed depends on how uncertain we were as to the outcome. For information to exist, there has to be a situation in which numbers of alternative outcomes are possible and certainty is impossible.

To get further, look at the simplest possible model for such a situation: We specify a finite universe $x_1, x_2, \ldots, x_n$ of possible outcomes, together with associated probabilities $P(x_1), P(x), \ldots, P(x_n)$. This list of outcomes and probabilities completely specifies what is sometimes called a random device, or a random experiment, or an information source. For example, a fair coin is a random device, and so is a die.

A random device is generally denoted by X. This random device in repeated operation *generates history*. Even if it is only a coin being tossed, if a record of all the outcomes is kept, then *history is being written and information is being generated*. Roughly, we say that we are given information whenever a random experiment is performed and we are told the outcome.

How much? In its crudest, simplest form, "how much information" means "how long," "how many words," "how many letters." Thus we might have 300 pages of information on the Civil War, or 1000 pages of information on World War II. Of course, this neglects the inhomogeneity of information, the fact that a small item on the back page of the newspaper may have more value or interest than all the material in the rest of the paper. This difficulty we leave for another theory. So far as we are concerned, we deal only with the simplest. Amount equals length. The idea is this: Let the random device be put into operation. It starts generating outcomes. We make a historical record of these outcomes from the very beginning. The length of the record per outcome is defined to be the rate at which the device produces information.

Now that we are writing history, there are certain conditions that our method of writing history must satisfy. If, eventually, numbers are going to come out of this theory, then all historians must used the same alphabet. This is so because, in general, the number of words or letters used to record will be dependent on what alphabet is used. Ordinarily, languages that have longer alphabets are able to use fewer letters per word. Since a standard alphabet has to be used, we may as well pick the simplest one: we shall use only the two symbols 0 or 1.

Rule I. Standard Alphabet. All history will be written as strings of 0's and 1's.

The next requirement is that historical embellishments will not be allowed. Good historians have the privilege in usual writings of describing what the queen was wearing on the day of battle. This we do not allow. For example, in coin tossing, we may record:

Outcome	Probability	Record by
H	$\frac{1}{2}$	0
T	$\frac{1}{2}$	1

Fine! But also, this is possible:

Outcome	Probability	Record by
H	$\frac{1}{2}$	00
T	$\frac{1}{2}$	11

The first recorder uses one digit per outcome to record; the other uses two. But the second digit is sheer literary embellishment, and is simply not allowed.

Rule II. No Historical Embellishment. *The recording method must use as few digits as possible.*

The third condition is that we write good history. Good history means that given the tape of 0's and 1's, we can deduce from this record exactly what happened. As an example, look at the device consisting of a six-sided die. Consider a recording method that puts down a 0 if face 1, 2, or 3 comes up, otherwise a 1:

Outcome	Probability	Recorded by
1	$\frac{1}{6}$	0
2	$\frac{1}{6}$	0
3	$\frac{1}{6}$	0
4	$\frac{1}{6}$	1
5	$\frac{1}{6}$	1
6	$\frac{1}{6}$	1

This is terrible history! If a 0 appears on the tape, it is impossible to tell which of the first three faces came up. A similar remark holds for a 1 and the last three faces.

Rule III. Good History. *Starting at the beginning of the record, it must be possible to reconstruct the entire history of outcomes of the device.*

These three rules shoehorn us into the following preliminary definition.

Definition (preliminary). *The rate of information production by a random device is the number of binary digits (Rule I) per outcome computed from a history of the device, this history being efficient (Rule II) and decipherable (Rule III).*

12.3 SOME EXAMPLES

Nothing takes the place of examples to illuminate difficulties and methods. In the examples below, we list the possible outcomes, their probabilities, and the proposed recording method.

Example 1. Fair-coin tossing.

Outcome	Probability	Record
H	$\frac{1}{2}$	0
T	$\frac{1}{2}$	1

The historical record is efficient and decipherable. Start at the beginning; a 0 means an H came up first, then a 1 implies that a T came up, and so on.

For a random device X, let $H(X)$ be the rate of information generation, that is, the average number of digits needed to record one outcome. Thus, for coin-tossing, we conclude that

$$H(X) = 1.$$

Example 2. This is a bit more complicated.

Outcome	Probability	Record
1	$\frac{1}{4}$	0
2	$\frac{1}{4}$	1
3	$\frac{1}{4}$	10
4	$\frac{1}{4}$	01

This recording method has been chosen to be as short as possible. It uses the two binary words of length one, and goes on to those of length two. Half the time one digit is used to record, half the time two. Thus

$$H(X) = \tfrac{1}{2} \cdot 1 + \tfrac{1}{2} \cdot 2 = \tfrac{3}{2}.$$

Mull over this result; there should be a little anxious worry and dismay. This recording method, even though it assigns different binary words to each outcome, is *bad history*! If, anywhere in a history, the symbols 01 occurs, this could be deciphered, perfectly accurately, as either of the following:

$$01 = \text{outcome 1 followed by outcome 2}$$

or

$$01 = \text{outcome 4.}$$

This recording method is therefore inadmissable, so let us try another:

Outcome	Probability	Record
1	$\frac{1}{4}$	00
2	$\frac{1}{4}$	01
3	$\frac{1}{4}$	10
4	$\frac{1}{4}$	11

This recording method is decipherable because, starting at the beginning, the instructions are to read the first two digits; if they are 01, for example, then 2 occurred. Read the next two, recording the result, and so on. Thus:

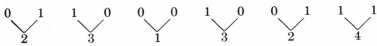

Since two digits are used every time,

$$H(X) = 2.$$

Now $H(X) = \frac{3}{2}$ we know to be too small. $H(X) = 2$ is attainable, but can this be lowered? The answer is "No," for the following reason. The only recording method that is any shorter will have to use at least one one-digit word—actually no more than one, or the same lack of decipherability would prevail as originally. So say that the symbol 0 is assigned to outcome 1. Then 00 cannot be used for anything else, since it would also look just like outcome 1 happening twice. Furthermore, three digits cannot be used to record anything since the advantage in using one digit to record outcome 1 would be offset. The only alternative left is an arrangement such as this:

Outcome	Probability	Record
1	$\frac{1}{4}$	0
2	$\frac{1}{4}$	10
3	$\frac{1}{4}$	01
4	$\frac{1}{4}$	11

This is bad history again. Look at the combination 0110. We have either of the following:

$$0110 = \text{outcome 3 followed by 2}$$

or

$$0110 = \text{outcome 1, then 4, then 1.}$$

With some degree of confidence, then, we conclude that $H(X) = 2$ is the correct answer.

Example 3. This is a three-outcome experiment.

Outcome	Probability	Record
1	$\frac{1}{2}$	0
2	$\frac{1}{4}$	10
3	$\frac{1}{4}$	11

This recording method is decipherable. The instructions are: Start reading. If you see a 0, 1 occurred; if you see a 1, read the next digit to conclude whether 2 or 3 occurred, then start as before. Thus you might have:

```
0   1  1   0   0   0   1  0   0   1  1  1   0
↓    \ /   ↓   ↓   ↓    \ /   ↓    \ /    \ /
1    3     1   1   1     2    1    3      2
```

A simple argument can be given here, very similar to the reasoning in Example 2, to show that there is no better recording system. To compute $H(X)$, note that half the time one digit is used, the other half, two, so that

$$H(X) = 1 \cdot \tfrac{1}{2} + 2 \cdot \tfrac{1}{2} = \tfrac{3}{2}.$$

12.4 BLOCK CODING

Example 3 has a purpose. Notice that the most efficient recording system associates the shortest word, 0, with the most probable outcome. This principle is used in all reasonable languages. The words used very frequently are short—consider "and," "if," "a," "but," "or." Further, reflect on the sobering thought of what would happen to the length of *The New York Times* if all these words were ten letters long.

Consider the following simple example involving unequal probabilities:

Outcome	Probability	Record
1	.9	0
2	.1	1

This recording method is certainly decipherable and is the shortest possible. Therefore $H(X) = 1$. But there is something bothersome and suspicious here. $H(X) = 1$ also for a fair-coin tossing device. This is nonsensical, because there is much less uncertainty in the preceding device. If we always predict that the outcome is 1, then 9 times out of 10 the prediction is correct. Make the example more extreme and let outcome 1 have probability .99. Then the prediction is correct 99 times out of 100, and there is very little uncertainty in this context. Only 1 time in 100 does something novel and unpredicted appear, but we still have $H(X) = 1$.

No matter how we twist and turn, this worry continues to nag us— somehow there is some intrinsic difference between the two experiments that is not yet reflected in our mathematics. Let us retrace our steps. It is time to point out something that may already have been obvious to some readers but no doubt mystifying to many others—*we are not yet utilizing the full potential of the various possible recording methods*. We have demanded of our recording methods only that they be decipherable, that we be able to read the outcomes of long strings of repetitions of the experiment. But so far we have restricted our attention to only those recording methods that give the outcome of one experiment at a time. One outcome is called out, we record; the next outcome is called out, we record again, and so on. But nothing that has been said prevents the use of a recording method that, for instance, waits for the outcomes of the first two experiments and then records, then waits for the outcomes of the next two, records again, and so on. We could call such a recording method recording in blocks of two, or as the engineers sometimes refer to it, as *block coding of length two* [2].

Returning to our example, we consider two independent experiments with our device. The possible outcomes of the two experiments are outcome 1 followed by outcome 1, outcome 1 followed by outcome 2, outcome 2 followed by outcome 1, and finally outcome 2 followed by outcome 2. In the following table, we again give a list of the outcomes, the corresponding probabilities, and a proposed recording method:

Outcome	Probability	Recording
1 (1,1)	.81	0
2 (1,2)	.09	10
3 (2,1)	.09	110
4 (2,2)	.01	111

This recording method is decipherable: If the first digit is a 0 we know that outcome 1 followed by outcome 1 occurred, and then we are ready to read the next digit. If the first digit is a 1, we know that one of the last three outcomes occurred, and we read on; if we then come to a 0, we know that outcome 1 followed by outcome 2 occurred, and we are ready to read the next outcomes; if we see another 1, we know that one of the last two outcomes occurred and that we must read on to the third digit to find out whether we got 2 followed by 1 or 2 followed by 2. But how many digits do we need on the average with this method of recording? On the average, to record two outcomes we need

$$.81 \cdot 1 + .09 \cdot 2 + .09 \cdot 3 + .01 \cdot 3,$$

or 1.29 digits for every two experiments. Dividing by 2, we see that we need on the average .645 digits per experiment, certainly significantly less than our previous result of 1.

Block coding of length three can also be used in this experiment; that is, now we wait for the outcomes of the first three experiments, record, wait for the outcomes of the next three, record, and so forth. Now we get the following table:

Outcome	Probability	Recording
1 (111)	$.9 \cdot .9 \cdot .9 = .729$	0
2 (112)	$.9 \cdot .9 \cdot .1 = .081$	100
3 (121)	$.9 \cdot .1 \cdot .9 = .081$	110
4 (122)	$.9 \cdot .1 \cdot .1 = .009$	101
5 (211)	$.1 \cdot .9 \cdot .9 = .081$	11100
6 (212)	$.1 \cdot .9 \cdot .1 = .009$	11101
7 (221)	$.1 \cdot .1 \cdot .9 = .009$	11110
8 (222)	$.1 \cdot .1 \cdot .1 = .001$	11111

This recording method is decipherable, and the average number of digits needed to record three outcomes is

$$.729 \cdot 1 + .081 \cdot 3 + .081 \cdot 3 + .081 \cdot 3 + .009 \cdot 5$$
$$+ .009 \cdot 5 + .009 \cdot 5 + .001 \cdot 5 = 1.598,$$

or .533 digits per outcome.

But why stop now? We can use block coding of length four, of length five, and so on. Looking at these various coding methods, we conclude that the longer the block the code uses, the better code it is; that is, the smaller the number of digits it uses per outcome.

Perhaps the list below, constructed for the experiment under discussion, will illuminate the matter:

Length of block code used	1	2	3	5
Number of digits used per outcome	1	.645	.533	.48

Here the world reveals its parsimonious nature. While block coding of length five, say, is considerably more effective than recording outcome by outcome, using on the average less than half the number of digits required by the latter method, it is also considerably less convenient. We have to wait and remember the outcomes of the first five experiments, then look up the appropriate coding in a table that now has no less than $2^5 = 32$ entries, before proceeding to the second block of five. Compare this to listening for the outcome and, if it is the first, jotting down a 0, while if it is the second, jotting down a 1.

But whatever the difficulties and complexities of block coding, we have the unexpected, startling, and somewhat gratifying result that the use of these more complicated codings can considerably reduce the average number of digits needed to record an outcome.

There is a difference in the amount of information inherent in the tossing of a fair coin and in the device with a bias of .9. Block coding clearly reveals the difference. Now the question becomes: What number shall be assigned as the rate of information generated by the device? From the preceding list, we see that if we use block coding of length 2, the answer is .654; blocks of length three result in .533; blocks of length five yield further improvement, and so on.

Faced once more with a serious methodological difficulty, we resolve it by an appeal to the reader's sense of fairness. It does not seem cricket to say that we shall consider only codes of block length at most ten, say, and ignore the improvement that can be made past this point. Instead, we define the rate of information generation as the *limiting value that we tend toward as we steadily improve our coding methods*—in our specific example, as that number which would stand (if such could be visualized) at the right-hand end of the preceding length-versus-number-of-digits list. This number would then represent our ultimate efficiency in coding, the shortest possible recording length per outcome we could even hope to achieve.

If only we knew how to compute this number for any given specific experiment, then we could check on the efficiency of any proposed coding method. For example, for some experiments, block coding of length three might be fairly close to optimum, whereas for other experiments we might have to go to blocks of length five in order to get the same. More concretely, if we knew in the example of this paragraph that the limiting value is .46 (which indeed it is), then the conclusion would be that by using block coding of length two, we are using .18 digits per outcome too much, an additional 18 digits for every 100 outcomes. An efficiency expert might demand that we use block coding of length five, which loses only 2 digits for every 100 experiments.

To summarize our position to date: To every random experiment X, with outcomes numbered $x_1, x_2, \ldots, x_n$ and corresponding probabilities $P(x_1)$, $P(x_2), \ldots, P(x_n)$, is attached a single, currently half-mythical, number [which we shall denote by $H(X)$]. This number has been called the *rate at which information is generated* by the device, or, synonomously, its *uncertainty*, and is defined as the lower limit of the average number of digits needed to record a single outcome of X, as increasingly efficient, but always decipherable, codes are used.

A semantic morass has been waded through, and hard ground has been reached. A reasonable and complete definition of uncertainty and rate of information generation by a random device has been arrived at. There remains only the problem of computing the number $H(X)$. Let us first, however, digress to review a notion that will be needed in this computation.

12.5 LOGARITHMS TO THE BASE 2

If a number can be written as 2 to a power, then its *logarithm to the base 2* (abbreviated $\log_2$) *is that power*. For example, $8 = 2^3$, whence $\log_2 8 = 3$; $4 = 2^2$, so that $\log_2 4 = 2$, and so on. Besides the numbers 2, 4, 8, 16, . . . , which can be written as integer powers of 2, there are the numbers which are equal to $2^{m/n}$, where $m > 0$ and $n > 0$, this number meaning the nth root of 2 raised to the mth power. Our definition extends to these. That is, $\log_2$ of such a number is m/n. Therefore, since $2^{1/2} \doteq 1.41$, we have $\log 1.41 \doteq \frac{1}{2}$; $2^{3/2} = (1.41)^3 \doteq 2.83$, whence $\log_2 2.83 \doteq \frac{3}{2}$. By using the numbers $2^{n/m}$, we can get $\log_2$ of any number to any degree of accuracy we wish. If we desire to compute $\log_2 5$ to two figures of accuracy, we begin by observing that 5 is between 4 and 8, so that its $\log_2$ is between 2 and 3. Now $2^{5/2} \doteq (1.41)^5 \doteq 5.66$, which is greater than 5, giving the result that $5/2$ is greater than $\log_2 5$. But $2^{7/3} \doteq 5.04$, so $7/3 \doteq 2.33$ must be quite close to $\log_2 5$, and further investigation can demonstrate that it is indeed accurate to two figures.

Finally, to get logarithms of positive numbers less than 1, we make the definition that the reciprocal of 2 to any power is 2 to the negative of that power, for example,

$$\tfrac{1}{2}^2 = 2^{-2}, \qquad \tfrac{1}{2}^3 = 2^{-3}, \qquad 1/\sqrt{2} = 2^{-1/2}.$$

This gives

$$\log_2 \tfrac{1}{2} = -1, \qquad \log_2 \tfrac{1}{4} = -2.$$

In general, logarithms to the base 2 of all positive numbers less than 1 have negative values.

12.6 THE THEOREM

The problem posed at the end of Section 12.4, that of computing $H(X)$, is answered in a remarkable theorem first stated and proved by C. E. Shannon [3]. Reason this way: If a random experiment X has outcomes $x_1, x_2, \ldots, x_n$ with probabilities $P(x_1), P(x_2), \ldots, P(x_n)$, then the entire structure of the experiment is specified by the list of numbers $P(x_1)$, $P(x_2), \ldots, P(x_n)$. It must follow, then, that the number $H(X)$, no matter how difficult to compute, must depend only on this list of numbers, and must be computable from the probabilities in this list.

Some more rough heuristic reasoning: Suppose that we have an experiment with n equally likely outcomes, and suppose further that n is large. Suppose even further that we wish to record all outcomes by combinations of 0's and 1's (synonomously, *binary words*) of *equal* length. Then what length is necessary? There are four code words of length 2, namely 11, 01, 10, 11, eight of length three, and in general 2^k of length k. Since a distinct binary word is necessary for each outcome, the length k must be such that, approximately, $2^k = n$ or $k = \log_2 n$. Here the probability of each outcome is $1/n$. In terms of this probability, then,

$$k = \log_2 n = -\log_2 1/n.$$

Our conclusion is that somehow, somewhere, $H(X)$ (which is the shortest length k) is related to the negative of the logarithms of the probabilities. This kind of reasoning gives a way of backing into the more general result.

Enough ado—now for that equation that is to modern communication almost what the Rosetta stone is to ancient Egyptian.

Shannon's First Theorem. *The number $H(X)$ may be computed as*

$$H(X) = -P(x_1) \log_2 P(x_1) - P(x_2) \log_2 P(x_2) - \ldots - P(x_n) \log_2 P(x_n),$$

or, in summation notation,

$$H(X) = - \sum_{x_i} P(x_i) \log_2 P(x_i).$$

Let us return to the examples of Section 12.3, which were considered before the notation of block coding was introduced. Is it possible that, by using the greater efficiency of block coding, we could improve the results obtained here? An application of Shannon's formula can settle this question once and for all, since it provides the lower limit attainable by any kind of coding. So back we go to compute $H(X)$ and compare it with our preliminary answers.

Example 1.

Outcome	Probability
1	$\frac{1}{2}$
2	$\frac{1}{2}$

$$H(X) = -\tfrac{1}{2} \log_2 \tfrac{1}{2} - \tfrac{1}{2} \log_2 \tfrac{1}{2} = - \log_2 \tfrac{1}{2} = 1$$

Example 2.

Outcome	Probability
1	$\frac{1}{4}$
2	$\frac{1}{4}$
3	$\frac{1}{4}$
4	$\frac{1}{4}$

$$H(X) = -\tfrac{1}{4} \log_2 \tfrac{1}{4} - \tfrac{1}{4} \log_2 \tfrac{1}{4} - \tfrac{1}{4} \log_2 \tfrac{1}{4} - \tfrac{1}{4} \log_2 \tfrac{1}{4} = -\log_2 \tfrac{1}{4} = 2$$

Example 3.

Outcome	Probability
1	$\frac{1}{2}$
2	$\frac{1}{4}$
3	$\frac{1}{4}$

$$H(X) = -\tfrac{1}{2} \log_2 \tfrac{1}{2} - \tfrac{1}{4} \log_2 \tfrac{1}{4} - \tfrac{1}{4} \log_2 \tfrac{1}{4}$$
$$= -\tfrac{1}{2} \log_2 \tfrac{1}{2} - \tfrac{1}{2} \log_2 \tfrac{1}{4} = 1 + \tfrac{1}{2} = \tfrac{3}{2}$$

The values $H(X)$ in these three examples result from our deliberate arranging. For in each of them, the previously proposed outcome-by-outcome coding methods are best, requiring exactly the average number of digits as given by Shannon's formula. But this sort of thing is a rare coincidence, rather than the rule, and it occurs only when all of the probabilities in an experiment are inverse powers of 2. Of course, our choice of these rare examples was not coincidence, but rather a result of our desire not to let block coding complicate things too early.

For the example of Section 12.4 that led to consideration of block coding, we have:

Outcome	Probability	
1	.9	$H(X) = .9 \log_2 .9 - .1 \log_2 .1$
2	.1	$\doteq .46$ (from a table of logarithms)

Suppose we look more generally at this sort of device, where the probabilities are as shown below:

Outcome	Probability	
1	P	$H(X) = -P \log_2 P - (1 - P) \log_2 (1 - P)$
2	$1 - P$	

The graph of $H(X)$ as a function of P is shown in Figure 12.1. Here $H(X)$ is, as we know, unity if $P = \frac{1}{2}$; but $H(X)$ drops rapidly as P gets close to 0 or 1. Thus the uncertainty becomes small as the probability of one outcome or the other becomes small.

Finally, harking back to the more recently familiar example at the beginning of the present section, we verify that our heuristic reasoning is consistent with Shannon's first theorem:

PROPOSITION. For a device with n equally probable outcomes,

$$H(X) = \log_2 n.$$

This follows directly from the fact that

$$-\frac{1}{n} \log_2 \frac{1}{n} - \frac{1}{n} \log_2 \frac{1}{n} \ldots - \frac{1}{n} \log_2 \frac{1}{n} = n\left(-\frac{1}{n} \log_2 \frac{1}{n}\right)$$

$$= -\log_2 \frac{1}{n}$$

$$= \log_2 n.$$

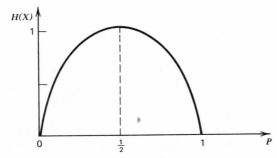

Fig. 12.1 Dependence of the rate of information generation $H(X)$ on the probability P.

12.7 A FINAL COMMENT

It is important to re-emphasize the conceptual connection between uncertainty and information. We began with a concept of uncertainty. The uncertainty in a random experiment depends on the entire universe of possible outcomes and their probabilities. In general, the more possible outcomes there are, the less we are able to predict the outcomes reliably and the higher is the uncertainty in the experiment. Now, we are told the outcome; the uncertainty is dispelled; we know what happened. It is natural then to say that the amount of information we have obtained is simply the extent of our a priori uncertainty as to what would happen. This is not a new definition, since the amount of uncertainty in an experiment has not yet been defined; but it would be offensive if an experiment having intuitively a high degree of uncertainty did not have also a high rate of information generation $H(X)$. This, however, does not occur, since the greater the number of equiprobable outcomes is, the greater is $H(X)$. (Recall that for n possible outcomes, $H(X) = \log_2 n$.)

Another important concept is illustrated by the definition of $H(X)$: The rate at which history is being made depends on the context of the entire device, that is, on the entire universe of possible outcomes. The rate at which information is generated depends essentially on the total structure of the device.

SHANNON'S SECOND THEOREM

12.8 COMMUNICATION CHANNELS

A communication channel will be, for the purpose of this chapter, the sort of thing that is illustrated in Figure 12.2. As far as this study is concerned, we take the "black box" point of view. What is inside the box and how the channel works are questions in another domain. The great simplification used here is to look only at the input-output relationships. The contrast between "How does it work?" and "What does it do?" has echoes in many fields. For example, the ear may be studied physiologically, by dissection, or study of nerve connections. Another recent approach is to put a sine wave into the ear at some given point, tap off the connecting nerves at another point, and compare the tapped-off signal with the original sine wave.

There is some conviction among psychologists that man can be defined and studied as the totality of his input-output relations. This subject is beyond the author's realm of competence.

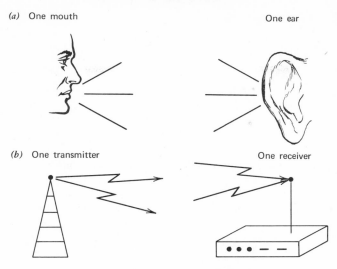

(a) One mouth   One ear

(b) One transmitter   One receiver

Fig. 12.2 Communication channels.

The black box diagrammed in → □ →, in order to be at all interesting, must contain a noise-generating device. For example, in a verbal or radio communication, there is always noise or distortion present.

The most dramatic example is in radio communication, where the meaning of the word "noise," as used here, originated. On every long-distance radio broadcast, there is superimposed the buzz and crackle of static. For a listener to overseas broadcasts, this is merely an annoyance. But in trying to receive information from the small transmitter in a satellite as it spins out past the sun, one may curse the day in which static was introduced into the universe.

The dominant characteristic of static (synonymously: noise) is its perversity, its almost complete unpredictablity. The voltages produced at a receiving antenna by noise might look something like what is shown in Figure 12.3. The magnitude and frequency of the noise depend on a near infinity of factors: the distribution of the electrical charge in the ionosphere, the location of various flocks of geese, etc.

The best that can be done here is statistical predictions, statements like "With probability .9, the noise magnitude will be less than .01 volts in 5 minutes." *The black box becomes a statistical animal.* The input-output relationships are not like: "When button No. 3 is pressed, light No. 8 goes on." They are more like: "When button No. 3 is pressed, with *probability* .9, light No. 8 goes on." Formally, we make the following definition.

Fig. 12.3 Random voltages produced by noise.

Definition. The communication channels to be studied are specified by two finite lists:

Input	Output
z_1	y_1
z_2	y_2
z_3	y_3
.	.
.	.
.	.
.	.

and the probabilities $P(y_j | z_i)$ of receiving the output signal y_j given that input button z_i was pressed.

The obvious question is *"How much information can you send across a channel?"* This question puts us into the realm of ideas that revolve around Shannon's second theorem. The interesting and marvelous result here is that we can define and study the transmission of information across a channel in two ways—seemingly completely dissimilar—but that then, at the end, Shannon's second theorem takes these two separate threads and ties them together.

12.9 ACCURATE TRANSMISSION BY REPETITION

Look at the channel of Figure 12.4, which has two inputs, 0, 1, and the same outputs, and which distorts with probability .1. This is called a *binary symmetric channel* with .1 error probability.

Is there any way of transmitting accurately over this channel? More specifically, suppose that a fair coin is tossed at the input end and that the channel is to be used to convey the outcome to the output end. If the channel is to be used only once, then no matter what is done, the proba-

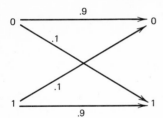

Fig. 12.4 A binary symmetric transmission channel with .1 error probability.

bility that the receiver will get the wrong information is .1. But suppose we are allowed to use this channel *more than once*. For example, suppose we can use this channel three times to try to inform the receiver as whether *H* or *T* occurred in the coin toss. Make the following "coding" agreement with the receiver:

If *H* occurs, send 0   0   0;
if *T* occurs, send 1   1   1.

He is to "decode" what he receives as follows: If he sees more 0's than 1's, *H* occurred, otherwise *T*. Look at the error probability. If *H* occurred, it is erroneously received only if

$$
\begin{array}{ccc}
0 \quad 0 \quad 0 & \longrightarrow & 1 \quad 1 \quad 1 \\
& & 1 \quad 1 \quad 0 \\
& & 1 \quad 0 \quad 1 \\
& & 0 \quad 1 \quad 1
\end{array}
$$

But the probabilities here (through all this chapter the assumption is made that the successive uses of the channel are independent) are as follows:

				Probability
0 0 0	$\longrightarrow$	1 1 1	$(.1)^3$	$= .001$
	$\longrightarrow$	1 1 0	$(.1)^2 .9$	$= .009$
	$\longrightarrow$	1 0 1	$(.1)^2 .9$	$= .009$
	$\longrightarrow$	0 1 1	$(.1)^2 .9$	$= .009$
			Total	$= .028$

The error probability has been reduced to less than a third of the error probability when the channel is used only once!

Continuing, we have the following probabilities:

Number of uses of channel	1	3	5
Error probability	.1	.028	.009

*It should be apparent by now that the information concerning the single coin
toss can be transmitted to the other end with as small an error probability as
desired by using the channel enough times.*

This all seems harmless and more or less obvious, but the foregoing
rather simple observation opens the door to the exciting realization that
accurate transmission is possible across a noisy channel. It is the systematic
exploitation and exploration of this possibility that is the basic material of
Shannon's theory of information.

What has to be done is to introduce a great dependency between the
successive input signals. A 1 is usually followed by a 1, a 0 by a 0. In
language, dependence between successive letters and words is called
redundancy. Redundancy in language is absolutely essential. Without it,
any conversation would be almost impossible. Redundancy allows us,
while listening, continually and automatically to fill in missing words from
the context around them. More concretely, suppose we receive a telegram:

I JM ARRIVING WEDNESDAY

From the context, we judge (with very small error probability) that this
should read:

I AM ARRIVING WEDNESDAY

Again, as with block coding, there is a balance. The more redundant a
language is, the more letters and words are needed per unit of communication. To transmit the outcome H or T with .01 probability of error takes
five times as many transmission periods as .1 error probability.

In the other direction, there are situations in which it is desired to decrease the redundancy of a language, gaining brevity of expression. For
example, the Speedwriting method seems to consist mainly of eliminating
highly dependent letters.

12.10 CODING

There is another method of getting information accurately across a noisy
channel, which can be illustrated as follows: Two hikers are proceeding up a
windy mountain about fifty yards apart. They have a signal agreement,
that if the lead hiker finds the going difficult, he yells back "Slow," while
if he comes across ice or snow, he yells "Snow." The yelling will probably
go something like this:

SNOW!   WHAT?   SNOW!   WHAT?

and so on. With enough repetitions, the message will finally get through.
But of course this is a foolish way to communicate. A far better signal

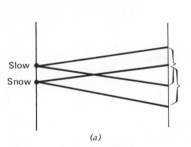
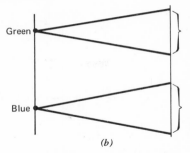

(a)   (b)

Fig. 12.5 Signals with (a) overlapping and (b) nonoverlapping distorted outputs.

arrangement is, for example, to yell "Green" instead of "Slow," and "Blue" instead of "Snow." These word sounds are so dissimilar that any reasonable wind distortion will not change either of them enough to sound like the other. Roughly, we have the situation pictured in Figure 12.5.

This is the basic idea of coding: If we want to discriminate between different signals accurately, then we use only inputs so far apart that outputs into which they can be distorted have little or no overlap. Again, this is a principle illustrated in language—words that are important to differentiate between ordinarily have sounds far apart. For example:

yes   right   go

no   left   stop

More mathematically, consider sending voltages between 0 and 1. The signal can be distorted a maximum of .09 volts. Then by coding we can send six messages perfectly accurately across this channel, as illustrated in Figure 12.6. The idea of coding here is the same—use only input messages far enough apart that their distortion sets have very small (or zero) overlap.

12.11 MATHEMATICAL DEFINITIONS

Let us consider again the binary channel of Figure 12.4. Recall that to send messages accurately across this channel, the channel had to be used more than once. To define accurate transmission, first an allowable error probability P_e must be preselected. This is at the choice of the channel users. Consider the channel used N times; then the set of all possible inputs is the set of all binary words of length N, that is, the set of all N-strings of 0's and 1's. There are 2^N of these. The set of all possible outputs is the same. We diagram these sets vertically as indicated in Figure 12.7.

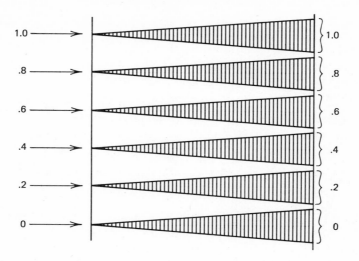

Fig. 12.6 Signals at intervals of .2 volts and distortions of not more than .09 volts have nonoverlapping outputs.

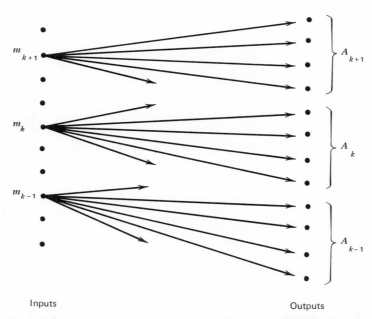

Inputs   Outputs

Fig. 12.7 A code of inputs m_k and output sets A_k with high probability that input m_k will result in output in A_k.

Definition. *If we can, from among the 2^N possible inputs, select J of them, say $m_1, m_2, \ldots m_J$, such there are $A_1, A_2, \ldots, A_J$ disjoint sets of output messages, and if, for each code word m_k, the probability that when m_k is sent, the received message is outside of A_k is less than P_e, then $m_1, m_2, \ldots, m_J$ is called a code of size J for transmitting with accuracy P_e. The $A_1, A_2, \ldots, A_J$ are called decoding sets.*

This definition is for a channel with two inputs and two outputs. But it is very clear that exactly the same definition holds for any channel. The only difference is that if there are r input buttons and s output lights, then in N uses of the channel there will be a total of r^N possible input words and s^N outputs.

If $m_1, m_2, \ldots, m_J$ is a code with error probability P_e, and $A_1, A_2, \ldots, A_J$ the decoding sets, then the "coding" agreement is that if anything in A_k is received, then message m_k was sent. The probability of an error is exactly the probability of receiving a signal outside of A_k, given that m_k was sent. By definition, for every m_k in the code, this probability is less than P_e.

Let J_N be the greatest possible number of messages in a code using words of length N that has accuracy P_e. Then the number J_N is a measure of how much information can accurately be sent across the channel. There is a way of transforming this which gives a much more interesting measure.

If J_N is the size of the largest code that has accuracy P_e, as defined above, then what we are prepared to do in N transmissions is to *communicate accurately to the receiver which outcome occurred in an experiment with J_N equally likely outcomes*. For example, if for $P_e = .01$ we have $J_7 = 6$, then in 7 transmissions we can tell the receiving end which one of the faces of a die thrown at the input end came up, and the probability that the receiving end will get the incorrect answer is less than .01.

From Shannon's first theorem, the information per outcome of an experiment with J_N equally likely outcomes is $\log_2 J_N$.

In N transmissions, then, the amount $\log_2 J_N$ of digits of information can accurately be communicated. The amount per transmission accordingly is $\log_2 J_N/N$. This last observation leads to the definition of a number that has made the third letter of the alphabet famous in engineering circles. A limiting value C exists for the amount $\log_2 J_N/N$ as N becomes greater and greater. That much is not difficult to prove.

Definition. *Let C = limiting value of $\log_2 J_N/N$ as $N \to \infty$. Then C is called the accurate-transmission capacity of the channel in binary digits per transmission.*

This brings to a close one way of looking at the problem of getting data across a channel. The only problem addressed is: Let the receiving end know with very small error probability exactly which one of J messages has been sent. The outstanding problem is: Compute C. This number governs the size of J_N for large N; equivalently, it governs the amount of information that can accurately be sent across the channel. No matter how complicated, C must be computable in terms of the channel probabilities $P(y_j|z_k)$. But to find out how, we have to circle around and look in a very different way at the question of getting information across a channel.

12.12 TRANSMISSION OF INFORMATION BY DIRECT HOOKUP

Instead of looking at the effective use of a channel over a large number of transmission periods, let us now hook a random device directly into the inputs of the channel, say the channel of Figure 12.4. For example, consider the hookup of Figure 12.8. This operates toss by toss: Flip the coin; if H comes up, press 0, but if T comes up, press 1. Flip again, press the appropriate input button, and so on. In general, hook up a random device X with outcomes $x_1, \ldots$ into the channel inputs as indicated in Figure 12.9. This is to be read: If x_1 occurs, send input z_3; if x_2 occurs, send z_5; and so on.

The situation here illustrated is not at all similar to the case of coding. There is no real coding going on, no operation by blocks of N transmissions.

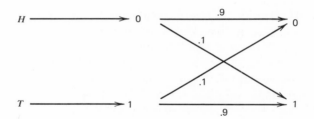

Fig. 12.8 Hookup of a particular random device and transmission channel.

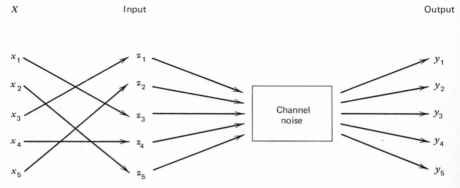

Fig. 12.9 General hookup of a random device and transmission channel.

Rather, we have a steady generation of repetitions of X and the corresponding use of the channel. The random device generates an output, the related channel input button is pressed, and one of the $y_1, y_2, \ldots$, flashes. The information being transmitted is by no means accurate. Thus in the first example above, at each transmission there is a probability .1 that the signal is distorted and H (or T) read as T (or H) on the receiving end.

Yet there can be no question that in some form or another information is being transmitted. If a gambler had a device that would give him inside information on a coin-tossing game and that was right 9 times out of 10 on the average, that device would be valuable! It would be worth a rental fee; its output signals would be attentively received and used.

The pertinent question is, of course: How much information per transmission is being transmitted through the channel? The basic approach we use is the measure of information in terms of digits per outcome needed to record. Accordingly, all the ideas, definitions, and results clustered around Shannon's first theorem are applicable. Consider two observers:

Observer A has no a priori information regarding outcomes of X.

Observer B has information concerning outcomes of X given by outputs of the channel.

The situation will work this way:

1. X is performed: the coin is tossed, the die thrown, etc.
2. The outcome is then sent over the channel to B, and he records it.
3. The outcome of X is then announced to both A and B.

The rate at which information is being generated for Observer A is, in terms of digits per outcome needed to record, exactly $H(X)$. But for Observer B, this is no longer true. Let us make the following definition.

Definition. Let $H(X|Y)$ be the number of digits per outcome that is needed by B to record the outcomes of X, given that he has a record of the channel outputs Y. $H(X|Y)$ is called the rate of information generated by X given Y, or the uncertainty in X given Y.

To illustrate, look at the example of Figure 12.8. If Observer B sees a zero, the probability is no longer $\frac{1}{2}$ that an H occurred, but is now .9. This is the key point, that when B looks at the output signal, the old probabilities for X are no longer applicable. There is a new set of relevant probabilities. In the preceding example, given that Observer B gets a 0, then the relevant probabilities for X are .9, .1 for H,T. If the output is a 1, then the altered probabilities are .1, .9 for H,T. Because of the symmetry, then, no matter what the channel output is, the X device has two outcomes with probabilities .9, .1. For such a device, we know that the rate of information generation is (by Shannon's first theorem)

$$.9 \log_2 .9 + .1 \log_2 .1 = .46.$$

This example gives the clue for the general computation of $H(X|Y)$. Let $P(x_i|y_j)$ be the altered probabilities on the X device, given that output y_j was received. Put another way, $P(x_i|y_j)$ is the probability[1] that x_i occurred, given that y_j was received. Then, by Shannon's first theorem, the average number of digits per outcome needed to record X every time y_j is received is given by

$$H(X|y_j) = - \sum_{x_i} P(x_i|y_j) \log_2 P(x_i|y_j)$$

(where the sum is only over the x_i). On the average, y_j is received a proportion $P(y_j)$ of the times, where $P(y_j)$ is the probability of output y_j. Therefore, $H(X|Y)$ is given by

$$H(X|Y) = \sum_{y_j} H(X|y_j) \, P(y_j).$$

We resort to an indirect method of analysis:

Observer A, with no channel, is getting information at the rate of $H(X)$ digits per outcome from X.

Observer B, with the channel, is getting information at the lesser rate $H(X|Y)$ on being directly informed of the X history.

The only difference between A and B is the channel. This fairly compels us to conclude that the channel is responsible for the difference

$$H(X) - H(X|Y)$$

in the rate of information flow to A and B. This indirect method of comparing the two observers, and using a "conservation of information" principle, impels us into the following definition.

Definition. *The rate of transmission across a channel with a random device X hooked into the input set is given by*

$$I(X,Y) = H(X) - H(X|Y).$$

[1] The probabilities $P(x_i|y_j)$ can be computed from the device probabilities $P(x_i)$ and $P(y_j|x_i)$, the probability of receiving y_j given that X resulted in x_i. These $P(y_j|x_i)$ are directly computable from the $P(y_j|z_i)$ and the knowledge of how the outcomes of the device are hooked into the inputs of the channel. The joint probability $P(y_j,x_i)$ that both x_i occurred and y_j was received is given by $P(y_j|x_i) \, P(x_i)$. The probability $P(y_j)$ of receiving y_j is now given by $\sum_{x_i} P(y_j,x_i)$. Finally, by definition of conditional (or a posteriori) probabilities,

$$P(x_i|y_j) = \frac{P(y_j,x_i)}{P(y_j)}.$$

12.13 REMARKS AND AN EXAMPLE

$I(X,Y)$ is the rate of transmission of information across the channel. The size of $I(X,Y)$ reveals nothing, however, about how accurate the information coming across is. The rough idea is that a balance goes on: If we try to send more information across, it becomes more distorted, so we may end with the same total amount of information. The number that measures the accuracy of the information outputs is $H(X|Y)$ because, if $H(X|Y)$ is small, the implication is that given the outputs Y, there is:

1. Very little uncertainty remaining in X.
2. A low rate of information generated by X.
3. A small number of digits per outcome needed to record X.

To illustrate the balance and the roles of $H(X|Y)$, $I(X,Y)$, look at a perfect binary channel:

$$0 \xrightarrow{1.0} 0$$
$$1 \xrightarrow{1.0} 1$$

Hook up a fair coin-tossing device X into this channel:

$$
\begin{array}{cc}
P(X) & X \\
\tfrac{1}{2} & H \longrightarrow 0 \longrightarrow 0 \\
\tfrac{1}{2} & T \longrightarrow 1 \longrightarrow 1
\end{array}
$$

The obvious computations are $H(X) = 1$ (from Example 1, Section 12.3). Given a record of outputs, we know exactly what happens in X. No additional digits are needed to record; that is, we have $H(X|Y) = 0$ and the information is completely accurate:

$$
\begin{aligned}
I(X,Y) &= H(X) - H(X|Y) \\
&= 1 - 0 = 1.
\end{aligned}
$$

Now, let us try to push much more information through this channel by hooking up the four-outcomes, $\tfrac{1}{4},\tfrac{1}{4},\tfrac{1}{4},\tfrac{1}{4}$, probability device X of Example 2, Section 12.3:

$$
\begin{array}{cc}
P(X) & X \\
\dfrac{1}{4} & 1 \\
 & \quad\searrow 0 \longrightarrow 0 \\
\dfrac{1}{4} & 2 \quad\nearrow \\
\dfrac{1}{4} & 3 \\
 & \quad\searrow 1 \longrightarrow 1 \\
\dfrac{1}{4} & 4 \quad\nearrow
\end{array}
$$

This time, $H(X) = 2$. If a 0 is received, then outcomes 1 or 2 must have occurred, each with equal probability, hence $\frac{1}{2}, \frac{1}{2}$. Similarly, if a 1 comes across the channel, then 3 or 4 must have occurred, with $\frac{1}{2}, \frac{1}{2}$ probabilities. In either case, X looks like a fair-coin-tossing game, so $H(X \mid Y) = 1$. The information is now quite ambiguous. $H(X \mid Y)$ is much larger, *but*

$$I(X,Y) = H(X) - H(X \mid Y)$$
$$= 2 - 1 = 1.$$

The total amount of information going through is the same.

We are now at the point where the two main threads of this second part of the chapter can be pulled together. First, notice that $I(X,Y)$ can certainly be computed without difficulty from the various given probabilities. A very pertinent question becomes: What is the maximum rate of information that can be achieved over a given channel? That is: What is the maximum of $I(X,Y)$ over all random devices X that can be hooked into the channel? This requires a standard computation. The device X depends only on the probabilities $P(x_1), P(x_2), \ldots, P(x_n)$, so that $I(X,Y)$ becomes a function of these n real variables. The problem is a calculus problem: Maximize a function of n variables. This is not always easy, but it is amenable to known classical methods.

This maximum is in general not achieved by transmitting accurately. For example, consider a binary symmetric channel with probability ϵ of error (Figure 12.10). The maximizing X is not hard to find. Suppose it had two outcomes, 1, 2. Think intuitively: By symmetry, $P(X)$ being something like $\frac{5}{8}, \frac{3}{8}$ just does not fit; the reasonable answer is $P(1) = \frac{1}{2}$, $P(2) = \frac{1}{2}$. It is also the correct answer!

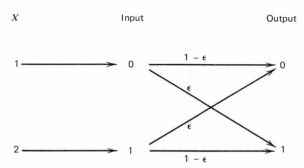

Fig. 12.10 Hookup of a random device X and a binary symmetric channel with error probability ϵ.

On the average, the input is distorted a proportion ϵ of the time. The X experiment, given Y, has probabilities $1 - \epsilon$, ϵ, so that

$$H(X \mid Y) = -(1 - \epsilon) \log_2 (1 - \epsilon) - \epsilon \log_2 \epsilon.$$

The maximum value of $I(X,Y)$ is therefore

$$I(X,Y) = H(X) - H(X \mid Y) = 1 + (1 - \epsilon) \log_2 (1 - \epsilon) + \epsilon \log_2 \epsilon.$$

For $\epsilon = .1$, therefore,

$$\max_x I(X,Y) = .54.$$

12.14 SHANNON'S SECOND THEOREM (THE NOISY-CODING THEOREM)

The basic statement of Shannon's second theorem is that the same amount of information in *any* degree of accuracy can be transmitted through the channel. More precisely, *if we can achieve a transmission rate of information $I(X,Y)$ by a direct hookup, then it is possible to transmit accurately at this same rate by using N-blocks of transmissions periods and the appropriate coding.* Still more precisely, Shannon's second theorem is the statement that

$$C = \max_x I(X,Y).$$

This is the promised intertwining. Consideration of the quantity C arose from looking at ways of transmitting accurately across the channel, using long blocks of transmitting periods and codes. But consideration of $\max_x I(X,Y)$ came from looking at a direct hookup transmission by transmission analysis where distorted signals were frequent.

To repeat: Shannon's second theorem states a sort of equivalence. *If information, no matter how distorted, can be sent at a given rate over a channel, then information can be sent accurately at that same rate by coding.*

12.15 SOME CLOSING REMARKS

One thing to notice from Shannon's second theorem is that C does not depend on the preassigned error probability P_e. That is, P_e nowhere appears in the definition of $I(X,Y)$, hence not in $\max_x I(X,Y)$. As a consequence, no matter how small P_e is set, for N large enough $(\log_2 J_N)/N$ is nearly equal to C. The joker here is "for N large enough." For example, in the binary symmetric channel with .1 distortion probability, we know from the above theorem that

$$C = 1.0 + .1 \log.1 + .9 \log.9 = .54.$$

How large does N have to be so that $(\log_2 J_N)/N$ is greater than .53? Here the answer does depend on P_e. For smaller P_e, N will be greater. The balancing process is operating again. To transmit at rate .53 digits per transmission with error probability .001, we must use coding over a number of transmission periods N much greater than if we would be satisfied with an error probability of .1. To realize what this entails, solve $(\log_2 J_N)/N = .53$ to get $J_N = 2^{.53N}$. To round numbers, we have the following:

N	4	7	11	20	30
J_N	4	10	56	1,500	59,000

As N increases in this table, the error probability gets smaller. But the other side of the ledger is that, for example, if we want to use a code for 30 transmission periods, then it is necessary to construct a good code with 59,000 entries. This in itself is difficult. Then to mechanize this transmission scheme, our machine would need a memory capable of storing 59,000 entries, and looking up the correct one every 30 transmission periods. This is not bad, with some of the high-speed computers now available. But what about a computer that can be placed on a small space probe?

This is as much as we set out to present concerning the Shannon theory of information. It is fine applied mathematics. Not only is it most relevant to engineers and scientists, and its conclusions significant, but from the mathematician's point of view the analysis is interesting and the theory contains at least two nontrivial results.

REFERENCES

1. Blackwell, David, "Information Theory," in Beckenbach, E. F. (editor), *Modern Mathematics for the Engineer*, Second Series, McGraw-Hill, New York, 1961, Chapter 7.
2. Hall, Marshall, Jr., "Block Designs," in Beckenbach, E. F. (editor), *Applied Combinatorial Mathematics*, Wiley, New York, 1964, Chapter 13.
3. Shannon, C. E., "A Mathematical Theory of Communication," *Bell System Tech. J.*, **27**, 1948, 379–423, 623–656.
4. Wolfowitz, Jacob, "Introduction to Information Theory," in Beckenbach, E. F. (editor), *Applied Combinatorial Mathematics*, Wiley, New York, 1964, Capter 14.

FURTHER READINGS

1. Berlekamp, Elwyn R., *Algebraic Coding Theory*, McGraw-Hill, New York, 1968.
2. Helstrom, Carl W., *Statistical Theory of Signal Detection*, Pergamon Press, New York, 1968.
3. Rényi, A. (editor), *Proceedings of the Colloquium on Information Theory*, Vols. I and II, János Bolyai Mathematical Society, Budapest, 1968.
4. Salomaa, Arto, *Theory of Automata*, Pergamon Press, New York, 1969.
5. Tou, Julius T. (editor), *Advances in Information Systems Science*, Plenum Press, New York, 1969.
6. Verhoeff, J., *Error Detecting Decimal Codes*, Mathematisch Centrum, Amsterdam, 1969.

CONCLUSION

What the eye sees is the mind's best guess
as to what is out in front.

A. AMES, JR.

The Morning Notes of Albert Ames, Jr.
Rutgers University Press, New Brunswick, 1960
(Reprinted by permission of the publishers.)

CHAPTER 13

On the Uses of Sensory Information by Animals and Men

EDWARD C. CARTERETTE

Professor of Psychology, University of California, Los Angeles

DONALD A. NORMAN

Professor of Psychology, University of California, San Diego

Contents

13.1   INTRODUCTION

In course, the reader may come to feel that we have been seduced into holding an exaggerated opinion about the importance of information processing. He may be right, but he should know that the attractions are strong:

A convergence of effort on the most difficult cognitive problems, those of perception and concept formation, has been building up at least since 1960, and we could well be on the edge of some genuinely spectacular results. Many scientists working on the problems feel we are getting very close to hitting on the one or two fundamental ideas needed to move rapidly ahead. If so, the theory of information processing and concept formation might even give quantum mechanics and molecular biology a run for their money for the title of most important scientific development of the twentieth century [68, pp. 26–27].

Suppes [68] argues cogently that the work in information processing and choice behavior embraces the most important new set of ideas in the social sciences in this century. These ideas have been developed largely since World War II. One of these ideas, at least 250 years old [10], recently was made explicit by the English mathematician and philosopher Ramsey [58]. It is the notion that a rational man chooses so as to make his expected utility as great as possible; thus:

1. He behaves as if there were a utility function on the outcome of his choice.
2. And he behaves as if there were a probability density function on the states of nature.
3. And he behaves as if he chose that decision which maximizes the expected utility with respect to his (subjective) probability function on the states of nature.

But suppose that the information does not suffice to assign probabilities to uncertain events, or that the uncertainty is perturbed further by rational (or irrational!) decisions made by other agents. In this context, "a second, absolutely fundamental new concept with respect to rationality has been introduced" [68], the concept of *randomness* of choice, which has been bound insuperably to the concept of rationality. Statistical decision theory, which has explored this relationship, is basic to our present discussion of information processing by men and animals.

"Information processing" is an imprecise term that is quite empty apart from the meaning it is given in a particular discussion. We use the term to refer to those experiments, methods, and theories that are concerned with examining the way in which an organism deals with the environment around it. The classical Gestalt psychologist considered the percept as given. He sought for little more than the set of laws describing the dynamics of percepts. The classical stimulus-response psychologist considered practically nothing as given beyond certain essential motor patterns and their neural substrata. He sought to explain most behavior by laws of learning. We shall accept both these views as correct in some measure. In our view, an information-processing theory attempts to account for the way in which an organism interacts with a structured environment on the basis of (1) sensory, motor, and neural mechanisms which are largely predetermined, and (2) rather flexible decision processes. We shall see that there exists in each organism complex, prewired procedures for dealing with some aspects of information. These relatively fixed input and output structures are connected through an algorithm which gives flexibility to an organism's responses by virtue of its power to vary the relative weights of information. (It should be clear that information ultimately must be given by biophysical quantities.) Often a nice duality can be drawn between the mechanistic workings of the sensory process and the flexible workings of the decision process.

This division of behavior into two components is an essentially new division in psychology. The need for such a division was early apparent to experimental psychologists and gave rise to amorphous concepts like "set," "attention," and "central processes." More precise meaning can now be given these words by use of tools and concepts from statistical decision theory and signal detection theory. It now appears possible to give a coherent account of the behavior under uncertainty of an organism which has relatively fixed sensory and motor structures.

Let us press this notion of randomness of choice into the realm of the senses. A weaker sound is heard less frequently than a stronger, and the variability of the responses is the greater for the weaker.

The notion of randomness is no less essential when sensory systems are considered. Randomness is at the heart of difficult discriminations or the detection of a stimulus at threshold. Even a series of judgments about the intensity of an unvarying physical stimulus will vary about a mean value. This kind of variability is attributed to noise. Obviously, there are external as well as internal sources of the noise. Recently psychophysicists [26, 48] have given much effort in identifying, separating, and giving the statistical laws of noise probability distributions.

Giving noise such a fundamental role has resulted in the abandonment of purely algebraic theories of behavior (with a normal error variance tacked on to give some jitter) in favor of stochastic theories of behavior [22, 13]. In many branches of psychology, only the steady state is of interest. Great pains often are taken in psychophysics and perception to obtain asymptotic performance. On the other hand, the learning psychologist is interested when some new or existing feature of the environment requires a new, changed behavior. The changing behavior is called learning; and when the stimulus-response-"reinforcement" sequences reach the steady state, learning is said to be "at a symptote." The fact that behavior is often stationary only in the statistical sense has widened the interests of both psychophysicists and learning psychologists.

In this chapter, our major concern is with asymptotic behavior, and we merely touch on the way in which parameters for learning may be introduced into such steady-state theories as signal-detection theory. (See Atkinson, Bower and Crothers [4] for a discussion of how steady-state theories can be extended by adding the axioms of learning theory. Applications are discussed, for example, by Atkinson, Carterette and Kinchla [5], and by Luce [42].)

INFORMATION THEORY AND SIMULATION MODELS

13.2 INFORMATION THEORY IN PSYCHOLOGY

Psychologists thought the Shannon-Wiener theory of selective information was heaven-sent because it offered a "dimensionless" metric. Heterogeneous classes of stimuli and responses could be compared. Important insights were expected into learning, memory, recognition, choice-reaction time, and the capacity for processing information. Symposia and conferences were held, new experiments were run, and old experiments were rerun. Old data were reanalyzed under the new rubric, often with the result that the precisely quantified data were degraded into classes so that it could be talked about in the new language of bits. Some fruit did come of the encounter, not the least of which was the recognition of the intimate relationship between stimulus and response classes, with their internal and external temporal and spatial constraints.

Let us consider a few representative applications. Miller, Heise, and Lichten [52] showed that, when monosyllables were recognized in noise with a fixed signal-to-noise ratio, vocabulary size had a profound effect on intelligibility. Test vocabularies were sets of 2, 4, 8, 16, 32, or 256 monosyllables having an a priori uncertainty of 1, 2, 3, 4, 5, and 8 bits. The percentage of words heard correctly decreased about 10 per cent for each added binary choice.

In many experiments like this, the subject knew what the set of possible stimuli was (as he must if the experiment is to have any meaning *vis à vis* information theory). The uncertainty *as seen by the experimenter* was shown clearly to affect behavior in learning or in perceptual recognition. But the important question of whether the critical factor is stimulus uncertainty or response uncertainty was not answered by these experiments. Pollack [55] among others attempted to answer this question. A subject was told which of several sets a message would be chosen from and had to make and record a choice from that set. The results shown in the lower curve of Figure 13.1 are as expected: accuracy declines as uncertainty increases. Following his first response, he had to make a second response by choosing one of two possible responses. The top curve shows that the accuracy does not depend on the stimulus uncertainty but rather on the response uncertainty.

Hyman [36] showed that mean reaction time increased from about 200 milliseconds for zero uncertainty to about 675 milliseconds for 3 bits worth of uncertainty. There is a suggestion, too, in reaction-time studies that it is

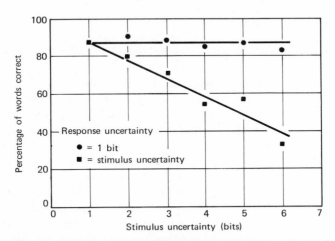

Fig. 13.1 Information transmitted by monosyllables heard in noise (ordinate) as a function of the size of the set of stimuli (2^0, 2^1, . . . 2^7). For the upper curve, responses were chosen from two categories. For the lower curve, response and stimulus categories were of equal size (After [55].)

the response uncertainty rather than the stimulus uncertainty which is the crucial factor.

So far we have looked only at univariate uncertainty. The notion of bivariate uncertainty may be used to talk about the capacity of a channel, or when rate is not a factor, about the amount of information transmitted over a channel. Without going into detail, it suffices to say that for a wide range of perceptual continua, the amount of information that can be transmitted when absolute judgments (that is to say, identification responses) are required is remarkably small [50]. For example, if we ask a subject to make absolute judgments of loudness of intensities ranging from 15 to 110 decibels (about 10^{-16} watt/square centimeter) using 4 to 20 categories, the information transmitted has a maximum of 2.1 bits. But this is only between 4 and 5 tones. Pollack, however, in 1952 found only 2.3 bits transmitted when pitch was judged [55]. Brightness gives 2.34 bits, size 2.84, and hue 3.08, according to the experiments of Eriksen and Hake [21].

In general, "channel capacity, or limiting amount of discrimination, is stable and low for most unidimensional continua, having a value of about 2.3 bits," an equivalent of about five stimulus categories. For stimuli having natural anchors, like hue, as much as 3.6 bits were transmitted, equivalent to nearly 12 different spectral colors. These values may appear astonishingly low to us, even paradoxical when we think of how easily we jockey our cars about on the freeway, while cursing other drivers, listening to a concerto, thinking about a problem in nozzle velocity, and even reading a newspaper! It is a relief to learn that quite large values have been obtained with multiple stimulus dimensions. Anderson and Fitts [2], using stimulus variables each of which had a high information transmission— several simultaneous stimuli differing in both form and color—showed that 17 bits can be obtained in a single brief exposure. This is truly astonishing when we think that perfect discriminability between 131,000 alternative stimuli is implied. Such experiments, says Garner [24], "induce a clear principle concerning human perceptual discrimination." *Discrimination is best when the stimuli to be discriminated vary simultaneously on many different dimensions.*

For most, disenchantment with information theory came early. McGill's paper [49], in which he demonstrated the structural similarity of the analysis of variance, correlational analysis, and informational analysis, was sobering. Generally speaking, the averaging required by information theory masked the quantitative structure of the data more than did variational or correlational analysis. Moreover, the information-measure average, $H(X)$ (often called "uncertainty"), taken over a subject's distribution of response probabilities, is a peculiar one [41, 42]. The potentially more important theorems on channel capacity and coding could not be used because the strong conditions of ergodicity and stationarity could not be met, or it was not clear whether or how they were applicable.

Only impoverished use of information theoretical measures has been made in psychology, and even this was possible only because agreement can be reached by subject and experimenter about a specification of signals and responses and their distributions. In a lucid discussion of the coding problem as the fundamental unsolved problem of information processing in nervous systems, Rapaport [59] points out that whereas an erg is always an erg, a bit is not always a bit: "Amount of information depends on how much discrimination is made. There is no way to decide this except by knowing which differences *make* a difference. To know this means being able to group neural events into equivalence classes." And so we should not be surprised to discover even less use of information measures by the neurophysiologist in spite of his working very much as the psychologist does, by supplying a stimulus and observing a response. For, thus far, practically nothing is known about which aspects of nervous activity carry information.

It is not to be supposed that all the work on information theory has been wasted. Although the early studies showed quite clearly that a naive treatment of information processed by humans was bound to failure, other concepts from the theory of information have proved to be very valuable. For example, the notion that there are some limitations on what can be processed in a finite processing time when noise enters the system has proved to be a valuable one for psychology. We cannot, in fact, do many things at the same time. To be more accurate, it appears that there is some upper limit to the amount of processing that the human or other organism can perform at any given time. When we wish to do more than one thing at a time, we can do so if the total processing required by these tasks does not exceed our capacity to handle the prerequisite information. As soon as overload occurs, performance on some task might suffer. We can choose to distribute our limited capacity in many ways. We might, for example, distribute our capacity equally among all tasks, so that all tasks suffer to some extent. We might choose to distribute our capacity unequally, so that some tasks are performed with little decrement, while others receive very skimpy treatment on our part. Or we might choose to switch rapidly among several tasks so that during any brief moment of time we attend only to a very small number of tasks, with the hope that we can skip rapidly among the tasks so that all will get performed. Thus, in a sense, we are much like modern time-shared computers. We have limited capacity, but we are able to use this limited capacity in many ways. Perhaps the best illustration of these limits on our capacity is the simple observation that if we listen to the radio while driving our automobile, we find that when we must drive through a busy intersection we no longer are aware of what occurs over the radio. A good review of the concepts involved here is presented in the book by Broadbent [12], although some of the concepts discussed in his book are by now outdated. A more recent account of some fruitful uses of the concepts of information theory has been given by Garner [24].

In retrospect, it turns out that another development with deeper roots is already seen as the harbinger of a new psychophysics. We refer to the theory of signal detectability as applied to the human observer. In some ways this development was like information theory. Both originated during World War II, mainly at MIT, and both were heavily motivated by applications of mathematics to problems arising in communication. As in the case of the entropy measure $H(X)$, the basic quantity of signal detectability theory—the index of detectability d'—is highly abstracted and contains almost no clue about the conditions that gave rise to the data it is intended to characterize. Without wishing to deny the usefulness of having available the response distributions themselves, later in this chapter we shall try to justify the use of the index d' precisely because it is very nearly free of the conditions under which the data were collected. It remains stable in the face of changing instructions, rewards, or penalties, or such other conditions of the experiment as, for example, the ratio of the number of occasions when only noise occurs to the number of occasions when a signal to be detected occurs.

13.3   INFORMATION-PROCESSING THEORIES AND SIMULATION

Information-processing theories and simulation in psychology are considered here only to give an impression of the state of the work to now. We do not have space for more, and two recent books will give the reader quick access to the concepts, methods, and many of the foundation papers: *Computers and Thought* by Feigenbaum and Feldman [23], and Reitman's *Cognition and Thought* [62].

Information-processing theories and simulation are often lumped under the name "simulation," as, for example, by Newell and Simon [54, p. 368]:

Simulation is the process of studying a system by (1) constructing a model, numerical or not, (2) examining time paths generated by the model, and (3) comparing these time paths with time paths of the phenomena under study. Thus simulation is one of the techniques for analyzing a numerical or nonnumerical theory . . . . It is the one most suited to the computer.

Most contemporary information-processing theories are frankly "cognitive." That is not necessary but merely incidental to the theorists. There are some "behavioristic" models of information-processing, and their proportion will increase. There is one theory [51] called by its authors "subjectively behavioristic," which clearly partakes of cognitive and behavioristic elements, though not necessarily in equal parts. Cognitive theories, models, and concepts are aimed at an analysis of complex central mechanisms in terms of the activity of cognitive elements—or, in a word, thought. The end of thought may be very definite—to play chess or checkers, or solve integration problems in freshman calculus. The end of thought may be (sometimes only apparently) very general—to prove theorems in logic or geometry, to compose Bach chorales, to solve problems generally. In fact, a model of human thought has been proposed by Reitman [62].

Certainly the most famous model is Newell and Simon's General Problem Solver (GPS) [53], "a program that simulates thought," and we shall sketch their influential ideas. The notions will be clearer if it is kept in mind that the program was successfully applied to a problem in elementary symbolic logic, namely to show that

$$(R \supset \sim P) \cdot (\sim R \supset Q)$$

may be transformed into

$$\sim (\sim Q \cdot P);$$

here GPS sits among a set of *objects* (logical expressions). His task is to transforms one object into another by applying any of a set of *operators* (logical rules). He detects differences (for example, such that he should change connective) between objects and organizes the information about objects and operators into three types of goals (see Figure 13.2):

$G(T)$: Transform object A into object B;
$G(D)$: Reduce difference D between A and B;
$G(Q)$: Apply operator Q to A.

GPS achieves a goal by first attaining subgoals on the way to the primary goal. He has a number of methods for doing this. For example, a method associated with $G(T)$ is to match the elements of A to the elements of B and determine the difference D; a method for achieving $G(D)$ is to hunt for an operator Q which may reduce D; and a method for achieving $G(Q)$ begins with seeing if the conditions are satisfied under which Q may be applied. In short, the methods of GPS form a recursive system such that a tree of subgoals is generated in trying to attain a given goal.

The procedures of the GPS are said to resemble set, insight, concept formation, and structure of the problem-subproblem hierarchy. GPS can take a hint, have an "Aha!" experience, and avoid what psychologists have called mechanical trial and error, at least excessive trial and error. Thus GPS solves a big problem by solving the smaller component problems first.

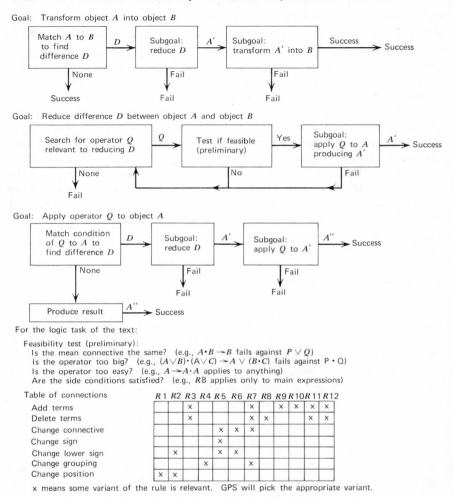

Fig. 13.2 The skeleton of the General Problem Solver. (After [54].)

For the logic task of the text:

Feasibility test (preliminary):
  Is the mean connective the same? (e.g., $A \cdot B \to B$ fails against $P \lor Q$)
  Is the operator too big? (e.g., $(A \lor B) \cdot (A \lor C) \to A \lor (B \cdot C)$ fails against $P \cdot Q$)
  Is the operator too easy? (e.g., $A \to A \cdot A$ applies to anything)
  Are the side conditions satisfied? (e.g., $R8$ applies only to main expressions)

Table of connections

	R1	R2	R3	R4	R5	R6	R7	R8	R9	R10	R11	R12
Add terms		x				x		x	x	x	x	
Delete terms		x				x	x			x	x	
Change connective				x	x	x						
Change sign					x							
Change lower sign		x			x	x						
Change grouping				x			x					
Change position	x	x										

x means some variant of the rule is relevant. GPS will pick the appropriate variant.

For some, an information-processing model *implies* a computer program: "A program is simultaneously a *statement* of a system, a sequence of *computer instructions*, and finally, an *operator* for achieving certain ends" [62]. It is widely and strongly held that these information-processing theories enable one's ideas of thinking and cognition to be stated with an arbitrary precision. A common way of testing such a theory or program is to attempt to put its critical responses into one-to-one correspondence with those of the person whose thought is being modeled. Obviously this test fails, as do more liberal versions of it such as setting the computer back on the track whenever it makes a wrong prediction, then restarting it until the subject's response sequence is mimicked exactly. The number of resets required would serve presumably as a kind of goodness-of-fit test.

Reitman and others argue at length that the usual methods of theory evaluation do not generally apply to simulation programs. They maintain that a program embodies its axioms, theorems, and proofs, and that it tests itself as well.[1] The notion is in many respects reasonable, but the fact neither invalidates the canons of theory construction nor absolves the theorist from the essential task of empirical verification of the model's adequacy. So far as we can discover, the studies of Hunt [34] and of Hunt, Stone, and Marin [35] are the only serious and extensive attempts to base a computer program on psychological assumptions derived from a study of the experimental literature, and to make very clear and explicit tests of the performance of the models devised. It would be remiss not to mention the very important work of Uhr [71] and Uhr and Vossler [73] on visual pattern recognition. Though they make some comparisons of human behavior with that of their model generated from theory, it is clear that their pattern-learning programs really were not intended directly to simulate human behavior. We wish to be most explicit that the criticisms or reservations voiced here are not intended to apply to programs designed to perform some task, however complicated and humanoid it may seem, in which *simulation* of behavior is not at issue. Artificial intelligences and brilliantly ingenious programs which prove theorems from geometry or from the *Principia Mathematica* are very important endeavors. However, the amount of light these programs cast on psychological information processing is usually very small. There is a recent implicit review of the attempts to use cognitive language aided by the computer in a search for abstractions of perception, language, and thought [62]. It may be too early after the brilliant pioneering work of Newell, Simon, and Shaw (see references in [23]) to see more than a hint of future success. But an examination of the studies listed in the bibliography (and of those published in *Behavioral Science*) clearly reveals that there have been few computer programs put forth as models of some class of human behavior and tested in any reasonable way. The substantial part of the list is unpublished papers or dissertations dating from about 1960, many from the Carnegie Institute of Technology.

Computers allow us to formulate more complex, even truer, theories. They permit us to make more exhaustive and deeper tests of a theory's adequacy. But, ironically, the cognitive theorist who was in the past con-

---

[1] The statement cannot be strictly true by virtue of Gödel's two theorems on formally undecidable systems.

tent with broad generalizations today makes incredible demands on his information-processing models for locally precise predictions. A consequence of the computer's power will be seen in heavier demands on the theorist to specify more precisely the way in which *humans* process information. He must ask: "How many memories are there? What are their capacities and connections? In what form are images stored and how do they decay and interact?" Such questions imply more precise and delicate experiments to reveal the fine temporal and spatial structures of perception and memory.

Care must be taken not to confuse what is necessary with what may be sufficient, and not to confuse the program with the process that it is meant to represent. That is to say, the complex list structure of information-processing languages and the microsecond time-base of the computer must not be assumed necessary for human cognition or perception. One mathematical form may be more propitious, or fecund, where another is not. In disagreement with Reitman, we think that it is not proper to say that the program *is* the model or theory of the thought processes any more than it is proper to say that a linear operator or a finite-state Markov system *is* the model or theory of probability learning.

The paradox of immense power having borne moribund models of psychological processes may be resolved in part. Many researchers recognize that the computer is capable of exploring *any* model or theory if only the model or theory has been stated adequately. Yet in spite of this freedom, programs are too often conceived as analogies with the computer, or are descriptions based often on a quicksand of verbal protocols. Programs depend on a set of rules which are little more than algorithms and are usually modified by expedience, rather than being based on unambiguously stated axioms or assumptions. Consequently, the output of a simulation program is unbelievably complicated. Even if it can be interpreted, it is unclear how an alternative result could be obtained from the theory or what its interpretation ought to be. To the extent that the theorist is delayed from giving his theory clear *mathematical* expression will he be delayed from attaining a systematic theory. It matters hardly at all whether the concepts are "behavioral" or "cognitive."

Information theory and simulation models have been concerned for the most part with "input-output" systems, that is, with the relationship between stimulus and response. No one believes the organism to be wholly empty; but it is often treated as if it were, or it is endowed with a conceptual nervous system made up of arbitrary and hypothetical structures. It is difficult to dissect or analyze the living, acting human (although new methods of telemetering information are bound to ease this difficulty). Let us turn then to a system in which we can look at what lies between input and output for a more general understanding of perception. The problem of perception is the problem of understanding the way in which the organism transforms, organizes, and structures information arising from the world in sense data or memory.

THE PROBLEM OF PERCEPTION

13.4 A VERY SIMPLE PERCEIVER

Recently many attempts have been made to exploit mathematical models of physiological and psychological processes of sensation and perception (see, for example, the papers in [64]). Such models usually consider an input of relatively complex form to a system made up of simple components or elements. There may be only a single kind of element, or several simple kinds of elements; or a subset or collection of elements may be treated as an element. Often but not always the model has a feedback loop which allows the output signal s_o to be compared to the input signal s_i. The comparison gives rise to a resultant signal s_r. In a system having a negative feedback loop, s_r may depend on the (absolute) difference $|s_i - s_o| = s_e$ (the error signal). Generally, some function on the s_e is minimized. The engineer and the applied mathematician are familiar with such systems. The mathematical model of the relation between the input and the output— the transfer function—has been extensively treated. Transfer functions, transform, and operational methods are very powerful and deeply motivated mathematically. Although many of these methods are quite old, the computer and new developments in mathematics has revitalized them. For example, recent work in stochastic processes depends heavily on generating functions (known as Z-transforms in electrical engineering) which were already well developed in 1812 by Laplace and may have been invented by de Moivre, who certainly used them by 1730 (see [15]).

To make the ideas concrete, consider Waterman's model of the basic control mechanism required by an azimuth-orienting animal [76]. The water flea, *Daphnia pulex* (a fresh-water crustacean) is observed to have an oriented response in a vertical beam of linearly polarized light. In an intense polarized beam in a nonreflecting environment (black screen), the distribution of *Daphnia's* horizontal swimming direction was nearly gaussian with the mean at 90° and practically all responses lying between $-45°$ and $+45°$ (that is, $2\sigma = 45°$) (Figure 13.3). In a weak beam against a black screen, or in a weak or strong beam against a white reflecting screen, the horizontal swimming directions gave peaked distributions, tending to symmetry about each of the four directions 0°, $+45°$, 90°, and $-45°$. These

Daphnia pulex

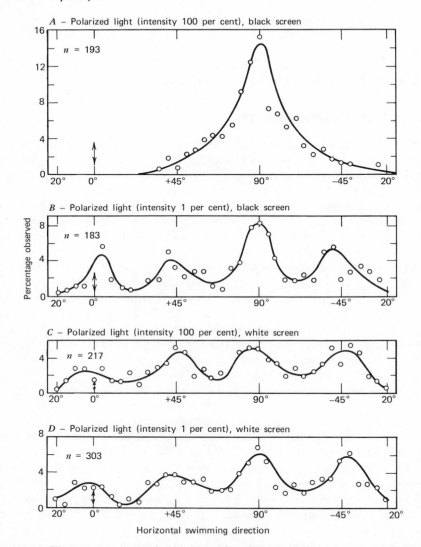

Fig. 13.3 The percentage of animals observed (ordinate) at different horizontal swimming directions (abscissa) in a vertical beam of linearly polarized light. In a high-intensity unreflected beam the distribution has a single, sharp peak as in (*A*). With a reduction in intensity (*B*), decrease in directionality (*C*), or both (*D*), directionality of orienting clearly shows four peaks. (After [76].)

data are consistent with a transfer function for which the turning tendency (torque) $s_e = \sin 2\theta$, where θ is the error angle, that is, the angular deviation of the orientation from the reference direction. Such behavior leads one to ask, "How much of this coding can be done by the receptor mechanism?" Work on facet eyes has ruled out the corneal lens, crystalline cone, or cone stalk as an analyzer and points rather at another element in the optic axis, the *rhabdom*. It is suspected, but not proved, that the rhabdom contains the photopigment rhodopsin. In any case, the rhabdom (Figure 13.4) has structural properties of the kind demanded for a phototactic analyzer. In the crustacean-eye rhabdom, several layers of microtubules are neatly stacked parallel to one another and perpendicular to the optic axis, much like a cord of neatly cut firewood. The eight cords in a stack are alternately at right angles to each other.

It appears that photosensitive rhodopsin molecules are arranged in a highly ordered crystal-like manner. Based on certain reasonable assumptions about the spatial orientation of the molecules relative to the cell walls, one of two perpendicular sets of microtubules would absorb light in proportion to $\sin^2 \theta$, the other to $\cos^2 \theta$ (Figure 13.5). The angle θ is the dif-

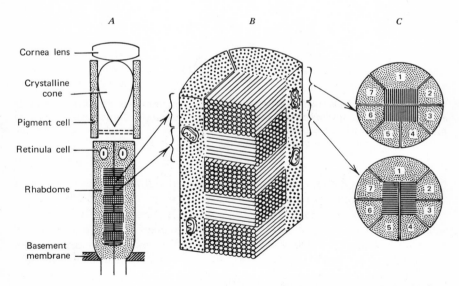

Fig. 13.4 The structure of the rhabdom in the crayfish (*Procambarus clarkii*). (*A*) Ommatidium. (*B*) Microtubule packing pattern. (*C*) The way in which the seven retinular cells of a retinula contribute. Note the strong periodicity at 90° in the orientation of microtubules. (After [76].)

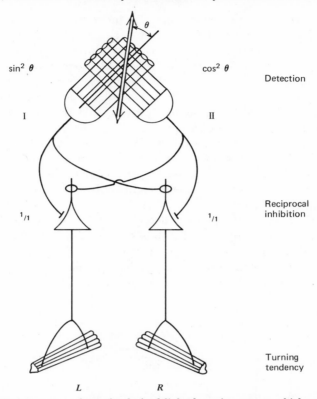

Fig. 13.5   Model of a two-channel polarized-light detecting system which could produce right and left turning tendencies. Because the microtubule patterns have alternating bands arranged with their long axes perpendicular to those of neighboring layers, the outputs would vary as $\sin^2 \theta$ and $\cos^2 \theta$ as indicated. (After [76].)

ference between the error vector of the incident light and the direction of the axis of the rhodopsin for which absorption is greater. A possible code is that the output of a single retinula gives the direction of vibration of linearly polarized light as two axon spike frequencies related to each other by some function, $f(\sin^2 \theta, \cos^2 \theta)$ (Figure 13.6). It may be an actual code. Waterman and Horch [77, p. 474] present evidence for two mutually perpendicular channels in the electroretinograms from the eye of the crab *Cardiosoma*. The paper is remarkable for its conclusion that the two-channel polarization analyzer "effectively accounts for the relevant spectrophotometric, fine-structural, electrophysiological, and behavioral data currently available for a considerable number of arthropods and cephalopods."

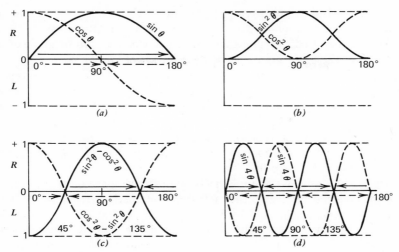

Fig. 13.6 (a) Graphical model for a system showing sinusoidal turning tendencies with a period of 360°. The positive quadrants of the function are assumed to determine a right turning tendency and the negative quadrants a turn to the left. Consequently, the arrows show the direction of the torques, and the amplitude of the trigonometric function shows their intensity for any given asimuth direction. In the case of sin θ, between 0° and 180° the organism should turn right until it is stabilized at 180°, heading directly away from the light source; between 180° and 360° (not drawn) the function would be negative and the animal would turn left, again to an asimuth of 180°. Thus a sin θ function would describe a negative phototaxis, whereas −sin θ would describe a positively phototactic case. Similarly, a system following a cos θ function would orient perpendicularly to the stimulus as suggested by the broken arrows. The well-known dorsal light reflex of swimming and flying animals is an example of such transverse orientation. (b) Sinusoidal functions representing the amount of polarized light absorbed by two dichroic elements oriented perpendicular to each other. Note that the period is 180° and no negative values appear. (c) If the two functions in b are subtracted from each other, two curves may be obtained as shown here. The turning tendencies shown by the arrows would produce steering at ±45° oblique to the ε-vector. (d) If the two systems' outputs are multiplied one could obtain functions of 4θ which would give orientation at 0° and 90° as well as ±45° depending on σ. Such models should suggest experiments capable of testing the information-processing hypotheses involved. (After [76].)

In the case of *Daphnia*, if the primary channels from a single retinula were added convergently in a secondary channel according to the function $f = K(\sin^2 \theta + \cos^2 \theta)$, information about intensity would be present, but that about the angle of polarization would be lost. Thus the orienting distribution would be uniform with respect to the angle of polarization. If the neural process were subtractive, the secondary channel code would be a function of ±cos 2θ. Or, if the outputs of the two channels interacted by multiplication (for which some experimental evidence exists), the neural output code in the secondary channel would be a function of cos 4θ. However, a function of cos 8θ is needed if a direct account is to be given of the *four* peaks in the orienting response distribution of *Daphnia*.

Such rudimentary explanations of very low-level tactic responses as these obviously do not account for the complex orienting of an animal homing on a nearby anemone, much less one homing on another continent. Nonetheless, these elementary systems are of considerable interest because we must know how information is coded, transferred, and recoded at or between the several key junctions if we hope ever to give a satisfactory account of human perception.

The structure of any system is decisive in the way the system works. It has been believed generally that effector systems had response patterns which were very firmly fixed by heredity, whereas receptor systems were thought to be much more labile. The last evidence suggests that receptors may carry out a large amount of the processing previously relegated to the brain. Since the processing is carried out by specialized elements within the receptor, it is almost certain that these response patterns are also fixed by the inherited structure of the organism.

13.5 MOTOR AND PERCEPTUAL REFLEXES

It is usual to find easy discussions of the way in which an organism processes information, but we shall not quote the versions of well-known authors. Let us recognize that we know many details about sensory systems, motor systems, and central nervous systems, but our knowledge of the manner in which they are linked together for interaction is fragmentary and confused. We are only beginning to have an inkling of the sensory codes, and we know even less about the number or kinds of encodings and decodings that occur from the first transformation on stimulus energy in a receptor to the last transformation in muscle or gland which acts on the outer or inner environment.

In spite of our ignorance, we are struck by the work of the past two decades, which is converging on a view that the precortical stages of a sensory system have a functionally autonomous organization similar to that of the postcortical effector system, that is, the movement system of the spinal animal. By 1900 the integrative action of an effector system independent of the cerebral cortex was undeniable. It was only after 1950 that such integrative actions in receptor systems were seen clearly as existing independently of the cortex.

It sometimes appears in man that the higher central nervous system is infinitely labile and teachable. Yet many are inclined, as are we, to believe that future work will compel the view that the central, as the peripheral, nervous system is to a high degree an autonomous functional organization. Its dynamics are built in. In this view, the interactions between the inner and outer nervous systems which give rise to rather complex intellectual activities such as language depend on inherently well-defined structures. As an example, an infinite number of different human languages can exist. Though each child learns his own language, it now appears that the development of normal speech is rigidly tied to temporal aspects of anatomy and physiology [39]. Certainly it is the case that psychologists have not been able yet to give a satisfactory account of language learning, especially of such a fact that an infant of 30 months talks according to a consistent grammar. The hypothesis all but forces itself: Natural (grammatical) languages of the child are basically maturational in nature, like creeping or walking. The patois which the child comes to speak results from his interaction with the environment, and that interaction is mediated by inner, outer, and central nervous systems, each of which has an organized, dynamical function fixed by anatomical structure. To quote the linguist Chomsky [14, p. 330]:

For acquisition of language to be possible at all there must be some sort of delimitation of the class of possible systems to which observed samples may conceivably pertain; the organism must, necessarily, be preset to search for and identify certain kinds of structural regularities.

Let us look at some of the preset functions in animals and men and the way they are governed by structural regularities.

13.6 MOTOR AND SENSORY SYSTEMS

One striking difference to be seen in the earlier work on sensory and motor systems lies in the degree to which the two were thought to depend on the brain and especially on the cerebral cortices for their integrity. In the third edition of *A Textbook of Physiology*, Foster in 1879 sought to make clear the improbability that all incoming nerve fibers went from the periphery to the brain and all outgoing fibers went from the brain to the periphery:

The phenomena of reflex action have shown us that the cord contains a number of more or less complicated mechanisms capable of producing, as reflex results, coordinated movement altogether similar to those which are called forth by the will. Now it must be an economy to the body, that the will should make use of these mechanisms already present, by acting directly on their centres, rather than that it should have recourse to a special apparatus of its own of a similar kind. And from an anatomical point of view, it is clear that the white matter of the upper cervical cord does not contain a sufficient number of fibers, even of attenuated dimensions, to connect the brain, by afferent or efferent ties, with every sensory and motor nerve-ending of the trunk and limbs [40, p. 101].

The independence and subtlety of such mechanisms was first shown fully by Sherrington (a student of Foster's) in his study of the scratch reflex of the spinal dog in 1906. In his Preface to the 1947 edition of that classic *The Integrative Action of the Nervous System* [67, pp. xv, xvi] Sherrington says:

> Again, in the dog a feeble electric current ("electric flea") applied by a minute entomological pin set lightly in the hair-bulb layer of the skin of the shoulder brings the hind paw of that side to the place, and with the unsheathed claws the foot performs a rhythmic grooming of the hairy coat there. If the point lie forward at the ear, the foot is directed thither, if far back in the loin the foot goes thither, and similarly at any intermediate spot. The list of such purposive movements is impressive . . . .

Furthermore, the regular rhythm of 4.8 beats per second was independent of the rate of stimulation, change in site of stimulation, or the combined effect of stimulating two different areas, and was unaffected by cutting the afferent roots of the scratching limb:

> The observation that the scratch reflex is not affected by section of the dorsal roots of the scratching limb is of special interest. It shows first that the organization of prime movers and synergists and the primary spatial orientation of the response is inherent in the pattern of reflex activation, and not in any "feed-back" mechanism [17, pp. 22–23].

In summarizing all the work done to date on the cerebral control of movement, Denny-Brown [17, p. 207] remarks:

> The patterns of activity of the spinal organization predetermine the patterns of pyramidal activation and selection. The network for co-operation of the two systems exists in the spinal segments. There is no need to postulate a network within the cerebral cortex for detailed co-operation of muscles.

In short, it is found in a relatively simple nervous system—the spinal cord—that complex effects rise out of the interplay of nearby pathways.

13.7   SENSORY ANALYZERS AND FILTERS

And what of the sensory systems? Do any of them show the simpler effects early demonstrated in the spinal cord, such as facilitation, inhibition, recruitment, and summation? The extensive lateral connections of the retina of the eye had led, before the twentieth century, to the conjecture that the retina was a miniature nervous system [57]. But an argument from anatomy was only presumptive; the functional proof was harder to make and had to wait really for the first primitive stages of the electronic amplifier.

It was not until 1928 that Adrian and Matthews [1] had strong evidence that the peripheral retina might be capable of performing a part of the analyzing and integrating functions. They showed that if the rate of discharge from the optic nerve were used as a measure, then there was spatial summation and the neurological mechanism for it lay in the retina. Their caution in speculating on other mechanisms drew a barb from Polyak [56, pp. 186–187]:

. . . it is possible that, if the retinal structures were better known, not all the more complex visual phenomena would have to be summarily charged to the account of some unknown "central factors," as is done at present (e.g., by Duke-Elder; Adrian and Matthews; *et al.*).

Hartline [28, 29] first showed directly that diverse complex operations could be performed on the visual image at a very early stage. He showed that the ganglion cells in the frog retina could be grouped into three response classes. When a small spot of light was directed to their receptive fields,[2] *on* cells fired at the offset of the light and *on-off* cells responded to both the on and the off of the light. (Oddly, Polyak does not remark on the 1940 paper [29] of Hartline; it is likely that the book was printed before the paper appeared. The bibliography of the original edition of Polyak's book seems to list no papers later than 1940.)

In a brilliantly interpreted experiment, Barlow [6] confirmed Hartline's work and showed further that light falling outside the receptive field of an *on-off* fiber had an inhibitory action. Barlow suggested in some detail the way in which *off* and *on-off* units could underlie visual functions in the frog such as the detection of movement, color discrimination, and simultaneous contrast effects. In effect, Barlow provided the (first?) speculation about an explicit mechanism for a fly detector. He believed that the retina introduced *meaningful* distortions in acting as a filter to reject unwanted information and pass useful information. It appears that he may have seen these mechanisms as "perceptual reflexes":

There is a great deal of convergence from the level at which light is detected to the level at which the resulting neurological activity is transmitted back to the central nervous system. In Sherringtonian language, an optic nerve fibre is the final common path for activity aroused over a considerable region of the retina, and if some purposive integration has taken place it should be possible to relate this to the visual behavior of the frog.

[2] A receptive field is a restricted region of the retina from which a neural firing pattern can be influenced by light.

A suggestion of Barlow's [6] about how a fly-detection system could work using elementary addition and subtraction was duly tested in an interesting series of demonstration experiments by Maturana, Lettvin, McCulloch, and Pitts [46, p. 131]:

> Spots of light are not natural stimuli for the frog in the way that a fly or worm is. Their use has given valuable information about the internal organization of the receptive fields, but on the whole it seems not to have led directly to the discovery of natural invariants in the function of ganglion cells. Rather, all of this has suggested that, although the ganglion cells integrate the function of many receptors and bipolars, they repeat to some extent, but in a coarser and inconstant manner, the original pattern of light and dark of the visual image weighted by local differences. Nevertheless, the perception of universals that is obvious in the behavior of the frog demands the presence of some functional invariants in the activity of the components of its visual system. Considering the anatomical arguments presented above . . . we thought that these invariants should appear in the function of the ganglions cells, although up to now they had not been found in the protean nature of the receptive fields.

The common American frog *Rana pipiens* was shown objects of various sizes and shapes. Light and dark objects were moved against dark or light background or a colored photograph of the frog's natural habitat. Direct recordings were taken at the optic nerve from the axons of single ganglion cells and also from their endings in the tectum. Maturana et al. found in essence that the ganglion cells formed five natural classes of detectors uniformly distributed across the retina and with great overlapping of receptive fields. The ganglion cells performed the following operations:

Class 1. Sustained-edge detection—with nonerasable holding (that is, activity continued in transient darkening).
Class 2. Convex-edge detection—with erasable holding.
Class 3. Changing-contrast detection.
Class 4. Dimming detection.
Class 5. Darkness detection.

There are many qualifying details, but the general functions are clear: "Four of them act on the visual image to perform complex analytical operations that remain invariant under changes of the general illumination and changes of the general outlook of the visible environment; the fifth class measures the light intensity" [46, p. 169]. Some of the details have abstracted from their paper and are shown in Table 13.1. It is interesting to speculate on the kinds of "concepts" that could be formed from such a collection of primitive operators. Of course there has been a very considerable amount of work on computer simulation of pattern-recognition models based on the recognition of such primitive distinctive features as

TABLE 13.1

Operations of Retinal Ganglion Cells in the Frog (Rana Pipiens)[a]

Class of Operation Performed: Detection of	Stimulus Properties					Response-Receptive Field	Ganglion-Cell Type
	Shape	Size	Brightness Relative to Background	Motion	Remarks		
1. Sustained edge[b] (coincides with Hartline's *on* units)	Sharp edge	Any	Dark or light	Moving (burst of activity); stopped (sustained activity); maximal or only response to unidirectional motion	Not erased by transient darkening	1° to 3° in diameter	Small, unmyelinated axions, conduction velocity <.5 meter/second
2. Convex edge[b] (no equivalent Hartline class)	Convex edge	Small	Dark; little or no response to light object	Moving (burst of activity); stopped (sustained activity); maximal or only response to unidirectional motion	Erased by transient darkening	2° to 5° in diameter	Same as class 1
3. Changing contrast[b] (*on-off* class of Barlow and Hartline)	Any	Any	Light or dark	Changing only	No response to a standing pattern	7° to 12° in diameter	Myelinated axons, 1 to 8 meter/second
4. Dimming[b] (*off* class of Barlow and Hartline)	—	Independent of shape, size ,or contrast	Darkening	Stopped; moving (response proportional to darkening produced by movement)	Prolonged off discharge	Up to 15° in diameter	Myelinated axons, conduction velocity fastest of all, averaging 8 meters/second
5. Darkness	—	—	Slow darkening only	No response to movement	—	Large, but not well determined	Not measured

[a] Data condensed and table prepared from Maturana, Lettvin, McCulloch, and Pitts [43].

[b] Response of ganglion cells in Classes 1, 2, 3, and 4 are independent of intensity of general illumination.

edges, angles, cursive lines, and loops (see Uhr [72] and especially the paper by Uhr and Vossler [73]). But there is very little definitive work on form perception in either animals [69] or humans [27] because, as Hake states, there is no psychophysics of shape or pattern as there is for pitch or hue, or loudness or brightness. That is, form as a stimulus cannot now be specified in a way which leads to psychologically relevant measures of form.

We remark on the fact that almost universally theories of form perception (see, for example, Deutsch [18]) or computational models (see, for example, Rosenblatt [63] and McCulloch and Pitts [47]) require that form recognition be invariant with respect to position or rotation in the retinal field. Even the present successful pursuit of elementary operators (such as ganglion cells) has been conditioned by the assumption that there is an invariance of form in perception. It has been pointed out by Hake [27] that this involves a belief in *form constancy* in spite of considerable evidence that the invariance is weak: there are illusions in form perception; form-shape judgments depend on location of objects in the visual field; form discrimination depends on specific methods and conditions of judgment. This weak invariance is, it seems, what we ought to expect on the evidence from studies at the receptor level. It is found, for example, by Barlow and Levick that the detection response of a cortical unit in rabbit, for stimuli belonging to the form class to which the receptor is responsive, falls off rapidly as the stimulus is rotated away from the orientation of maximal response [8].

Strong confirmation has been provided recently that complex analysis of sensory information occurs at the periphery in rabbit retinal ganglion cells, prior to its projection to the higher centers. Barlow, Hill, and Levick [7] showed that the rabbit's retinal ganglion cells responded selectively to orientation and speed and direction of image movement, and Barlow and Levick [8] gave a detailed analysis of the mechanism of the direction-sensitive neurons.

The main characteristics of the five classes of units found by Barlow, Hill, and Levick are shown in the abbreviated Table 13.2. Figure 13.7 illustrates the striking asymmetry in response magnitude of a single directionally selective unit to a spot of light moved in different directions across the receptive field.

There are some similarities and quite a few differences between these results in the rabbit and those we have just seen in the frog. Some of the differences arise because rabbits are not frogs. Other differences may arise from experimental methods or procedures. For example, Maturana et al. [46] found the two classes of receptors with small fields (first two listed in Table 13.2) to show unidirectionality but not directional selectivity. Their description suggests, however, that these two classes may in fact show directional selectivity [7] but might appear not to if the stimulating spot

TABLE 13.2

Main Characteristics of the Five Classes of Unit

Receptive Field	Most Effective Stimulus	Percentage	Number	Average Diameter (deg. ± s.d.)	Average Eccentricity (deg. ± s.d.)	Regression of Diameter on Eccentricity. (Slope: deg./deg. ± s.e. of Slope)
On–off, directionally selective	Movement of a small object in a particular direction within a localized region of the retina	30	17	3.1 ± 1.1	23 ± 13.4	+0.043 ± 0.016
On, directionally selective		11	6	3.3 ± 1.0	15 ± 6.6	
On-center concentric	Local brightening	25	14	3.6 ± 1.0	27 ± 16.3	+0.0054 ± 0.018
Off-center concentric	Local dimming	23	13	5.0 ± 1.1	22 ± 12.1	+0.021 ± 0.029
Large-field	Fast movement in any direction within a larger region of retina	11	6	8.7 ± 1.7	29 ± 13	−0.10 ± 0.045

NOTE: Standard deviations are for the populations of diameters and eccentricities. Standard errors are for the estimates of the slopes of the regression lines. The figures were analyzed statistically and the following selection of t-test results shows which differences between classes are significant. The figure given after each pair is the probability of obtaining as big a difference in means by random sampling from a single population. (1) For diameters, on–off directionally selective were smaller than off-center concentric (<0.001): 'on' directionally selective were smaller than off-center concentric (0.007): on-center concentric were smaller than off-center concentric (0.003): off-center concentric were smaller than large-field type (<0.001). (2) For eccentricities the most significant difference was between the 'on' directionally selective group and the large-field type (0.04): other differences were not significant. (3) For regression of diameter on eccentricity, t tests showed that the probability of obtaining as steep a slope if diameter did not depend upon eccentricity was 0.013 for the whole directionally selective group: the probability was 0.08 for the large-field type, even higher for other classes.

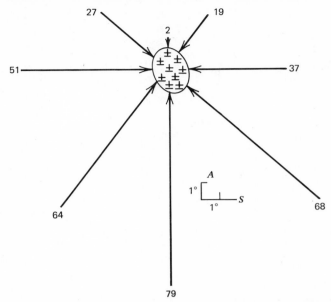

Fig. 13.7 Schematic diagram showing responses of a directionally selective unit to motion in different directions. Response (recorded from axon) occurred to stationary spot at onset (+) and offset (−) of light. There were no responses outside the receptive field (elliptical region). The arrows show the direction in which the light spot was moved across the receptive field, and the number of spikes elicited by it. A is the anterior-posterior axis, and S is the superior-inferior axis, of the eye (After [7].)

was not moved all the way through the receptive field. As another example, the "convex-edge detectors" of Maturana et al. (Table 13.1) are probably ganglion cells whose operation is explicable by lateral inhibition. Barlow, Hill, and Levick also feel that "erasability" and "muttering" are "interesting phenomena [but] should be examined further in an anesthetic-free preparation, for the level of anesthesia certainly has a big effect on the maintained discharge" [7, p. 403].

In their discussion of the coding problem, Barlow, Hill, and Levick point out that the breaking of the code may be delayed, for:

When doing these experiments one's first problem is to establish experimental grounds for differentiating one class of unit from another. One may easily fail to take the next step, which is the important one for the coding problem, namely, the attempt to discover what part of the information provided by the animal's normal environment each class of unit transmits: what normally triggers its response? What feature does it abstract from the spatio-temporal pattern of quantal absorptions in the receptors? Tests which are adequate to differentiate different classes of unit may fail to give one useful clues about this, as our own experience shows. The response to static spots of light turned on and off enables one to differentiate "on-off" units from the others, but one has to test with moving spots to understand that these units signal the direction of motion of objects in the visual field. If one's apparatus is inflexible, or if one's attention is too narrowly confined to the problem of differentiating classes of units, one may easily omit the relatively crude observations and experiments that tell one most clearly what are the trigger features, and hence reveal most about the code.

The mechanism of directional selectivity in the retinal cells of the rabbit is explicated in experiment and theory in a recent paper by Barlow and Levick [8]. They found in essence that *on-off* units respond to one direction of motion (preferred) but not to the opposite (null). The directional-response property does not depend on crossing a boundary or region of the receptive field, but it is found in small subregions. The effect is strong for two regions about $\frac{1}{2}°$ apart and declines with increasing separation. When two subregions are stimulated successively, the response "depends upon whether the order corresponds to motion in the preferred or null direction." From these and other facts, the authors concluded that directional selectivity is the result of the discrimination of the sequence of pairs of regions. In Figure 13.8, two models of the sequence discriminating mechanism are compared. A possible anatomical basis is depicted in Figure 13.9.

13.8 VISUAL ANALYZERS

Not so dramatic as the study of Maturana et al. [43], but more carefully analytic and more relevant to sensory and perceptual coding by humans, are the studies of De Valois and his associates [19]. Using psychophysical techniques, they demonstrated that the macaque monkey and normal man have the same sensitivity to light and the same color vision. Consequently, the electrophysiological records obtained by them from single cells in the macaque's lateral geniculate nucleus may be treated as if they were obtained from humans. No attempt was made to assess form and spatial vision. Only diffuse monochromatic and white light stimulation was used in an attempt to discover how information about intensity and wavelength of light was coded in neurons.

De Valois and his associates found two general classes of cells, broad-band cells and spectrally opponent cells. The broad-band cells underlie brightness vision, showing "either excitation to all wavelengths or, more commonly, inhibition." Opponent cells show inhibition to some wavelengths and excitation to others. For example, Figure 13.10 shows the average number of spikes given in response to the various wavelengths of an equal-luminosity spectrum. The $+G—R$ cells show a decrease in firing rate as wave-

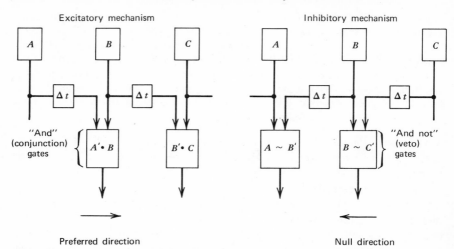

Fig. 13.8 Two hypothetical methods for discriminating sequence. For both, the preferred direction would be from left to right, null from right to left. In the excitatory scheme, activity from the groups of receptors A and B is delayed before it is passed laterally in the preferred direction to the "and" (conjunction) gates. If motion is in the preferred direction, A' (delayed A) occurs synchronously with B, B' occurs synchronously with C, and these conjunctions cause the units in the next layer to fire. In the scheme on the right, the activity spreads laterally, but in the null direction, from the groups of receptors B and C, and it has an inhibitory action at the units in the next layer; hence these act as "and not" (veto) gates. The inhibition prevents activity from A and B passing through these gates if motion is in the null direction, but it arrives too late to have an effect if motion is in the preferred direction. Notice that a special delay unit is not really necessary, for this scheme works if inhibition simply persists longer than excitation and can thus continue to be effective after a lapse of time. The excitatory scheme works by picking out those stimuli with the desired property, whereas the inhibitory scheme works by vetoing responses to unwanted stimuli; the latter is the one favored by the experimental evidence. (After [7].)

length is changed from short (green) to long (red), whereas +R—G cells show an increase in firing rate. One of the most important interpretations of their results is that the color code is not contained in some absolute rate of firing but, rather [19, p. 161]:

These results tend to support the notion that the spontaneous firing rate of afferent neurones serves as sort of a carrier frequency around which signals are modulated, with decreases from this frequency as well as increases carrying information about the stimulus.

Both the exquisite sensitivity to wavelength changes, and the similarity of these changes to those exhibited by humans in a hue-discrimination

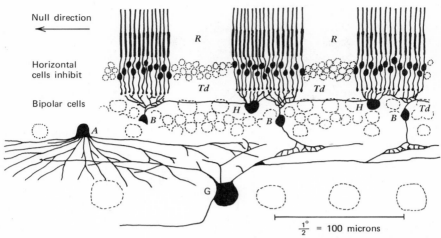

Null direction

Horizontal
cells inhibit

Bipolar cells

$\frac{1}{2}^{\circ}$ = 100 microns

Fig. 13.9 Suggested functional connections of the retinal elements concerned with directional selectivity. The elements are freely adapted from Cajal (1893) and are assembled in accordance with the functional organization suggested in this paper. The scale of the diagram is approximate and a posterior nodal distance of 11.5 millimeters has been assumed. The pathway of excitation is from receptors R, through bipolars B, to the ganglion cell G, but activity in this direct pathway is modified by the associational cells. The horizontal cells H pick up from receptors, conduct laterally in the null direction through a teledendron Td, and inhibit bipolars in the neighboring region. This prevents responses when an image moves in the null direction but has no effect when motion is in the preferred direction. Horizontal cells have the function of the laterally conducting elements in the inhibitory scheme shown in Fig. 13.8. The amacrine cells A are thought to pick up from bipolar endings in the inner plexiform layer and to conduct activity throughout their axodendritic ramifications; they are assumed to make synaptic connection with the ganglion cells and inhibit them, thus mediating lateral inhibition of the type illustrated in Fig. 5 of Barlow et al. [7] and Fig. 13.8 of this chapter. The off-responding mechanism is not illustrated, but it seems to require duplicate horizontal cells and bipolar cells. Notice that the ganglion cell must connect selectively to those particular bipolars which respond selectively to the sequences for one particular direction. Its response is specific for this pattern of stimulation but is invariant with respect to contrast and position in the receptive field. It may be said to achieve some degree of "stimulus generalization." (After [7].)

experiment, are shown in Figure 13.11. The ordinate ($\Delta\lambda$) gives the least change in wavelength which can be detected as a function of wavelength in microns. Data for humans were obtained in standard psychophysical experiments. In the case of single cells, data are based on a criterion difference, that $\Delta\lambda$ required to produce a change of one impulse per second in the average rate of firing.

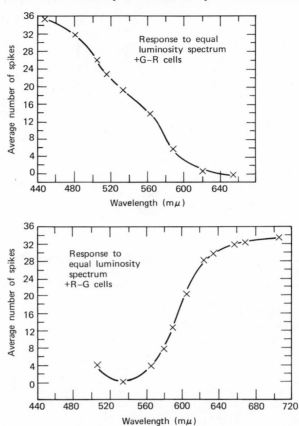

Fig. 13.10   Plot of the averaged responses of +R—G and +C—R cells to an equal-luminosity spectrum. ([19].)

There is an enormous literature on the physical, biological, and physiological aspects of the eye. Already in 1896 Helmholtz gave nearly 8000 references. In spite of the prodigious work since then, there is as yet no generally acceptable theory of the visual detection process or of color vision. Let us sketch, in outrageously brief form, what appear to be the essential facts and conclusions about the visual process. (A recent critical review has been given by Sheppard [66], from the standpoint of the engineer.) The visual process begins with the object in Euclidean space. An object emits, reflects, or refracts electromagnetic radiant energy. The radiation from the object has a unique spectral composition, of very narrow wavelength. That region of special interest for vision lies between .38 and

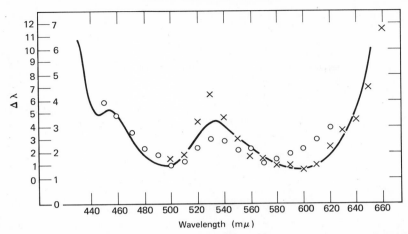

Fig. 13.11 The differentiated responses of the +G—R and +R—G cells to an equal-luminosity spectrum are compared with the human hue-discrimination function. W. D. Wright average of 5 human observers; ✕ = average +R—C cells; ○ = average +G—R cell. ([19].)

.78 × 10⁻³ millimeter, or 380 and 780 nanometers. These spectral limits have the special name (visible) *light*, for the form of energy radiated as a transverse harmonic vibration having frequency limits of about 7.8 × 10¹⁴ hertz (shortwave) and 3.8 × 10¹⁴ hertz (longwave).

13.9 SENSITIVITY OF THE RETINA

There is an essential duplicity in the function of the retinal receptor mechanism. There appear to be two interwoven retinas in a single, normal human eye, and the two have different functions and different sensitivities. The distinction between the bright vision (*photopic*) and dim vision (*scotopic*) functions rests on firm experimental ground—in particular, these phenomena:

1. Anatomically, the two kinds of retinal elements, rods and cones, are different, wherever they may be located.

2. From psychophysical measurements there result two distinct relative luminous efficiency functions, one at low, the other at high luminances. The transition from bright to dim vision is called the Purkinje effect.

3. The rod outer segments yield the photopigment *rhodopsin*, whose absorption curve correlates with the spectral sensitivity of dim vision (Figure 13.12).

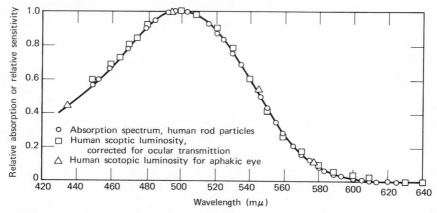

Fig. 13.12 Comparison of human rhodopsin absorption spectrum and the spectral sensitivity of scoptopic vision. (After [66].)

4. The central fovea contains only cones. Cones have not yielded up rhodopsin. The Purkinje effect is absent in the central fovea.

5. The central fovea is blind in dim vision.

6. In visibility threshold measurements, it is generally true at all wavelengths that rod-mediated sensations are "colorless," whereas cone-mediated sensations are "colored."

It can be concluded that rod receptors are different from cone receptors, rods are the principal receptors of dim vision, and cones are the principal receptors of bright vision. Further, since color sensations are well developed only in bright vision, cones are the principal receptors of color vision. These generalities are widely held, even though according to Sheppard [66]:

It may be said without serious qualification that there is no generally acceptable mechanism known for either the rods or the cones to explain the *details* of the receptor process that begins when radiation strikes the receptor and ends with the first synapse.

In the case of hearing, an analogous situation exists in respect to the transformation of mechanical energy into nerve impulses.

13.10 STAGES IN THE OVERALL PROCESS OF VISUAL PERCEPTION

Radiation reflected or emitted by an object is focused by the rather simple optical system of the eye on to the retinal receptors. These receptors (see above) are called rods and cones. Estimates of their numbers are about

6.5 million cones, and 100 million rods. The radiation which is absorbed in the receptor neurons depends on the spectral composition of the radiation and the way in which it is modified by the various parts of the eye. The absorption at the retinal element initiates a process that is not yet well understood. What is clear is that a series of electrical impulses arises and is propagated along the optic nerve fibers in the general direction of the brain. At the optic chiasma, half the fibers cross and half the fibers remain on the same side as the eye. The left halves of both retinas project to the left occipital lobe, and the right halves of the two retinas project to the right occipital lobe (see Figure 13.13). Note that there are no electrical (synaptic) connections at the chiasma. The retinal nerve fibers that arise from each

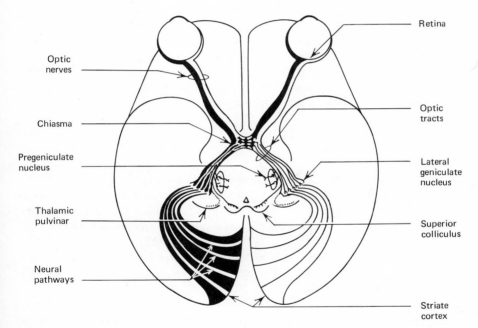

Fig. 13.13 Diagram of the human visual system drawn into an outline of the brain. (Adapted from [56].)

· The subcortical portion consists of the retinas, optic nerves, chiasma, and optic tracts, the latter terminating in subcortical visual centers, principally the lateral geniculate nucleus, with subsidiary pregeniculate nucleus, superior colliculus, and thalamic pulvinar.

· The supranuclear division consists of the neutral pathways originating in the lateral geniculate nuclei and terminating in the striate areas of the occipital lobes.

· Fibers originating in the inner or nasal halves of the retinas intercross in the chiasma.

mixed optic tract end in the subcortical lateral geniculate nucleus. Cortical nerve fibers arise in the geniculate nuclei and end on the striate areas of the occipital lobes of the visual cortex. There is a vast amount known about each one of these stages. Sheppard [66] says the completeness of such a description is deceptive, however, as "becomes apparent when it is realized that the mechanism for the initial radiation reaction in the cone receptors is still unknown, to say nothing of the nature of the final emergence of a color sensation in human consciousness." (Sheppard takes visual scientists to task for glossing over what he believes to be fundamental difficulties.)

Without going into the computational or experimental details, let us look at the most recent estimate of the absolute sensitivity of the eye. It appears that one quantum of energy suffices to stimulate a rod. According to Hecht, Shlaer, and Pirenne a one-millisecond flash of green light delivered at threshold is seen on 60 per cent of the occasions if it contains between 54 and 148 quanta as measured at the retina [30]. The expected number of quanta absorbed by rhodopsin is 14 or less after reflection and absorption losses, even for the 148 quantum flash illuminating about 500 rods. The probability of at least one of these 500 rods receiving two or more quanta is, according to Brindley [11],

$$1 - \exp{(-14)}\left(1 + \frac{14}{500}\right)^{500} = 0.178,$$

which is much less than 0.60, the probability of seeing the flash. It follows that two quanta are not necessary; thus one quantum must be sufficient to excite a rod. The ear also has remarkable sensitivity with energy requirements at detection threshold of the same order of magnitude as those of the eye.

We do not have space here to treat the incredibly rich topic of color vision. The interested reader is referred to the standard literature. See, for example, Davson [16, Chapters 12–16].

From the human optic nerve, approximately three-quarters of the fibers pass to the lateral geniculate body (see Figure 13.13), while the other quarter (about 250,000) passes to the superior colliculi and pretectal region (the tectum is in the dorsal part of the midbrain). It seems that the only well-established function of these nongeniculate fibers is to control the pupil size, although there is a little evidence that they may play a role in spatial discrimination.

Those fibers going on to the cerebral cortex synapse with cells in the lateral geniculate body of the thalamus. The axons of these cells go on to the cerebral cortex. Whenever an anatomist encounters a node like the lateral geniculate body, his first question is, "What is it for, what is its function, its advantage?" As we have seen, more than one hundred million retinal units feed into about one million fibers and only three-quarters of these arrive at the lateral geniculate. This amounts to considerable loss and compression of information. According to Brindley [11] the lateral geniculate compresses information into a smaller number of channels, or discards unimportant information, or both. It is also possible that it may translate information into a code more suitable for the operations yet to be done by the cerebral cortex. For example, the messages from the two eyes may be sent out over one set of fibers as the two-eye average, and over another set as the difference between the messages, withal "an elegant economy achieved." Brindley does not believe this conjecture, for experimental evidence makes it unlikely. De Valois and Jones [20] have provided strong evidence against binocular interaction in the primate lateral geniculate nucleus.

The preceding discussion amounts to the hypothesis that the lateral geniculate body is (1) an information-processing system. Two other hypotheses are (2) that the optical tract is not the only afferent input to the lateral geniculate, and (3) that the lateral geniculate performs no function.

The evidence is that compression of visual information by the lateral geniculate body into fewer channels may occur in man (and rat), for some 700,000 optic nerve fibers feed into 570,000 cell bodies. But in rhesus monkey, 120,000 optic nerve fibers feed into 450,000 cells of the lateral geniculate body.

There is no clear evidence, from records of electrical activity, that recoding takes place in the lateral geniculate body of cat, or monkey, or, by extension from the monkey, of man.

Anatomical and physiological evidence strongly suggests that the optic nerve of vertebrates contains centrifugal fibers—fibers whose cell bodies lie not in the retina but in the brain. In fish, such fibers may control movement of receptors and pigment cells. But Brindley [11, p. 110] reports:

In mammals, photomechanical responses probably do not occur, and at least in them another function for centrifugal fibers must be sought. It is at present very fashionable, perhaps with good reason, to ascribe to them the function of modifying the message sent to the brain from the retina according to whether the animal is directing its attention mainly to visual or non-visual stimuli.

On the other hand, evidence from sensory experiments with humans [11, p. 113] "suggests that the human brain cannot decrease or increase the informational content of the message sent to it by the optic nerve when a given pattern of illumination is received on the retina."

The cells of the lateral geniculate body send axons collected in a well-defined tract mainly to the striate field of the occipital cortex. It is clear from evidence of localized lesions made in this tract, or the optic nerve, or striate cortex, that corresponding points of the two retinas and their neighborhoods remain close together.

Work before 1960 established that responses of single cortical units fell roughly into five classes: (1) about 70 per cent responded with a train of impulses at high frequency falling exponentially to a steady, slower rate for the duration of illumination; (2) some 20 per cent responded in a similar way both to onset and offset of light; (3) about 6 per cent gave *off* responses; (4) the remainder were unaffected by steady light but could be briefly inhibited by a very bright flash [11, p. 122]:

> The most striking feature of the patterns of discharge of neurones of the visual cortex in relation to illumination of the eyes is their close similarity to those of ganglion cells of the retina. As for the lateral geniculate body, so also for the cortex, there is no evidence from inspection of the records from single cells that anything has been done with the information received from the optic nerve except its transmission in essentially unchanged form.

Brindley did not, however, believe that no transformations occurred at the striate cortex. He pointed out that light stimuli used in most studies were large uniform fields, whereas to get any indication that complex transformations were taking place it would be necessary to use a variety of spatial patterns of stimulus. Brindley had not then seen the work of Hubel and Wiesel [32] or Maturana, Lettvin, McCulloch, and Pitts [46] in which complex spatial and temporal stimulus patterns were used to reveal that transformations occurred as early as the retinal ganglion cells.

The receptive fields of single cortical units had excitatory and inhibitory regions, thus being similar to the receptive fields of ganglion cells. However, the shapes and arrangements of the regions were very different from the usual concentric pattern (excitatory area with inhibitory surround) of the ganglion cells [32].

13.11 MACH'S BANDS—APPEARANCE AND REALITY

There is great excitement nowadays among neurophysiologists, zoologists, and psychologists as new discoveries in neural structure and function revitalize work in sensory and perceptual psychology. Let us illustrate this by showing how many of the effects of perception known as "contrast" and "sharpening" must be mediated at very early, peripheral stages.

One hundred years ago the physicist Ernst Mach wrote with great insight about an ubiquitous "subjective" phenomenon which when noticed is apt to be explained away on "objective" grounds. Mach's own description is all but impossible to improve:

By chance, I have noticed a phenomenon involving rotating discs with black and white sectors, the further investigation of which has led me to a more general law of physiological optics.

I will first of all describe this phenomenon. When one rapidly rotates the discs in Figure 13.14, the image *1.c* results. It appears gray, increasing in darkness toward the rim, but is interrupted by narrow, brighter, somewhat washed-out rings in regions where the black sectors end in points or inflect. The phenomenon of the bright rings will astonish anyone who seeks its theoretical explanation, because it is apparent that when both discs *1.a* and *1.b* are rotated they should show the same brightness relation, according to the Talbot-Plateau law . . . .

. . . Figure 13.15*a* gives the brightness of the rotating discs according to the Talbot-Plateau law, in which the radius is plotted as abscissa (*x*) and the light intensity as ordinate (*y*). In the same way, Figure 13.15*b* shows the actual appearance of the rotating disc (see Ratliff [60, pp. 254–255]).

Mach noted that photographs appeared exactly like the rotating discs, but warned against concluding that the bright and dark rings were objective phenomena because they appear in the photograph. On the contrary, he had shown that objective photography followed the Talbot-Plateau law and,

. . . since the rings are not explainable in terms of this law, the subjective nature is demonstrated . . . there can be no doubt about its subjectivity. Its cause is not in the object, but in the visual organ. Places are seen as brighter or darker which are of equal intensity with their neighboring surroundings, or which, to mention intermittent light also, reflect in equal time equal quantities of light as their immediate surroundings.

Since the local effect depended always on the surroundings, Mach classified the rings with contrast phenomena. The only question was whether it belonged to successive or to simultaneous contrast. In the light of a spark from a Leyden jar, Mach "surprised" the retina and found the bands still present, albeit weaker. He therefore concluded that the bands' effect belongs to simultaneous contrast and, by virtue of the briefness of the flash, must not depend on eye movement.

It appeared to Mach that the phenomena could be explained only on the basis of a reciprocal action of neighboring areas of the retina. This was some 75 years before a clear physiological basis was demonstrated by Hartline [28]. He had no doubt, however, that many of his contemporaries would prefer an explanation of the phenomenon we now call "Mach bands," based on unconscious inferences and judgments (Helmholtz's doctrine of

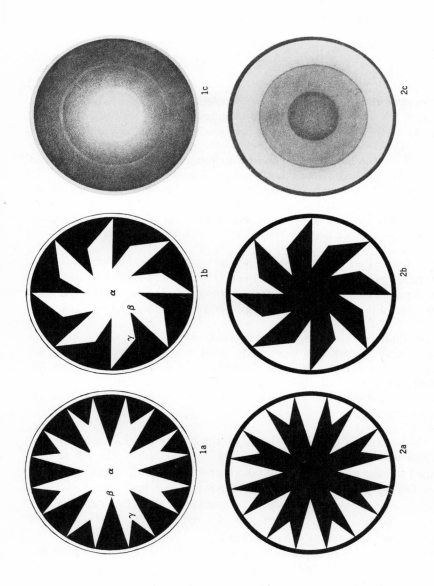

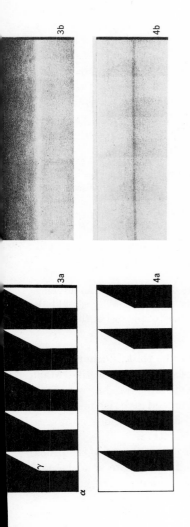

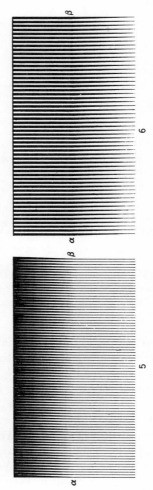

Fig. 13.14 "When one rapidly rotates the discs in Plate *1.a* or *1.b*, the image *1.c* results. It appears gray, increasing in darkness toward the rim, but is interrupted by narrow, brighter, somewhat washed-out rings in regions where the black sectors end in points or inflect. The phenomenon of the bright rings will astonish anyone who seeks its theoretical explanation, because it is apparent that when both discs *1.a* and *1.b* are rotated they should show the same brightness relation according to the Talbot-Plateau law. From the center X to the ring going through β they should appear uniformly white. At β the black sectors begin and should cause a gray increasing uniformly in darkness toward γ. From γ on, where the sector is inflected, or respectively a new sector begins, the darkness should increase more rapidly. A priori, we would not expect that the rings β and γ would be brighter than their surroundings, but that their brightness would lie between that of the next outer and next inner rings. Accordingly, they would not interrupt the continuity of the illumination." (Mach [45], translated by Ratliff [69].)

The discs in Plate *2.a* and *2.b* are the negative images of *1.a* and *1.b*, as are their subjective appearances.

397

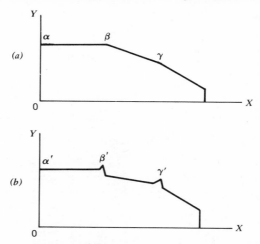

Fig. 13.15 The graph (a) gives the brightness of the rotating disc according to the Talbot-Plateau law (ordinate) as a function of the radius of the disc (abscissa). Graph (b) plots the actual appearance of the disc.

unbewusster Schluss), rather than on the structure of the retina and its physical processes. With a tinge of irony Mach said [60, p. 269]:

> I consider even this conception of the sense organs as somewhat of an advancement. Why should not the sense organs have a certain logic? Why should the ganglion cells of these organs behave differently than those of the rest of the nervous system and the brain?

An implication of Mach's remark would appear to be that, if other parts of the brain also have a certain logic, then contrast phenomena like Mach bands could be subserved by the central nervous system. We shall see that a cortical model with very weak connectivity does indeed give rise to sharpening, as was pointed out by Kabrisky [37]. But first let us look at several mathematical models of reciprocal action in the retina.

We condense Ratliff's (1965) version of Mach's (1868) theory of reciprocal action of neighboring areas of the retina, so modified by him as to be consistent with contemporary electrophysiological evidence.

Two retinal receptors j and p (Figure 13.16a), each with surface area a, mutually act on each other. The nearer together the two receptors are, the greater their mutual influence becomes. At small separations, influence falls off rapidly and perhaps linearly at greater separations, according to some function $q(X_{jp})$ of the distance X_{jp} between the receptors j and p. We omit the details, but it can be shown that the neural activity of receptor p

illuminated by intensity I_p interacting with $n - 1$ other receptors is $r_p = I_p \cdot S$, where S is the ratio of excitation to total inhibition. It is a nonlinear system.

Using this equation, Ratliff calculated responses $R_1(X)$ and $R_2(X)$ to two intensity distributions $I_1(X)$ and $I_2(X)$, using the distance function q of Figure 13.16b. The important features to note (Figure 13.17) are these: (1) the general form of $I(X)$ is approximately reproduced; (2) maxima appear where the curves $I(X)$ are *concave* with respect to the abscissa; (3) minima appear where $I(X)$ are *convex* with respect to the abscissa; and (4) as in Mach bands, maxima are more pronounced than minima (cf. Figure 13.15).

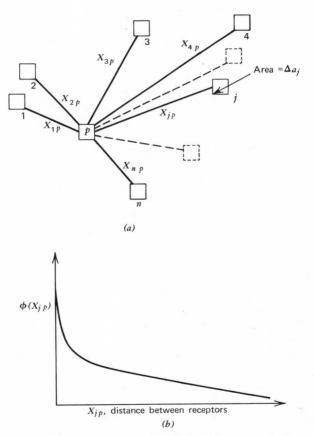

(a)

(b)

Fig. 13.16   (a) An arbitrary subset of n retinal receptors each having area Δa_j. X_{jp} is the distance between receptor p and receptor j. (b) The mutual influence between receptors j and p, $\phi(X_{jp})$ (ordinate) plotted as a function of X_{jp}, their distance apart.

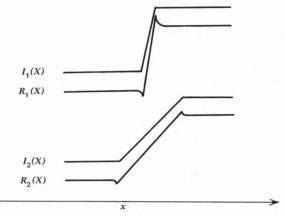

Fig. 13.17 Calculated responses, $R_1(X)$ and $R_2(X)$ of two intensity distributions $I_1(X)$ and $I_2(X)$, using the distance function of Fig. 13.16*b*. (After [60].)

The work of Hartline, Ratliff, and their associates makes it possible to give a quantitative description of an actual neural network of a retina in action *in vivo*. The lateral eye of the horseshoe crab *Limulus* has a small number of interacting receptor elements (ca. 1000 ommatidia) whose mutual connections form a true retina. Moreover, only inhibition travels over the lateral fibers of the network. Excitatory effects can be observed directly in a single optic nerve fiber, as can their modification by inhibition arising in the lateral network (Figure 13.18). Figure 13.19 shows how two receptors mutually inhibit. From such experiments as these, a set of equations can be obtained. The result is roughly that the receptor activity is given by the external excitation minus the inhibition resulting from the activity of nearby receptors. However, one receptor can inhibit another only if the one's activity exceeds some least value. Furthermore, there is a time delay between the onset of activity in one receptor and its inhibition of another.

Now for the crucial question. Does *Limulus* see Mach bands? We cannot ask *Limulus*, and a definitive experiment is probably (at the present time) a technical impossibility. Let us try a related but easier question. Does a single receptor unit in a *Limulus'* eye behave as if it sees Mach bands? The answer is *yes*. To show the effect ideally, a pattern would be shown to the retina and the response of receptors would be measured over the retinal mosaic. Another less tedious way of proceeding, equivalent under certain assumptions, is to fix a single receptor and move the pattern in small steps relative to it. Ratliff and Hartline did just this [61]. A simple gradient of illumination (Figure 13.20) was moved in small steps across the retina.

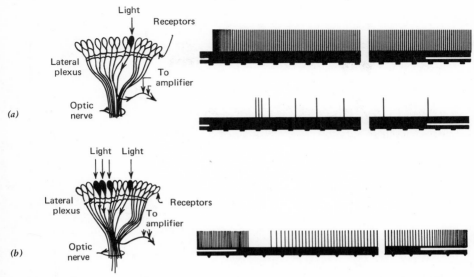

Fig. 13.18 Oscillograms of action potentials in single optic nerve fibers of *Limulus*. The experimental arrangements are indicated in the schematic diagrams. (*a*) Response to steady illumination of a single ommatidium. For the upper record the intensity of the stimulating light was 10,000 times that used to obtain the lower record. The signal of exposure to light blackens out the white line above the $\frac{1}{5}$-second time marks. Each record interrupted for approximately 7 seconds. (*b*) Inhibition of the activity of a steadily illuminated ommatidium produced by illumination of a number of other ommatidia near it. The blackening of the white line above the $\frac{1}{5}$-second time marks signals the illumination of the neighboring ommatidia. Record from Hartline, Wagner, and Ratliff (1956). ([60].)

All receptors but one were masked from the light. The single receptor unit "reproduced" the illumination gradient in the graph of its firing rate. When the mask was removed so that mutual interaction among the receptor and its neighbors took place, the expected effect occurred. The response curve of the single receptor unit shows it to be in the presence of a Mach band! A maximum occurs where the intensity curve is concave with respect to the abscissa, a minimum where it is convex!

Masking and inhibition have turned up almost everywhere in perception and sensory physiology. Ratliff examined six different models in all, of which two (those of Békésy [9] and of Huggins and Licklider [33]) arose from work on the auditory system. They all (Figure 13.21) have a common property—the second derivative of the spatial pattern gives sharpening at borders characteristic of Mach bands. Differences among the models are often only apparent. Discrete models may be rewritten as continuous

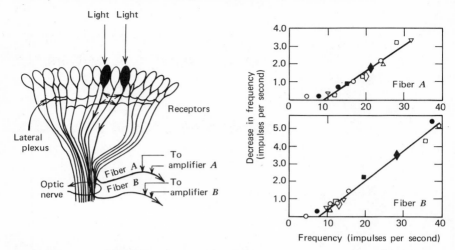

Fig. 13.19 Mutual inhibition of two receptor units in the lateral eye of *Limulus*. Action potentials were recorded simultaneously from two optic-nerve fibers as indicated in the schematic. In each graph the magnitude of the inhibitory action (decrease in frequency of discharge) of one of the receptor units is plotted on the ordinate as a function of the degree of concurrent activity (frequency) of the other on the abscissa. The different points were obtained by using various intensities of illumination on receptor units *A* and *B* in various combinations. Data for points indicated by the same symbol were obtained simultaneously. The slope of the line gives the value of the inhibitory coefficient; the intercept with the *x* axis gives the value of the threshold. ([60].)

models, and vice versa. Some models treat single retinal elements as the basic unit, whereas others make retinal regions the elementary unit. When the optical blurring of the stimulus spatial distribution is introduced, as it must be in a complete account, a point source cannot be imaged on a single receptor. The limited resolving power of the discrete system makes it behave like those models which assume light to spread over a region about a stimulated point, with decreasing intensity from the point of stimulation. As a concrete example, the convolution of a gaussian blurring function with the response of Mach's model, which has a narrow excitatory component (Figure 13.21c) gives a composite weighting function very much like those of the continuous models of Békésy (Figure 13.21b) and Huggins and Licklider (Figure 13.21a).

It does not appear that Mach anywhere discussed the sharpening and contrast in other sense modalities. But the ubiquity of Mach bands in vision suggests that if sharpening and contrast occur in other sense modes, then inhibitory networks must also occur there. Békésy stated this clearly experimentally and theoretically in 1928 for audition, and later [9] for the

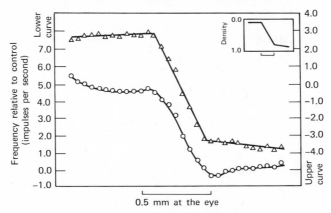

Fig. 13.20 The discharge of impulses from a single receptor unit in response to a simple gradient of illumination moved in small steps across the retina. The upper curve (triangles) shows the form of the response of this receptor unit relative to control measurements when the illumination was occluded from the rest of the eye by a mask with a small aperture, thus preventing neighboring receptors from inhibiting the test receptor. The lower curve (open circles) is the response of the same receptor unit when the mask was removed from the eye and the test receptor was then inhibited by the activity of its neighbors. ([60].)

skin senses. Actually, it was experiments made on two-point thresholds on the skin which led Békésy to a model of neural inhibitory networks.

That Mach bands can be embarrassingly everywhere is indicated by a number of other paradoxes of appearance and reality discussed by Ratliff in his interesting monograph on Mach bands. For example, an early attempt to demonstrate that X-rays were wavelike and to measure their wavelength was for a time led astray by Mach bands in photograph plates exposed to X-rays emanating from a narrow slit. An old puzzle, the apparent enlargement of the earth's shadow falling on the moon during an eclipse, was resolved too as arising from Mach bands. Ratliff states that "The apparent enlargement was taking place in the observer's visual system" [60, p. 217].

The phenomenon of Mach bands is not limited to black and white, but occurs also in color. Ratliff [60] relates the way in which the French color scientist Chevreul investigated the complaints involving the quality of pigments used in the tapestries produced by the famous Gobelin tapestry works. A few complaints had a remediable chemical cause and were justified. But complaints about the vigor of blacks used in blue and violet draperies were not justified. Chevreul theorized and then proved by experiment that the appearance of a yarn's color in a finished drapery depended both on its own color and tone and on the color and tone of the other yarns entwined in it.

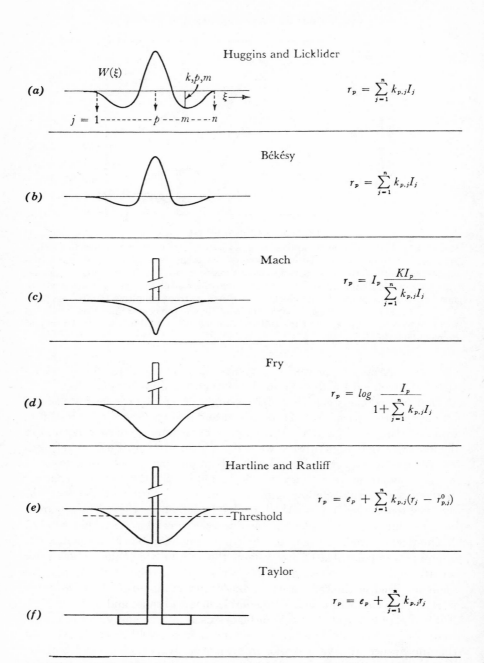

Fig. 13.21 Graphical and mathematical representations of the six models of inhibitory networks. (After [60].)

It is instructive to look at the most recent attempt [37] to model the assumed biological processes of visual-information processing in the human brain. Kabrisky here assumes (correctly) from anatomical evidence that the flow of data within the cortex is *"vertical* to the plane of the sheet of cortex . . . and the output corresponding to a particular input departs the cortex at the same point where the input went in. There is essentially *no* transmission of data across the sheet of cortex.'' The elementary datum sent on is a variable pulse-repetition rate. The pulse heights are of constant amplitude (the all-or-none property). A collection of cell-like structures (Figure 13.22) is made up of the cortical basic computational elements (BCEs). He suggests, again on anatomical evidence, that the grain of the cortical copy seen by the BCEs need be no coarser than the grain at the retina.

Thinking on the sloppiness of nature's workmanship in laying out neuronal tracts convinces Kabrisky that the inevitable cross-coupling between BCEs would lead to some smearing. Thus a graph of output density versus location for a "point" input would be more like a bivariate gaussian than a bivariate uniform distribution. Because of proximity, the activity field of one BCE would merge into those of its neighbors.

The calculation made by a BCE is assumed to depend on both the present inputs and prior inputs; that is, a BCE has a memory. The model was simulated on a digital computer for a $10 \times 10 = 100$ square planar array of BCEs. Such a sheet of basic calculating elements can receive a two-dimensional pattern (for example, from a "retina") and transmit it in a

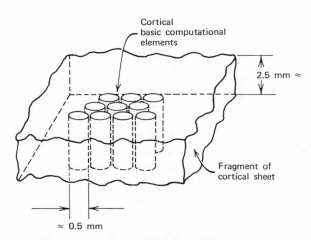

Fig. 13.22 Cortical basic computational elements (BCE). (Redrawn by permission from [37].)

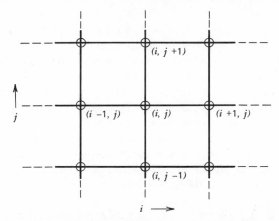

Fig. 13.23 Schema of localized cross-coupling of basic computational elements at point (i, j) to its nearest neighbors at $(i \pm 1, j \pm 1)$.

form modified by the short-term memory store. Interesting consequences of the assumption of cross-coupling and short-term memory are: (1) a limited cross-coupling blurs granularity, and too much blurs sharp resolution of the system, whereas localized cross-coupling (to nearest neighbor as in Figure 13.23) can sharpen edges; (2) local scintillations in the value of the short-term memory function can occur under certain circumstances; and (3) pattern recognition is not invariant under rotation if only a single target pattern is stored.

Kabrisky says [37, p. 48]:

Therefore, it seems reasonable to conjecture that the brain is a two-dimensional pattern manipulator; this is the "computation" which it performs and its variables are not numbers, but the models of worldly things which it erects, in two dimensional patterns, in its cortex.[3]

The intriguing fact we wish to point out here is that Kabrisky's final analytical equation simulated on the computer amounts to an autocorrelation function (in time), which is itself a function of a spatial cross-correlation function. The similarity of his model to a neural inhibitory network model with time-varying inputs leads us to expect both contour sharpening and intensity scintillation.

[3] Kabrisky's model is biologically inaccurate. It does not take account of the funneling and spread of information at various stages of the visual pathway, or of the sizable receptive fields of single cells, or of the very complex operations made possible by connections among the visual system and other cortical and subcortical systems.

We end by noting an implication which follows if a model like of that of Kabrisky approaches the truth: Perception is not to be understood as an elaboration or informing of sensory input by a central nervous mechanism, which in turn issues a set of commands in the right code to be carried out as behavior by the muscles and glands; rather, perception must be understood as the dynamic product of afferent and efferent systems with brain systems. Each of these systems is relatively fixed in the way it processes neural information, and each works according to similar principles. If we take into account the four dimensions of time and space, number and diversity of receptors and effectors, and the complexity of the environment, it is not difficult to understand how one perceives his world as having a familiar constancy in the midst of infinite variety.

No doubt Mach would expect such a result, just as he would not be surprised that Kabrisky does not allude to Mach bands. For by 1906 Mach had said of his 1865–1868 papers, "My reports have remained almost unknown or unnoticed for a long time, such that, indeed, the facts were again discovered by observers more than 30 years later" (see [60, p. 322]).

PSYCHOPHYSICS AND MATHEMATICS

13.12 SENSITIVITY AND CRITERIA IN DECISION MAKING: THE NEW PSYCHOPHYSICS

Detecting and deciding are ubiquitous acts of animals and men. A sudden rustling in a forest causes a doe to freeze for a few seconds, then run. Was it a signal (a predator) or a noise (a gust of wind)? Was running the right decision or a false alarm? What is the value of staying or running? What the cost? Signal-detection theorists think of the doe's behavior as having two independent and separable parts, *sensitivity* and *criterion*. These notions have put the *sensory threshold* on trial for its life, questioning even whether it exists.

Fechner refined the ancient concept of sensory threshold in his *Elemente der Psychophysik* (1860) and set down *the* three psychophysical methods for assigning to the threshold (*limen*) a numerical value. A signal was either above or below the threshold. If above, it was always detected; if below, its presence was merely guessed at. The facts of behavior made necessary the assumption that the threshold varied randomly according, say, to a gaussian probability law. The guessing rate was estimated from the proportion of false reports on trials when the signal was deliberately omitted ("catch" trials).

The threshold and its associated methods are still viable after 120 years. No event for almost 100 years seriously perturbed these notions, although the fixed threshold was called in question by Thurstone in this equation or *law of comparative judgment.* He reasoned somewhat as follows.

If on every occasion when it is presented, a stimulus always causes the same internal effect and if on repeated presentations of a pair of stimuli the same decision rule is used in judging the internal effect of one of the pair to be larger than that of the other, then two stimuli should never be confused with each other. This is patently false. Hence either a stimulus causes a variable effect, or the decision rule changes, from one presentation to another. The former seems the more natural assumption. At any rate, it was the one Thurstone chose to make.

For example, Figure 13.24 shows a psychological continuum (scale) of discriminal processes, along with the distributions associated with four stimuli, 1, 2, 3, and 4. The scale value s_i of the ith stimulus is defined as the modal value of its discriminal process.

Thurstone in 1927 assumed that (1) a stimulus gave rise to a *discriminal process* which had some value on a psychological continuum and that (2) any given stimulus gave rise to a *discriminal* dispersion (standard deviation) about a mean value.

Thurstone assumed as a fixed decision rule:

(13.1) $\qquad$ stimulus x is judged $\left\{ \begin{array}{c} \text{larger} \\ \text{smaller} \end{array} \right\}$ than y if $X \left\{ \begin{array}{c} > \\ < \end{array} \right\} Y$.

In short, successive presentations of stimuli x and y generate the random variables X and Y having the real numbers as their range. It is very likely that X and Y are correlated in many experiments because x and y will occur close together in time or space. The probability that x is judged greater than y, $p(x,y)$, is just the probability that $X - Y > 0$,

(13.2) $\qquad\qquad p(x,y) = \Pr(X - Y > 0).$

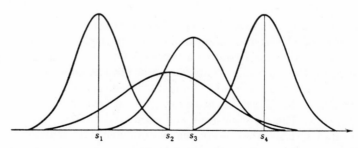

Fig. 13.24 Distributions on the psychological continuum of discriminal processes associated with four stimuli. (After [43].)

Thurstone called the set $(X - Y)$ the *discriminal differences*. It is necessary to know the distribution of the differences $X - Y$ in order to compute $p(x,y)$. Under the assumptions that X and Y are normally distributed with means $\mu(x)$, $\mu(y)$ and standard deviations $\sigma(x)$, $\sigma(y)$, respectively, the correlation is denoted by $r(x,y)$. It follows that $X - Y$ has the normal distribution with mean $\mu(x) - \mu(y)$ and variance

$$\sigma^2(x,y) = \sigma^2(x) + \sigma^2(y) - 2r(x,y)\ \sigma(x)\ \sigma(y).$$

Under the decision rule (13.1), where

$$(13.3) \qquad p(x,y) = (2\pi)^{-1/2} \int_{-\infty}^{[\mu(x)-\mu(y)]/\sigma(x,y)} \exp\left(-\tfrac{1}{2}t^2\right) dt$$

$$= \int_0^\infty N[\mu(x) - \mu(y), \sigma(x,y)],$$

$N(\mu,\sigma)$ is the normal distribution with mean μ and standard deviation σ. If $p(x,y)$ is written as its normal deviate $z(x,y)$ with respect to $N(0,1)$, (13.3) becomes

$$(13.4) \qquad \mu(x) - \mu(y) = z(x,y)[\sigma(x)^2 + \sigma^2(y) - 2\sigma(x)\cdot\sigma(y)\cdot r(x,y)]^{1/2},$$

which is the law of comparative judgment as given by Thurstone. (The development given above was abridged from Luce and Galanter [41] rather than from Thurstone in order to use more familiar notation.)

Equation (13.4) is not uniquely solvable as it stands, since with n stimuli, even when the zero point is arbitrarily set and the scale unit is taken equal to one of the discriminal dispersions, the number of unknowns exceeds the number of equations by $(2n - 1)$. However, further very strong assumptions make the equation useful in practice. Torgerson in 1958 presented an extensive treatment of the simplified law known as case V, together with methods of solution and computation. Luce and Galanter point out that the law of comparative judgment "took up Fechner's approach from a new point of view, one which has since dominated theoretical work in psychophysics and, even more, psychometrics." It appears, nonetheless, that Thurstone's model has not been widely used in psychophysics but rather for scaling psychological attributes that are not easily quantified, for example, favorableness toward the church, pleasantness, handwriting, and beauty. For a discussion of the reasons, see [26].

13.13 SIGNAL-DETECTION THEORY

Of much more importance to psychophysics than Thurstone's 1927 paper was Tanner and Swets' 1954 paper on a decision-making theory of visual detection by humans. The signal-detection theory sketched by them was formally the same as Wald's 1950 statistical decision model for testing which of two simple hypotheses to accept [75]. Signal-detection theory was conditioned most directly by the work on detection and extraction of signals in noise done by communication theorists [38, 74]; see also [65] for a good exposition of selected topics for the engineer and mathematician.

The basic idea of signal-detection theory as applied to the human observer is that a stimulus produces a sensory process and the information about the process can be summarized by a number. Just as with Thurstone's discriminal process, on repetition the same stimulus does not always produce the same number, but rather a distribution of numbers. The subject behaves as if he knew the distributions associated with different stimuli. The number resulting from a particular trial is evaluated with respect to those distributions from which it could have arisen.

It is assumed[4] that the effect of a stimulus-stimulation presentation s can be described by a random vector $\mathbf{s}$ having k components in a Euclidean space E_k of k dimensions. If $\mathbf{x} \in E_k$, the probability density that stimulus s produces the effect $\mathbf{x}$, $p(\mathbf{x}|s)$, is assumed to exist. Suppose that on each trial one of two stimuli, s or s', occurs, and that on a given trial the effect $\mathbf{x}$ is observed by the subject. He has to decide whether s or s' gave rise to the observation $\mathbf{x}$ on the basis of what he knows about the distributions $p(\cdot|s)$ and $p(\cdot|s')$. Let us now assume that in his uncertainty the subject somehow is able to compute the likelihood ratio

$$(13.5) \qquad l(\mathbf{x}) = \frac{p(\mathbf{x}|s)}{p(\mathbf{x}|s')}.$$

If the ratio is large, he says the effect $\mathbf{x}$ was produced by s, if small, by s'. By setting a criterion number c, he can use the decision rule

$$(13.6) \qquad \text{say} \begin{Bmatrix} s \\ s' \end{Bmatrix} \text{produced the effect } \mathbf{x} \text{ if } \log l(\mathbf{x}) \begin{Bmatrix} > \\ < \end{Bmatrix} c.$$

Given such a rule, response probabilities can be computed if expressions are found for the distributions of log likelihood ratio for stimuli s and s'. Let $L(z)$ be the set $[\mathbf{x}|\log l(\mathbf{x}) = z]$. Then the distributions are

$$(13.7) \qquad \begin{aligned} p(z|s) &= \int_{L(z)} p(\mathbf{x}|s)\, d\mathbf{x}, \\ p(z|s') &= \int_{L(z)} p(\mathbf{x}|s')\, d\mathbf{x}, \end{aligned}$$

---

[4] The development given here is abridged from Luce [42].

provided they exist. They are usually assumed normal. Using the decision rule (13.6), we have the probabilities of the response S that s occurred,

(13.8)
$$p(S \mid s) = \int_c^\infty p(z \mid s) \, dz,$$

$$p(S \mid s') = \int_c^\infty p(z \mid s') \, dz.$$

More than plausibility dictates assuming the decision-axis scale to be a likelihood ratio or a monotonic function of it (as in log l). If an optimal decision rule, one which maximizes expected payoff, is assumed, then the decision axis *must* be measured by the likelihood-ratio axis. A cutting-point decision rule is not just reasonable for such distributions as shown in Figure 13.25, but an observer's behavior is optimal for several definitions of optimality when these distributions are of likelihood ratios. Obviously a decision rule like that of (13.6) would not be sensible for the pair of many-peaked distributions of Figure 13.26. Happily, it can be shown that such distributions are impossible if the decision-axis scale is a monotone function of likelihood ratio.

13.14 THE YES–NO EXPERIMENT

What is the weakest signal energy man can detect? This basic problem of psychophysics is interpreted in signal-detection theory as the problem of deciding whether the sensory event on a particular trial was produced

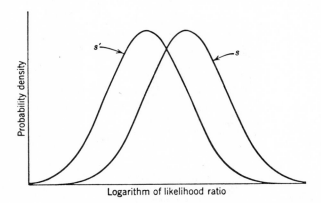

Fig. 13.25 Typical normal distributions of the logarithm of the likelihood ratio for two different stimulus presentations. (After [43].)

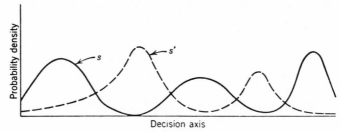

Fig. 13.26 Multimodal distributions for which a cut-point decision rule is not appropriate but which cannot occur if the decision-axis scale is a monotonic function of likelihood ratio. (After [43].)

by the signal or by some random process. The problem is often attacked by means of the yes-no experiment, in which the subject's task is to decide whether the presentation on a single trial was the signal *s* added to a background of noise, or the noise *n* alone. The observer must choose between the two mutually exclusive events by giving one of two responses: *yes*, it was the signal (*S*), or *no*, it was not the signal (*N*). For theoretical reasons, the observer is almost always told the a priori probabilities for the binary events. A typical sequence of events is shown in Figure 13.27.

The stimulus-response matrix resulting from the yes-no procedure is shown in Figure 13.28. There are only two degrees of freedom in the matrix, so that all its information is contained in a point $P: (x,y)$, $0 \leq x$, $y \leq 1$, in a two-dimensional graph (Figure 13.29).

The point marked by an open circle in Figure 3.29 arose from an experiment in which the observer responded S on a proportion of about .45 of the

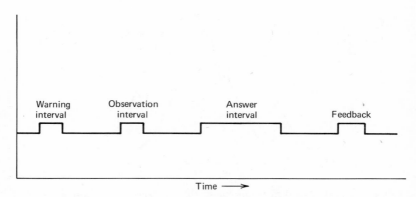

Fig. 13.27 Events in a trial of the yes-no procedure. (After [26].)

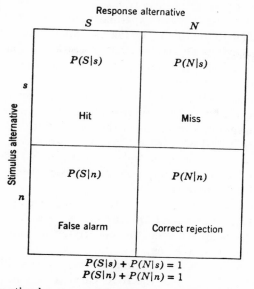

$$P(S|s) + P(N|s) = 1$$
$$P(S|n) + P(N|n) = 1$$

Fig. 13.28 The stimulus-response matrix of the yes-no procedure. (After [26].)

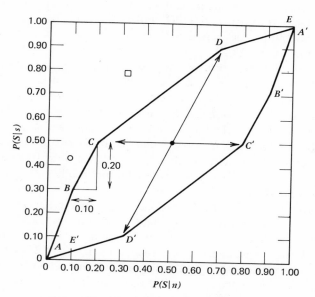

Fig. 13.29 The ROC graph. (After [26].)

s trials and S on about .10 of the n trials. Even though we do not know how his decision rule was set in that experiment, it is safe to say that we could induce him to change the rule by giving him something useful (a quarter of a dollar, say) each time he says *yes*. His new hit probability $P(S|s)$ might move up almost double at .80 (the open square in Figure 13.29). But note that his false-alarm probability has trebled at .30. By such means as monetary rewards, instructions about accuracy, or praise, it is possible to "bias" the observer's decision rule so as to generate a sequence of points. The smooth curve obtained in one of these ways with the other conditions and signal energy fixed is called the receiver's operating characteristic, or just ROC, curve. *It is important to realize that only the observer's rule for choosing among alternatives has altered. The physical parameters which define the environment and stimulus remain unchanged.*

It appears that when we induce the observer to change his decision rule, we obtain a new point on his ROC curve. Let us look more closely at the important relationship between the underlying decision process and the observed points on the ROC curve.

The first important result that follows from our assumptions and equation (13.6) is that the slope of the ROC curve at any point is equal to the cutting point of the likelihood ratio which generates the point. Green and Swets [26] exemplify this property well with a simple decision rule (Table 13.3). The probabilities that sensory event e ($e = 1, 2, 3,$ or 4) arises given that n or s occurred and the likelihood $l(e)$ are shown in part (a). Part (b) gives five decision rules: $A, B, C, D,$ and E. Part (c) shows the false-alarm and hit probabilities associated with each decision rule, and these points are plotted in Figure 13.29.

Clearly rule A is conservative in that a false alarm is never made. But there are no hits, either. Rule B is conservative, too, because even though the hit probability is .30, the false-alarm probability is only .10. If we think of lower values of $l(e)$ as being less conservative, we notice that (1) the lower $l(e)$ is, the higher the hit probability becomes, and (2) increasing the hit probability from that of a particular point always induces an increase in the associated false-alarm probability, and hence an ROC curve based on likelihood-ratio decision rules has a hit probability that is monotone decreasing with the false-alarm probability.

A few other properties of the ROC curve are interesting or useful. On the average, other decision rules will produce worse behavior than a decision rule based on likelihood ratio. The worst possible rule (although optimal in a perverted sense) will generate the reflection $A'B'C'D'E'$ about the main diagonal. Any other less efficient rule will generate points in the region bounded by the two curves. It is useful for setting signal power to a level

TABLE 13.3
A Simple Decision Example

(a) Sensory events (e)	$p(e\|n)$ = Probability, given n, of e occurring	$p(e\|s)$ = Probability, given s, of e occurring	$l(e) = \dfrac{p(e\|s)}{p(e\|n)}$
$e = 1$	0.10	0.20	2.00
$e = 2$	0.30	0.10	0.33
$e = 3$	0.50	0.40	0.80
$e = 4$	0.10	0.30	3.00

(b) Decision rule		Equivalent decision rule
A	Say S if $l(e) > 3.00$	Never say S
B	Say S if $l(e) \geq 3.00$	Say S only if event 4 occurs
C	Say S if $l(e) \geq 2.00$	Say S only if event 1 or 4 occurs
D	Say S if $l(e) \geq 0.80$	Say S only if event 1, 3, or 4 occurs
E	Say S if $l(e) \geq 0.33$	Always say S

(c) Given decision rule	Probability, if n occurs, that response is S, a false alarm $p(S\|n)$	Probability, if s occurs, that response is S, a hit $p(S\|s)$
A	0.00	0.00
B	0.10	0.30
C	0.20	0.50
D	0.70	0.90
E	1.00	1.00

at which an observer can detect reliably to have a simple measure describing the ROC curve. Such a measure is the area under the ROC curve. When

$$p(S\,|\,s) = p(S\,|\,n),$$

the area is .5. When the area is 1.0, the observer makes no errors at all. But most important is a fact relating the yes-no ROC curve to another widely used psychophysical procedure, the two-alternative forced-choice task. The essence of this latter task is that on each trial *two* observation intervals occur in time or space, the signal *always* occurs in the first or second in-

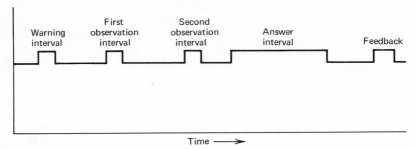

Fig. 13.30   Events in a trial of the forced-choice procedure. (After [26].)

terval, and the observer is forced to choose one. Usually the observer is instructed to "choose the interval most likely to have contained the signal" (see Figure 13.30). The percentage correct in a two-alternative forced-choice task is equal to the area under the yes-no ROC curve. (See Section 13.15, below.)

The decision-theory aspect of signal detection theory is really quite elegant, in view of the simplicity of the assumptions made. As Green and Swets [26, p. 53] point out, the relationships are nonparametric, that is:

. . . No particular form for the probability distribution of sensory events was assumed. One need only assume that the observer partitions sensory events into equivalence classes. For each equivalence class there is an associated response. A stimulus causes an event that falls into either one or the other of these classes, and the response associated with that class is produced.

The freedom from knowing underlying distributions has made the yes-no task and the forced-choice task favorite methods for investigating problems bordering on human psychophysics—in animal psychophysics, sensory physiology, reaction time, time discrimination, vigilance, attention, subliminal perception, recognition memory, and, recently, problems even in personality and social psychology. This nonparametric aspect of signal-detection theory is an extremely useful "methodology" whose use has led to the clarification or integration of disparate findings.

13.15   ON THE ASSUMED DISTRIBUTION OF SENSORY EVENTS, ESPECIALLY GAUSSIAN

In our discussion of Thurstone's work, we developed the likelihood-decision model assuming the two classes of events underlying n and s to have the normal (gaussian) distribution. ROC curves for two underlying distributions, each normally distributed with means m_n and m_s and equal variances,

$$\sigma_n{}^2 = \sigma_s{}^2 = \sigma^2,$$

are shown in Figure 13.31. The parameter d' is the difference between the means of the two distributions divided by the standard deviation,

$$(13.9) \qquad\qquad d' = \frac{m_s - m_n}{\sigma}.$$

The greater the parameter d' is, the greater the separation of the means of the two "hypotheses" becomes, and the closer the area under the curve approaches the area of the unit square.

The abscissa and ordinate are linear in probability. If hit and false-alarm probabilities undergo z (standard score) transformations, the resulting ROC curves become straight lines with slope 1 when plotted on double-probability axes.

Figure 13.32 shows ROC curves to be expected when the underlying variances are not equal. In this instance, likelihood ratio is not monotonic with x. The case of $\sigma_s > \sigma_n$ is illustrated in the top row, that of $\sigma_s < \sigma_n$ in the third row, of Figure 13.32.

In the unequal-variance cases, the likelihood ratio is equal to 1 at the two different points at which the probability density of x under either hypothesis n or s is the same (points a, b, and d, e). We know already that $l(x) = 1$ at only one point c when $\sigma_n = \sigma_s = \sigma$. At c, the ROC curve intersects the negative diagonal of the unit square.

Under the assumptions that observations from each interval are independent, weighted equally, and combined linearly, it is not difficult to show that d' (forced-choice) $= \sqrt{2}\, d'$ (yes-no).

13.16   THEORY OF THE IDEAL OBSERVER

We have just seen how statistical decision theory is used in the analysis of simple detection experiments whereby *decision criteria* are separated from *sensory variables*. The *ideal detector* of communication theory provides the second basic aspect of signal-detection theory. The crucial feature is the interpretation of the parameters of the theory in terms of the measurable physical properties of electronic devices and several classes of signals and noises. The theory thus specifies the ideal and a way of calculating the relative efficiency of real devices for which there exists an uncertainty or an inability to use a particular parameter (for example, phase angle). Further, by manipulating these parameters in experiments with observers, it may

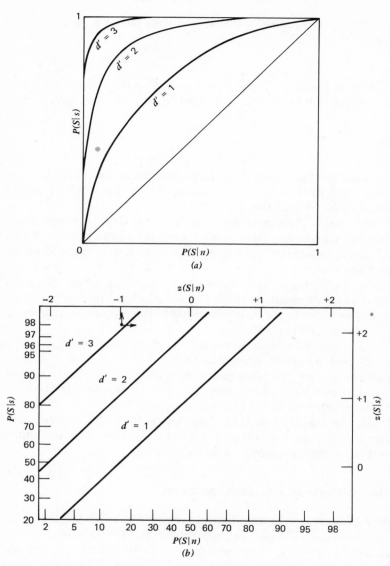

Fig. 13.31 (a) ROC curves assuming that the two underlying distributions are gaussian with equal variance. The hit and false-alarm probabilities are plotted on linear scales. The parameter d' is the distance between the means of the two distributions divided by the common standard deviation. (b) ROC curves plotted on double-probability paper. These are the same curves plotted in (a) except that the Gaussian transform has been used to scale the ordinate and abscissa. For an explanation of these transformations, see the text. (After [26].)

418

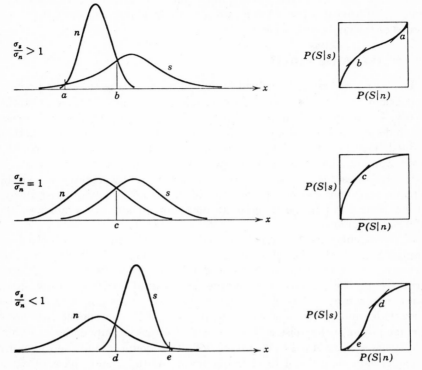

Fig. 13.32 The expected ROC curve for the unequal-variance gaussian case. At the top of the figure the distribution under s has a variance larger than the variance under the n hypothesis. At the points marked a and b on the variable x the probability density given either hypothesis is the same; hence the likelihood ratio is 1. These two points are labeled in the ROC curve to the right of the distribution, and, as indicated, the slope of the ROC curve is unity at the points marked a and b. In the middle of the figure is shown the equal-variance gaussian case. Only at the point c is the likelihood ratio equal to 1. At higher values of x the likelihood ratio is greater than 1, and at lower values the likelihood ratio is less than 1. On the ROC curve the only point at which the slope is 1 is marked on the graph. The slopes below and above that point are less than 1 and greater than 1, respectively. At the bottom of the figure we consider the case in which the variance under s is less than is the variance under n. At the points marked e and d the likelihood ratio is 1; thus the slope of the ROC curve is 1 at these points, as indicated in the accompanying ROC curve. (After [26].)

be possible, say Green and Swets [26], to infer how much and what kind of sensory information can be used or something about the structures and modes of sensory processes.

13.17 THE NOISE PROCESS

The first problem to be solved is that of representing the noise process. It is taken for granted that the signal may be specified exactly or statistically. For example, it may be a sinusoid or a sample of Rayleigh noise. Given descriptions of signal and noise, the ideal or optimal detector is then derived. We emphasize that "ideal" means a relative best. The particular description of the ideal detector will depend on specific conditions of signal and noise as well as on the information or uncertainty which the detector has about physical parameters of the signal. Behavior must always be less than ideal if the detector is uncertain about, or cannot use, the information given it.

The particular noise waveform used in experiments is most often an amplified thermal noise. The model is a gaussian noise containing frequencies no higher than W hertz and is represented by a finite Fourier series. We omit the derivation and give the essential result: The total power in a single component is N_0/T, where N_0 is the noise power in a band 1 hertz wide and T is the period. Since there are WT components, the total average power of the noise is WN_0 measured across an impedance of 1 ohm.

The signal is assumed to be a fixed definite waveform, and the waveform of choice is a sinusoid of fixed frequency, amplitude, and phase. Because it is desirable for the signal $s(t)$ to have the same representation as the noise, it too is represented by a finite Fourier series. When measured across an impedance of 1 ohm, the signal has an energy E_s.

13.18 IDEAL DETECTOR FOR SIGNAL SPECIFIED EXACTLY

We sketch the derivation of an ideal detector for the basic detection task in which the signal is specified exactly using the temporal representation (see Figure 13.33). The observed waveform will be

$$(13.10) \qquad x(t) = s(t) + n(t)$$

for signal plus noise, and

$$(13.11) \qquad x(t) = n(t)$$

for noise alone. Given the hypothesis of signal plus noise, H_s, the probability density function is

$$(13.12) \qquad f(x_m \mid s) = \frac{1}{\sqrt{2\pi N_0 W}} \exp\left[-\frac{1}{2}\left(\frac{x_m - s_m}{N_0 W} \right)^2 \right].$$

Given the hypothesis of noise alone, H_n, the probability density function is

$$(13.13) \qquad f\left(x_m \,|\, n\right) \;=\; \frac{1}{\sqrt{2\pi N_0 W}} \, \exp\left[-\frac{1}{2}\left(\frac{x_m{}^2}{N_0 W} \right) \right].$$

Then the probability density function of the total waveform $x(t)$, given H_s, is

$$(13.14) \qquad f\left(x(t) \,|\, n\right) \;=\; \prod_{m=1}^{2WT} f\left(x_m \,|\, n\right),$$

or given H_n,

$$(13.15) \qquad f\left(x(t) \,|\, s\right) \;=\; \prod_{m=1}^{2WT} f\left(x_m \,|\, s\right).$$

Since each x_m is independent, it can be seen that the log-likelihood function is given by

$$(13.16) \qquad \log[x(t)] \;=\; \log\left(\frac{f(x(t)\,|\,s)}{f(x(t)\,|\,n)} \right)$$

$$= \frac{1}{N_0 W}\left(\sum_{m=1}^{2WT} x_m s_m - \frac{1}{2} \sum_{m=1}^{2WT} s_m{}^2 \right).$$

The term $\sum s_m{}^2$ is constant; hence the cross-correlation term

$$z \;=\; \sum_{m=1}^{2WT} x_m s_m$$

is a monotonic function of likelihood ratio. We have the result then that a receiver, which computes the value of cross-correlation and accepts the hypothesis that a signal was present only if the value of the cross-correlation is larger than a criterion value, is an optimal detector.

There are other optimal detectors. One is based on the Fourier-series representation, and the critical quantity it computes is cross-correlation in frequency. Another optimal detector is based on the impulse response of a filter and correlates the incoming waveform with the delayed impulse response to the expected signal of a "matching filter." But all are equal in that they all are optimal.

Finally, we might ask how these detectors perform. Since likelihood ratio is monotone with

$$z \;=\; \sum_{m=1}^{2WT} x_m s_m,$$

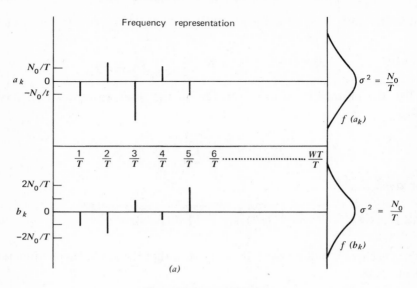

Frequency representation

$$\hat{x}(t) = \sum_{k=1}^{WT} a_k \cos \frac{2\pi}{T} kt + b_k \sin \frac{2\pi}{T} kt$$

$$a_k = \frac{2}{T} \int_0^T x(t) \cos \frac{2\pi}{T} kt \, dt$$

$$b_k = \frac{2}{T} \int_0^T x(t) \sin \frac{2\pi}{T} kt \, dt$$

Probability density

$$f(a_k) = \frac{1}{\sqrt{2\pi N_0/T}} \exp\left(-\frac{1}{2} \frac{a_k^2}{N_0/T}\right)$$

$$f(b_k) = \frac{1}{\sqrt{2\pi N_0/T}} \exp\left(-\frac{1}{2} \frac{b_k^2}{N_0/T}\right)$$

Parameters: mean $(a_k) = 0$ variance $(a_k) = N_0/T$
mean $(b_k) = 0$ variance $(b_k) = N_0/T$
a_k and b_k all independent

Fig. 13.33 Two equivalent representations of the waveform. (a) Finite frequency representation of the waveform. The waveform is represented by a Fourier series having a fundamental frequency of $1/T$ and containing the indicated value at all harmonics of this fundamental. The value of a_2 is the contribution of the cosine component; the value of b_2 is the contribution of the sine component. Given noise alone, the distribution of the values in frequency is assumed to be gaussian with mean 0 and standard deviation N_0/T.

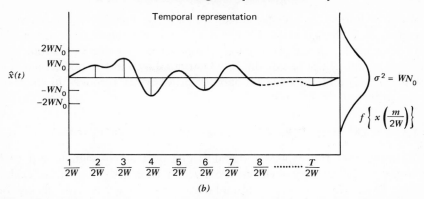

Fig. 13.33 (cont.) (b) Finite temporal representation of the waveform. This is simply the value of the waveform at successive, equally spaced intervals in time. The distribution of these samples is assumed to be gaussian with mean 0 and variance WN_0. (After [26].)

we require the distribution of z under both hypotheses. Now z is normally distributed because it is a sum of variables x_i each of which is normally distributed. Given H_n,

(13.17) $$E(x_i) = 0, \qquad E(x_i^2) = N_0 W,$$

and given H_s,

(13.18) $$E(x_i) = s_i, \qquad E(x_i - s_i)^2 = N_0 W.$$

By summing these expectations $E(x)$ over all i components ($i = 1, 2, \ldots,$ $2WT$), it is easy to show that the means and variances under the two hypotheses are, for H_n,

(13.19) $$E(z_n) = 0, \qquad \text{var } (z_n) = 2W^2 N_0 E_s,$$

and, for H_s,

(13.20) $$E(z_s) = 2WE_s, \qquad \text{var } (z_s) = 2W^2 N_0 E_s.$$

Note that adding the signal to the noise increases the mean but not the variance.

The basic parameter of signal-detection theory, d', can now be stated:

(13.21) $$d' = \frac{E(z_s) - E(z_n)}{\sigma(z)} = \frac{2WE_s}{2W^2 N_0 E_s} = \sqrt{\frac{2E_s}{N_0}}.$$

The quantity d', which was introduced earlier in the parametric decision model, thus relates parameters of the physical situation to signal and noise distributions on a decision axis which is parametrized by a monotone function of likelihood ratio. This d' is of deeper significance because a step has been made toward specifying a biophysical relationship. From this, we can predict the shape of the ROC curve (shown in the middle panel of Figure 13.32) and thus the probability of a correct response in the two-interval forced-choice task.

13.19 IDEAL DETECTORS FOR SIGNAL SPECIFIED STATISTICALLY

Suppose that the expected signal is one of a set of signals and each member of the set may occur on a particular trial with some finite probability. The derivation of the optimal observer is carried out just as before, except that the probability density function for the waveform must take uncertainty into account. An interesting case is that of a sinusoid of fixed amplitude, known frequency, but unknown phase. The probability density function for H_n is the Rayleigh distribution, for H_s is accepted only when the amplitude of the *envelope* of the waveform exceeds the criterion value.

The probability density function and the family of ROC curves derived for the envelope-detection model are shown in Figure 13.34. Jeffress in 1964 made a case for the envelope detector as a good model for the human who is detecting weak, pure tones in noise. He fitted with apparent success some rating data (from a particular form of the yes-no task) by means of the envelope-detection model (Figure 13.35).

13.20 UNCERTAINTY AND STRUCTURE AS PSYCHOLOGICAL CONCEPTS

Garner [24] combined information theory and set theoretical constructs in his rather general analysis of structure in perception. We shall consider his recent [25] thinking about three aspects of perception: (1) perceiving is knowing; (2) what is perceived relates to properties of sets of stimuli, not of single stimuli; (3) perceiving is an active process in which the perceiver participates fully. Garner's view is that perceiving is a cognitive process. It involves "knowing, understanding, comprehending, organizing, even cognizing." Although perception depends on sensing and discriminating, it is more akin to classifying, forming concepts, or learning with free recall. The crucial point for Garner is that a single stimulus has no meaning apart from its relation to a set of stimuli. This is due to the fact that the attributes which define a single stimulus can be specified only if the alternatives are known.

Consider the stimuli in Figure 13.36. Binary attributes of the pairs of dots which could be perceived are *position P* (left or right of center), *distance D* between dots, and *orientation O* (rotation to right or left of vertical). Suppose that a subject in an experiment on classification were

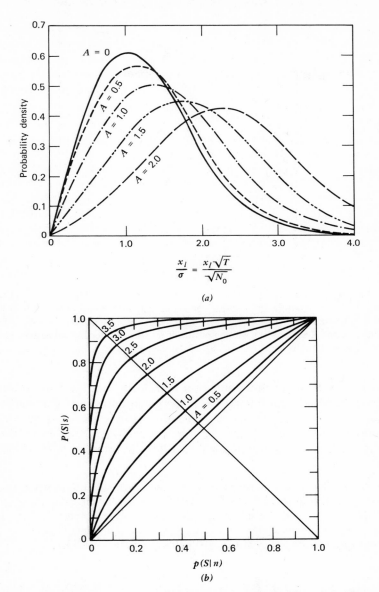

$$\frac{x_l}{\sigma} = \frac{x_l \sqrt{T}}{\sqrt{N_0}}$$

(a)

(b)

Fig. 13.34 The distribution function and the corresponding ROC curve for the envelope detector. (a) Probability density of the amplitude of the envelope of a narrow-band gaussian process. The parameter A is the amplitude of the sinusoidal signal relative to the rms value of the noise. The curve $A = 0$ is the distribution for the case of noise alone. The curve labeled $A = 2$ is the density when a sinusoid with amplitude twice the rms noise voltage is added to the noise. (b) The ROC curves corresponding to selected values of signal amplitude. (After [26].)

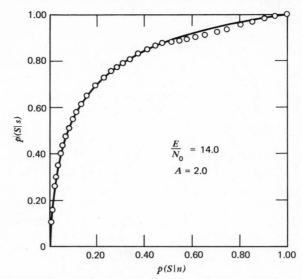

Fig. 13.35 Rating data fitted by the envelope-detection model. The data were obtained from an observer listening for a weak sinusoidal signal in noise. The ratio of signal energy to noise-power density, E/N_0, is 14.0. The theoretical ROC curve is for an envelope detector of a sine wave whose amplitude is twice the root-mean-square value of the narrow-band noise process ($A = 2.0$). (After [26].)

shown only examples from the subset of four in the top row. The perception *right rotation* of *near* dot pairs *left of center* could not occur. This may seem obvious, but some psychologists have unwittingly assumed that every attribute of an entire stimulus set was present in a random or "representative" sample from it. Garner [25, p. 11] puts this important point as follows:

How the single stimulus is perceived is a function not so much of what it is, but is rather a function of what the total set and the particular subset are. The properties of the total set and the subset are also the perceived properties of the single stimulus, so we cannot understand the knowing of the single stimulus without understanding the properties of the sets within which it is considered.

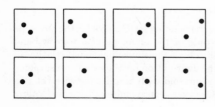

Fig. 13.36 Binary attributes of pairs of dots: position (left or right of center), distance (close or far), and orientation (rotated to left or right of vertical). (After [24].)

When a subject sorted as fast as he could cards bearing the stimuli of Figure 13.36, according to one of the three attributes D, O, or P, chosen arbitrarily by the experimenter his sorting times (Figure 13.37) were found to be about the same whether he sorted with only a single attribute present or with one or two competing attributes present. However, the higher the relative discriminability (abscissa) is, the shorter the sorting time becomes. The conclusion drawn from these results is that the perceived organization is affected only by the degree to which the stimuli can be discriminated. This conclusion was bolstered by the results from subjects who freely chose an attribute for the sorting task. The latter results made it clear that subjects tended strongly to sort on the preferred attribute (*no* subject preferred P) but there were strong individual differences in preference. In another experiment, it was shown that a subject always chose his preferred attribute for sorting when its relative discriminability is high. But when his preferred attribute had low discriminability, a non-preferred attribute might be chosen for sorting and, depending on its relative discriminability, might even be chosen more often than the preferred attribute.

Garner [25, p. 13] interprets these results to mean that a subject can pay attention to the differentiating attribute alone of a stimulus while ignoring those others which define the larger set. The subject does just as well with one attribute as with another. Yet he has definite personal preferences for attributes, and all of the attributes defining the set affect his perceptual organization. "To perceive is to know—all properties of the stimulus set, not just those immediately relevant to discrimination."

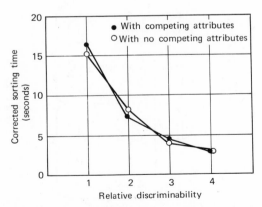

Fig. 13.37 Sorting time in seconds (ordinate) as a function of relative discriminability (abscissa). The open circles are for the case of no competing attributes, the filled circles for the case of competing attributes. (After [24].)

In concept or classification learning, the subject's task is to perform according to the rules set by the experimenter. The subject may have to discover the rules that define the classes or subclasses of stimuli to be learned. Whitman and Garner [78] used the stimuli in Figure 13.38 to answer the question whether or not ease of learning was affected by the nature of the classification system.

The stimuli belonging to the two classes A and B with simple structure (columns) had been shown previously to be easy to learn. Class A has four triangles and four circles, as does B. The two classes also agree in gap location, number of vertical lines, and dot location. Within each class one attribute is perfectly correlated with another. Thus in A, triangles are left-gapped, circles right-gapped. Just the opposite holds in B. Rows J and K, however, are classes with complex structure in that these two classes have no correlation between any pair of attributes (the reader should show this to himself as an exercise).

Now it is usual in concept learning to present stimuli singly from both classes in random order. Whitman and Garner used this method as well as a second method in which one class was presented alone. By the first method, the subject was shown each of the 16 stimuli labeled A or B (J or K for the complex set). The subject read aloud each label and immediately afterward sorted an unlabeled, randomized deck of the same stimuli into two classes, A and B. The complex classification was learned as easily as the simple classification. "The conclusion with this method is that the nature of the structure in the subset does not affect the ease of learning."

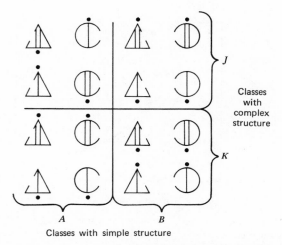

Fig. 13.38   Classes of stimuli having simple or complex structure. (After [24].)

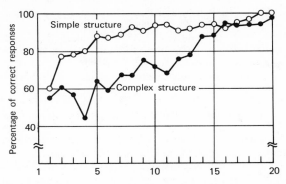

Fig. 13.39 The course of learning for the simple and complex structures of Figure 13.38. (After [24].)

With the second method, just one class of eight stimuli (A or J) was shown to the subject, who read aloud the same label eight times. Then, just as for the first method, he sorted the full set into two classes A and B or J and K. Figure 13.39 shows that the simple classification was much easier to learn than the complex classification. (The course of learning for both simple and complex structures by the first method was much like the lower curve of Figure 13.39.)

From this experiment, Garner [25, p. 15] concludes that there exist facilitating properties of sets of stimuli, that people do perceive these properties, and that these properties affect ease of learning. "But the stimuli must be presented so that it is clear to the subject what constitutes a single class or group or subset."

Garner's concern with "cognition," organization, and relations, and his view that the part is defined by the whole, make him seem at first glance to be a present-day Gestaltist. But it would be fallacious to affix the label "Gestalt" to him, for at least two reasons. Classical Gestalt psychology dealt almost exclusively with the single stimulus and the static, "as given" state. Garner deals with the vital way in which elements of a set and the set are related, and the way in which this relation grows or can be altered. Cognitive yes, Gestalt no.

REFERENCES

1. Adrian, E. D., and R. Matthews, "The Action of Light on the Eye, Part III. The Interaction of Retinal Neurons," *J. Physiol.*, **65**, 1928, 273–298.

2. Anderson, N. S., and P. M. Fitts, "Amount of Information Gained during Brief Exposures of Numerals and Colors," *J. Exp. Psychol.*, **56**, 1958, 362–369.

3. Atkinson, R. C., "A Variable Sensitivity Theory of Signal Detection," *Psychol. Rev.*, **70**, 1963, 91–106.

4. Atkinson, R. C., G. H. Bower, and E. J. Crothers, *Introduction to Mathematical Learning Theory*, Wiley, New York, 1965.
5. Atkinson, R. C., E. C. Carterette, and R. A. Kinchla, "Sequential Phenomena in Psychophysical Judgments: A Theoretical Analysis," *Inst. Radio Engineers, Transactions on Information Theory*, IT–8, 1958, 155–162.
6. Barlow, H. B., "Summation and Inhibition in the Frog's Retina," *J. Physiol.*, **119**, 1953, 69–88.
7. Barlow, H. B., R. M. Hill, and W. R. Levick, "Retinal Ganglion Cells Responding Selectivity to Direction and Speed of Motion in the Rabbit," *J. Physiol.*, **173**, 1964, 377–407.
8. Barlow, H. B., and W. R. Levick, "The Mechanism of Directionally Selective Units in Rabbit's Retina," *J. Physiol.*, **178**, 1965, 477–504.
9. Békésy, G. v., *Experiments in Hearing*, McGraw-Hill, New York, 1960.
10. Bernoulli, D., "Exposition of a New Theory on the Measurement of Risk," [1738] (translated by L. Sommer), *Econometrica*, **22**, 1954, 23–36.
11. Brindley, G. S., *Physiology of the Retina and the Visual Pathway*, Arnold, London, 1960.
12. Broadbent, D. E., *Perception and Communication*, Pergamon Press, New York, 1958.
13. Bush, R. R., and F. Mosteller, *Stochastic Models for Learning*, Wiley, New York, 1955.
14. Chomsky, N., "Formal Properties of Grammar," in Luce, R. D., R. R. Bush, and E. Galanter (editors), *Handbook of Mathematical Psychology*, Vol. 2, Wiley, New York, 1963, pp. 323–418.
15. David, F. N., and D. E. Barton, *Combinatorial Chance*, Griffin, London, 1962.
16. Davson, H. (editor), "The Visual Process," in *The Eye*, Vol. 2, Academic Press, New York, 1962.
17. Denny-Brown, D., *The Cerebral Control of Movement*, Liverpool University Press, 1966.
18. Deutsch, J. A., "Theory of Shape Recognition," *British J. of Psychology*, **46**, 1955, 30–37.
19. De Valois, R. L., "Behavioral and Electrophysiological Studies of Primate Vision," in Neff, W. D. (editor), *Contributions to Sensory Physiology*, Vol. 1, Academic Press, New York, 1965.
20. De Valois, R. L., and A. E. Jones, "Single-Cell Analysis of the Primate Color-Vision System," in Jung, R., and H. Kornhuber (editors), *The Visual System: Neurophysiology and Psychophysics*, Springer, Berlin, 1961, pp. 178–192.
21. Eriksen, C. W., and H. W. Hake, "Multidimensional Stimulus Differences and Accuracy of Discrimination," *J. Exp. Psychol.*, **50,**, 1955, 153–160.
22. Estes, W. K., "Toward a Statistical Theory of Learning," *Psychol. Rev.*, **57**, 1950, 94–107.
23. Feigenbaum, E. A., and J. Feldman (editors), *Computers and Thought*, McGraw-Hill, New York, 1963.
24. Garner, W. R., *Uncertainty and Structure as Psychological Concepts*, Wiley, New York, 1962.
25. Garner, W. R., "To Perceive Is to Know," *American Psychologist*, **21**, 1966, 11–19.
26. Green, D. M., and J. A. Swets, *Signal Detection and Psychophysics*, Wiley, New York, 1966.
27. Hake, H. W., *Contributions of Psychology to the Study of Pattern Vision*, WADC Technical Report 57–621, Wright Air Development Center, Ohio, October, 1957 [Excerpted in Uhr, L. (editor), *Pattern Recognition*, Wiley, New York, 1966].

28. Hartline, H. K., "The Response of Single Nerve Fibers of the Vertebrate Eye to Illumination of the Retina," *Amer. J. Physiol.*, **121**, 1938, 400–415.
29. Hartline, H. K., "The Effects of Spatial Summation in the Retina on the Excitation of the Fibers in the Optic Nerve," *Amer. J. Physiol.*, **130**, 1940, 700–711.
30. Hecht, S., S. Shlaer, and M. Pirenne, "Energy, Quanta, and Vision," *J. Gen. Physiol.*, **25**, 1942, 185–190.
31. Helmholtz, H. V., *Helmholtz's Treatise on Physiological Optics*, Southall, J. P. (editor); translated from 3rd German edition and published by the Optical Society of America, Dover, New York, 1924.
32. Hubel, D. H., and T. M. Wiesel, "Receptive Fields of Single Nuerons in the Cat's Striate Cortex," *J. Physiol.*, **148**, 1959, 574–591.
33. Huggins, W. H., and J. C. R. Licklider, "Place Mechanisms of Auditory Frequency Analysis," *J. Acoust. Soc. Amer.*, **23**, 1951, 290–299.
34. Hunt, E. A., *Concept Learning: An Information-Processing Problem*, Wiley, New York, 1962.
35. Hunt, E. B., J. Marin, and P. J. Stone, *"Experiments in Induction*, Academic Press, New York, 1966.
36. Hyman, R., "Stimulus Information as a Determinant of Reaction Time," *J. Exp. Psychol.*, **45**, 1953, 188–196.
37. Kabrisky, M., *A Proposed Model for Visual Information Processing in the Brain*, University of Illinois Press, Urbana, 1966.
38. Lawson, J. L., and G. E. Uhlenbeck, *Threshold Signals*, McGraw-Hill, New York, 1950.
39. Lenneberg, E. H., "Speech Development: Its Anatomical and Physiological Concomitants," in Carterette, E. C. (editor), *Brain Function*, Vol. III: *Speech, Language, and Communication*, UCLA Forum Med. Sci. No. 4, University of California Press, Los Angeles, 1966.
40. Liddell, E. G. T., *The Discovery of Reflexes*, Clarendon Press, Oxford, 1960.
41. Luce, R. D., "A Threshold Theory for Simple Detection Experiments," *Psychol. Rev.*, **70**, 1963, 61–79.
42. Luce, R. D., "Detection and Recognition," in Luce, R. D., R. R. Bush, and E. Galanter (editors), *Handbook of Mathematical Psychology*, Vol. I, Wiley, New York, 1963, pp. 103–190.
43. Luce, R. D., R. R. Bush, and E. Galanter (editors), *Handbook of Mathematical Psychology*, Vol. I. Wiley, New York, 1963.
44. Luce, R. D., and E. Galanter, "Discrimination," in Luce, R. D., R. R. Bush, and E. Galanter (editors), *Handbook of Mathematical Psychology*, Vol. I, Wiley, New York, 1963, pp. 191–243.
45. Mach, E., (1) "On the Effect of the Spatial Distribution of the Light Stimulus on the Retina" (1865); (2, 3, 4) "On the Physiological Effect of Spatially Distributed Light Stimuli (1865, 1866, 1866); (5) On the Dependence of Retinal Points on One Another" (1868); (6) "On the Influence of Spatially and Temporally Varying Light Stimuli on Visual Perception "(1906). [Papers 1, 2, 3, 4 and 6 all appeared in *Sitzungsberichte der mathematisch naturwissenschaftlichen Classe der kaiserlichen Akademie der Wissenschaften*, Wien, (Vols. 52, 54, 54, 57, and 116, respectively), and Paper 5 appeared in *Vierteljahresschrift für Psychiatrie in ihren Beziehungen zur Morphologie und Pathologie des Central-Nerve-systems*, **2**, 1868, 38–51. Ratliff has translated all six papers, and they are collected in his book.]
46. Maturana, H. R., J. Y. Lettvin, W. S. McCulloch, and W. A. Pitts, "Anatomy and Physiology of Vision in the Frog," *J. Gen. Physiol.*, **43** (Part 2), 1960, 129–175.

47. McCulloch, W. S., and W. Pitt, "A Logical Calculus of the Ideas Immanent in Nervous Activity," *Bull. Math. Biophysics*, **5**, 1943, 115–137.

48. McGill, W. J., *Introduction to Counter Theory in Psychophysics*, Academic Press, New York, 1967.

49. McGill, W. J., "Multivariate Information Transmission," *Psychometrika*, **19**, 1954, 97–116.

50. Miller, G. A., "The Magical Number Seven, Plus or Minus Two," *Psychol. Rev.*, **63**, 1956, 81–97.

51. Miller, G. A., E. Galanter, and K. Pribram, *"Plans and the Structure of Behavior,* Holt, New York, 1960.

52. Miller, G. A., G. A. Heise, and W. Lichten, "The Intelligibility of Speech as a Function of the Context of the Test Materials," *J. Exp. Psychol.*, **41**, 1951, 329–335.

53. Newell, A., and H. A. Simon, "GPS, a Program that Simulates Human Thought," in Billing, H., *Lernende Automaten*, Oldenbourg, Munich, 1961. [Reprinted in Feigenbaum, E. A., and J. Feldman (editors), *Computers and Thought*, McGraw-Hill, New York, 1963.]

54. Newell, A., and H. A. Simon, "Computers in Psychology," in Luce, R. D., R. R. Bush, and E. Galanter (editors), *Handbook of Mathematical Psychology*, Vol. I, Wiley, New York, 1963, pp. 361–428.

55. Pollack, I., "Message Uncertainty and Message Reception," *J. Acoust. Soc. Amer.*, **31**, 1959, 1500–1508.

56. Polyak, S. L., *The Retina*, The University of Chicago Press, 1941.

57. Ramon y Cajal, S., *Histologie du Systéme Nerveux de l'Homme et des Vertébrés*, A. Maloine, Paris, 1909–1911 (reprinted, Madrid, 1955).

58. Ramsey, F. P., *The Foundations of Mathematics*, Routledge and Kegan Paul, London, 1931.

59. Rapoport, A., "Information Processing in the Nervous System," in Gerard, R. W., and J. W. Duyff (editors), *Information Processing in the Nervous System* (1962 Proceedings of the International Union of Physiological Sciences, Vol. 3), Excerpta Medica Foundation, Amsterdam, 1964, pp. 16–23.

60. Ratliff, F., *Mach Bands: Quantitative Studies on Neural Networks in the Retina*, Holden-Day, San Francisco, 1965.

61. Ratliff, F., and H. K. Hartline, "The Response of *Limulus* Optic Nerve Fibers to Patterns of Illumination on the Receptor Mosaic," *J. Gen. Physiol.*, **42**, 1959, 1241–1255.

62. Reitman, W. R., *Cognition and Thought*, Wiley, New York, 1965.

63. Rosenblatt, F., "The Perceptron: A Probabilistic Model for Information Storage and Organization in the Brain," *Psychol. Rev.*, **65**, 1958, 386–407.

64. Rosenblith, W. R. (editor), *Sensory Communication*, Wiley, New York, 1961.

65. Selin, I., *Detection Theory*, Princeton University Press, Princeton, N. J., 1965.

66. Sheppard, J. J., Jr., *Human Color Perception: A Critical Study of the Experimental Foundation*, American Elsevier, New York, 1968.

67. Sherrington, Sir Charles, *The Integrative Action of the Nervous System*, The University Press, Cambridge, 1947.

68. Suppes, P., "Information Processing and Choice Behavior," in Lakatos, I., and A. Musgrave, *Problems in the Philosophy of Science*, North-Holland Publishing Company, Amsterdam, 1968, pp. 278–304.

69. Sutherland, N. S., *The Methods and Findings of Experiments on the Visual Discrimination of Shape by Animals*, Experimental Psychology Society (Gr. Britain) Monog. No. 1, 1961.

70. Swets, J. A. (editor), *Signal Detection and Recognition by Humans: Contemporary Readings*, Wiley, New York, 1964.
71. Uhr, L., " 'Pattern Recognition' Computers as Models for Form Perception," *Psychol. Bull.*, **60**, 1963, 40–73.
72. Uhr, L. (editor), *Pattern Recognition*, Wiley, New York, 1966.
73. Uhr, L., and C. Vosller, "A Pattern-Recognition Program that Generates, Evaluates, and Adjusts Its Own Operators," *Proceedings of the Western Joint Computer Conference*, **1961**, 555–569.
74. Van Meter, D., and D. Middleton, "Modern Statistical Approaches to Reception in Communication Theory," *IRE Transactions of the Professional Group on Information Theory*, IT **4**, 1954, 119–145.
75. Wald, A., *Statistical Decision Functions*, Wiley, New York, 1950.
76. Waterman, T. H., "Systems Analysis and the Visual Orientation of Animals," *American Scientist*, **54**, 1966, 15–45.
77. Waterman, T. H., and K. W. Horch, "Mechanism of Polarized Light Perception," *Science*, **154**, 1966, 467–475.
78. Whitman, J. R., and W. R. Garner, "Concept Learning as a Function of Form of Internal Structure," *Journal of Verbal Learning and Verbal Behavior*, **2**, 1963, 195–202.

FURTHER READINGS

1. Broadbent, D. E., *Decision and Stress*, Academic Press, London, 1971.
2. Brindley, G. S., *Physiology of the Retina and the Visual Pathway*, 2nd ed., Edward Arnold, London, 1970.
3. Dodwell, P., *Visual Pattern Recognition*, Holt, Rinehart and Winston, New York, 1970.
4. Gibson, E. J., *Principles of Perceptual Learning and Development*, Appleton-Century-Crofts, New York, 1969.
5. Gibson, J. J., *The Senses Considered as Perceptual Systems*, Houghton-Mifflin, Boston, 1966.
6. Minsky, M. (editor), *Semantic Information Processing*, M.I.T. Press, Cambridge, 1968.
7. Minsky, M., and S. Papert, *Perceptrons: An Introduction to Computational Geometries*, M.I.T. Press, Cambridge, 1969.
8. Neisser, U., *Cognitive Psychology*, Appleton-Century-Crofts, New York, 1967.
9. Nilsson, N. J., *Problem-Solving Methods in Artificial Intelligence*, McGraw-Hill, New York, 1971.
10. Norman, D. A., *Memory and Attention*, Wiley, New York, 1969.
11. Noton, D., and L. Stark, "Eye Movements and Visual Perception," *Scientific American*, **224**, 1971, 34–43.
12. Plomp, R., and G. F. Smoorenburg (editors), *Frequency Analysis and Periodicity Detection in Hearing*, A. W. Sijthoff, Leiden, 1971.
13. Wathen-Dunn, W. (editor), *Models for the Perception of Speech and Visual Form*, M.I.T. Press, Cambridge, 1967.
14. Whitfield, I. C., *The Auditory Pathway*, Edward Arnold, London 1967.

AUTHOR INDEX

SUBJECT INDEX _____